HIGH VISIBILITY

HIGH VISIBILITY

Irving J. Rein
Philip Kotler
Martin R. Stoller

Heinemann Professional Publishing

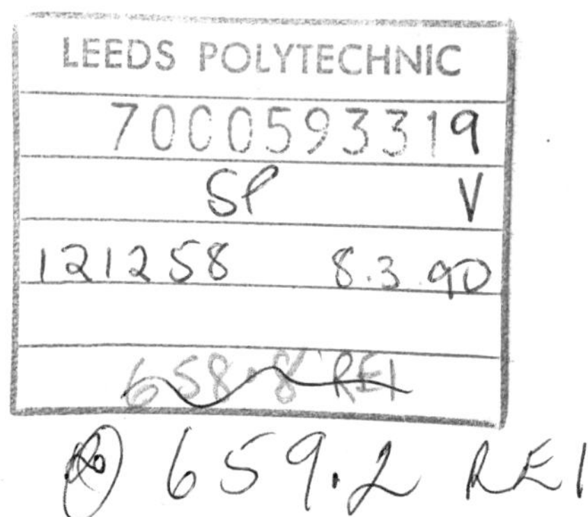

Heinemann Professional Publishing Ltd
Halley Court, Jordan Hill, Oxford OX2 8EJ

OXFORD LONDON MELBOURNE AUCKLAND SINGAPORE
IBADAN NAIROBI GABORONE KINGSTON

First published in Great Britain by William Heinemann Ltd 1987
First published as a paperback edition 1990

British Library Cataloguing in Publication Data
Rein, Irving J.
High visibility: the professional guide
to celebrity marketing.
1. Success 2. Celebrities
I. Title II. Kotler, Philip III. Stoller,
Martin R.
158'.1 BF637.S8

ISBN 0 434 91024 4

Printed in Great Britain by
Billing & Sons Ltd, Worcester

to Lynn Miller, Neil Kotler, and Janey

Contents

Preface

At one time or another, each of us has thought, "What would it be like to be famous?" Whether we are children pretending to be TV stars, or adults daydreaming about being on the cover of *Time* or *Forbes*, fame is one of our strongest recurring fantasies.

It is also, more and more often, a recurring reality. Changes in American society are affording more and more people the luxury of becoming well known. Celebrity, once possible for only a few, is now a real possibility—often a necessity—for people in all walks of life. Open any newspaper in any city or town and celebrity names spill out—the business leaders, homebuilders, lawyers, doctors, sports stars, religious figures, entertainers, academics, restaurant owners, and many others. For these celebrities, being highly visible generates more clients, attracts more patients, and commands a dollar more per pizza. For people in all areas of endeavor, high visibility has become a powerful tool. The key question is, What are the marketing and communications strategies that can create it?

The possibilities for a study of celebrityhood first hit home for the authors during a lunchtime encounter with Maureen Taylor, a waitress at The Third Rail, a restaurant in Evanston, Illinois. Between serving courses, Taylor related her dream of becoming an opera star. The authors, specialists in marketing and communication, began to speculate on how these powerful processes could help an aspirant in opera—or, for that matter, how they could help aspirants in other arts, in entertainment, in business, in the professions, and in all other careers. Because we already had spent years consulting with politicians and business-people, Taylor's dream intrigued us. Could we develop a systematic plan for seekers of high visibility?

We had no idea what we had got ourselves into. Ultimately, our research would involve interviews with hundreds of celebrities and celebrity-makers, research trips to celebrity-manufacturing centers in New York, Los Angeles, and Nashville, participation in auditions for network TV talent, and the development and teaching of several courses in celebrity-communication and celebrity-marketing at Northwestern University.

Ironically, it was the celebrities who were least able to cope with the systematic study of celebrity. One famous actor, upon hearing about our research, sniffed, "What are they going to teach people? How to talk to their chauffeurs?" A syndicated columnist for the *Chicago Sun-Times*, even after interviewing enthusiastic students and sitting in on a class session, maintained that celebrityhood wasn't a fit subject for investigation. In her opinion, students would be better off studying *Beowolf*. And for every interview with people such as Garry Marshall and Pia Zadora, who understood and appreciated the value of studying celebrity, there were interviews with William Simon and Senator Bill Bradley, who claimed that high visibility was superfluous to professional success. Still other celebrities, such as personal/celebrity manager Jay Bernstein, whom we called fourteen times, didn't even respond. It may be that celebrities, isolated from the process of their own manufacturing and marketing, have been unable to grasp the total scope of their own creation.

This book is meant to clarify the ambiguity that surrounds the celebrity culture. The fact is that everyone is involved in either producing or consuming celebrities. Through TV advertisements, restaurant openings, charity balls, trade shows, and sports events, our lives are celebrity-saturated. But for all its impact, celebrity has scarcely been understood. *High Visibility* explains the mechanisms that create celebrities and sustain them. *Importantly, it is designed for readers who want to understand and use visibility in their own careers and lives.*

This book is not a quick fix. If our research has proven anything, it is that high visibility is powerful, complex, and high-risk. Unfortunately, many writers on celebrity and high visibility have emphasized short-term goals, simplistic formulas, and common folk wisdom couched in behind-the-scenes anecdotes. The emphasis in *High Visibility* is on long-term goals, realistic marketing strategies, and uncommon approaches to celebrity. Any quest for high visibility should be thoughtful and deliberate, for the quest—while an adventure—needs to be managed.

Acknowledgments

A book on a subject as complex and all-encompassing as celebrity requires a great deal of help. In our three-and-a-half-year investigation of visibility-seeking and the celebrity industry, we were assisted by a large number of people. It is impossible to cite the names of everyone we spoke with or who helped steer us in profitable directions, but the people we acknowledge below were of particular help. We are indebted to them.

Our research was informed—and speeded along—by the work of a number of researchers who have explored celebrity and related areas from different perspectives. Foremost among them are Daniel Boorstin, whose pioneering work on image prepared the ground for our work; Erving Goffman, whose work on impression management was very helpful in our understanding of transformation strategies; Richard Dyer, whose work on stars in cinema and literature helped round out our view of character analysis; and Orrin Klapp, who inspired our understanding of social types and their importance to celebrity-making.

High Visibility would not have been written but for the generosity of Ted and LouAnn Van Zelst, whose Van Zelst research chair provided Irv Rein with support for a year of research into celebrity. Once begun, the project rapidly assumed the status of a small cottage industry, with invaluable help being provided by a wide range of people. Foremost among these contributors are our chief research assistants, Dara Carr and Jane Steiner, who made contacts, ferreted out obscure research, conducted interviews, and helped review the manuscript.

For thoughtful editorial guidance, we are indebted to Andrew Ade, whose encyclopaedic knowledge of the entertainment world nearly matched his skill at recognizing split infinitives. Eric Newman's editorial review was thoughtful, while Lynn Miller's editing saved us numerous embarrassments. In the early stages of the manuscript's development, the comments of Susan Tucker and Jeff Seglin were invaluable. Throughout, Leigh Stoller's computer assistance and knowledge of word processing technology was extraordinarily helpful.

Of course, no book on celebrity would be possible without the help of many celebrities and their associates. We express our thanks to the celebrities and celebrity managers who visited our classes or participated in interviews: Pia Zadora, Tim Kazurinsky, Bobby Vinton, John Jakes, Larry Gelbart, Jerry Paris, Ed Feldman, Chuck Binder, David Friendly, Richard Kind, Edgar Scherick, David Skepner, Shelley Berman, Patrick Goldstein, Jack Childers, Margie Korshak, Del Close, Paul Barrosse, Rush Pearson, Garry Marshall, Michael Emery, Rich Frank, Jane Heitz, Dick Kordos, Harisse Davidson, Mark Murdoh, Robert Fischer, Phil Krone, Steve Lewis, Paul Shefrin, John Leven, Steve Stark, Bill Nuss, and Stanley Garfinkle.

Helping us locate and interview these and other celebrities were Terry Bearman, Joan Hyler, and Carole Yumkas. We are especially grateful to Rac Clark, Jr. and Dan Paulson for allowing us to participate in auditions and project planning. In addition, celebrities ranging from William F. Buckley to Christie Hefner, from Andrew Greeley to Milton Friedman, graciously consented to interviews conducted by our research associates and students.

Making contact with and investigating these and numerous other celebrities were our Northwestern University researchers, including Kerri Ginsberg, Mary Deeley, Neil Kornfeld, Jeff Colin, Tim Alevizos, Doug Mazer, Jacquie Sinclair, Marilyn Hill, Chris Tralmer, David Harris, Nina Harlan, Julie Noack, Richard Monturo, Cara Titus, Jeff Kwatinetz, Jill Obmascik, Martha Hawtrey, Kevin Richert, Michael Parker, Charles Martinez, Jeff Sikes, Jeff Cory, Lynn Turner, Bonnie Landes, Benjamin Pohn, Jeff Berger, Cyndi Zale, Paula-Barri Whitehorn, Mike Mertz, Cheri Pugh, Mark Bloom, Jon Nemeth, David Kohn, and Darcy Eikenberg.

Contributing additional research to *High Visibility* were Tim Blaney, Mike Sable, Jill Langendorff, Jennifer Stone, Greg Brooks, Jodie Gerson, Sue Berkey, Jeff Greenfield, Jeffrey Jacobs, Scott Whalley, Peggy Fethke, Felicia Rubloff, Katy Schlesinger, Jennifer Smyth, Brian Rusted, Heather Buchanan, Tad Meyer, Sharon Cunningham, Donna Orlovitz, Tom Holt, Diane Donnelly, Eva Lucido, Jillisa Brittan, Mark Wright, Craig Springer, Mary Davidson, Toni Perling, Suzette Adouth, and David Rosen.

We would also like to thank Muadi Dibinga, who continually tried to make order out of our notes and files, and Lauren Rein for invaluable research assistance. We would also like to thank Richard Radutzky for allowing us to help produce his *David Letterman* appearance, and Richard Kaplan for his help in simulating David Letterman.

Throughout the publication process, we have received the enthusiastic support and help of Lynne Lumsden, publisher of Dodd, Mead, who had the foresight to understand the potential in this project. Robin Bartlett and Joyce Levatino have likewise shown great skill in shepherding the book through to completion.

CHAPTER ONE

The Pygmalion Principle

Lee Iacocca, chairman of Chrysler Corporation, is holding a press conference. TV camera crews, newspaper reporters, and local officials all wait expectantly. As Iacocca enters, there is a hush generally accorded to presidents. He quickly diffuses the tension with a joke about the local press and a self-deprecating comment about being the star of Chrysler's television commercials. But once the press conference begins, Iacocca is direct, dramatic, and blunt. He attacks the timid U.S. trade policy toward Japan, sounding like the 1943 head of Naval Operations in the Pacific theater of war. He praises Chrysler cars and workers, speaks out on the federal deficit, and again denies that he will run for president. When he leaves the press conference, Iacocca's comments will be scrutinized by the public and policy makers alike, for in the hierarchy of celebrities, Lee Iacocca—a businessperson, not an entertainer—ranks at the top.

The arena is filled to the rafters, the crowd buzzing in anticipation. Suddenly, the lights dim. Rosalynn Sumners, world champion figure skater, glides out onto the ice. Casting graceful shadows in the dazzling spotlights, Sumners manages to create the impression of being alone, vulnerable, and unprotected amid the vast expanse of ice. Little girls crane their necks; adults unconsciously move a little closer to the edges of their seats. Rosalynn Sumners, solo artist, is about to perform.

Judge Wayne Olson is about to be launched. News of his indictment in an undercover investigation of judicial graft has just flashed over the airwaves. Now, he leaves his chambers, walking slowly down the hall toward the gauntlet: shouting reporters, jostling cameras, blinding lights. But as he confronts his first waving microphone, the judge is curiously at ease. He has seen this all before. Edwin Moses . . . Mary Cunningham . . . Gary Gilmore . . . T. Boone Pickens . . . Billie Jean King . . . Oral Roberts . . . Richard Pryor . . . it is deja vu. *Without conscious thought, Judge Olson turns to the cameras and begins smoothly fielding questions, acting out a role he has never played. He is on the launching pad, poised to soar into celebrity orbit.*

The chairman, the ice skater, and the judge are worlds apart, but they share a very powerful bond: high visibility.

For Lee Iacocca, high visibility is a strategic tool. As have Victor Kiam for shavers, Frank Perdue for chickens, and Frank Borman for plane tickets, Iacocca has become a celebrity in order to sell cars. To do so, a whole support system was assembled: policy planners, media advisors, ad agencies—all orchestrating the production of Iacocca's image as decisive, tough, in control. But creating the image of the confident chairman on the sixty-second TV ad requires eight hours of filming, weeks of editing, and months of planning and research. Iacocca's public image as the old-style street fighter is the result of careful crafting by hard-working ghostwriters and Iacocca's own meticulous preparation and practice. Lee Iacocca's transformation into a celebrity is as deliberate as the manufacture of his cars—calculated to use his high visibility to bring the buyers to the showrooms.

Rosalyn Sumners is a study in high visibility, too. She has pursued it for her entire life, desiring it so intensely that she has conscripted an army to help her capture it: coaches, costume designers, press agent, nutritionist, choreographer, sports psychologist, trainer, sponsors, and venue agents. Sumners is the ultimate manufactured celebrity.[1] Trained, managed, and prodded by her "support system," her name marketed throughout the world, she skates onto the ice as much a product as a Sony Walkman or Hamilton Beach mixer. Her transformation into a celebrity is no accident; all that is in doubt is how successfully she can translate it into the rewards she craves.

possible to change. The industry operates not by whim but by design, not for pride but for profit. In fact, the ability to transform people into celebrities has become so sophisticated, and the rewards of high visibility have become so great, that the Pygmalion Principle is now at work in virtually every area of life.

The Power of Visibility

Most of us in American society are invisible. We have a small network of people who know us: in our work place, our neighborhood, our place of worship. It might be 50 people, 100, or 500—a far cry from those whose high visibility earns them the freedom to vacation on private islands, slip in through side doors at theaters, glide about in limousines behind smoked glass, and book entire restaurants for an undisturbed meal. For most of us, life rarely holds such pleasures.

But what is happening in society is that, as our power to distribute images expands, the ranks of the highly visible are growing rapidly, as those who understand the Pygmalion Principle use it to enhance their opportunities and rewards. Thanks to modern communication technology, society's capacity to transmit images—and, therefore, create visibility—has grown a thousandfold. Television, radio, film, cable, magazines, billboards, satellite dish receivers—all help make possible worldwide person-image transmission. Inspired by the modern notion of universal distribution, enabled by transportation and sophisticated communication and marketing tools, we have developed the ability to create, in Daniel Boorstin's terminology, *well-knownness*—and to blanket the world with it.[4]

When Boorstin first proposed his theory of the power of communication technology to create "artificial fame," the practical knowledge about how it could be accomplished was far less sophisticated than it is today.[5] Little was known about how particular individuals could be processed through the visibility-generating machinery, or about how to take maximum commercial advantage of their resulting celebrity. But in the past twenty-five years, many of the processes that Boorstin first suggested have become knowable and do-able.

This book explains how the manufacturing and marketing of people into celebrities has become an institution fueled by an army of consultants, mentors, coaches, advisors, agents, managers, promoters, and headhunters. It tells why celebrity is so profitable and deciphers the industry that produces it. *High Visibility* applies marketing science to the quest for celebrity and discusses what is required for celebrity in sectors ranging from business to entertainment. It reveals how audience appeal is measured and how audiences are attracted and used. Throughout the book, a recurring theme is the importance of celebrities' images—their design, refinement, and delivery to audiences. *High Visibility* explores how the common myths of great talent, magnetic charisma, the right attitude, incredible luck, electric personality, and perfect timing often obscure the path to high visibility. In place of these myths, this book offers a four-step transformation process, a marketing and communication plan to systematically elevate visibility seekers into celebrities. Finally, the book discusses how high visibility can be sustained over time, and what its rewards, and costs, can be.

The End of Heroes, the Rise of Celebrities

What do Ron Reagan Jr., Princess Diana, Jimmy the Greek, Charles Nelson Reilly, Priscilla Presley, and Leo Buscaglia have in common? They are benefactors of the celebrity industry's ability to turn people with scant claim to fame into household names.

Richard Schickel, in his biography of Douglas Fairbanks and Mary Pickford, identifies the years 1915 to 1925 as the period when the perception arose that people could be *made* well known, and that there was great value in doing so.[6] Published sources between the years 1900 and 1980 confirm that this period marked a shift in the public's perception of celebrity. As Figure 1 demonstrates, uses of the term *fame* peaked early in the 1900s.[7] In contrast, *celebrity* germinates in the 1920s, then grows in use at a dizzying pace. In Figure 2, where major events of the century are superimposed upon the shift from fame to celebrity, the effects of entertainment and technology on celebrities is clear: The ascendancy of "celebrity" coincided with the flooding of the marketplace with highly visible people.

Today, the highly visible permeate our media, our economy, our very lifestyles. *They are manufactured, just as are cars, clothes, and computers.* Moreover, an entire industry has evolved whose very existence depends upon producing—and profiting from—highly visible persons. It is an industry that virtually all other industries have come to depend upon. That is because high visibility has developed into an asset with an independent identity and function, a propellant energizing a wide variety of activities: attracting clients; selling movie tickets; generating charity donations; promoting political and social causes; and selling jeans, health club memberships, and virtually everything else.

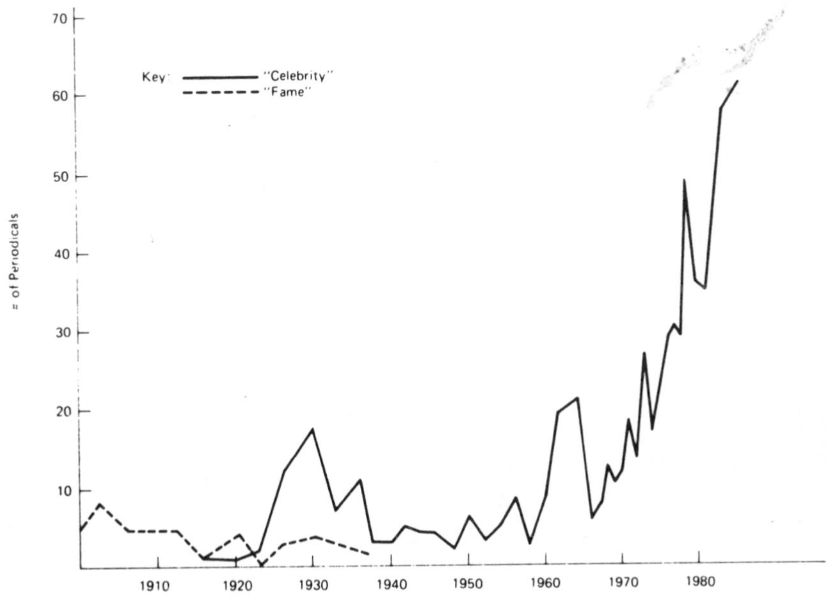

Figure 1: Displays the Number of Times the Words "Fame" and "Celebrity" Appeared in Magazine Article Titles, 1900–1983.

The Rise of the Celebrity Industry

Given the pervasiveness of celebrity, why hasn't society recognized the "celebrity industry" as more than just a group of loosely affiliated producers of artifacts—of records, concerts, T-shirts, and TV shows? Why haven't we accorded the celebrity industry the same status as our other, more overtly strategy-based, marketing-centered, and research-oriented industries? Because as the central producer of high visibility, the celebrity industry has a vested interest in maintaining its own invisibility. And it does so in a number of ways.

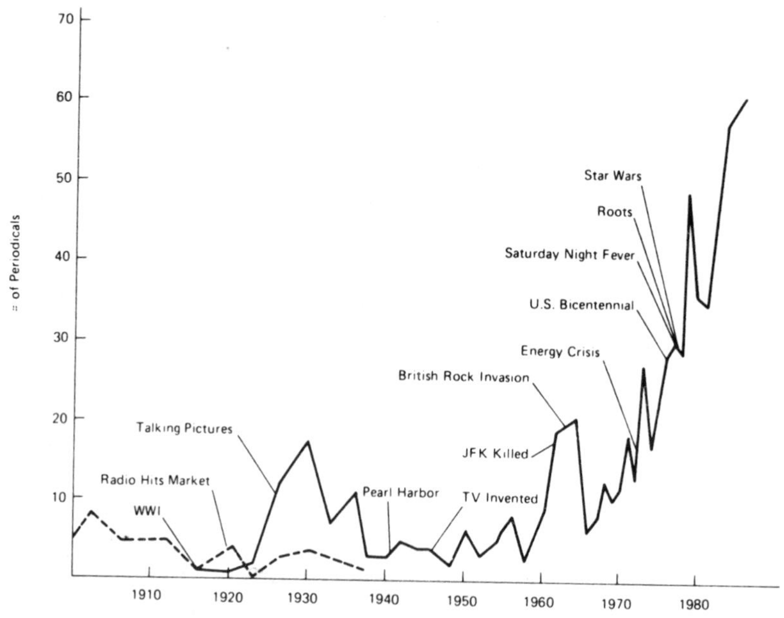

Figure 2: Shows Correlation of Major Cultural Events with Figure 1.

First, there are the industry's self-cloaking strategies. This is the industry whose products are identified as having "talent," "charisma," "magic," "electricity," "presence," "star quality"—and where the producers have "luck," "timing," and "gut instinct." Deliberately mystified by the people who run it, the celebrity industry is rife with terms and practices meant to cloak its complex infrastructure, proprietary patents, and designs. It is an industry with few laws mandating what it must tell consumers—the fans who worship its products. There are no safe-packaging standards or truth-in-advertising laws in the celebrity industry.

Second, the celebrity industry is shielded from public understanding by our culture's deep-seated belief that people are unique, that they are *not* interchangeable parts or manipulable machines. Cultural beliefs that talent wins out, that the routes to power are obscure, that genius cannot be denied—all are part of the folklore of celebrity. "Barbra Streisand," screamed a film producer during an interview, "is just *there*—a great talent."

Third, the industry's own character interferes with our understanding it as we would a traditional industry. The celebrity industry is *new wave*, a product-based industry that breaks new ground by manufacturing and marketing a concept—high visibility—using a mixture of traditional and nontraditional strategies and tools. Like the software industry and the new interstate banking business, the celebrity industry does not even have a single, consolidated headquarters. It exists almost everywhere: in Nashville, Los Angeles, Minneapolis, New York, or Athens, Georgia.

Fourth, the celebrity industry does not produce a recognizable product—at least, not one that we think of in traditional ways. A light bulb is a product we understand; it has a function that its design is suited for. We have a clear need for it. People make it. We can trace the paths through which it is distributed. We have business schools that teach courses in how to manage the light bulb industry. But the manufacturing and marketing of people as products is not systematically taught anywhere.

Finally, there is the fact that traditional industries can be easily studied. We can analyze the evolution of their marketing, pricing, and advertising strategies. They have histories, whereas the celebrity industry has not—at least, not a reported one. Its products are consumed daily by millions, but its personnel and operations are cloaked in vague generalities.

Thinkers and Doers

While the celebrity manufacturing business has been growing, two major perspectives have come to dominate the discussion over "artificial fame." On the one hand are the social critics, who feel very strongly that there is something terribly wrong about the manufacturing of images, that celebrities constitute a highly visible assault on old-fashioned values. Essentially, what the critics have done is to dissect the celebrity world into pieces, isolate what they perceive to be its effects, and theorize from them, proclaiming that society elevates precisely the wrong people into popular acclaim. To the critics, celebrities are paid far too much, embody harmful role models for children, are too powerful, and generally debase society.

These critics, seeing themselves as the conservators and defenders of American values, are preoccupied with the fear that the manufacturing and marketing of celebrities is destroying the fabric of society. The critics' conception of a perfectly ordered hierarchy is under relentless attack by the celebrity world. As stated by critic Barbara Goldsmith:

> What Boorstin could not have predicted was how the swiftness of our technological achievements, combined with the personal disillusionments of the last two decades, would encourage us to manufacture our fantasies while simultaneously ripping away the guideposts of the past.[8]

In the world conceived by Goldsmith, pop star Madonna is an object of misguided adoration, whose huge popularity is clear evidence of a lowering of standards. For the critics, caught up in their fears for society, dealing objectively with the process through which celebrities are mass produced is impossible.

The other popular view of celebrity is that held by the celebrity industry's practitioners—the agents, producers, managers, PR specialists, media personnel, and others—who treat celebrity manufacturing as a trade. To these people, the major concerns are what will sell, what can be marketed, who can be motivated to consume the celebrity product, and what the net profit will be. Busily working within the system, perfecting their techniques, shaping and delivering the product, they have come to see themselves as isolated specialists, never considering the broader consequences of what they individually, and collectively, do. Like the critics, they do not see the celebrity industry in its totality. The only time they consider its impact on society is when there's a profit– or image-threatening crisis: when publisher Rupert Murdoch's controversial high profile causes mass resignations at a newspaper he has taken over; when Mark David Chapman shoots John Lennon; when the statements of highly visible Interior Secretary James Watt force his resignation; when commercially valuable sports celebrity Len Bias dies of a cocaine overdose. The practitioners do not ask whether Bruce Springsteen should be as powerful as he is, or if anyone should be. As a result, the critics don't understand *how* celebrities are manufactured, and the manufacturers don't care about the consequences. What is needed is a position that respects celebrity's value yet recognizes its dangers.

The Urgency for Celebrity

One well-respected lawyer reflecting on the importance of visibility observed, "It's something everyone is anxious about." He went on to explain that in his office, the junior and senior partners constantly consider and discuss the various places in which they are on display—in court, bar conferences, media interviews, professional association dinners, high-profile trusteeships, and directorships for charities and universities. The same scenario is repeated in accounting offices, locker rooms, diocesan headquarters, charity board rooms, and legislative hallways. For most people trying to launch or maintain their visibility, the path is not only obscure but also littered with land mines.

One real problem is that the idea that people can be transformed into celebrities runs counter to some very deep-seated, almost sacred notions in our culture. To some degree, we all cling to the traditional conception of fame: that it is a pure and usually merited reward for significant accomplishment. But although occasionally a tool of value, fame in the past was useful only to the individual who had rightly earned it.

Today, for our visibility-conscious lawyer, all that has changed. Well-knownness or high visibility has become a marketable commodity. Wholly divorced from great deeds and accomplishments, *well-knownness itself* has obtained tremendous commercial value. Well-knownness has evolved into celebrity, and celebrity in today's society means power and money—not just to its possessor, but, critically, to businesses, institutions, political parties, causes, entrepreneurs, charities, and others.

We are now a society in which change—evolution—has become the norm. People in all walks of life no longer find it strange to consider making radical changes in their lives and images in order to gain high visibility and its power. Although celebrity for many people remains an intriguing idea, the fact is that high visibility is becoming a necessity. Critics will criticize celebrity, but they won't stop people from wanting it or using it.

To be marketed successfully, individuals need to gain control of their images, making decisions based on a thorough understanding of all aspects of how marketing operates in the celebrity industry. The person trying to execute a high-visibility plan needs to understand not just the tricks of projecting the right images, but how the best images are determined and how they can be produced. The first stop on this road is to understand why celebrity is economically, socially, and emotionally one of the strongest forces in our culture.

CHAPTER TWO

The Quest for Celebrity

Deborah Jones is dead. Everyone in the chapel is in that sad state preceding the final words for a lost friend. Suddenly, in through the side door walks a nationally known sportswriter, followed by a high school classmate who played character roles in B-movies, the president of the local Right To Life chapter, and the deputy mayor. Deborah Jones is now celebrity-linked. The audience buzzes with conjecture about the relationships implied by these visits. The minister, irritated by the audience's excitement and change of mood, launches into final words for Deborah Jones.

Deborah Jones's funeral is at once disrupted and enhanced by the arrival of celebrities. People turn their heads to view these mourners who "stand out from the crowd." Many of us have had our lives disrupted and enhanced by celebrities. People often define their lives by when and where they have encountered them. Who are these people who command such attention, while most of us scarcely cast a shadow?

A first glance at a definition of *celebrity* quickly reveals a source of confusion. There are many person-types who are somehow bound up with celebrity: heroes, leaders, legends, idols, stars, superstars, gurus, and luminaries.

With the older of these terms—heroes, leaders, legends—high visibility was usually associated with merit. In older cultures, invisibility was generally regarded as the normal state of affairs. The exceptions—victorious generals, daring heroes, popes, mystics, mass murderers—were people elevated into high visibility by their deeds, their birthright, or their leadership of institutions. These heroes were well known for their deeds: fighting off the French, delivering the rain, saving the bankrupt nation. The leader was often well known for his or her so-called charismatic appeal and ability to inspire. Luminaries were distinguished for activities in business, science, or some other useful field.

It is not that these individuals lacked rudimentary understanding of promotion techniques; they understood very well that images and symbols had power, and they employed them effectively to exert control over their publics. It was not by accident that Richard became the Lion Hearted, William became The Conqueror, Jesus became the symbol of a vast church, Napoleon became indelibly linked to a forbidding hand-over-abdomen portraiture, and Clara Barton became the embodiment of the American Red Cross.

Today, the terms we use to describe the highly visible—*celebrities, stars, superstars, icons, gurus*—are very different. Intrinsic to *their* meaning is the fact that high visibility has become a valuable commodity *all by itself*. It is an entity that stands alone, independent of accomplishment, sacrifice, or heroics.

The term *celebrity* comes from the Latin *celeber*—meaning "much frequented" or "thronged."[1] No less an authority than the *Oxford English Dictionary* defines *celebrity* as "a person of celebrity, a celebrity person, a public character"[2]—hardly an illuminating definition. Some definitions emphasize numbers, such as "a celebrity is a person (or name) who is known by a larger number of people than average." Another definition uses the same theme, but with the twist of anonymity: "a celebrity is a person who is known by people whom he does not know," or "a person who is talked about." Most of the definitions concentrate on reputation, praise, and popularity. In some cases, the definition revolves around the short-lived, ephemeral quality of celebrity. There is the implication that memory is a crucial dimension, that celebrity tends to be fleeting, less permanent than fame or greatness.

The fact is that the traditional definitions fail to illuminate the core essence of celebrity as we perceive it today: the commercial value of high visibility. Can the celebrity sell newspapers, laundry soap, Saab turbos, or Head tennis racquets? Can he generate attendance at the charity ball? Can she draw media attention to her own pet political cause? *The Celebrity Register* hints at a useful definition when it suggests that "a celebrity i- name which, once made by news, now makes news by itsel This definition at least suggests the critical profit-generating rc played by celebrity.

How do we define a celebrity? *A celebrity is a person whose name has attention-getting, interest-riveting, profit-generating value.* Such a definition allows us to consider at once the Media Meteor, the Infamous Murderer, the Top-Selling Local Real Estate Broker, the Situation Comedy Star—*all* as players in the celebrity industry. The definition encompasses the notorious Rosie Ruiz streaking across the celebrity landscape after faking a victory in the Boston Marathon; John Hinckley's psychoanalyst; the biggest homebuilder in Mobile, Alabama; and the rise, fall, rise, and fall again of Suzanne Somers.

Why the Quest?

Why is celebrity so sought after? Because attaining high visibility generates substantial rewards for celebrities and their support systems. The celebrity personally achieves a degree of privilege, power, pay, and perquisites that make achieving and sustaining celebrity compellingly attractive.

Consider the "pay differential" or "premium" that celebrity confers—that is, the difference between what a celebrity earns *as* a celebrity, and what a celebrity *would* earn in his or her best use in the noncelebrity world. This pay differential has two causes.

First, celebrities are rewarded merely for choosing to compete in high-risk/high-profit sectors instead of low-risk/low-profit ones. An athlete with certain physical skills might excel equally in football or rugby. Quarterback Doug Flutie, selecting to specialize in the more visible (and thus more competitive) sport of football, earns a premium over what he would have earned in the less popular sport of rugby.

Second, celebrities earn a premium because they are better known than other members of their professions or sectors. When the United States Football League was trying to establish itself as a credible rival to the National Football League, the drawing power of its players was as important as their skills. Although shorter than the traditional quarterback, Doug Flutie was signed by the New Jersey Generals for a significant premium over the salary of other USFL quarterbacks. The Generals had analyzed the impact of Flutie's visibility on Boston College—increased ticket revenues, a higher media profile for the entire football program, and even an increase in applications to attend—and anticipated that his high visibility would generate greater revenues for the USFL as well. One way to measure this premium is to take Flutie's performance statistics, find other players with similar performance statistics, and compare their average earnings with Flutie's. Every dollar that Flutie earned above and beyond comparable players' salaries constitutes his celebrity-generated rent or premium. When the USFL's activities were suspended, and Flutie approached the only other available marketplace—the NFL—he found that his value to the already established league was significantly lower than his value to the celebrity-conscious USFL. As a result, he was "sold" to the Chicago Bears at a discount. Flutie's case is a dramatic way of demonstrating that celebrity has a market value all its own.

This is no less true of other sectors, although the performance statistics may be more difficult to measure. What Walter Cronkite earns for a speech to a major convention versus what Topeka's top newscaster commands constitutes Cronkite's celebrity-generated premium. What celebrity fitness expert Richard Simmons receives for his services versus what the equally skilled aerobics instructor at the local "Y" charges is Simmons's celebrity-generated premium.

In our society we willingly pay this "celebrity premium" to reward those who take the risks to become the highly visible people we so love to revere or revile. It is the great size of this premium that motivates so many aspirants to join the quest for celebrity *despite* the high risks. *People* magazine's celebrity earnings issue shows that the rewards to aspirants who succeed are tremendous indeed, not just for them, but also for the people surrounding them.[4] At such astronomical salaries—talk show host Merv Griffin earning $3,000,000 per year; journalist Diane Sawyer, $1,000,000; actor Clint Eastwood, $10,000,000 per year; sportscaster Brent Musburger signing a $10,000,000 five-year contract—parents, spouses, lovers, and children all potentially benefit from celebrities' pay, privileges, and reflected glory. Also dependent upon celebrities' prodigious cash flows are those who develop and promote them. Publicists, agents, coaches, personal managers—all derive their incomes from helping produce and sustain their celebrity's success. All said, the celebrity's high visibility confers economic and psychological benefit to members of a far-flung (and continually expanding) support system.

But celebrity is not merely a reward unto its possessors and their intimates. It also helps meet the crucial public need for role models. Celebrities provide us with stories, entertainment, diversion, uplift, and even moral instruction. Through them, we enjoy vicarious emotions and experiences rarely found in our own daily lives.

On a more basic level, most of us would hate a society without names. Recall the "no name" entities of the recent past: the no-name defense of the Miami Dolphins; generic peanut butter; no-brand gas. Such commodities are strongly identified for their very lack of identifying characteristics. How many people would like a genuinely no-name government, unidentifiable TV stars, or a wholly generic life? The very idea strikes a strong chord of uneasiness and distaste in our celebrity-adoring society.

Finally, celebrities meet the needs of institutions for representatives and advocates. Charities, schools, sports teams, and organizations of all stripes compete for attention, funds, and market share. To the extent that they can adopt, create, or flaunt some well-known (and, one hopes, dramatic) personality as *their* celebrity, they can more successfully achieve their goals. In such cases, the celebrity becomes a symbol for the entire institution. Thus, Chrysler benefits when Lee Iacocca is made into a business celebrity. Chanel No. 5 sells better because Catherine Deneuve and her image mingle with the perceived qualities of the product. Universities seeking funds tout the names of their Nobel Prize winners or celebrated graduates to give donors a sense of the exciting and exotic. In some cases, universities use coaches to personify their marketable qualities.

The contribution that celebrities can make to institutions is clearly displayed in the large number of television preachers who make up the "electronic ministry." Celebrity evangelists such as Robert H. Schuller, Jerry Falwell, and Ernest Angley have all invested heavily in the recognizability of their names. They are every bit as leveraged into celebrity promotion as film and sports stars. Where would they be—what would they be earning—if they were only as visible, as well known, as the local corner minister or parish priest? Would Schuller's opulent Crystal Cathedral ever have been built—with all that that would mean in lost or uncreated jobs, lost TV revenue, lost book sales—were Schuller *not* a celebrity? How would it affect the impact of Schuller's message of religious faith? Personal name recognition is essential for TV evangelists, virtually their paramount marketing tool. How many audience members even know the names of the celebrity preachers' organizations? How many contributors say, "I give to Liberty College"? Not many. The vast majority say, "I give to Jerry Falwell." The contributions flooding in to Falwell and his compatriots reaffirm the power of people standing for whole institutions, and the importance we have come to place on person-images.

LUNCH WITH THE COACH

How would you like to have lunch with Coach Ray Meyer? Whether you've a basketball fan or not, if you're an alumnus of DePaul University, you're likely to get a call from DePaul's Department of Alumni Relations, asking you that question. Coach Meyer, though now retired, through his winning basketball teams and carefully promoted grandfatherly image, still has great power to draw alumni contributions. It was Meyer's successful teams that moved the little-known, small Catholic inner-city university into the consciousness of American television audiences. Network TV basketball announcer Al McGuire would look down on the floor and wax effusive about the gruff but courtly coach. Meyer, coaching in his seventies, far after his peers had retired, would pace the floor as a human symbol of anachronistic values and concern for students as people and not just players. Ray Meyer stands for DePaul, and DePaul stands for Ray Meyer. The luncheon guests enjoy being in the presence of a celebrity, and whether the eventual donation is for the basketball program or the philosophy department, the check is paid. How much do the values of the real Ray Meyer actually infuse the real DePaul University? To those involved, such a question simply isn't sporting. . . .

Perhaps most important of all is the fact that the same function that high visibility serves for Schuller and for business at large, it serves for people in *all* walks of life. The most visible lawyer in the small town; the most well-known young manager at the national sales meeting; the most recognizable ingenue in the regional theater troupe: The careers of each will be energized by their being more visible than their peers.

TOP GUN IN THE SOCIALITE WORLD

In every sector of life, there is the party world—the charities, the balls, the fundraisers—where people congregate to do business, have fun, and be seen. In any of these sectors, there are aspiring socialites arrayed in a hierarchy. But there are very few of them who make it to this sector's zenith. One of them is Sugar Rautbord, a leading socialite who interviews celebrities for Andy Warhol's *Interview* magazine, sits on the State Department's Fine Arts Committee, and is on the board of the New York City Ballet.

Born Donna Louise Kaplan, she married Clayton Rautbord, president of Photocopy Machine Corporation. Rautbord has, according to a close friend, "structured her life around being in the right places in the right times, wearing the right furs."[5] Rautbord is rich, but there are a lot of rich people. Many people are also good-looking and bright. But Rautbord's extra dimension is that she understands the difference between just being seen, and marketing herself. She has professionalized the socialite world, strategically parlaying one level of visibility into successively higher ones. Rautbord has taken visibility to the rewards stage: writing novels, posing for high-fashion photographers, hosting State Department dinners, and selling her consulting services.

Every town had its lady in the dark blue Buick, the head of the Garden Club and the Library Board. She drove slowly and received her recognition in subtle ways. Today, we have a new generation of do-gooders—fronting larger and larger affairs, and driving a whole lot faster.

Where Did the Quest Begin?

Chuck Binder's house is almost impossible to find. His neighborhood in Beverly Hills' Benedict Canyon is a lush maze of twists and turns, swimming pools and seclusion. Resting at the end of a cul-de-sac, the house perches precariously on the edge of a cliff, only the sleek Mercedes sports car in the driveway a clue that anyone is home.

The door is opened by Jennifer—tall, barefoot, one of the most beautiful women in the world. Beyond her, the only furniture in sight are a small table and four chairs. Binder enters the room in a coordinated red and white tennis outfit, a phone wedged between his shoulder and cheek. The story of Binder's rise to the cliffs of Benedict Canyon is the Hollywood Model of celebrity marketing come to life.[6]

Chuck Binder began his career in the visibility industry as an itinerant tennis instructor, helping entertainment stars polish their strokes on their backyard tennis courts. Deciding that he'd enjoy some visibility, too, Binder found a job in the legendary mail room of the William Morris talent agency. Binder's kernel inspiration came while delivering a package to superagent Jerry Weintraub. One look at Weintraub's opulent quarters was enough to crystallize Binder's conviction that power and visibility were his ultimate goals.

Binder's opportunity finally came when tennis client Janet Leigh's daughter, on vacation from school, implored her mother to allow her to seek an acting job in films. Leigh agreed, with the proviso that her daughter spend a maximum of two weeks seeking a role before returning to school. Binder, interceding, offered to represent the young woman. His first days as a celebrity marketer were inauspicious: He wasn't even able to get through Universal's front gate. Finally, a friend counseled him to barrel up to gate, wave jauntily, and drive on through. Once inside, Binder canvassed from office to office, finally managing to interest a Universal producer in his client, and to sign her to a contract. He was now a full-fledged personal manager. And client Jamie Lee Curtis was no longer in school. Following his success with client Daryl Hannah, who made the hit movie *Splash*, Binder was soon "hot," powerful, a man who got his calls answered in Hollywood.

The Hollywood Model is, simply, the marriage of entertainment and fame building to create and sell highly visible products called celebrities—products with a short shelf life, strong emphasis on intangibles (style and personality), and luxurious, often wastrel lifestyles; products that appear to be manufactured under mysterious circumstances by shadowy figures working under great tension. In the Hollywood Model, the emphasis is on product development, coaching, story building, drama, public relations, and manipulation of free media. Chuck Binder, specializing in this year's blonde, emphasizing his good eye for talent, rising quickly to power, and possessing seemingly unknowable business skills, embodies the Hollywood Model in all its glory.

Binder is part of something that, although popularly and critically perceived as more of an ephemeral curiosity than a genuine industry, has more ancillary support mechanisms than any industry in the world: celebrity restaurants, clubs, boutiques, funeral homes, registers, hotels, doctors and dentists, drug dealers, dressmakers, and tailors. Few places illustrate the depth of the visibility industry's support systems better than West Los Angeles. A trip through Santa Monica's Upper Rustic Canyon resembles a television commercial for the state of the art in military tactics applied to home protection: ominous warnings of killer dogs, roving guards, piercing alarms. To keep the lines of communication secure and free from fan interference there are unlisted phone numbers and elite answering services in abundance. Traveling celebrities arrange for private planes and limo-to-runway service—or even, as in the case of Dick Clark's trip to China, an exclusive, personally conducted tour. In West Los Angeles, there is apparently no end to the special services celebrities command: car washes, parking lots, even pet motels for the celebrities' lucky nonhuman companions.

The Spread of the Quest

In Hollywood, celebrity marketing is an established, institutionalized form of life, the accepted way that highly visible persons—celebrities—are created in the entertainment sector. But crucial to the growth of the visibility industry worldwide is that, just by the force of its presence, the Hollywood Model of visibility-building causes pressure for imitative behavior in Aspen, Colorado; Little Rock, Arkansas; and Munster, Indiana.[7] Hollywood's visibility-generating strategies—widely portrayed in Hollywood films and on network television—have been absorbed throughout the country. The press agent in the film *The Harder They Fall,* the trials and tribulations of Mickey Rooney, the deification of James Dean, the manufacturing of the political candidate played by Robert Redford in the movie *The Candidate*—all are lessons in celebrity manufacturing, Hollywood style. All contribute to the public's awareness of, and predisposition to use, Hollywood techniques.

Much PR activity in this era came out of New York, but it was Hollywood that codified and disseminated PR more efficiently than any other institution in the world. While Hollywood films were seeding the American consciousness with notions of fame-building, the support systems that Hollywood helped develop were expanding, spreading visibility-building know-how across the country. PR firms, agents, local promoters, managers, publicists, and other agencies developed to serve the entertainment sector in local markets began applying their skills to clients in sectors other than entertainment. These two factors—the awareness of visibility-building as a practice, and the availability of the expertise needed to accomplish it—spread the Hollywood Model, "celebritizing" more and more sectors of life.

Moving aggressively, the ad agencies, PR experts, publicists, dressing consultants, image designers, and charity coordinators have since permeated almost every area of American culture. The result is that the once dominant Hollywood star-making system has been superceded by its offspring—a worldwide, multi-sectoral system to generate high visibility and create celebrities. It is a system already well entrenched in the sports and political sectors, and growing fast with the celebritization of the business, religion, science, academic, and art sectors. The trend seems clear, illustrated by everything from the heavily promoted campaign for money manager Fred Alger to the media-multiplied image of environmental artist Christo: The proficiency, penetration, and saturation of the Visibility Industry is growing.

Fueling the cycle is the public's recently acquired belief that achievements are not achievements unless they are reported in the media. High visibility, even at the most local level, has become the validating mechanism for accomplishment, a sort of society-wide imitation of the high school football quarterback's rifling of the local paper's sports section to see if he's mentioned. For many of us, the public reporting of the achievement becomes more important than the achievement itself.

Not only is the Hollywood Model moving out into local markets, but local markets are becoming increasingly sophisticated in transforming the ordinary into the visible, and the visible into the highly visible. In the widely reported 1983 Chicago mayorality race, the product development model spawned by Hollywood was clearly in evidence.[8] Though eventually losing in a close race, incumbent Jane Byrne managed, through transformation, to achieve a spectacular rise in the polls. Under attack, Byrne hired New York political consultant and former filmmaker David Sawyer to guide her faltering campaign. Sawyer completely changed Byrne's look—hair, dress, makeup, walk—even managing to alter her abrasive personal demeanor. He created commercials to support her new image and then delivered that image to the voters. As a consultant, he used all the elements of the Hollywood Model: product development, story enhancement, manipulation of free media, paid advertising, and strategic use of appearance venues. The new Jane Byrne was now soft-spoken, level-headed, responsible—a blurred merger of fact and fiction.

The successful grafting of the Hollywood Model onto the political sector has triggered controversy. After all, manufacturing celebrities for entertainment purposes seems far less offensive than manufacturing our elected leaders. But the same ethical problem exists in other newly celebritized sectors, such as science and medicine, where pressure on individuals to achieve high visibility has spawned such aberrations as the lawsuits between French and American researchers over who shall receive credit for discovering the AIDS virus.

In this spread of celebrity-making throughout our culture, an important change has occurred. Visibility-building in its original Hollywood form relied on systematically refining aspirants who had been randomly discovered. Today, however, we have moved from this "discovery model" to a breeding model, to a system that is transforming unknown aspirants into high visibles in much the same way that Sumo wrestlers are grown in Japan, or ballerinas built in the Soviet Union. All over this country, from *Fame*-type high school talent banks in New York City to ice-skating schools in Denver and gymnastics camps in California, we are breeding the highly visible instead of discovering them. For example, for years, towns that wished to promote themselves and stimulate commerce have used celebrities to highlight some local feature or attraction, using a fairly standard formula:

1. Stage a competition to select the local beauty queen.
2. Have her pose with the local avocados, prize cattle, or other local feature attraction.
3. Promote the new celebrity in an elaborate stage show featuring local musical talent.
4. Promote the beauty queen to the local press as a centerpiece for stories about the region and its products.

Today, however, the Pygmalion Principle is beginning to transform Fishing Derbies and Strawberry Festivals across America. The most important changes are those being made in the participants themselves. Not far off is the day when Strawberry Kings and Queens and Bass Derby majorettes will be identified in elementary school and placed into clinics and summer camps, to be systematically bred to play their roles. Soon, seminars will be instituted for instructing parade organizers and band members, and acting lessons given to the most archetypal, quaint, colorful members of the town, creating on demand a celebrity showcase. Festival organizers will combine the manufactured celebrities with the marketing formulas designed by consultants, selecting the most appropriate festival colors, designing logos, and manufacturing cheap peripherals for on-the-spot sale to tourists. Ultimately, the whole spectacle will be packaged for sale to regional and state television, with T-shirts, beach balls, and logo-imprinted Frisbees available for sale through late-night direct-response TV commercials.

That the spread of the quest is leading to the breeding of beauty queens as well as political candidates and CEOs is testimony to the drive to produce new and improved celebrities on demand. But as the quest spreads, so does the intensity of its detractors' attacks.

Attacks on the Quest

Critics and commentators often compare the celebrity world to the scourges of humankind: to pestilence, drought, and depravity. The litany of complaints is by now familiar.

1. *Celebrities have too much power.* They are a special elite who are not subject to society's rules or mores. Why are celebrities frequently quoted as authorities on subjects they know little if anything about? Why should actor Paul Newman have any more say in our political decision-making process than Aunt Sally? At least we know that Aunt Sally is going to caucus meetings, circulating petitions, and speaking before the Village Board.
2. *Celebrities have too much power to attract audiences to events*—especially audiences who have little if any real interest outside the opportunity to celebrity-gaze. Condemned as well is the practice of recruiting celebrities to head university or organization fund-raising drives. In many cases, critics point out, the celebrity fronting for the institution did not even graduate, attend, or belong. When celebrities front for institutions, there is always the danger that their names, and not a legitimate cause, will attract people. Investment brokers A. J. Obie and Associates and Diamond Mortgage Company went bankrupt leaving 400 investors with 20 million dollars in potential losses. The companies' two celebrity endorsers, actors George Hamilton and Lloyd Bridges, suffered more than image damage in the bankruptcy: they were named in a class action lawsuit as "salespeople who participated and aided and abetted in the sale of the securities."[9] The argument was that the investors were lured into the financial arrangement because they believed in the trustworthiness of the celebrities.
3. *Celebrities are synthetic creatures of our media-dominated society.* In return for what real achievements, critics ask, do our celebrities merit their great power? Why, for example, did Mr. T, formerly a bouncer in a Chicago bar, come to dominate the media with his own TV show (live action *and* animated), children's cereal, and support industry peripherals: T-shirts, whistles, posters, dolls, and board games? To the critics, Mr. T takes us one more step from reality to a fake world of warped values, of violence and simplistic answers.
4. *Celebrity is intruding into every sector of American life.* It is one thing to "create" a Mr. T, but quite another to manufacture and market political leaders, sports heroes, religious figures, academics, scientists, and doctors. Gymnast Mary Lou Retton, multiplying her Olympic fame with the help of a retinue of agents and publicists into a whole range of endorsed products, including a line of designer clothes, fuels the controversy. Six months after the Games, Retton was ensconced in a Hyatt suite giving out programmed "interviews" that were tantamount to endorsements for everything from clothing to makeup to her own upcoming per-

> sonal appearances. Upon retiring from active competition, Retton staged a full-scale press conference to announce that she was returning to school, and would be available for broadcasting duties.

In some ways, these criticisms are understandable. The highly visible often earn huge sums of money, get the best tables at restaurants, have their cars parked in special places, and receive VIP treatment at airports, hotels, and shops. Moreover, they seem to live in a state of perpetual grace, insulated from the annoyances and abuses of modern life.

LIFESTYLES OF THE RICH AND FAMOUS

At singer Bobby Vinton's home, the electronic gate swings aside to the tune of one of Vinton's hits. Up the drive, the singer stands in a navy blue tennis outfit, silhouetted against his palatial mansion and the Pacific Ocean beyond. A quick tour of the multi-million dollar home reveals expensive cars, a full recording studio, and a lifestyle reminiscent of the great kings.[10] Living behind his gates, shielded from the cares of everyday life, Vinton probably will never know when Scott's Turfbuilder is on sale at the hardware store.

The special needs of celebrities often lead critics to charge that celebrities have contentious relationships with their admirers. It is a paradox that is unavoidable: the need to set up barriers to keep fans, clients, and audiences at bay, balanced against the need to foster a public perception that the celebrity is close to his or her public. These two competing pressures create the celebrity version of Hide and Seek, typified by the award-winning television and film producer who, while enthusiastically and patiently cooperating throughout our interview, suddenly suspiciously asked, "The interesting thing is, why are *you* doing this book?" It accounts for comedian Shelley Berman graciously consenting to an interview with a group of college students, yet turning suddenly hostile at being asked a question about a career setback.[11] The celebrity, whether baseball manager Billy Martin battling a patron in a bar, or actress Cloris Leachman buying out the contents of a high-fashion boutique to the astonishment of gawking customers, is always juggling the public's envy and admiration. It is not surprising that critics—and fans—sometimes find fault with them.

While possibly exaggerated by folklore and the media, the charge that celebrities are exempt from common rules of behavior, aloof from the publics who support them, is largely accurate. It is a criticism that is important. But it does not lie at the heart of the anti-celebrity question. The truly critical indictment argues that people with less and less actual substance and achievement to justify their claim to well-knownness are becoming more and more highly visible—and, thus, powerful. Rather than the by-product of heroism or achievement, say the critics, visibility (and its pursuit) has become an end in itself. Richard Schickel sums up the feelings of many of celebrity's detractors when he describes the roles that Douglas Fairbanks and his contemporary stars played in the new realities of the media:

> What happened in this period is that the public ceased to insist that there be an obvious correlation between achievement and fame. It was no longer absolutely necessary for its favorites to perform a real-life heroic act, to invent a boon for mankind, to create a mighty business enterprise.... Beginning with the rise of the star system in Hollywood, it was possible to achieve "celebrity" through attainments in the realms of play—spectator sports, acting—and almost immediately thereafter it became possible to become a celebrity (a new coinage describing a new phenomenon) simply by becoming . . . a celebrity. . . .[12]

Many forces helped drive this change in attitude toward achievement, but underlying them all was a rise in the power of audiences. As modern technology created new sports, new forms of entertainment, and whole new areas of human activity, as well as the means to popularize them, audiences developed new interests and needs. The rise of such phenomena as motorcycle racing, corporate takeover warfare, and environmental art—coupled with all the free time and resources that people now had to commit to them—created specialized audiences for legions of new celebrities.

Not only were more celebrities created; increased media exposure and world travel sharply changed the relationship between celebrities and audiences. Now, celebrities are seen often and in rich detail. Previously a distant and alien presence, a celebrity such as the Pope now visits every corner of the globe, reaching much of his audiences in person, and the rest through the media. He is distributed through every conceivable channel: on T-shirts, balloons, and buttons; in instant books and TV specials; in Sunday-paper features and on-the-spot radio reports.

But such universal exposure doesn't just tighten the grip of a select elite of celebrities on audiences; it creates competition, too. A TV viewer not only has the opportunity to embrace the image of the Pope, but also that of evangelist Robert Schuller—or, for that matter, the images of Julia Child, Peter Jennings, or Diane Von Furstenberg.

Why did audiences, as Schickel argues, cease to insist that there be an obvious correlation between achievement and fame? Because as new sectors opened up, the highly visible created within them began to merge their primary function of entertaining with the older hero's functions of inspiring us and reflecting a code of values. Today, business celebrity Saul Steinberg, Reliance Group chairman and corporate raider, is portrayed as a tough gunslinger on the corporate frontier. Jane Fonda, an actress, is promoted as a superwoman for all women to emulate. Astronomer Carl Sagan is presented as a far-seeing prophet warning of apocalyptic visions of the future.

This merging of entertainment, inspiration, and moral instruction creates ambiguities and occasional outrages. Often, when real-life figures do not play out their stories with sufficient attention to drama and values, the celebrity industry's entertainment division takes over completely, recreating the event in order to amplify the drama. Actor Robby Benson—not an athlete, but well known—plays the Olympic 5,000-meter gold medal winner Billy Mills in the film *Running Brave*. For most viewers, Benson *is* Mills. What has become of the real hero? If he's lucky, he's had a good agent hold out for a decent deal for the rights to his story. He may even get a two-minute interview on "The Today Show." But as far as the public's memory goes, Mills has surrendered his identity forever.

The ultimate case of matching a celebrity's actions to the expectations of the marketplace finds a former B-movie actor assuming the real-life role of president—and looking and acting more like a president than almost any president in history. Actor Benson, in the public's consciousness, takes on aspects of the real-life character he portrays; former actor Ronald Reagan, in the public's consciousness, adds desirable fiction-like trimmings to the performance of a real-life task. Granted, Reagan actually was elected president, while Benson is only playing a role. But what is important is that both are trafficking in illusion. By doing so, both Benson and Reagan help meet society's needs. But don't ask the former to run in the Olympics, or the latter to speak without notes.

All of these charges are part of the critics' basic indictment: that celebrities are fundamentally bad for us. But the indictment misses the point. While our social critics attack the highly visible and denounce them as undeserving of their tremendous salaries, power, privilege, and control over society's opinions, what the critics *really* seem to be angry about is that they themselves don't control the process. Critics of celebrity culture will never be able to control image formation. The root causes of why people want—indeed, *need*—celebrities are so basic as to render the critics' complaints superfluous. That the public chooses to worship David Bowie and not the editor of *Commentary* is not necessarily destructive or damaging. It is, to the contrary, often valuable and certainly worth understanding.

High Visibility and the Quest

For aspirants, becoming a celebrity seems to involve a bewildering barrage of illusion-making and transformations. In the process, one can easily lose control of one's identity—and lose touch with one's sense of self. When an image that is designed to meet an audience's expectations is properly crafted, it can be picked up by the media and driven through the culture with a velocity that is sometimes terrifying. When actor-playwright Sam Shepard appeared as test pilot Chuck Yeager in the film *The Right Stuff*, the celebrity publicity machinery churned Shepard's image through *Newsweek*, *Time*, *New York*, *The Atlantic*, the TV networks, the local press—every nook and cranny of American media life. Shepard was "a man's man," "brilliant," "self-educated," "stoic"—characteristics oddly similar to the genuine qualities of the real Yeager (who was himself soon to surface doing Delco TV commercials). Far more people were fed information about this purportedly "real" Shepard than actually saw the film—information so detailed that the public could almost construct a complete imaginary relationship with him. Shepard's relationship with actress Jessica Lange provided even more fuel for the engine that drove his image through the media and into our consciousness. But how many people stopped to consider who the *real* Sam Shepard is—or how severely the demands of celebrity have affected him?

The truth is that very few people care. The reason is that the confusing of real life and "role" life is now a fixture of business and politics as much as entertainment. It is a deliberate strategy to make celebrities knowable to their publics as friends, while taking advantage of the audience's desire to see traditional story lines embodied in celebrities' real lives as well as in their public, media-delivered "performance" lives. Celebrities in old Hollywood had a perfect system for taking advantage of the power of associating themselves with images: the fictional tales they enacted in their films, and the gossip columnists' delivery of the images of their private lives to large publics. Today, the highly visible in every sector are marketing the images they supposedly live. Is Federal Reserve Chairman Paul Volcker *really* the "second most powerful person in America"? Is author Erica Jong *always* so open and vulnerable? Does actress Goldie Hawn *never* get depressed? Who are these people?

Clearly, the controllers of celebrity images have learned from the past that certain stories have power, that the themes a celebrity takes on and projects are potentially very powerful. They learned from the public's fascination with drama in real life—wars, sporting events, military heroism—that drama disguised as real life could set their celebrities apart from less-textured, blander celebrities. The results include the sagas of Jim and Tammy Bakker, Chuck Colson, T. Boone Pickens, Mary Tyler Moore, Bernhard Goetz, and Joan Collins—long-running dramas that intrigue and involve us, with far more staying power than ordinary fiction. As celebrity–manufacturing spreads throughout the culture, it has become common for aspirants in Topeka or Boise to retain public relations advisors to create, refine, tell, and reinforce their stories. The image becomes the celebrity's trademark and new reality.

For some of us, the quest for high visibility will always be controversial. The word *celebrity* will continue to be an alien term suggesting high risk, plasticity, and unnaturalness. For many people, celebrities will still seem to come and go at random, selling us our ice cream and automobiles, getting us to contribute to charities, and influencing the way we vote. For others, celebrity is a goal, an unrelenting desire for high visibility in their sector. But to ignore this phenomenon is to undervalue a key concept of our culture. Without highly visible individuals, most of the business of our culture could not be conducted. The manufacturing and marketing of celebrities is a complex industry—one that all aspirants must understand and that all enlightened citizens must explore.

CHAPTER THREE

The Celebrity Industry

The elevator door opens. In strides the business leader, followed by his media advisor, head speechwriter, operations manager, chief of staff, personal photographer, and his dinner guest, a presidential candidate.

"Are you still driving that old Jaguar?" the candidate asks the businessman.

"No, I just got a Mercedes 560 SEL last week," the businessman replies. "It's a real tank."

"Who picked it out?" the candidate asks.

The businessman nods imperceptibly in the direction of his chief of staff.

The candidate smiles. "So, who picked the color?" he asks.

The businessman smiles. "I don't remember," he says, to knowing laughter. The elevator has reached the penthouse.

One might consider this businessman to be somewhat extravagant, assembling so large a personal staff. But the businessman has a reason. He is committed to high visibility—a commitment requiring that his image be distributed on television and in print, through interviews, live speeches, guest columns, expert testimony, and charity appearances. By assembling so many different experts, he is taking advantage of the opportunities offered by a young industry. It is an industry that serves more consumers than Sears, yet it has no stores. It employs more people than the airlines, but it has few unions. It is as important to the national economy as agriculture, yet it has few lobbyists. It is an industry that is everywhere, yet it is mostly unseen. It is the celebrity industry.

Dedicated to the manufacturing and marketing of highly visible persons, it is the celebrity industry that ultimately arbitrates who, out of the millions who aspire to high visibility, actually achieve it. As businesspeople and others increase their use of celebrity industry services, our businessman is simply attempting to compete. Yet neither he nor the other aspirants it serves understand very well how the celebrity industry works.

As for the public, it is scarcely aware that the celebrity industry exists.

What is the celebrity industry?

Classically, an industry is *a collection of people, materials, equipment, and processes that collectively produce an output that has value to a market.* Just as the automobile industry consists of workers, tools, and designs that turn materials into cars, the celebrity industry consists of specialists who take unknown and well-known people, design and manufacture their images, supervise their distribution, and manage their rise to high visibility. Consider these examples of the celebrity industry at work:

- Jack Kemp, deciding to run for president, would not set out on his quest alone. His campaign will be run much as a national corporation is, with a Washington headquarters coordinating the operations of field offices scattered throughout the country. Supporting Kemp will be press secretaries, ghost writers, media coaches, advertising agencies, political consultants, TV commercial directors, fund-raising experts, direct-mail specialists, and many others whose job it will be to increase Kemp's well-knownness and design an effective Kemp image.
- Wayne Gretzky, star center of the National Hockey League's Edmonton Oilers, is a virtual one-person multinational corporation. Gretzky, "more famous than everyone else in Canada combined," endorses or does commercials for Canon cameras, Titan hockey sticks, Nike sportswear, Travelers Insurance, Mattel Toys, and many others.[1] He even has his own General Mills cereal, Pro-Stars.[2] Four companies handle Gretzky's multi-million-dollar business affairs in Canada and the United States. His activities, which have a significant impact on the Canadian economy and consumer trends and fashions, are handled by a whole corps of image, marketing, and manufacturing specialists.

These industry specialists, working to fulfill the public's great demand for their product, help make the celebrity industry one of the nation's largest. Such items as record and book sales, concert revenue, and the $3.75 billion in movie tickets sold in 1985 are just the more obvious indicators of the industry's size.[3] But just as dependent on celebrities are the sale of cars (George C. Scott for AMC and James Garner for Mazda), stocks and bonds (Bill Cosby for E. F. Hutton, John Houseman for Smith-Barney), fashion (Calvin Klein and Halston), and virtually every other item and service offered in our culture.

It is impossible to put exact numbers on the celebrity industry's gross sales, total employment, or taxes paid. But we know that if it disappeared tomorrow, vanishing also would be the record business, film industry, electronic ministry, television business, and professional sports sector. Law firms and ad agencies, dependent on "name" partners, would suddenly be competing just on their merits. Charities, lacking spokespeople, would see dramatic drop-offs in contributions. The fashion industry, dependent upon "name" designers, would atomize. The entire consumer goods and services sector, so celebritized in recent years through use of endorsers, would have to find an entirely new way to attract consumer attention.

But the celebrity industry *does* exist, and its function is clear: to design, create, and market *faces*, to produce and sustain celebrities in all sectors. The worldwide distribution of Wayne Gretzky's image demonstrates the industry in its present state of the art. But the industry did not reach this level of sophistication overnight. What are the stages through which the celebrity industry evolved? What are the sub-industries and occupations that make it up?

The Evolution of the Celebrity Industry

The celebrity industry has evolved through four stages: the cottage industry stage, the industrializing stage, the factory stage, and the decentralizing stage (see Figure 3).

Through most of its history, until about the early 1920s, celebrity manufacturing and marketing operated largely as a cottage industry. It was only under the influence of an emerging Hollywood that celebrity manufacturing underwent an industrializing process. After World War II, the industry moved into a sophisticated factory stage, and its methodology spread to politics, sports, and business. Today, the celebrity industry is entering a fourth stage, marked by the spread of "transformation factories" from New York and Hollywood to locations all across the country, and by the invasion of organized celebrity manufacturing and marketing into every sector of American life.

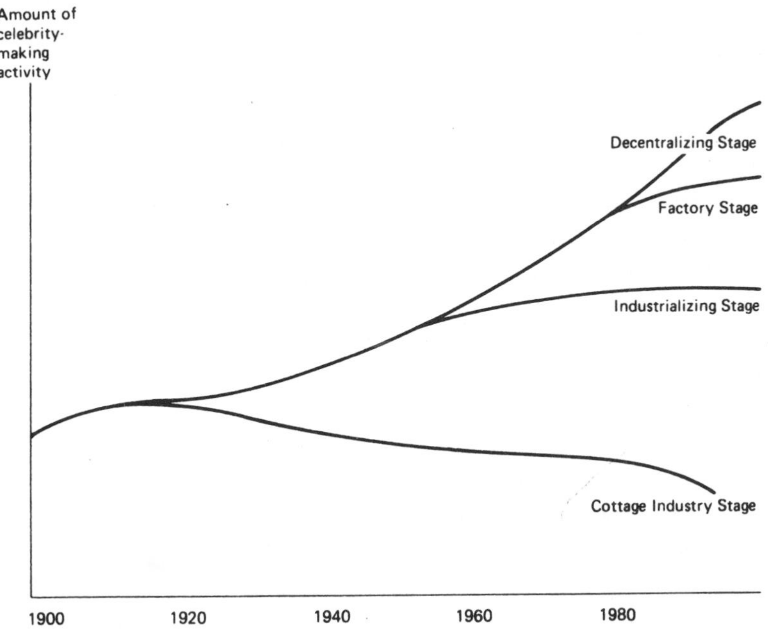

Figure 3: Approximate Evolution of Celebrity-Making Activity and Stages.

Clearly, the manufacturing of celebrities is a growth industry. Each year, more and more people become involved in producing celebrities, more ways are found by businesses and institutions to use them, and more satellite industries spring up to service them. From the agent-training academies of William Morris and International Creative Management (ICM) to the burgeoning business in celebrity endorsements (Pepsi-Cola USA signing Michael Jackson to a record $15 million endorsement package—and not even requiring him to drink the product!); to specialists like Peggy Ganopole of the Ask Mr. Foster travel agency, whose whole function is to smooth celebrities' movements through airports ("Jack Nicholson won't budge from his limousine" unless she's there[4]); to the proliferation of image and style consultants catering to businesspeople, the celebrity industry is booming.

Interestingly, unlike the growth profile of traditional industries, all four stages of the celebrity industry still coexist today: Celebrity manufacturing and marketing still operates as cottage industry in some sectors; in an industrializing stage in many others; in a factory stage in some others; and in a decentralized stage in a few. But although the sophistication of celebrity-making varies from sector to sector, overall sophistication is sharply on the rise. Successful aspirants rarely remain in one stage; as cottage-industry strategies propel an aspirant to higher visibility, industrializing-stage strategies will be attempted. A successful industrial-stage celebrity may be absorbed into a larger factory-stage system. And an unsuccessful aspirant may move through the stages in reverse.

Let's look at the stages in detail, using examples of celebrities who are using the various stages' strategies *today*.

THE COTTAGE INDUSTRY STAGE

Throughout modern history, before the well-knownness of celebrity had replaced achievement-oriented fame, high visibility was created by small "mom and pop" operations that, together in a patchwork, formed a cottage industry. The few professionals who existed were usually in the service of royalty or the church, hired to spread the glory of their employers. Fame seekers in the cottage industry stage were largely on their own.

Consider the situation facing fame seekers in the early 1900s. Many young children were pushed by their parents into taking singing, dancing, piano, or acting lessons in the hope that their achievements would lead to fame and fortune. Most dropped out. Some persevered, landing entry-level jobs in entertainment. Many of these dropped out, too, but some continued performing minor roles, and some of these survivors eventually rose to the top. Factors contributing to their success included the amount of help and encouragement they received from their friends and relatives, their support from teachers and backers, and their "luck" in being in the right place at the right time.

Today, many aspirants are striving for celebrity in the same primitive way, using the cottage-industry resources shown in Figure 4. Typically, "talent" is recognized in a young female vocalist, who is encouraged by family and friends to retain teachers. Along the way, she arranges for a composite of semi-professional photographs and prepares write-ups of her background, previous engagements, and abilities. She contacts venue managers who own or manage bars and nightclubs and asks for a chance to sing. If turned down on all fronts, she may alter her style and start again; or, in extreme cases, she may even begin singing for free on the streets of large cities where crowds gather to hear free entertainment. Most likely, our aspirant will drop out of the celebrity industry altogether—a product that did not make it off the drawing board.

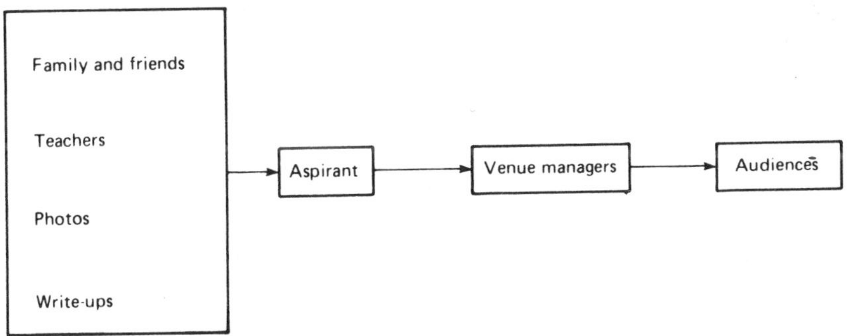

Figure 4: The Cottage Industry Model.

Still, some modern aspirants *do* use cottage-stage strategies successfully. Considered "auteurs" in the arts, entrepreneurs in business, or gadflies in politics, they rely on their own energy and initiative to put their own master plans into action. John Sayles, the critically praised director of independent films such as *The Return of the Secaucus Seven* and *The Brother From Another Planet*, has perfected cottage-stage strategies in the film sector. Maintaining complete creative control of his films, Sayles, in addition to writing and directing, has a hand in production and editing and even appears in small parts.[5] He also maintains economic control of his product, funding the low-budget projects out of his own pocket, getting actors to work for deferred payments, and going on long publicity tours to pitch his films. Despite these competitive disadvantages, Sayles has achieved critical acclaim and high visibility among a widening public.

BECOMING A COLLEGE PRESIDENT

John Evans (a pseudonym) was a successful young politician who was elected to state office at an early age. Hailed as a "boy wonder," he subsequently ran for high office but was defeated several times. Having developed an image as a perennial loser who lacked content or depth, Evans resorted to cottage-stage strategies to continue a quest for celebrity. Reducing his visibility as a politician, Evans took a university position. He then hired a publicist, who generated speaking engagements, media appearances, and mentions in newspaper columns. To reinforce his new image as a serious figure, Evans managed a political campaign and wrote several foundation reports. The cottage-stage techniques paid off: A major university found his image appealing and his visibility useful, and it hired him as its president. For Evans, it was time to close the cottage.

Cottage-industry tactics can be used even by international celebrities. Consider Nobel laureate Milton Friedman:

"We're a staff of two, Professor Friedman and me. . . . So far as I know it was always that way," said Friedman's secretary, Gloria Valentine.[6] "He's quite different from a number of university professors, who have a coterie of people working for them." With this staff of two, Friedman functions effectively as an internationally celebrated economist. Friedman partially credits cottage-industry methods with his comment that he's "never personally had any agent whatsoever."[7]

Both Sayles, and to a lesser extent Friedman, illustrate the major characteristics of the cottage-industry stage of celebrity-making:

1. The aspirant's major backing and support come from family and friends, and organizational support comes from tiny staffs.
2. The aspirant is heavily dependent on self-training, self-initiative, and perseverance.
3. The aspirant initially may lack both an understanding of the nature of markets and information about what the market is looking for and make little if any use of celebrity-industry specialists.

4. The extremely low cost of entry encourages a flood of aspirants to compete for the available slots. It is a buyers' market, with the aspirants dependent upon venue managers whose selection criteria are highly subjective.
5. Successful auditions (or their nonentertainment equivalent) are the key means by which aspirants move up the celebrity pyramid.
6. "Word of mouth" is important in spreading the aspirants' reputation because their use of mass communication is underdeveloped or nonexistent.
7. The venues are highly independent and not organized into local, regional, or national chains, networks, or markets.

THE INDUSTRIALIZING STAGE

In the second stage of the celebrity industry's development, specialists emerge—talent agents, personal managers, publicists, professional coaches, and financial managers—who are able to judge aspirants' talent, develop their potential, solicit interest from venues where they can perform, and negotiate salaries and fees. (See Figure 5.) In this stage, the first specialist whom an aspirant might retain is an agent, publicist, or lawyer. If the aspirant begins to achieve some visibility, he or she might hire a personal manager to handle their personal and financial affairs. The personal manager in turn might hire publicists, professional coaches, business managers, accountants, lawyers, and investment specialists and might also manage the aspirant's relationship with the agent. The publicist, in turn, will work with the communication media to disseminate the aspirant's image and name to venue managers and audiences. The hope is that this promotion activity will help the aspirant's talent agent locate more opportunities for his or her client.

All of the specialists above also exist in the celebrity industry's next level of evolution, the factory stage; in the industrializing stage, however, they simply have not yet reached full professional status. Also central to the industrializing stage, the soliciting of these specialists' help, and the coordination of their efforts, is often handled *by the aspirant*. Decisions and strategies evolve moment to moment, more on an as-needed basis than as a result of a comprehensive strategic plan. Celebrity manufacturing in the industrializing stage is more the work of firemen than architects.

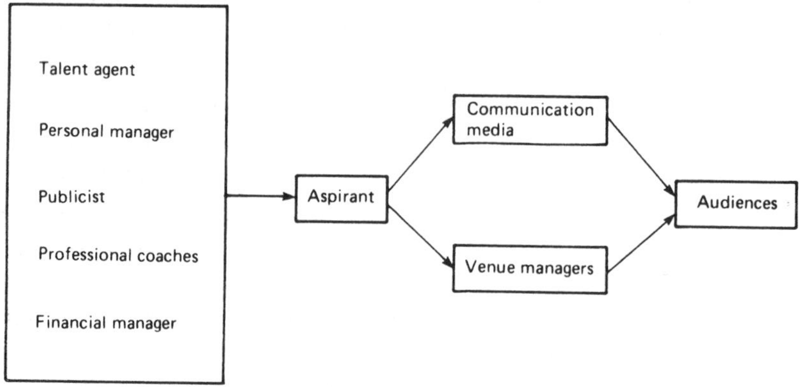

Figure 5: The Industrializing Stage.

Nevertheless, industrializing-stage tactics can be very successful. Consider dentist Dr. Robert William Donovan.[8] Graduating from dental school in 1950, Donovan eventually achieved high visibility using industrializing-stage tactics. Among his many strategic moves, Donovan takes credit for:

1. Expanding the normal distribution of a dentist's traditional "product"—his services—by opening 200 branch offices around the world.
2. Using a market pricing strategy—reduced fees—to increase his visibility among potential patients, and, in the 1980s, moving aggressively into the Health Maintenance Organization market.
3. Establishing an academy that taught orthodontics to general dental practitioners, enabling Donovan to further increase visibility by lecturing at universities all over the country.
4. Providing graduate dental students offices in which to intern, thus assuring himself of a steady flow of future consultation referrals and wide geographic reach—ultimately achieving a consulting practice in New York, Miami, Los Angeles, Dallas, San Juan, and Chicago.
5. Assembling a consortium of specialists (plastic surgeons, dentists, cosmetologists, orthodontists, hair stylists, and dermatologists) to create a total Face Clinic, where, as Donovan says, "You can turn in your head and get a whole new one."[9]

In the entertainment sector, internationally known reggae musician Bob Marley (of Bob Marley and the Wailers) also used industrializing-stage techniques. These included using mentor relationships (Clement Dodd, Johnny Nash, Allan Cole), attempting self-promotion with his own record label, and strategically linking himself with political causes to help build his image.

What placed Marley's quest in the industrializing stage was its hit-or-miss style planning, and its reliance on other specialists to help the quest succeed. As the Wailers' guitarist Peter Tosh (who would achieve celebrity in his own right after Marley's death) commented, "We were too young for producing. We never understood certain important things, like how to get on the radio or sell our records. We only knew how to make them."[10] As far as promotional and marketing sophistication, Marley, early in his career, was still firmly in the cottage-industry stage, at one point employing hoodlums to bully Jamaican radio stations into playing his songs. But slowly, Marley began to take advantage of other specialists' expertise. He joined forces with an already-visible singer, Johnny Nash, and provided backup music for Nash's albums. He adopted and changed managers and mentors. He even started his own record label and sold his records out of his own store in Jamaica. The strategies succeeded, with Marley eventually selling more than 200 million records worldwide.

For aspirants ranging from dentists to musicians, the industrializing-stage model of celebrity-making incorporates the following features:

1. Aspirants design their own self-promotion strategies to link themselves to existing institutions and aggressively use pricing and marketing techniques.
2. The stage is marked by the emergence of specialists such as talent agents, personal managers, publicists, professional coaches, business managers, and venue managers.
3. With the exception of the business managers and talent coaches, the other specialists are not highly professional; they operate on a need-fulfillment basis, dealing with crises as they occur; they run small-scale operations and vary greatly in their level of competence.
4. Entry into these specialist fields is very easy; many of them lack training or licensing requirements. Professional knowledge and evaluation criteria are neither well developed nor well disseminated.

5. Much of the action is controlled by venue managers, who conduct fairly active searches for qualified performers.

THE FACTORY STAGE

Two key developments characterize celebrity manufacturing in the factory stage: The operations of industry specialists grow more sophisticated, with master organizations appearing to coordinate their services; and the control of the celebrity marketing process passes from the aspirant into the hands of others. New specialists emerge, such as costumers, photographers, hair stylists, makeup artists, communication experts, psychologists, marketing researchers, commercial marketers—all ready to assist in the process of transforming unknowns into celebrities, and translating high visibility into profits. Concurrently, the specialists who emerged in the cottage-industry and industrializing stages—agents, personal managers, publicists—are improving their craft and becoming more systematic and knowledgeable. Professional associations are formed to protect and promote specialists' interests and offer training; a few even initiate licensing procedures. Some specialists, notably agents, build large firms with national and sometimes international coverage and connections. Various complementary specialists link themselves into networks and embark on joint ventures. Transformation budgets grow larger, and more sectors of the society now draw upon the machinery of the industry.

In this stage, aspirants are transformed in "factories" very much like the Hollywood factories of the 1930s, wherein studio makeup artists, costumers, and coaches prepared the stars for filming while publicists supplied the hype and distributors bought and sold the filmed wares.

An excellent example of the factory stage of celebrity manufacturing is Motown, the largest black-owned business enterprise in the United States. In its early days, Motown's founder, Berry Gordy, established a hugely successful factory for manufacturing black pop singers. Gordy painstakingly groomed his performers, teaching them to evoke a strategically designed musical style in order to reinforce Motown's image. His power over image was complete, involving the total transformation of aspirants who were sometimes recruited straight out of high school. Operating on the same principle that had made Detroit the car capital of the world, Gordy's factory employed specialists to handle songwriting, artist development, repertoire, artist management, production, distribution, even choreography. No aspect of the potential celebrities' images—their songs, sounds, styles, clothes, dance routines, or work schedules—was left to chance.[11]

Gordy went so far as to set up International Talent Management Inc., which put his promising stars through up to six months of "finishing school" training. Said Motown performer and later top executive Smokey Robinson, "We taught our artists everything from hygiene to doing interviews, even what to say to people on the street."[12]

Celebrity-factory techniques of the type used by Motown and other entertainment organizations are now being used by image makers to launch business leaders, politicians, starlets, artists, sports figures, and others. The factory system's purpose is straightforward: to launch aspirants in much the same way that new products are launched by professional marketers working for major consumer goods companies. The aspirants' potential audiences are selected and analyzed, the aspirants' concept and story are refined and positioned for the audience, and their clothing, appearance, and behavior are designed to reinforce their roles and types. In its factory stage:

1. The industry has attracted a number of new specialists beyond the agents, personal managers, publicists, and specialists who characterized the industrializing stage.
2. The various specialists have organized professional associations to protect and promote their interests, and they have established rating and licensing procedures. The result is higher (though not formidable) barriers to entry and an increase in specialist skill levels.
3. Rather than being controlled by the aspirant, strategy and tactics are handled by independent managers, or by large vertically integrated firms that have national and international coverage and connections. These firms are prepared to spend larger budgets to launch or support celebrities.
4. Celebrity manufacturing has moved into sectors beyond entertainment—notably sports, politics, art, business, and religion.
5. Aspirants and celebrities in this stage routinely give away not 10 percent of their income, but up to 50 percent support the various

specialists who surround them. Actor William Petersen, star of the films *To Live and Die in L.A.* and *Manhunter,* complained:

> It's expensive to be successful in acting. The largest percentage goes to the federal government in a big way—they take 40 percent. . . . I pay 10 percent to my personal manager and 5 percent to my business manager. So off the top, 15 percent goes to just the people who handle my money. . . . About 15 to 20 percent goes to expenses, literally expenses—being an actor. So that gets it up to about 75 percent. I'm left with about 25 percent of my salary.[13]

In the factory stage, celebrity production begins to echo even more subtle aspects of modern manufacturing and marketing. There is less random guesswork and more marketing research and design; fewer errors and more planning. Packaging, pricing, advertising, and distribution are all fully integrated. In an ideal factory stage, the celebrity industry has identified consumer needs, developed a corps of experienced managers, and established a repertory of visibility-generating formulas based on experience and research. (See Figure 6.) In all these ways, it mimics traditional business practice.

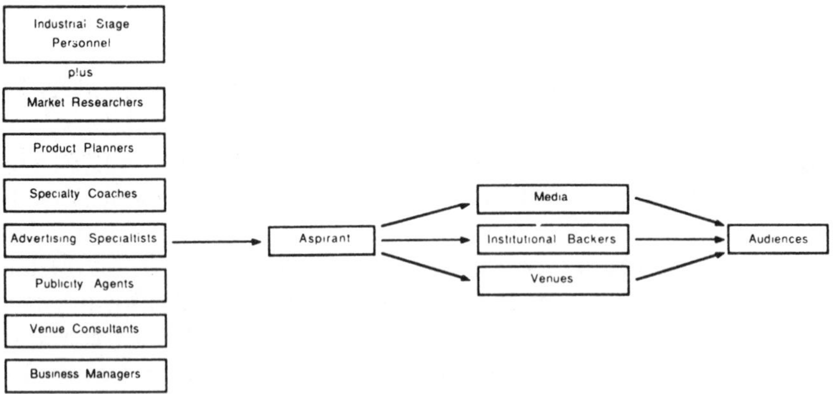

Figure 6: The Factory Stage.

In the celebrity industry's next stage, however, tradition is augmented by innovation.

draws upon several industries to help turn unknown aspirants into *its* products. Figure 8 shows the major participating sub-industries whose services must be coordinated to produce and promote celebrities. Not every sub-industry is used by every sector, of course. Religious celebrities have not yet turned to agents; some celebrities who have, such as business executives, do not yet contract for manufacturers to reproduce their likenesses on dolls and lunch boxes. But as celebrity continues to spread, new sectors are making use of more of the sub-industries all the time. What are the sub-industries?

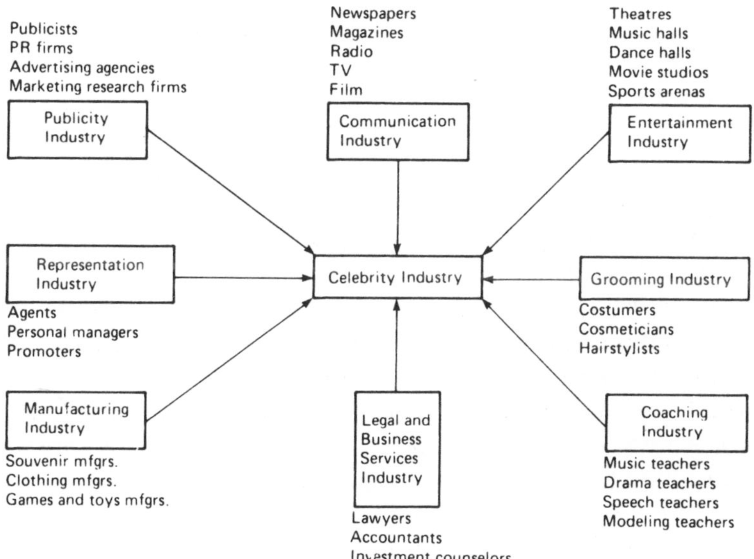

Figure 8: Structure of the Celebrity Industry.

ENTERTAINMENT INDUSTRY

The entertainment industry consists of all the organizations involved in producing entertainment and entertainers. Working within it are actors, actresses, directors, producers, makeup artists, wardrobe advisors, film editors, musicians, photographers—all dedicated to advancing the art of illusion. But the entertainment industry is not limited to the traditional media of film, radio, and television. The celebrity industry is today making increased use of such entertainment venues as museums (as platforms for celebrities' charity appearances), county fairs (to afford celebrities in-the-flesh exposure to audiences), baseball games (having celebrities sing the national anthem or throw out ceremonial pitches), and many other venues. Because of the celebrity industry's deep roots in Hollywood, many of its component industries whose descriptions follow also began as support services of the entertainment sector.

REPRESENTATION INDUSTRY

The representation industry includes all those who solicit for or negotiate engagements for aspirants for a fee, typically a commission. Formerly confined to the entertainment sector, the ranks of the representation industry are swelling as its activities spread rapidly into every sector of American life. Because the representation profession lacks a clear structure and is still dominated by entrepreneurs, its members operate at very different levels of skill and creativity. Many representatives work in the capacity of representing celebrities. There is often confusion even as to what they should be called.

"I'm not an agent," Mark McCormack insists. "Agents are fat bald guys with cigars. Agents book bands. I'm a manager, sort of an engineer, not only of careers and lives, but of things, concepts, ideas."[14]

Whatever McCormack calls himself, he has generated great wealth for his clients. Bjorn Borg, for example, earned about $7 million in 1983 (the year he retired) because McCormack got him lucrative contracts to endorse Italian Fila sportswear, Belgian Donnay racquets, and many other products. Of course, not every agent or manager achieves this success for his or her clients. Woody Allen portrayed (if comically exaggerated) the less successful type of agent in *Broadway Danny Rose*. His character represents a stable of woeful performers, including a blind xylophonist, a one-legged tap dancer, a parrot who sings "I've Gotta Be Me," and a fumbling hypnotist who can't get his subjects out of their trances. Rose barely makes a nickel for his clients, or himself. Although fictional, Rose illustrates the wide range in skill levels of all the different types of representatives: agents, personal managers, and promoters.

The Agent. Agents generate employment for their clientele—often a large group of aspirants, each of whom may command only a small part of the agent's time. For all but the most highly visible, aspirants tend to need agents more than agents need aspirants. That is because agents function as filters, as buffers between aspirants and those who employ them. Their compensation is a percentage (generally 10 percent, but not always so limited) of the client's earnings. In recent times, agents have moved toward more professionalism by holding conferences, staging anniversary banquets, starting newsletters such as *ATA* (Association of Talent Agents), and generally attempting to upgrade their public image.

THE SUPREME REPRESENTATIVE

Mark McCormack has had an interesting variety of clients. As the best-selling author of *What They Don't Teach You At Harvard Business School,*[15] he cites his management of Jean-Claude Killy, Jackie Stewart, Bjorn Borg, Herschel Walker, Martina Navratilova, Chris Evert-Lloyd, and over five hundred others whom he represents in their search for high visibility. Among other clients are groups as unlikely as the English Catholic Church and the Nobel Foundation. McCormack was even retained to work on the Pope's tour of the United Kingdom in 1981. According to John Wild of McCormack's International Management Group, "With the visit of any huge celebrity, there are a lot of souvenirs sold. The Vatican wanted to make sure that any souvenirs sold in connection with the Pope's visit were officially licensed."[16] The assignment to handle the merchandising of the Pope's image, while seemingly somewhat of a stretch for a sports representative, is really only the harbinger of a trend. "I have dealt," said McCormack, "with heads of state and heads of corporations, with international bankers and small-town advisors, with bureaucratic governing sports bodies and autocratic empire builders."[17] In a growing world culture where the likenesses of sports figures, media personalities, heads of states, and religious leaders are fair game for reproduction on T-shirts, balloons, and clocks, getting a fair cut must be negotiated by experts.

The Personal Manager. These specialists represent fewer clients than agents, but they do so more comprehensively. Some personal managers completely orchestrate their clients' lives—answering their mail, investing their money, buying their real estate, planning their schedules, placing their children in schools, even hiring the gardener and firing the maid. Singer Laura Branigan's former personal manager, Sid Bernstein, described himself as her "wet nurse, her shrink, her accountant, her handholder."[18] Danny Goldberg, who helps guide the career of *Miami Vice* star Don Johnson, explained, "I'm part negotiator, part public relations man, part idea man, and part therapist. Right now, I'm involved in about fifteen things at the same time."[19]

Promoters. These individuals arrange, fund, and advertise events, be they firetrap club performances of unknown rock groups, convention appearances by former *Star Trek* performers, or world heavyweight title fights. Promoters do not work for the client on a permanent basis but contact the client or the client's agent for particular engagements. Promoters are primarily interested in highly visible, "hot" performers. The key difference between promoters and traditional agents and personal managers is that the promoter is taking on great personal risk by financing events. Promoters raise money from investors, hire the necessary personnel, advertise the event, and hope that their profit projections are accurate.

Agents, personal managers, and promoters work primarily for the celebrity, or "seller." They should not be confused with *booking agents, venue managers*, and *casting directors*, who represent buyers. *Booking agents* run their own businesses and are hired to find talent for theaters and concert halls and sign the talent to contracts; they are paid a commission by the venues. *Venue managers* are paid a salary; they often contact performers or their agents directly. *Casting directors* are hired by film studios, theaters, and advertising agencies to find the right persons to cast in specified roles.

DEVELOPMENT OF AGENTS

Some people just stumble into agentry accidentally. This can happen as a result of being Brooke Shields' mother, marrying Loretta Lynn, spotting the Beatles in a Liverpool nightclub, or coaching Olympic sprinter Carl Lewis. The random nature of agent development is illustrated by the rapid rise of punk rock manager and promoter Eric Nihilist. As a high school student, Nihilist began befriending members of newly emerging punk rock bands in the Midwest. Soon he formalized his role, supplying food and other necessities for the musicians. In the process he started to understand their problems and perform minor managerial tasks. He ultimately began to perform as an agent at the age of eighteen. Nihilist had two advantages:

1. He was in the same age group as the performers. They were his class. In the agent business, the word *class* describes the groups of people that the agent first launched. As the agent ages, generating new clients can become a serious problem.
2. Punk rock music was not attractive to well-established agents and promoters at the time. This provided Nihilist's opportunity.

The accidental route, with its emphasis on entrepreneurism, is the least professional of several routes to agentry. More likely to be successful are those who enter the agentry business through a natural career evolution. Marvin Josephson started as a CBS lawyer, decided to become an agent, misfired with his first client (a TV announcer), succeeded with Captain Kangaroo, and then acquired a series of agencies. Now he is the president of International Creative Management (ICM), one of the largest representation companies in the world.

Jay Bernstein, on the other hand, started in the mail room at the William Morris Agency. Moving to a competitive agency as a junior publicist, he eventually began his own firm. Moving next into talent development, Bernstein became a personal manager for Farrah Fawcett and is now a packager of TV and film projects. The natural evolution route also includes accountants who moved to agentry, and even stage designers who hook up with an aspirant and then begin to function as agents. Recently, courses in entertainment law have begun to appear, along with courses in agenting that might lead to celebrity management.

The most conventional route to agentry is institutional. This means finding work with William Morris, ICM, or another established firm. In this case, the trick is getting hired. There are many more applicants than jobs. The applicant who is hired may begin in the mail room, move to secretarial work, then to junior agent, and finally to agent. John Leven started in the William Morris parking lot and later moved to the mail room. He then began to bring into William Morris his talented college classmates—literally, his "class." He eventually turned to his supervisors and said, "I'm bringing you business; make me an agent." They did.

An agent's most important task is to find work for the client. This includes scanning for opportunities, phoning or visiting booking agents and venue managers, making the case for the client, negotiating the terms, and making sure the client shows up for the engagement.

Agents also feed information to their clients about what is happening in the client's sector. Whether it is advice on which teams are looking for players, where clients should eat or be seen, or which corporations are quietly looking for new CEOs, agents are expected to be conversant with the sector's rules and activities. They also try to arrange introductions to the right people. Every agent has a network of acquaintances and influential people to whom he or she may introduce the client.

Agents also provide advice and coaching help to improve their clients' marketability. Agents may offer pointers on effective dress, speech, deportment, and strategy, but more often they urge their clients to obtain training from coaches.

Agents may also arrange publicity for clients. The agent may dream up events or stunts to create greater client visibility. Or the agent may recommend a publicist for the client to employ.

Agents also attempt to line up other projects for the client. These may include poster deals, commercial endorsements, speaking engagements, trade show appearances, or TV commercials. These supplemental opportunities, originally seen as fun money or bonuses, are fast becoming the primary interest of agent-client relationships.

All six functions—finding work, passing on information, advising and coaching, arranging introductions, publicizing, and finding appearance opportunities—are rarely performed by all agents. Most agents try to sell their existing clients as they are. *It is the rare agent who takes such interest in his or her clients as to put in the time to improve as well as sell the product*. But as the celebrity industry becomes more sophisticated, "total service agents" are becoming very important to their clients, playing the roles of surrogate parents and spouses, offering friendship, guidance, and hand holding.

COMING AND GOING

On a warm spring day, sports agent Jack Childers arrives for the interview in a bright red Mercedes.[20] He's on the phone. He could have selected his '37 Cord convertible or a '72 DeTomaso Pantera. But somehow the Mercedes fits the day. Beginning by recounting his past, Childers quickly moves to the story of how he moved into agentry through the back door: being one of the first to handle licensing agreements for merchandise bearing the likenesses of film and television figures. Childers is asked about his strategies, techniques, operations. But he clearly would rather tell stories about his clients; about the lucrative connections he made between client Oscar Robertson and Spaghetti-Os, and between Dick Butkus and Prestone Antifreeze; about Kareem Abdul-Jabbar appearing in the hit film *Airplane,* and about his successful negotiations with Oakland A's owner Charlie Finley over Reggie Jackson. He is, according to airline magazine *Republic Scene,* the Babe Ruth of agents: managing money, counseling career moves, and helping his clients to extend their visibility after their playing days are over. Jack Childers, leaving the interview, can rest assured that he's covered everything.

PUBLICITY INDUSTRY

The publicity sub-industry includes a host of individuals and firms that are skilled in boosting aspirant visibility through the skillful generating of publicity. Populating this industry are publicists, public relations firms, and advertising agencies, all of which rely heavily on the work of marketing researchers.

Publicists were, in fact, the first celebrity promoters—individuals with a flair for writing and for generating attention for their clients. Originally called "press agents," they knew how to get their clients "ink." Many in fact were former journalists whose ties to their ex-employers helped their clients gain publicity.

Public relations firms are another important arm of the publicity industry. These firms were started by people who offered to defend and promote corporations to counteract the pressure from the public, legislators, and other interest groups. Thus Ivy Lee, hired by Standard Oil of New Jersey to defend the company's image, eventually attracted additional clients who wanted representation. Today, large public relations firms such as Hill and Knowlton, Burson–Marsteller, and Daniel Edelman strive to raise the visibility of individuals, organizations, cities—even countries—using such tools as press relations, product publicity, corporate communications, lobbying, and client counseling.

Advertising agencies constitute the largest branch of the publicity industry, responsible for touting hundreds of thousands of products, services, persons, places, ideas, and causes. One of the largest sub-industries of the celebrity industry, advertising is a $70 billion industry staffed with media experts, art directors, marketing researchers, account executives, and others. The advertising industry is also one of the largest employers of celebrities, using them four basic ways:

- as actors (when celebrities dramatically demonstrate a product or service)
- as spokespeople (when celebrities are employed *over a long period of time* to promote products or services, often becoming very closely identified with them)
- as testimonial givers (when, having used the product or service in their careers, they can attest to its quality or value)
- as endorsers (when *not necessarily* having used the product or service, celebrities lend their names to the products)

Celebrity advertising, while fast growing, presents a whole series of controversial issues. From the celebrities' point of view, endorsements can create overexposure, tarnishing their images with their audiences. Mark Spitz, seven-medal-winning Olympic swimmer, demonstrated such risks by simultaneously signing deals with the Schick Razor Company, Adidas, Elton Corporation, Kransco Watergames, Spartan Pools, and Regal Apparel for a Mark Spitz line of shirts. "They thought I was a money grubber," said Spitz. "What's wrong with making a dollar?"[21]

From the advertisers' or manufacturers' point of view, should the image of the product be risked on the fallibility of a single person? Ideal Toy Company invested a great deal of money in its Evel Knievel toy line, only to see the money lost when Knievel gained some unintended publicity by assaulting a television executive with a baseball bat. Celebrity endorsements and testimonials have become so lucrative that a special branch of the publicity sub-industry has evolved to manage them.

Although the various components of the publicity sub-industry partially rely on creativity and improvisation, they depend more upon proven techniques, formulas, and research, gathering information about audience demographics, needs, perceptions and preferences, venues, media costs, and geographical markets. For this, they often rely on marketing research specialists to provide information.

COMMUNICATION INDUSTRY

How do we *know* celebrities? With rare exceptions, we know them entirely through the media. Celebrities' images, products, stories—most of what we consume of the celebrity product is distributed through media channels. The finest strategy, deftest timing, most brilliant story use—all will fail without the help of the communication industry. Countless aspirants have had all the elements of transformation and marketing operating in sync, only to misfire spectacularly because they failed to come across effectively through the media. Hubert Humphrey was regarded as one of the most dynamic, exciting politicians ever to light up a rally; on TV, he was perceived as a hyperactive, if kindly, bumbler.

Network television, cable, radio, film, newspapers, magazines—each of these has developed specialized ways to take advantage of the celebrity phenomenon. Magazines such as *People* and *Us*, national live telephone call-in shows such as "Rockline" and "Larry King Live," "infotainment" TV venues such as "Entertainment Tonight," and the scores of TV talk shows—all cater to the celebrity industry's needs. Those who understand these forums have tremendous advantages; those who don't are restricted to live encounters and small local markets.

"ASK ME ABOUT MARK HUGHES"

Some celebrities seem to exist *solely* as media images, as electronic leaders who hardly ever appear in the flesh. Mark Hughes, founder of the HerbalLife nutrition and diet products empire, has effectively used communications media to attract customers among the public, as well as to recruit his salespeople and distributors. "With the fervor of a tent-show preacher and the glitz of a TV huckster," Hughes hosts coast-to-coast cable TV training sessions and promotional shows.[22] Announcing new packages of obscure powders, awarding prizes to top salespeople, and delivering rambling, emotional rebuttals to attacks on his person and products, Hughes blends the features of many different TV formats—game shows, press conferences, and religious revivals—to take advantage of the latest technology to distribute his image as widely as did presidents in a former age.

APPEARANCE INDUSTRY

With image so critical to celebrity manufacturing and marketing, the appearance business is one of the celebrity industry's fastest-growing components. Makeup specialists always were important to the entertainment sector; now, ironically, businesspeople are demanding a greater share of the grooming business' services. The alteration or enhancement of appearance is now handled not merely by hair stylists and cosmeticians but by clothing counselors, color consultants, image coordinators—even plastic surgeons. As Dr. Robert Donovan, whose new Face Clinic provides complete image makeovers, says, "You must have the basic ability, but your success is determined by your visibility."[23] What are the general going rates for plastic surgery? Try $3,000 for eye lifts, $7,750 for face lifts, $5,000 for tummy tucks, $4,500 for breast enlargement, and between $1,500 and $4,000 for cellulite suctioning.[24]

More than just the transformation of facial appearance and body shape is being industrialized. More than 250 total image consulting firms appeared in 1984's *Directory of Personal Image*

Consultants; clothing and color consultants earn between $50 and $75 an hour, with "personal shoppers" earning between $25 and $250 an hour.[25, 26]

COACHING INDUSTRY

Who is it that actually designs a celebrity's transformation? Depending on the sector, the strategy design may be in the hands of an agent, personal manager, campaign manager, gallery owner, or the aspirant. Singers need singing lessons, politicians need speech lessons, tennis players need serving lessons. Of course, not everyone who seeks to improve a skill aspires to celebrity; but many do, and it is to the coaching industry that this critical task of improvement falls.

The coaching industry is expanding at an extraordinary rate, and it is for several reasons. With celebrity sectors understood better than ever before, more and more is becoming known about which images succeed and which fail. With the rise of media, celebrities have fewer chances to hone their images at low-cost, low-risk, small venues. The old-fashioned system of accidentally finding someone to help you perfect your baseball swing, polish your courtroom presentation style, or improve your bedside manner has given way to a huge market for formal coaching services.

Of course, many of the coaches and trainers who supply these services still operate in the cottage-industry stage. In any city, one can find communication consultants for business-people, freelance singing and dancing teachers, piano instructors, speech coaches, and others. But the size and sophistication of the coaching sector are growing. In what is probably an understated figure, speech consultants alone were reported to have grossed $88 million in 1984.[27] Annual salaries for most experienced speech consultants are put between $50,000 and $150,000[28], with daily billing rates for top consultants averaging $843.[29] With so much profit potential, some coaches have founded schools to train the most talented or the most moneyed: Communispond trains public speakers, Julliard trains singers and musicians, The Studio trains actors. Driven by economies of scale, a franchise system of coaching is beginning to emerge on the model of Berlitz or McDonald's, where particular styles of training are featured.

LEGAL AND BUSINESS SERVICES INDUSTRY

Most celebrities do not know much about managing themselves as businesses; few have the time to learn. Considering that many are suddenly confronted with the need to manage and invest large amounts of money, develop such legal entities as corporations, and prepare estate plans, it's not surprising that most celebrities turn to lawyers, accountants, and investment advisors. Marvin Snyder, a former tax accountant who has acted as business manager for Ed Asner, Lily Tomlin, Kenny Rogers, John Ritter, and many others, says:

> With celebrity clients, you have to assume that the job they have right now may be the last job they ever have . . . that the assets may have to last for a long period of time.[30]

There's also the issue of protection. As Snyder says,

> Being in the public eye, the celebrity is prone to being hit upon by every guy in the country who is trying to sell something—people who are putting together deals that are less than what you might call "sound." Not versed in the business world, the celebrity is very gullible, an easy target. That's why the business manager is so important; he is the alter ego, he tries to restrain the celebrity from jumping off the deep end and going into a lot of programs that are just scams. One of the business manager's most important functions is to say no, without disrupting the celebrity's ego.[31]

Seeing the potential in this area, some law and accounting firms have specialized in providing services to entertainers, sports figures, and politicians. Many celebrities have, in fact, "relinquished control over every conceivable facet of their financial lives—save actually earning the money—to one of a growing number of firms that, for a not insubstantial sum, receive all their income, pay all their bills, manage their myriad investments, purchase their insurance, pay their taxes, and even shop for their houses and find them good deals on their cars."[32]

But financial managers go beyond even these functions. As Snyder described it,

> The business manager serves many purposes. He is a personal advisor and a psychiatrist, because when you deal with money you're dealing with a disruptive force, something involved with the celebrity's marriage, family, children, girlfriend. Depending on how strong a relationship you have with the client, the celebrity may divulge things to you that he doesn't talk about to other people.[33]

ENDORSEMENT INDUSTRY

With the celebrity industry growing more sophisticated, no longer can celebrities themselves pursue endorsement deals, record contracts, or rights agreements. Expert help is becoming crucial. This is because the *image* of a celebrity, like the proverbial hog in the slaughterhouse, is now being cut up and used in many ways. "Tools of the trade" endorsements are when celebrities endorse items they depend on in the course of their work—for example, John McEnroe endorsing tennis shoes. "Non-tool" endorsement involve products they *don't* depend on—for example, McEnroe endorsing Bic razors. A third major use of celebrity images is as an attention-getting device displayed on manufactured goods (McEnroe's image adorning a beach towel).

These practices can generate profit far above a celebrity's main activity. John Hauser, former executive with ProServ, Inc., said, "Top athletes can expect to have a three-to-one ratio in terms of endorsements versus salary."[34] William "the Refrigerator" Perry signed a contract for $1.35 million over four years as an NFL rookie, but he stands to take in many times that sum in endorsements and peripherals.[35] Perry also demonstrates the importance of "hotness" in the endorsement industry: In just the first two months after the 1986 Super Bowl, he visited "Dallas for a shoe convention, Indianapolis for a truck-refrigeration company, New York for a macaroni-and-cheese company, Miami for a big-and-tall men's convention, Cleveland for a bacon commercial, Chicago for an auto show and soda commercial, Denver for an auto show, Chicago for a paint company, a jeans commercial, and a paper-towel company."[36]

> **SHOULD NEW JERSEY HAVE CELEBRITY LICENSE PLATES?**
>
> A concept being explored for generating revenue is to enable drivers to feature names or pictures of their favorite celebrities on their license plates. While many motorists have for years displayed plates featuring their own names or favorite sayings, the practice pales before the possibility of teaming your Toyota Corolla with the likeness of Frank Sinatra. This new practice might find the New Jersey Turnpike flooded with "Frankie," "F. Sinatra," "Old Blue Eyes," and "Ch of Bd." Coming next? Perhaps the naming of streets, airports, and forests after teen idols and business heroes.

Manufacturers of peripherals—coffee mugs, sunglasses, paper towels, lunch boxes—show little interest in low-level celebrities. As mass marketers, they prefer the faces and names of "hot" celebrities, such as Diane Von Furstenberg perfume and Jimmy Bakker's Heritage USA Condominiums, to buy or license for brand use. When successful, the strategy can almost merge the product's perceived qualities with the celebrity's (James Garner and Mariette Hartley for Polaroid cameras; Burgess Meredith for Honda). Other manufacturers create games centering on celebrities, or they manufacture dolls and toys with their likenesses. It is the power of visibility at work. A lunch box bearing the likeness of a children's favorite TV star will far outsell a comparable generic product. In the film sector, the profits that accrue from the sales of peripherals may equal or surpass earnings from ticket sales.  The key from a marketing standpoint is that the celebrity's likeness will draw the attention not just of the celebrity's fans, but also of those many consumers who are not members of the celebrity's main audience but still liable to be influenced in their purchase decision by their familiarity with the celebrity's image. Studies by ad agencies indicate that consumers will not assume that an endorsed product will be any better than its competition. What the consumer will do is pay closer attention to advertising that features celebrities, absorbing more of the sales message.[37]

The use of endorsements may be poised on the brink of a dramatic expansion. Until now, endorsements and peripherals have been limited mainly to the sports and entertainment sectors. But the power of visibility is catching on in other sectors.

DR. BARNARD'S MIRACLE CREAM

The first heart transplant was performed by South African surgeon Dr. Christiaan Barnard, an achievement that made Barnard a medical legend. What role is appropriate to such an achiever? Chairing foundations, giving lectures, endowing professorships, and lending prestige to important medical research are just a few examples. So it was with some shock that the medical community confronted the image of Dr. Barnard peering out from daily newspaper ads endorsing a miracle face cream called Glycel. Even more disturbing to doctors was the public's reaction to Barnard's endorsement. What a heart surgeon knew about cosmetics was of little concern to consumers. When it came to buying a $75 ounce of wrinkle cream, Dr. Barnard's name was good enough for them.[38] How far off is the day when the Chief Justice of the United States endorses a do-it-yourself divorce kit?

CELEBRITY SERVICE INDUSTRY

A growing sub-industry within the celebrity industry consists of the many different firms that meet unusual celebrity- or audience-related needs and interests. One such firm is Celebrity Service International, which operates in the United States and in Europe.[39] Its sole function is to closely track the movements of celebrities in various sectors. "What we are selling is access" to celebrities, said Donna Schor, the service's marketing director. For a fee of $1,500 per year, subscribers are entitled to receive tracking bulletins, as well as call in to ascertain a particular celebrity's exact whereabouts. "If Lee Iacocca is in Washington," said Schor, "you want to know about it. You want to know how to contact him, what he is doing, where he is staying." And the company's service is in high demand. Said *The Wall Street Journal* about Celebrity Service's daily bulletin on celebrity whereabouts, "Because today's bulletin items are next week's talk-show guests or newspaper profile subjects, subscribers scramble for copies. About 30 messengers from TV networks and newspapers line up outside the New York office every morning to take early delivery of the bulletin."[40]

Another firm directly generated by the celebrity industry is Ron Smith's Celebrity Lookalikes, a modeling and talent agency that provides look-a-likes to ad agencies and others. Other businesses sustain themselves by playing off the celebrity world: publishers who specialize in "Where Are They Now"–type books, or such items as the *New York Celebrity Locator*, which, for $5, will tell fans that Henry Kissinger lives at 435 E. 52nd Street.[41] In the United States there are currently 50,000 celebrities who are immortalized in 600 Halls of Fame, including country music performers, swift pickle-packers, hard-riding dog mushers, and dead-eye shuffle board players.[42] There are even purveyors of high-quality goods who solicit a celebrity clientele (such as the Manhattan butcher who is in such high demand that there is a long waiting list to become his customer). Celebrities are even catered to by hypnotists. Harvey Meisel of the Institute for Hypnosis specializes in applying his technique to major league baseball players.

Even more numerous than these specialists are the businesses and entrepreneurs of the celebrity support industry. As celebrities rise in visibility, they acquire two types of support personnel.[43] The "home office" staff consists of the celebrity's agent, personal manager, PR person, and others whose roles are fairly defined, and who operate out of a fixed address. But celebrities are, by nature, mobile. In all sectors, they travel a great deal. In the case of international celebrities and legends, the money may be available to transport the celebrity's home support staff wherever he or she goes. But many celebrities cannot afford the huge cost. That's why a whole cottage industry has sprung up to service the needs of celebrities on the road. Ranging from seamstresses to dentists, drug dealers to phone-answering services, these individuals offer celebrities discretion. With old-fashioned rules of fair play routinely discarded by today's more aggressive celebrity press, celebrities live in constant fear of the indiscriminate information leak. The treatment of a common venereal disease could end the sports hero's pursuit of lucrative endorsement contracts; the insomnia of a children's television star, relieved by an ordinary prescription of sleeping pills, could chill career prospects; the world-class model coping with an outbreak of skin problems could face a flood of canceled modeling contracts. For these simple problems, as well as to fulfill unusual or illicit requests, celebrities—both at home *and* on the road—rely on special support personnel to keep secret potentially embarrassing, even threatening, information.

Buttressing this growing service sector are the personnel of limousine companies, bodyguard and security firms, exclusive resorts, four-star restaurants, health spas, and many others whose clientele is made up largely of the highly visible. In total, their contribution to the national economy is incalculable.

Resistance to the idea of people as manufactured, marketable products has kept the celebrity industry perpetually hidden from view. Its lack of a central headquarters city, its abstract codes of behavior, its obscure traditions and formulas—all of these have helped the industry to evolve almost without interference. Scholars have not analyzed it. Think tanks do not commission studies of it. But the celebrity industry has woven itself so deeply into the fabric of our economy and culture that it simply can no longer be ignored. Like it or not, the industry has tremendous impacts; it has philosophies and methodologies; it has complex interrelationships with almost every institution of society.

Each year at the Academy Awards, the president of the Academy of Motion Picture Arts and Sciences stands up and intones, "We are members of a great industry." Yet the viewer feels that there is something wrong. People understandably feel that no one who spends time making movies, acting, or hobnobbing with the stars should be speaking about the rigors of *working* in an *industry*. The fact is that the movie business *is* an industry, part of the far larger entity called the celebrity industry. But before one may fully comprehend this industry, before one can learn to operate inside it, one vital process must be understood: the celebrity–marketing process.

CHAPTER FOUR

The Celebrity-Marketing Process

When language expert Henry Higgins bets Colonel Pickering that he can pass off a common Cockney flower girl as a member of high society, the idea immediately captures our imagination. The story is appealing for many reasons, not the least of which is that it embodies the fantasy that, with the proper support and training, one can do or become anything. In the tradition of Cinderella and Snow White, Shaw celebrates one of the human psyche's foundation fantasies: that of transforming a common person into a princess or prince. Henry Higgins, in modern terms, is the "starmaker," the "super-agent," the "Merlin" who has the talent to produce the transformation.

What Higgins did in fiction is being attempted today in reality. Higgins would immediately recognize a process that is underway right now: the selection of a Democratic candidate for president of the United States. Many different candidates are mentioned as possible challengers. All share one thing in common: a reliance on the marketing perspective. Each potential candidate has a circle of strategists who ask, How can our candidate be as popular as Ronald Reagan was in the presidential campaigns of 1980 and 1984? Which of Reagan's characteristics does *our* candidate have to have in order to win the election? The exact answers—the need for likability, warmth, sincerity—are not the main issue. What *is* the issue is the process: that candidates are redesigning their images much as automobile manufacturers change body styles—by looking at the most successful products in the marketplace, figuring out *why* they are successful, and trying to duplicate those features.

Today, long after Shaw, people remain intrigued by the *Pygmalion* myth of design and transformation. In the film *The Idolmaker*, a frustrated male singer decides to give up his own ambitions for stardom and instead coach others to succeed. He shows great aptitude as both coach and agent, turning two "nobodies" into teen idols. He teaches them how to sing, what to sing, and how to act so as to meet the public's expectations, desires, and needs. His only problem is that the two manufactured stars turn against him, something not unheard of in the stormy world of celebrity manufacturing and marketing.

In another recent film, *Rhinestone*, Dolly Parton's character, a country singer in a local nightclub, bets the club owner that she can make a country singing star out of anyone. The owner, frustrated by the lack of good male singers to feature in his club, and tempted by the prize he would win if she loses, agrees. The first person they encounter is a macho taxicab driver, played by Sylvester Stallone, and although he sees it as a joke and goes along half-heartedly with his training, he eventually makes it as a country-and-western star.

These movies, while fictional, are based on a fundamental truth: that performers achieve stardom not as a result of irrepressible talent or accident, but because of a strategic process. Today, this process is undertaken by large institutions that have a need for highly visible people; by agents, managers, and other celebrity entrepreneurs; and by individuals who desire to be celebrities themselves. Institutions and individuals can scan the full range of celebrity sectors, choose one that is viable for their purposes, and manufacture their representatives or themselves into products that the audience covets.

Although they scarcely ever perceive what they are doing as a marketing process, what these institutions and individuals are engaged in is precisely that: studying a sector's audience, then searching for the right attributes and characteristics to distinguish their clients or themselves from the competition.

Sometimes the distinguishing characteristic can be small. In Garson Kanin's novel *Moviola*, an aging movie mogul tells his associates:

> Tell you what I want. You, Allan, and Freddie, you—you like that name "Alan"? Alan Bolt? Nothing. Let's get a name for him, somebody. Make up a list. Check it with Max. Max is good on names. A long one. That one is too short. It's over before you know it. I like long names. They look bigger on the billing. People think they're getting more for their money.[1]

The search for the right combination of "name," "look," "voice," and other features is a staple of the marketing process. Every manager of a fledgling rock band hopes to find the mixture that will catapult the group to high visibility. Typically, it won't be the group's sound, since many groups sound similar. It *might* be the group's look (androgynous as in Boy George, unisexual as in David Bowie), the group's antics (The Who smashing guitars; The Plasmatics' use of nudity), or the group's social or political manifesto (Jackson Browne; U–2). But the same marketing principle applies to aspirants in all sectors: Analyze the image and characteristics that the *aspirant* possesses, as well as those that the sector expects, and transform the person to bring the two closer together. This is how the Pygmalion Principle works.

Transformation and the Idea of Marketing

Some people naturally develop the skills, traits, appearances, and behaviors that audiences value or desire. Sometimes, these individuals obtain high visibility almost effortlessly. But for most others, high visibility and its rewards must be actively pursued. And the key feature of this pursuit is change—change from the status quo to the behaviors, expectations, material, and countless other characteristics that are the prerequisites for celebrity.

Indeed, the steps that visibility seekers must take mimic the steps involved in launching a new brand of soap, jam, or automobile. Procter & Gamble does not simply put detergent powder into a box, give it an arbitrary name, establish a large advertising budget, and ask retailers to carry it. If companies were that casual about launching new products, the failure rate of new products would be even higher than its current level of 50 percent. Instead, a company such as Procter & Gamble gives careful thought to the people who make up the detergent-using market (the "audience"). They consider how people use detergents, the benefits they are seeking (whiteness, soapiness, fresh smell), their feelings toward competitive brands, consumer reactions to different package sizes, colors and possible brand names, retailers' expectations and requirements for carrying the brand. Good marketing work requires careful *marketing research, product design, packaging, pricing, promotion*, and *distribution*. Major manufacturers follow this marketing process with a certain degree of rigor, whether they are producing detergents, ice cream, or motorcycles. The same process is followed by service businesses such as airlines, hotels, and restaurants, too, for they need to know what the public wants or will accept, what their competitors are doing, and what will constitute a winning service.

The fact is that launching a personal quest for high visibility is very much like launching a new product or service. To some extent, one must be transformed. And a successful transformation demands the understanding and mastering of the marketing process. For too long, specialists who worked behind the scenes to assist aspiring celebrities failed to apply marketing principles. Mike Gormley, national publicity director of Mercury Records, displayed such a nonmarketing focus in his description of a typical publicity meeting: "We get together every six weeks. We'll go down our sales figures. If we decide a group is getting 'no action'—meaning no air play or album sales—we'll drop them. If promotion doesn't get results, you just don't throw away more money."[2]

Gormley's implied attitude toward investment spending on groups—that once an act has failed to find an audience, the best remedy is to find a new act—is shared by many skeptics. Underlying this attitude is the idea that a group or act is only so malleable. Such skeptics usually raise two objections to the idea that visibility seekers can be transformed and marketed like products. The first is that products are moldable, but people are not. The second is that even if people were moldable, marketing would produce only limited results.

Both views are flawed.

CAN PEOPLE BE SHAPED INTO PRODUCTS?

The observation is often made that products don't have to be transformed at all; they can be designed from scratch and shaped into exactly what buyers want, whereas human beings can be "stretched" only so much. In this view, a builder can build a Georgian, Colonial, Cape Cod, or whatever style home a buyer wants—but the seeker of visibility begins as a real person with set features. In the skeptic's view, the lawyer aspiring to high visibility cannot be rebuilt into a duplicate of celebrity attorney Marvin Mitchelson even if potential clients abound. There is no way to turn the young actress into an exact duplicate of Jessica Lange even if the public yearns for a new Lange. Conventional wisdom holds that a human being can be stretched or altered only so much.

The truth, however, is that the limits of "stretchability" are expanding all the time. What were once "givens" about an aspirant's limitations are now being addressed by many different celebrity support industries. These support groups are providing cosmetic surgery, coaching, interpersonal skill building, psychiatric counseling, and the vast array of services resulting in what has been termed "the makeover"—a term once limited to cosmetics but now referring to the complete transformation of aspirants, be they fast-track executives, ambitious congressmen, or promising artists. Our young actress may not wish to become a new Jessica Lange, but the technology now exists to transform her into a replica of Lange should she change her mind.

THE ULTIMATE STRETCH

Seka is the uncontested leader of the pornographic movie sector.[3] Her earnings top those of all competitors in her sector: "$100,000 or so for a film, $15,000 for a one-day film appearance, 'four figures' for a one-day live appearance, $60 for a five-minute phone conversation."[4] She even gets $14.95 for a pair of her used underwear. Most importantly, Seka is a celebrity made by transformation. Under the guidance of her mentor/manager, she undertook a physical regimen involving diet, four-and-one-half hours of daily exercise, diction and drama lessons, and improvements in her posture, appearance, and deportment. With her trademark platinum locks, she is instantly recognizable. Even her invented name is memorable. It's short and exotic. Her competition—X-rated performers Marilyn Chambers and Sylvia Crystal—while still making films, cannot match the sophistication of Seka's approach to marketing.

It may be that people are becoming more easily transformable than traditional products are. After all, Heinz ketchup cannot be turned into Lipton tea; Volkswagens cannot be turned into Jaguars. Performers, however, *have* shown the ability to transform themselves—sometimes radically—over and over again. Bob Dylan went from folk singer to rock singer to gospel singer and back to rock singer; Richard Nixon went from militant anti-Communist to champion of détente to national embarrassment and then to elder statesman. Carl Sagan began in academics, expanded into entertainment, and finally added political activism to his menu of activities.

One way that people *do* differ from products is in ease of management. A box of detergent sits on a supermarket shelf. It does not talk back. It does not take drugs, punch reporters, or fire its managers. But people do, often displaying a variability and inconsistency that complicates efforts to transform them and build strategic images. Ronald Reagan, in each of his meetings with the public or press, has his advisors paralyzed in fear of what he might say. Surgeons, executives, lawyers, singers—all have their off-days and will inevitably lapse into some behavior potentially lethal to even the most carefully constructed image.

Yet traditional products also have performance problems. Manufacturers of new computers or aircraft pray before a test demonstration that their machines will not break down. Whether handling a person or a product, care must be taken that both perform up to their advertised expectations.

CAN MARKETING MAKE A SUCCESS OUT OF ANYONE?

Marketing is primarily a process of examining a product in relation to a market and determining how to maximize the product's potential—that is, its need-filling ability. This does *not* mean that an aspirant can be marketed into any desired level of visibility in any market sector. The best marketing advice for Walter Mondale might have eaten into Ronald Reagan's 1984 landslide by a few percentage points; Mondale would still have lost. In a less unbalanced campaign, however, a different marketing approach could easily have made the difference. And in the type of transformations and image-building campaigns waged by most aspirants, small differentiations *can* be played to great advantage.

Marketing's potential contribution to the quest for visibility varies in different sectors. In the hundred-yard dash, visibility goes to the swiftest, and marketing can make no difference in who wins. (It *will* make a big difference in the victor's commercial reward, however.) But in other sectors such as business, law, medicine, religion, politics, and entertainment, where there are thousands of aspirants with the baseline minimum qualifications, marketing's impact can be enormous.

Can marketing make a success out of anyone? No. But it can identify the best sector in which to compete, determine the best role for one to play, and help isolate the most productive audiences to approach.

Three Marketing Styles for Launching Aspirants

The idea of marketing oneself is not new. For many aspirants of the past, undertaking a quest for visibility involved a number of strategies. One of the most popular, as succinctly expressed in *Moviola,* was a form of personal marketing:

> You're doing it the wrong way, honey [said an aging movie mogul to a new star]. There used to be a nice actress from the stage, Ina Claire, and somebody once said to her, "Do you really have to sleep with all the producers and directors to make good?" And Ina Claire said, "Of course you do—if you haven't got any *talent*."[5]

For Ina Claire, and for real aspirants of the time, there was a grab bag of strategies that were learned through trial and error. A systematic approach to marketing oneself, to assessing one's strengths, weaknesses, and best positioning concept, was not widely known or understood.

Today, not all marketing professionals would approach the quest for visibility in the same way. Most would agree that marketing principles could help aspirants in their quests. But what are the best ways to apply marketing? Three very different marketing styles can be distinguished.

Suppose a female pop singer, unable to obtain booking engagements on her own, hires an agent to help market her. The agent faces three basic strategy options:

1. *Pure Selling Approach*. Here the agent would present photos and tapes of the singer to several venue managers to persuade them to book her. The singer is satisfied if her agent succeeds, and she is extremely satisfied if the venues are prestigious, visible, or well paying. In the pure selling mode, the agent sees the client as a fixed product that simply has to be sold, as is, to the "best" market that can be found.
2. *Product Improvement Approach*. Not content to work with a fixed quantity, here the agent takes an inventory of the singer's characteristics and suggests ways in which she could improve her songs, appearance, personality, and other modifiable characteristics. The agent is taking a value-added approach, adding value to the performer's ability to attract the market's interest.
3. *Market Fulfillment Approach*. Here the agent decides that the singer does not possess the minimum skills or flexibility to be sold as is or molded into a viable product. So the agent declines to help her specifically. Instead, he scans the market to see what kind of public entertainment needs exist and are not being adequately satisfied. The scan may reveal that the market is ready for, perhaps, another Anne Murray–type singer. The agent then searches among the pool of minimally qualified aspirants for the one who is most promotable into this role. Finding the right person, the agent proceeds to develop her systematically into a new Anne Murray—the product the market wants.

The three styles are clearly illustrated in the film *The Idolmaker* referred to earlier. The idolmaker first tries to promote himself as a singer but without much success (pure selling approach). He gives up his own dream of fame and spots an acquaintance who has raw talent that needs shaping and goes about "improving the product" until his client becomes extremely successful (product improvement approach). The idolmaker and his client have a falling out, and the idolmaker decides to search for the kind of talent that the public wants. Sensing the public's wish for a new teen idol, he finds an ideal candidate and modifies that candidate's character to the market's wants (market fulfillment approach).

Today, the same three marketing styles are in use in the nonentertainment sectors. In the political sector, the pure selling approach means trying to attract more votes for existing candidates as they are; the key is to create in the voters an attraction to the qualities and characteristics that the candidate already possesses. In the product improvement approach, the candidate is transformed—trained to speak more effectively, dress more in line with the audience's (voters') expectations, and express views shown by polling to be already popular. The third approach, market fulfillment, is used, if discreetly, by political machines and parties that analyze what the public wants in the way of public officials and find candidates who meet voter desires and expectations.

Already, today's political parties are becoming more sophisticated, moving steadily toward the market fulfillment approach, searching for potential candidates who can fulfill market expectations. Striving for success in the marketplace, political parties, and other celebrity-using institutions are moving from pure selling to market fulfillment. Of course, some experienced celebrity-makers still claim that they rely on "gut instinct" for selecting high-potential entertainers, politicians, business executives, or religious leaders. And some do have better "feel"—in actuality, a better intuitive understanding of the celebrity-marketing process—than others. But with the stakes riding so high on the launch of a major aspirant, new-style celebrity-makers are increasingly turning to such modern marketing tools as audience analysis, public opinion research, and focus groups, in which a selected group of consumers is deeply probed to reveal their views on products, services, or celebrities.

Ironically, as celebrity-makers adopt more of traditional industry's tools, traditional industry is adopting more of the visibility industry's tools. Today, new products are launched as if they were humans, using show-business techniques. The new Diet Coke was introduced at a gala Radio City Music Hall premiere that would have been the envy of any aspiring performer. But whether it is business promoting products and services by treating them as if they had personalities, or people seeking the greatest reward from their careers, the marketing process is the new foundation.

Steps in the Marketing Process

There are four major steps in the marketing of celebrities: market analysis, product development, distribution planning, and promotion strategy. Each step contains "sub-routines" that make it a science all its own, involving special strategies, jargon, and both written and implicit rules. Later, we will deal with product development, distribution, and promotion. But before a celebrity can be distributed and promoted, the market must be analyzed.

MARKET ANALYSIS

Visualize a celebrity-making agency that operates on the ideal marketing model. Who would be the agency's hypothetical clients? Some are aspirants who look very promising; others are minor celebrities seeking larger markets; some are major celebrities who are at the top of the pyramid; still others are celebrities in decline who hope to extend their commercial value or be relaunched. In order to market its clients intelligently, the Agency first has to master market analysis.

To do so, the Agency must constantly monitor the changing environment to identify new opportunities and anticipate new problems. Such monitoring would show investment banking now overshadowing law as the field for high-stakes deal making; comedy films surpassing war pictures in popularity; romance novels booming as cowboy fiction declines. Monitoring the environment breaks down into three separate tasks: environmental scanning, market segmentation, and market selection.

Environmental Scanning. The Agency monitors the environment for indicators of new opportunities and new threats. This scanning can be casual, as when executives read newspapers, listen to street talk, and make inquiries about interesting developments. Or the scanning can be more formal, as when companies set up an intelligence department to screen and sort information to feed back into the Agency.

Our cultural environment consists of so many streams of events that no organization can monitor them all. There are, however, five focal areas that the Agency must watch: the demographic, economic, technological, political/legal, and social/cultural environments.

Demographics reveal pertinent facts about the population, such as its size, age distribution, racial and national composition, geographical distribution, birth rates, marriage and divorce rates, and mortality rates. The Agency would be especially interested in such demographic data as the size of the teenage population (because they are the heaviest purchasers of pop musicians' and other entertainers' products) and in the geographical shift of the population to the South (because this suggests cities in which potential audiences are growing.) The Agency would also be interested in the rapid growth of the Hispanic population, of senior citizens, and of single-person households, as suggestive of new celebrity opportunities.

The Agency would also pay attention to trends in the *economy*, specifically to income levels and distribution, inflation, unemployment, and leisure spending. Rising unemployment historically has meant more television viewing and movie attendance. Inflation means that performers need to charge more for their engagements. Rising disposable income levels among minority or ethnic groups mean new opportunities to promote celebrities who appeal to such groups. The Agency would continuously monitor economic trends and translate them into celebrity-making plans.

Technological changes also have a significant impact on the celebrity world. Before the days of radio and television, newspapers were the primary medium of generating visibility. Many people, only vaguely aware of what their favorite celebrities looked like, had to rely on what they wrote or what was said about them. Radio added the dimension of voice, and television added images. The movies, in their switch from silents to "talkies," made and broke careers. Film star John Gilbert was ruined when he made his first talkie, *His Glorious Night*, because his voice, which was normal in person, sounded high-pitched and whiny, completely out of character with his image as the great lover in silent movies.

Each medium seems to favor some aspirants over others. In the pivotal first 1960 presidential debate, John Kennedy, understanding the demands of television technology, projected confidence and coolness by giving careful attention to makeup and lighting, talking specifically to the audience, and lightening his schedule to have adequate time to prepare. Richard Nixon treated the debate as a standard campaign appearance. Not adapting to the demands of the new technology, and having injured himself prior to the debate, he appeared wan, sweaty, and uncomfortable. More recently, cable technology and music video have come to favor musicians with videogenic talents; business news coverage has created the need for executives to hone media skills; and the televising of Congress has created a whole new image consciousness (of appearance and speaking style) among national politicians. The upshot is that the Agency has to monitor changing technologies because they can make or break their clients' quest for visibility.

Another important environmental area is that of *law and politics*. When, in the 1948 Paramount case, the Supreme Court dissolved the ties between movie studios, distributors, and exhibition houses, the studios' power to force exhibitors to show their own films was reduced, radically changing the economics of the industry and the composition of its celebrity mix. When, in the 1952 *Miracle* case, the Supreme Court restricted film censorship, filmmakers began to explore a wider range of themes and subjects. When the federal government in 1971 authorized public funding of political campaigns, the large influx of money created whole new opportunities for employing expensive consultants and image strategists. In the religious sector, a single ruling of the Federal Communications Commission—the 1960 decision that TV stations could apply paid-for broadcasts toward their required quota of public-service programming—opened the way for a new type of religious celebrity: the marketing-oriented TV evangelist. Today, such figures as Pat Robertson, Jimmy Swaggart, and Ernest Angley, the direct benefactors of the FCC ruling, control hundreds of millions of dollars in cash flow annually.[6] The Agency, in order to maximize opportunities for its clients, must watch these legal and political developments to determine their impact on the celebrity industry.

Finally, the Agency needs to monitor *socio/cultural* trends. When young people's political consciousness was raised by the Vietnam War and the protest movement was ushered in, new types of entertainers flourished while others were swept away. In the late 1970s the lower-class punk movement in England created new opportunities for politically oriented entertainers. More recently, the trend to celebrity-supported charity drives such as Live Aid, Farm Aid, and the Amnesty International tour presents many showcase opportunities for celebrities. With the recent rehabilitation of business as a highly respected profession, opportunities for businesspeople to take advantage of high visibility have expanded into advertising, endorsements, and politics.

JIM AND TAMMY

TV evangelist Jim Bakker has built an empire on market analysis. Technologically, Bakker was one of the first to appreciate the potential in promoting religion through cable and satellite signal distribution. Demographically, he understood in which areas of the country his gospel message would be most strongly appreciated. Socio-culturally, Bakker realized that his audience could be encouraged to consume his image in other ways, too. As a result, he built Heritage USA, described by Bakker as a "Christian camp ground" that combines the theme park strategy of Walt Disney with an array of worship venues. The park was so well designed that it attracted 4.9 million visitors in 1985, making it, after the two Disney parks, the third biggest tourist draw in the United States. Featured at Heritage are such attractions as a Water Park, petting zoo, reproduction of the site of the "Last Supper," and evangelist Billy Graham's actual boyhood home. Under development at Heritage: an amusement ride trip through heaven and hell.

Analyzing market expectations, Bakker determined that he could be most persuasive by presenting his sermons in tandem with entertainment. Today, his "PTL Club" and "Jim and Tammy Show" rival network television shows for professional production, fast pacing, and variety. What Bakker calls "Christian entertainers" sing, dance, and converse in a set designed as a lavish country living room. Legally and politically, Bakker has mastered the intricacies of tax-exemption status and charity law. Finally, analyzing prevailing public attitudes toward big government, Bakker launched such satellite operations as "New Vine Fellowship" alcoholism treatment centers, "Crisis Pregnancy" clinics, the "Tender Loving Care Adoption Agency," and the "People That Love" family counseling operations—all aimed at applying private-sector management to services that the government, in Bakker's view, was failing to provide. In all these areas, Bakker was astute in measuring and executing the opportunities made clear by market analysis.

Market Segmentation and the Visibility Seeker. *A market consists of all of the people who have actual or potential interest in some class of product or service. And each market contains sub-markets*. Celebrity-marketers such as the Agency must not only watch the broad demographic, economic, technological, political/legal, and socio/cultural trends but must also monitor the markets and sub-markets, such as the filmgoers' market, the sports fans' market, the voters' market, the art appreciators' market, and the worshippers' market. And, through economies of scale and division of labor, a large agency would be capable of doing so. But individual visibility seekers, who have most likely already *selected* a market sector, such as law, entertainment, or business, can do so too. For example, lawyers need to monitor not just the broad law market but all the smaller markets that make up law: the large and small firms, the courts, the legislatures.

It is remarkable how, even within broad markets, so much variation exists. The pop music market consists of sub-markets who consume rock, jazz, blues, country, folk, and other genres. Even within a sub-market, such as rock music lovers, members will differ as to their preferences for hard rock, soft rock, new wave, or even for individual performers. Within the broad business market, there is an almost infinite variety of specialties; even within one, such as the securities industry, there is great variation: commodities, municipal bonds, equities, options, and others.

The overall heterogeneity of markets means that visibility seekers must carefully select a target market upon which to concentrate. *A mass-market approach—trying to appeal to all music listeners, or all sports fans—should be avoided*. It leads to sloppy thinking and wasteful spending; it does not suggest how the aspirant should shape oneself or one's material; it does not indicate which venues the aspirant should pursue. The truth is that today's markets are individualized. People in an affluent society grow more differentiated in their lifestyles, tastes, and activities as a result of higher incomes and more education. They face a growing supply of different entertainment and leisure opportunities. Communication media become more differentiated. No longer is there a *Life* or *Look* magazine to reach everyone, nor an "Ed Sullivan Show" that the whole nation watches on Sunday evening. Instead, there are more than 15,000 magazines catering to every conceivable interest. City dwellers have a choice of scores of radio and TV stations to satisfy their varying entertainment preferences. People are reading books, watching videotapes, listening to recorded music, attending sports events, or traveling. It is increasingly difficult to reach a mass audience with one or even a few media vehicles; at the same time, it is becoming increasingly easy to reach a targeted audience with a single vehicle.

The lesson is that *the more precisely the visibility seeker defines the target market, the easier it is to design the necessary transformation: to build the appropriate image and launching plan for the aspirant.* If a female singer can perform both country and folk music, it would be better to position her strongly in one of the markets than to have her sing on the fringe of both. If the religious aspirant is both a skilled scholar and an exciting orator, it would be better to concentrate either on fellow theologians, or on the public market of worshippers. Given limited resources, it would be far better for a boutique owner seeking local celebrity to try to generate the attraction of high-fashion clothes buyers, rather than the attraction of all clothes buyers in the entire community.

In the selection of the aspirant's initial target market, two extremes must be avoided. If the target market is defined too broadly, it may be impossible for the aspirant to craft a distinctive image. The resulting image might be too diffused to inspire audience attraction and loyalty. Then again, if the target market is defined too narrowly, there may not be enough people (clients, voters, fans) to appeal to, and the aspirant might become overtyped and frozen in the role. Initial target market selection must avoid *image diffusion* on the one hand and *image freeze* on the other.

To target the right market, aspirants have to creatively segment the market. Any market can be segmented in several ways; the key is to weigh different factors that might shed light on important audience differences. A rock singer may have great appeal to the teenage market—but *which* teenage market? Teenagers differ in *age* (early, middle, and late teens), *sex* (male and female), *income* (low, medium, and high), *education* (low, medium, and high) and *geographic region*. And these few demographic variables do not capture all the differences. Teenagers also show psychographic or lifestyle differences, ranging from conformity-oriented conservatives all the way to rebellious, anti-establishment individualists. Finally, teenagers vary in their product use and purchase habits: there are heavy consumers, medium consumers, and light consumers of rock music.

The politician's market consists of voters. But no politician can appeal to all the sub-markets within the electorate. Specific constituencies must be targeted, just as an aspirant seeking visibility within a large corporation must identify sub-groups and key individuals upon which to target an image-building strategy.

Figure 9 illustrates the variety of market segments that emerge when applying different variables to analyze a market. Using only three variables (sex, age, and race), we can distinguish at least eighteen target markets making up the teenage market. A new performer can try to appeal to the black female early-teen market, or the white male late-teen market, or any of sixteen other segments. Or the performer can try to appeal to a macrosegment, such as black females, or even all females.

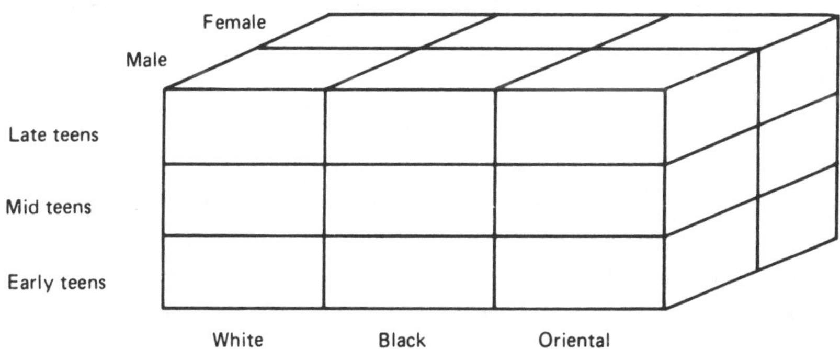

Figure 9: Illustration of Market Segmentation of Teen Age Market by Age, Sex, and Race.

Market Selection. Visibility seekers have to think very carefully about the best initial target market to attack. Selecting this initial target market is not an easy task. Several considerations come into play.

Market size is a key factor. Seeking the greatest possible rewards, many aspirants try to appeal to large market segments. Political aspirants on the national level are not going to go far by choosing to appeal exclusively to minority voters; there simply aren't enough of them for reward (election). But bigger is not always better; limited resources, or the value of appealing to small, influential markets, may come into play and help shape market size decisions.

Market growth rate is also important, especially if the aspirant expects to entertain the same group for many years. Consider the plight of a young corporate lawyer just starting a quest for visibility. The lawyer would need to take a long, hard look at the large number of competitors entering his or her sector. In contrast, a science aspirant would benefit from a fast-growth area like artificial intelligence, where aspirant supply has not caught up with demand. Other things being equal, aspirants would prefer to target audiences that are experiencing steady and sustainable growth.

The *audience's purchasing power* is also important. If older teenagers spend more money on concerts and recordings than younger teenagers, performers could clearly earn more by targeting the former group rather than the latter. If urban couples have disposable income to spend on paintings and sculpture, and a great disposition to do so, art aspirants would be advised to market themselves accordingly.

Another consideration is the degree of *accessibility* into a given market. Some markets are overcrowded with aspirants; each new aspirant finds it harder to break in and draw a market share. Or the entry costs into that market may be very high. The cutting, promotion, and national distribution of a new album can cost $250,000, an amount that few new performers can afford. Finally, accessibility might be a problem because of audience or gatekeeper prejudices against certain types of aspirants. Black singers, for example, might encounter resistance in rural southern nightclubs, while engineering-trained plant managers are blocked from breaking into the MBA-dominated financial hierarchy of their corporation.

Even when the market *is* accessible, the aspirant needs to feel comfortable with the market, capable of displaying the behaviors necessary to appeal to it. A comedian used to younger audiences in urban improvisation clubs might have difficulty making the transition to entertaining older audiences in Las Vegas, even if the latter audience is larger, growing more rapidly, and spending more on entertainment. If the aspirant wants to attain high visibility in a target market, he or she must feel well prepared to work with that audience.

These considerations will not all favor the same target market. An executive offered a high-visibility position in New York might be far happier remaining in a familiar region. A performer might feel more comfortable entertaining an older group, although more money could be made entertaining a younger one. Or the aspirant might prefer working in a small but highly accessible market to fighting for entry in a larger but less accessible market. There are always trade-offs among desirable ends. Nevertheless, market selection must be carefully done, because it sets the stage for the next step in the marketing process: bringing the aspirant and the market together.

Market Beachhead: Driving into the Marketplace

Any marketing theory is only as good as the image maker's ability to make it work. The *market beachhead plan* initially launches the aspirant. It is this plan that ultimately brings aspirants and the market together. Understanding the three major drivers that bond aspirants and audiences is critical to getting the beachhead plan off the ground. What are these forces that initially drive or restrain an aspirant's ascent to high visibility? They are: *audiences, backers*, and the *communication media*.

DRIVER ONE: *THE AUDIENCE*

Some performers are initially launched toward high visibility by their audience. Folksinger Joan Baez started performing in small Boston bars without the benefit of backers or the communication media. Although she appeared at the 1959 Newport Folk Festival and was offered several record contracts, Baez chose to continue honing her material and building audience contact in the coffeehouses. After another appearance at Newport, she signed with Vanguard records. With the addition of this institutional backer, all the elements driving a quest for high visibility came together. Soon, Baez was recording best-selling records. While unintentional, Baez's experience illustrates a key principle: Often it is the audience that dominates the process of marketing. Pop psychologist Leo Buscaglia activated his high visibility by making such a powerful, direct emotional appeal to his audience that on two occasions, publishers in the audience were moved to sign him to contracts. The resulting exposure helped put three of Buscaglia's books on the best-seller list at the same time and made him one of the most sought-after lecturers in the country.[7]

DRIVER TWO: *BACKERS*

Backers are the second driver that can initiate a quest for celebrity—either individuals who act as *patrons* or whole *institutions*.

Patrons. Some aspirants are initially supported and guided by patrons or mentors. Patronage is an ancient practice. Caesar sponsored Mark Antony. The great musicians—Bach, Mozart, and Beethoven, for example—had their patrons. In more recent times, Vincent Van Gogh's brother Theo supported him, art collector Peggy Guggenheim sponsored Jackson Pollock, and southern California tennis mentor Perry Jones sponsored many successful tennis stars, including Jack Kramer and Pancho Gonzales.

Patrons perform many critical services for aspirants. Among them are:

- funding them so that they can live, afford training and materials, and pursue their "art" without having to work at something else for a living
- advising and guiding them on the best way to approach their markets and develop support systems
- encouraging them to believe in themselves and not give up
- introducing them to sector decision makers who can help their quests

Not all aspirants find a patron willing to do this for them; nor do all patrons who back an aspirant succeed in their plans. If, ultimately, the aspirant fails to attract audience or media support, the patron's efforts generally come to naught.

Institutions. Another way that aspirants are first introduced to audiences is through the help of institutions. Corporations and nonprofit institutions have developed elaborate programs to build up "stars," because the better known their leaders, the more recognizable their products and services are to consumers. Sports teams have a vested interest in building up the visibility of their players so that they can draw larger crowds. Political parties strive to make celebrities of their candidates for the same reason.

The underlying reason why institutions drive the celebrity-making process is that they receive value from creating "icons." By an icon, we mean someone who serves as a symbol, a role model, an inspiration whose glow settles on the institution itself. The institution, in the minds of its audience, takes on the positive attributes of its icons. That's why institutions create or invest in an iconic figure in order to gain one or more of the following advantages:

1. *Building more awareness of the institution.* Many institutions are relatively obscure. One way of becoming better known is to promote their association with someone who already has high visibility.
2. *Building a specific personality for the institution.* The institution may have an unclear or unfocused image that leaves audiences lukewarm. By publicly promoting one of its inside personalities, it can broadcast its values and personality. For example, what is a hotel? It is merely a collection of rooms and services. The designers can change its exterior and call the rooms by various names in order to affect its appeal to consumers. But far more effective is a marketing plan that uses celebrities to communicate a sense of the hotel's "personality." In New York, Helmsley Hotel ads feature the image of a tough but elegant Leona Helmsley. Helmsley is portrayed paying meticulous attention to small details, keeping unyielding pressure on the staff, and seeing to it personally that each and every guest has a quality experience. "I run my hotels the way I run my home," says Leona in one ad, adding, "I love to read in bed, so most rooms have swing-arm lamps on both sides of the bed."[8] Helmsley Hotels has chosen to make a folk hero out of Leona. By lionizing her, the hotels, in the minds of consumers, acquire her qualities: meticulous attention to detail, coupled with indulgent luxury.
3. *Changing the institution's image.* Some institutions have an image they would like to shed or revise. The Soviet Union decided to eradicate Stalin's image; China moved to submerge Mao's. Both countries chose successors whose traits would cancel or reverse their former leaders' images. One of the best ways for an institution to re-profile itself is to find or create an icon out of someone with the currently desired qualities. Not only does the institution gain from "iconizing" one of its members; the icon also gains. More fame can mean more income and/or power to the icon. Or the icon might cooperate simply out of a wish to help his or her institution. New York Yankee owner George Steinbrenner's frequent resurrection of Billy Martin as manager and NASA's decision to bring back James Fletcher as chief administrator are both examples of institu-

tions' addressing image problems through the use of previously successful icons.

ALMA MATER

"I'm Making It," proclaimed Christine Huston, a successful graduate in a newspaper ad for the City Colleges of Chicago. "Had it not been for the excellent opportunity and education I received at Kennedy-King, I am sure there would be no Christine Huston, television comedy writer, in Hollywood today. Not only did I learn much of my craft at Kennedy-King, there I wrote the play that helped launch me, a comedy entitled, '227.' It will be an NBC-TV network series debuting this fall on Saturday nights."[9]

Along with the potential rewards, both icons and institutions assume some risk in the process. The celebrity gets more role-typed and has more visibility-related responsibilities and burdens, potentially suffering harm to his or her reputation if the institution suffers a scandal or decline. The institution has even more to risk. Its icon might be caught in a crisis, badmouth it, or fail to create the expected level of interest or affection for the institution. Or the celebrity's aura might overdefine the institution and make it difficult to reverse the image later when a new one is needed. The main point, however, is that institutions can be a major force in promoting or expanding an aspirant's prominence. They can be strong drivers and allies in the effort to gain visibility and its rewards.

THE CHARGING BULL

If ever a sports team needed an icon it was the Chicago Bulls. A perennial loser in professional basketball, the team changed hands, with the new owners promising the fans a new era. The new era's name was Michael Jordan, a dazzling, twisting, soaring talent with an appealing personality to match. The mere announcement of his signing began to boost season-ticket sales. Instantly, he became the symbol of the Bulls' reemergence. Then, in the fourth game of his second season, Jordan was injured. After a long recovery, Jordan was cleared to play on a limited basis. But the Bulls management, expressing fear of playing Jordan too hard, too soon, restricted the star's playing time. Jordan's reaction? He accused the management of trying to finish lower in the standings, in order to get a higher pick in next year's draft. Though the differences between Jordan and his employers were quickly repaired in a press conference, the icon's attack was permanently etched in the public's mind. Never cross an icon.

DRIVER THREE: *COMMUNICATION MEDIA*

The media can play an important role in driving an aspirant's marketing plan by *discovering* the aspirant before the audience or backers even appear. MTV, the music cable network, operates on the principle of elevating unknown aspirants to instant high visibility. *Interview* magazine does the same for lifestyle and fashion aspirants as does *People* for aspirants of all types. But all three media organizations illustrate the difference between backer launchers and media launchers: Not committed to the aspirants in any way, the media function only to provide the introduction to a larger audience.

Driver Sequencing

Three drivers—audiences, backers, and the communication media—can combine in a variety of ways to implement a celebrity-marketing plan.

ABC Pattern. In this scenario, the celebrity is initially audience-launched—for example, a state senator who first appeals to a county constituency, or a field manager who is extremely popular with employees. Ultimately, as the aspirant's audience grows, more powerful backers take notice. Their efforts raise aspirants' visibility levels dramatically, bringing them to the attention of the media.

BAC Pattern. In this instance, the celebrity first finds, or is found by, a backer, whether a patron or an institution. The backer helps provide a showcase opportunity that, if successful, is followed by media attention. It was a customary practice of art patron Peggy Guggenheim, for example, to advance the cause of unknown artists whom she had discovered. Promoting them to galleries, Guggenheim would help stage elaborate openings, hoping that the newspapers would subsequently report the artists' shows as successful.

CAB Pattern. In this pattern the communication media decide to publicize a person; this draws an audience; then a backer appears who offers to help. Artist Christo's dramatic environmental structures, some of which drastically altered the landscape (building a fence across the state of California), were first brought to public notice by the media. Once his public visibility grew, institutions such as museums and even national governments began to endorse and back his projects. Ultimately, he formed a corporation complete with project directors, prestigious legal counsel, general contractors, consulting engineers, and a blue-ribbon list of sponsors, including the major museums of Europe and wealthy art patrons from all over the world.[10]

These three linear sequences are admittedly oversimplified. An aspirant might attract a backer, audience, and communication media all at the same time. The aspirant might cycle through several backers. Or he or she might draw a small audience, find a backer who arranges for a larger audience, then find a new and more powerful backer. Many patterns are possible, but all involve the same three drivers, namely audience, backers, and communication media.

Once these patterns are understood, certain conclusions naturally follow:

1. Persons who lack audience impact will generally not get far as celebrities, no matter how strong their backing or communication media support.
2. Persons lacking backer support will be handicapped in the early stages of their career; they will need high audience impact to overcome this.
3. People who lack media support need an extremely loyal audience, one that will search out information about the aspirant, and his or her products, without the help of the media.

4. Persons who have audience impact, backer support, and media coverage will go the furthest. A marketing plan should provide and account for all three.

Memory Locks: The Marketing Objective

A central function of a celebrity-marketing plan should be to lock a celebrity's image into the long-term memory of audiences. We call this the Memory Lock. Of the thousands of past major league baseball players, only a few are remembered or revered. Ask several people to name the most famous baseball players and they are likely to say Ruth, Cobb, and Gehrig. The same question asked about football players produces the names Grange, Unitas, and Brown. If asked to name the greats of opera, they will say Caruso, Bjorling, and Callas. All of these celebrities have earned a permanent place in the *memory channel*—the ultimate sign of celebrity success. Historically, there were several classic routes into the memory channel:

1. *The "first or the most"*: Some people established a place in history because they were the first to do something. Charles Lindbergh earned a permanent place in history as the first to make a nonstop solo flight across the Atlantic. Sir Edmund Hillary was the first to climb to the top of Mount Everest. *The Guinness Book of Records* thrives on publicizing people who achieved the first or the most.
2. *Connected with a great event.* Abraham Lincoln's fame rests partly on the fact that he freed the slaves and led the nation during a great war. He would not likely have become as celebrated a president had he served during peacetime. Paul Revere owes his fame to his fateful ride when he realized that "the British were coming."
3. *Lending the name.* Celebrities often are memorialized by having their name lent to something that lasts—a museum (Hirshhorn Museum), a college (Bob Jones University), a foundation (The Ford Foundation), a prize (Nobel Prize), a street (Madison Avenue), a city (Lincoln, Nebraska). Another is to become an expression in the language such as "in like Flynn" (Errol Flynn), "Rabelaisian humor," "Napoleonic leadership."

Today, most aspiring celebrities cannot count upon such circumstances. Far more valuable is the marketing approach—deciding what sector to attack, which markets to appeal to in that sector, and whether to use pure selling, product improvement, or market fulfillment. This is the modern approach to achieving a memory lock.

This chapter introduced the marketing process that guides the launching of aspirants. As we will soon see, the marketing approach also involves putting the performer into test markets to see how well he or she performs and determine what kind of product improvement (transformation) is required. If the test market results are good, then an extended distribution plan must be developed, specifying the markets where the product will be rolled into, and at what times. A publicity plan must be developed to maximize the likelihood that consumers will hear about the product, get to believe that there is something special about it, and "buy" it. If enough buyers are satisfied, their word-of-mouth and repurchasing will move the product from newly launched status into that of an accepted staple. Sooner or later, the celebrity's visibility will be eclipsed, and valiant efforts will be made to arrest the decline or launch a comeback. Thus the celebrity life cycle closely resembles the standard product life cycle, with its stages of introduction, growth, maturity, and decline.

But for the visibility seeker, there is far more to active strategy making than has even been hinted at here. Activating the celebrity-marketing process requires a wide range of skills and the mastery of many specialized techniques. The first of these is for the visibility seeker to understand where celebrities exist, where they fit, and how long they last.

CHAPTER FIVE

Celebrity Sectors, Hierarchies, and Life Cycles

Imagine a New Year's Eve party thrown by a wealthy Southern Californian. The guests include:

- Mary Martin, famed musical comedy star, now in her seventies
- Larry Hagman, well-known actor playing the villain J. R. Ewing in the TV series "Dallas," who also happens to be Mary Martin's son
- James Tobin, a Nobel Prize–winning economist from Yale University
- Dr. Stanley Boucree, president of the American Dental Association
- Ivan Lendl, top-ranked world tennis star
- Lionel Richie, pop music superstar

How might the other guests at the party behave? Many of the younger guests would be starry-eyed, hovering by Richie and Lendl. Slightly older guests would pay attention to Hagman because of his popularity on the weekly TV series "Dallas." Still-older guests will respond to Martin, reliving, through her presence, memories of the past. James Tobin, although a Nobel laureate, will be more of a listener than a talker; few guests will have heard of him. Besides, economics is "dull talk." Hardly anyone will notice Dr. Boucree, although among dentists he is known far and wide, indeed.

A party very much like this was held in Hollywood not long ago, and a reporter overheard the following exchange between Mary Martin and Larry Hagman. Hagman, delighted with the media attention he had been receiving, edged over to his mother, who was drawing far less attention than he. "Mom, I hope you're proud of me," Hagman is reported to have said. "I'm a star, just like you." Mary Martin, it is said, turned to her son and replied, "You're a star, Larry, true. But I am a legend."

The story illustrates several important points about visibility. First, each *sector* of society—entertainment, academia, business, the professions—has its own constellation of high visibles. These people are not always known outside of their sectors, but within their sectors they command recognition, respect, and rewards.

Second, the celebrities in certain sectors—notably entertainment, sports, and politics—will be visible to the broader general public beyond their own sectors—because their performances reach more people and generate more news. The superstars in these three sectors—Paul Newman, Diana Ross, Kareem Abdul-Jabbar, Martina Navratilova, Ronald Reagan, Ted Kennedy—will tower over celebrities in other sectors, no matter how high the others stand within their own sectors. Such is the status hierarchy among sectors.

Third, people pay more attention to those who are "hot"—highly visible *right now*—than to fading celebrities. Celebrities, like products, move through a *life cycle* of take-off, growth, maturity, and decline. Celebrities want to rise as high as possible and stay at the top as long as possible.

Many visibility seekers overlook a central consideration: how to tailor themselves to sector conditions. A good marketing plan requires that aspirants consider the opportunities, rules, and restraints that are unique to each sector. Too often, aspirants rush into their quests for visibility without surveying their sectors. Avoiding false starts and poor plans involves understanding visibility sectors, hierarchies, and life cycles.

Visibility Sectors

People gain visibility in a number of ways: through occupational achievement, demographic leadership, distinctive personality and lifestyle, inheritance, accident, and sensational behavior. Occupational achievement is the most common route to high visibility.

Every field, however, has a pyramidal structure, with most members, especially the new ones, standing at the base. At the middle level are practitioners who have attained some level of skill and repute. A few stand at the very top: in medical research, Dr. Robert Jarvik; in Bible preaching, Jerry Falwell; in broadcast interviewing, Barbara Walters. Every field, no matter how visible or obscure, produces its own celebrities.

High visibility is also achieved by leaders of demographic groups, which include blacks, Hispanics, gays, socialites, and others. Each group has a need for leaders, even icons, through which to present itself to the world and to set an example for its members. Phyllis Schlafly is a celebrity in the New Right's traditional-values movement; Mayor Henry Cisneros of San Antonio is one in the civil rights movement; Representative Claude Pepper serves the same purpose for the senior citizens' movement.

Some people attain high visibility through their unusual personalities or lifestyles. Zsa Zsa Gabor has never attained serious status as an actress, but her flamboyant, effusive personality filled a slot on talk shows and the party circuit. Buckminster Fuller excelled in many occupations (architect, businessman, mathematician, engineer), but he never became preeminent in any one of them; his visibility rested on a personality that continuously challenged the status quo. Truman Capote and Orson Welles began their careers with serious, critically acclaimed work, but they evolved into mere media personalities.

Another lifestyle sector with its pantheon of heroes is the "counterculture." Over the years, this sub-group has included Bohemians, beatniks, hippies, flower children, and punks. The conservative trend of today's culture has limited this particular route to visibility, but this was not always the case. Abbie Hoffman, Alan Ginsberg, Ken Kesey, Ram Dass, and Timothy Leary were all celebrated for their promotion of new values and their unorthodox personal lifestyles. Most of them relied on self-promotion skills, amplified by the praise of their followers, rather than on the services of professional publicists.

Other people acquire well-knownness derivatively through being born into a well-known family. Princess Anne of Great Britain achieved worldwide recognition not because of her charm but because her mother is Queen Elizabeth. All members of the Ford, Rockefeller, and Kennedy families gain instant visibility; a few enlarge their well-knownness because they skillfully build their inheritance (Henry Ford, Jr.) or misuse it (Tommy Manville and his thirteen marriages to eleven women). Visibility seekers cannot create inherited fame; managing it to their best advantage is something they *can* do.

Another route to high visibility is to be an arbitrary beneficiary—or victim—of coincidence. W. G. Sutter discovered gold in California. Barney Clark became notable because he was the first to receive an artificial heart. Many people attain fame because they are in the right place at the right time or do the right thing at the right time.

Finally, some people gain visibility by performing sensational acts. Evel Knievel executed frequent death-defying stunts to grab public attention. Others thirsting after celebrity have climbed office towers, dog-sledded to the North Pole, or sailed around the world in a rowboat hoping to win a line in *The Guinness Book of World Records*, or at least a headline in the local newspaper. Some even commit murder to gain attention, a motive frequently cited by psychologists to explain the actions of many assassins.

Each path taken to high visibility has certain implications. Inherited or accidental celebrity provides an initial kickoff; sustaining and expanding it is often difficult or impossible. Sensation-staging tends to produce very brief periods of high visibility but often involves high long-term costs. For most people who deliberately seek high visibility, the intentional routes are obviously more productive. (One can deliberately achieve leadership of a demographic group, but no one can "create" wealthy parents.) Of all the possible sectors to become visible in, some are better candidates for deliberate celebrity-making strategy than others.

Nine sectors in particular contain the bulk of celebrity-making activity:

- entertainment
- sports
- politics
- culture
- business
- religion
- science
- the professions
- academics

At the top of the list stands the entertainment sector. Here, high visibility is axiomatic: Entertainers earn their living by attracting attention. The better known they are, the larger their audience, and the larger their income. Not surprisingly, entertainers were among the earliest users of the machinery of visibility seeking. Needing constantly to manage their image with audiences, entertainers depend heavily on publicists, agents, managers, and coaches.

In sports, aspirants must possess certain minimum physical and mental abilities before they can even hope to compete. Still, there are many strategic decisions athletes must make to position themselves for the greatest visibility. One involves the market the athlete chooses to attack. The sports sector's markets are widespread. For example, each country has its favorite sports: baseball, football, and basketball in the United States; soccer in Argentina; rugby in Australia. In recent years, sports celebrities have attracted unprecedented salaries—salaries made possible by television coverage that delivers large at-home audiences to commercial sponsors. Television, a relatively new distribution channel, made it profitable to build up stars in this sector; as a result, the sports industry is undergoing a transformation, moving closer to the entertainment industry in how much attention it pays to the images of its members. At the same time, many other sports in the United States, such as handball and endurance bicycle racing, languish from lack of public attention. Their "stars" are known only to a few fans. Managers in these minor sports keep trying to promote these sports into high visibility.

A sector in which image building and transformation truly dominate is politics. Politicians, who need well-knownness in order to win elections, use all available visibility-generating resources, including political consultants, public relations experts, media contacts, advertising agencies, marketing research firms, and political-party resources. Because there is money to be made in helping politicians get elected, the availability of these support personnel is steadily on the rise. At the same time, the way the transformation issue is handled in this sector is extremely delicate. Entertainers may have their bodies reworked and their stories changed at will; their publics almost expect it. But politicians must be extremely careful about how much of their image-making strategy is revealed to the public.

Members of the art and culture sector—consisting of writers, poets, artists, intellectuals—also use self-marketing strategies. Compared with the past, when artists and writers often labored anonymously (often becoming well known only posthumously), today's art environment is frenetic with celebrity making. In today's competitive environment, many institutions are using artists to improve their images, producing new opportunities for artists and writers to earn commissions and gain exposure.

Because religions are organized hierarchically, every sect produces local, regional, national, and sometimes international "well-knowns." The aspirants at each level compete for the limited positions at the next level: priests compete for the post of bishop; bishops for archbishop; archbishops for cardinal. But even in this highly conservative sector, success depends to some extent on image building among one's peers and superiors. Transformation in the religious sector, however, needs to be handled delicately. Institutional codes of propriety have to be observed; besides, making worshippers aware of celebrity making would only invite condemnation. For these reasons, religious careerists do not normally hire agents or publicists. The main exceptions are those who are challenging the establishment, who need media attention to draw audience members away from their churches into new sects.

The business sector has seen an evolution in its complement of heroes and leaders. During the Middle Ages and early Industrial Revolution, business was not a laudable calling; those highly visible within business were mainly known to other businessmen. Those who *were* widely known—Rockefeller, Morgan, Ford, Gould—were perceived mainly negatively. But as business became more respectable, it became possible to cultivate business heroes, especially in the capitalist economies of the West. Some of today's business leaders publicly disparage the rewards of high visibility, but this is a sector in which transformation and image building can have a great effect. Today, the trend in business is for chief executive officers to pursue fame building as a means of building their company's fortunes as well as their own. David Finn of the PR agency Ruder, Finn, Rotman, Inc., argued in the *Harvard Business Review* that business leaders should *seek* the public limelight rather than shun it, to boost their own stock and their companies':

> That a great many business leaders do care [about society's welfare], there can be little doubt. The problem is that they hide their human qualities behind a mask of corporate anonymity. . . . Leadership [means] exercising the courage to create an environment that reflects a top executive's image of the way he or she wants to do business. It means resisting the temptation to be inconspicuous and anonymous in order to avoid reporters' questions and public gossip. Sometimes corporate leaders act as if they feared a raised eyebrow more than a deficit. . . .[1]

The science sector has a long history of spawning well-known names: Galileo, Copernicus, Newton, Pasteur, Freud, Curie, Einstein. But such activity is accelerating. Margaret Mead, Jonas Salk, James Van Allen, Herbert Simon, and many others have been partially aided by celebrity industry techniques. Even though their well-knownness was originally inspired by their discoveries, the value of visibility for scientists' sponsors is so huge that more and more celebrity making is taking place. As competition for vanishing funding increases, institutions are encouraging, or actively building, the visibility of their scientists.

In the professions—law, medicine, engineering, architecture, and others—most practitioners were, for years, content to ply their craft without pursuing high visibility; in fact, in several professions, seeking visibility through self-promotion was heavily regulated. But with the growing deregulation of advertising by lawyers, doctors, and others, the professions are undergoing a dramatic change. Transformation and image building are expanding rapidly throughout these sectors. Dr. Joyce Brothers (psychology), Melvin Belli (law), and Philip Johnson (architecture) are successful examples of this phenomenon. Their pursuit of high visibility is not a compensation for lack of talent—they all possess at least the minimum qualifications for their sectors—but rather a reflection of a new competitive reality: Merely possessing the skill qualifications is no longer enough to guarantee high levels of success.

The entire academic sector has become more visible as educational institutions seek higher visibility and the media search for experts. University public relations departments pound out press releases extolling research reports, unusual classes, and faculty appointments to commissions and foundations. Slowly, the range of permissible visibility-generating activities available for academicians is widening. The nuclear physicist, who not long ago would have been hired by a university only to staff the department, now is profiled by the alumni magazine, lectures to wealthy alumni, and is trotted out to impress prospective freshmen.

For all the celebrity-making activity in these sectors, visibility seeking in other areas is actually on the decline. The military sector, for example, has produced few heroes in recent times: While Caesar had his publicists, today's generals, particularly since Douglas MacArthur and his controversial cult of personality, have shied away from personal image making. In some countries, however, where the military leaders and the political leaders are the same, use of image-making machinery is on the rise.

Image Making in the Sectors

As far as the intensity of image-making activity, the various sectors fall into three general categories.

The first group consists of those sectors whose members do the least to seek or promote public visibility, usually because traditionally, image making has offered little in the way of financial, social, or ego-related reward. But with institutions making greater use of celebrities, new conflicts have been created. Members of this group now have to make conscious decisions about seeking visibility, trading off costs and rewards. A research biologist may earn a large supplemental income by becoming a science "popularizer" in the media but at the same time risk losing the esteem of professional colleagues. Members in these sectors must decide whether they are trying to please themselves, their colleagues, or the general public, for these three audiences cannot always be simultaneously satisfied.

A second group consists of sectors whose members could benefit greatly from high visibility, but where organized image-making machinery is still in its infancy stage. This is the case with doctors, lawyers, architects, and other professional groups. Architects stand to gain more clients if they go on public-speaking tours, write articles for the right magazines, gain high office in their professional society, and in other ways market themselves and their practices. Although these sectors are catching up quickly, their image-making activity is likely to be sporadic, even amateurish. Aspirants often attempt to promote themselves without the benefit of professional guidance, as is typical of the cottage industry stage. They may occasionally buy the services of a marketing researcher, marketing consultant, or public relations firm, but not with enough continuity or commitment to expenditure.

A third group of sectors consists of those whose members derive substantial benefit from image making and where sophisticated machinery is already in place. One such sector is entertainment, whose members benefit from successful image making. Another is the business sector, in which many chief executives would benefit from image-creation and for which image-creating resources are available (speechwriters and clothes consultants, for example), but in which many executives still resist using these resources. Nevertheless, even the less image-intensive sectors are gradually increasing their image-building activity. Intensive transformation and image-building activity, while varying from sector to sector, is accelerating in all sectors.

Several factors explain why transformation and image-building are rising at different rates in different sectors:

1. *Image making can contribute more in sectors with low or ill-defined skill requirements*. For example, people with little or no skill can enter politics; image-makers in this case can be of great assistance. Modern painters can also benefit from image-making; the so-called "skills" required to compete in this sector are so variable that we need art critics to tell us which artists are good. On the other hand, a violinist, whose craft is evaluated on more specific criteria, cannot hope to become famous unless possessing a virtuoso level of skill.
2. *Image making can contribute more in sectors that command a high level of public and media interest*. People have a high interest in entertainment, sports, and politics; aspirants in these sectors command more media coverage. The media need much material to fill their daily time and space requirements. Dramatic image-making stories are an accepted tradition in these sectors. On the other hand, the public has little interest in such very specialized sectors as barbershop quartets, quilt-making, or dog-sled racing, and these sectors do not reward their leaders with nearly enough money to justify image-making activity.

3. *Image making can contribute more in sectors in which many aspirants compete for too few positions.* So many able actresses compete for roles in Hollywood that image-making investments can often make the difference. Conversely, so few people compete to become the leading scholar in the history of Liechtenstein that any competent individual could achieve this reputation without much image-building activity.
4. *Image making can contribute more in sectors that require an extensive amount of promotional activity for success.* For example, politicians cannot win elections simply by converting a few voters into supporters. The workload required to reach the necessary numbers of people is so great that politicians need image-making help—to research public attitudes, write strong speeches, and prepare commercial advertising.
5. *Image making is likely to expand in sectors in which image-making professionals can earn more.* Professional transformers and image-makers concentrate on sectors in which their skills command high prices. Because entertainment, sports, and political celebrities compete for high stakes, and image-making can contribute to their success, image-makers are more common in these sectors.

Visibility Hierarchies

High visibility does not have a single fixed dimension; the degree of well-knownness among the highly visible varies greatly. Lionel Richie is far better known than the current head of the American Dental Association, just as Ivan Lendl is more visible than any Nobel laureate in economics. Lendl and Richie stand higher in their sectors' *visibility hierarchy.*

To understand the visibility hierarchy, we need to recognize that well-knownness has two major dimensions: *space* and *time.* The first asks *how far the aspirant's well-knownness reaches.* Is it only local visibility, or is it regional, national, or even international in scope? The second concerns *how long an aspirant's well-knownness lasts.* Is it for only one day, a week, a year? Is it for a generation? Or is it forever?

These two dimensions combine to create at least twenty types of high visibles (see Table 1). Type 1 is the person who made news for one day in his town, such as a swimmer who rescued a boy from drowning. Type 8 is the person whose name makes news around the world for a week; for example, Dr.

William DeVries, who implanted an artificial heart in William Schroeder. Type 9 is the local person who enjoyed high visibility in his community for a year; a good example would be the town's mayor that year. Type 15 is the person who achieves, in one country, celebrity that lasts a generation; an example would be baseball's Stan Musial, who was well known in the United States but not elsewhere, as baseball is largely an American sport. Type 20 is reserved for those rare souls who have achieved the peak of fame: They are known all over the world, and their fame lasts forever. Generally, they have been borne along by perpetual institutions such as religions, cultures, or nations: Jesus Christ, Mohammed, Buddha, Herod, Catherine the Great, or George Washington.

Table 1. Levels in the Visibility Hierarchy.

Visibility Reach					
International	4	8	12	16	20
National	3	7	11	15	19
Regional	2	6	10	14	18
Local	1	5	9	13	17
	one day	one year	one week	one generation	forever
			Visibility Duration		

Clearly, Type 1s have the least visibility, and Type 20s have the most. Furthermore, a high visible's fame increases as he or she moves from the lower left of Table 1 to the upper right. However, it is not possible to compare the relative fame between someone in the upper left or lower right. Is someone whose name reaches the whole world for one day more well known than someone who is remembered forever in only his or her local community? More reach and more duration mean more fame, but the relative contribution of each cannot be compared.

VISIBILITY REACH

The reach, or space over which an aspirant's name is known, can be portrayed as a pyramid (see Table 2). The base of the pyramid consists of many *invisibles*. Just above these are *local celebrities*—who are somewhat well known in their own local areas. Above them are *regional celebrities* whose names are known beyond their own immediate areas, such as throughout the South or on the West Coast. Above them are still fewer *national celebrities*, who are in turn overshadowed by *international celebrities* who are well known in two or more countries.

Table 2. Visibility Reach Pyramid.

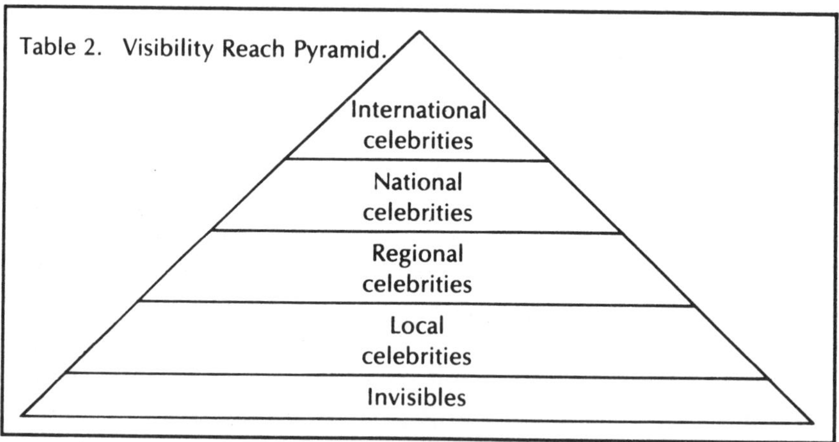

In the typical celebrity sector, the base of invisibles is very broad, and the higher levels thin out rapidly until only a few people are left commanding the highest visibility. The shape of the pyramid also alters as the sector matures. In an emerging sector, such as mountain climbing, many amateurs would be found, with just a few professionals who are well known primarily to the amateurs. As interest increases in the activity, more aspirants enter the base. This aspirant invasion means that the pyramid will develop more interim levels of visibility. Profit-seeking entrepreneurs will enter the sector to promote events, launch trade magazines, and organize fan clubs. They will try to immortalize certain mountain climbers, to create legends that will inspire others. Eventually, the sector will stabilize with a certain breadth (number of entrants) and height (number of visibility levels).

The highly visible in most sectors are well known only to

members of those sectors. David Bohardt, executive director of the National Funeral Directors Association, is very well known in the funeral industry but virtually invisible to members or audiences of other sectors. The general public has very little interest in the elites of these sectors. But other sectors have high *cross-sector* appeal; their elites will be widely known. For example, actors and singers who reach the top of their respective sectors are likely to be well known to a very high percentage of the general public. The activities in these highly visible sectors have inherent interest to the general public, a major reason why transformation and image-making machinery operates full time to create events and broadcast news about aspirants in these sectors.

Now let's take a closer look at the celebrities who occupy each level of the pyramid.

Local Celebrities. Celebrity is usually thought of as something that only an elite few enjoy. But every community contains people who are more visible than others. And every community, no matter how small, has its own celebrity pyramid. It includes the leaders of the community's *major institutions*: the mayor, leading banker, lawyer, physician, businessperson, football coach, and social host. Others are well known because they fill out the community's story needs, such as the local "bad girl," "bad boy," "Scrooge," "playboy," "philanthropist," "eccentric," "young widow," and "leading athlete." Every community boasts an intricate web of personalities whose stories constitute its history and drama. And the local celebrity process is abetted by local newspapers and broadcasters who search for stories to tell.

In the past, most local celebrities did not *seek* visibility; they acquired it as a by-product of their occupations or lifestyles. But increasingly, local celebrities are turning to professional transformers, image consultants, and marketing professionals to help increase their well-knownness. Still, lacking either resources or drive, most who attain local celebrity are content to remain locally elite. They would rather be the mayor of a small town than one of dozens of ward committeemen in a large city. The beauty queen of Shawnee Mission, Kansas, may not even place in the statewide contest or make it into the Miss America pageant. Feelings of local pride can be so strong that even striving for celebrity in a larger arena may lower the person's local standing among his or her peers. The local celebrity often has to choose between "standing out" or "fitting in" in his or her community.

ELECT YOUR LOCAL SHERIFF

For most people, the idea of a local sheriff brings to mind actor Andy Griffith's amiable, low-key "Mayberry" character who methodically solved the missing garbage can caper at the high school. In Virginia City, Montana, the local sheriff, Johnny France, was a gun-toting, rangy, ex-rodeo star who achieved national celebrity by single-handedly apprehending two killers hiding out in the mountains of Montana. The six-month chase captured the imagination of the country, and as a result, France wrote and promoted the book *Incident at Big Sky*, sold story rights to the movies, and did the usual meet-the-president routine. Back home in Virginia City, the local citizens were not as enamored of their pistol-flashing media hero. In the next election, they voted him out and his deputy sheriff in. France, reflecting on the matter, commented, "I think some people thought I was just too big for my britches."[2]

Local celebrities who aim for higher levels of visibility frequently have to leave their communities to succeed. The local singer or painter often moves to the larger cultural centers, and the local politician to the state capital or to Washington, D.C. If their quest is successful, they might become glorified by the local community, treated with some measure of respect during their visits back home. Yet many will be viewed ambivalently: They are part of the community and yet apart from it.

Local celebrities are in many ways more meaningful models for the people in their communities than those who are well known on the national level, because they are real and tangible to the people around them. They have undergone the most minimal of transformations; they have usually not been managed as images unrelated to their actual selves. As people rise in their sector's visibility pyramid, they engage in more image-making, becoming "bigger than life" to their audiences and, often, less real to themselves.

 ***Regional Celebrities.*** Some people enjoy a regional rather than a local reputation. Ask Californians to identify Herb Caen, and most will correctly identify him as a San Francisco columnist, but he would likely be unknown in the Midwest. Floridians would easily recognize politician Harry Johnston, while Californians would fail to identify him. Both of these people are regional celebrities, enjoying high name recognition, attention from the media, and high social status.

The regional celebrity phenomenon even has its own networks. A good example is radio and television newscasting, which by its very definition is region-based. Each city has its newscasters, who are well known within the city and surrounding areas. Other regional celebrities are drawn from the ranks of business leaders, fashion trend setters, and college athletes.

Regional celebrities who aspire to higher visibility can use their regional visibility as a stepping stone. Margie Korshak, a leading public relations personality, has very high visibility in Chicago—something that is beginning to establish her reputation with the public relations sector in New York and elsewhere. Her regional identification is so strong that she can use it as a lever to open up new markets.

Some people make the jump from regional to national celebrity not by climbing the ladder within their sector but by crossing over to a more popular, active sector, at the same time using their regional base to acquaint larger markets with their existence. Often, celebrities attempting this jump will move up and down in terms of visibility. A good example is Jesse Jackson, who began operating in the political sector as a civil rights activist on a local level, but who was elevated to national visibility through his association with Dr. Martin Luther King, Jr. Using his enhanced visibility to establish himself in Chicago as a strong regional political celebrity, Jackson was eventually able to translate his regional celebrity into even higher national visibility as a candidate for president in 1984. Although he did not gain the Democratic nomination, his name and oratory became familiar to most Americans. In moving from religion to politics, he managed to move from regional to national prominence.

 ***National Celebrities.*** Three types of national celebrities can be pinpointed. The first are *sector celebrities*: well known to people within their sector but hardly known by others. They include all

the national heads of associations such as the American Medical Association, American Bar Association, and the Council of Churches. Also included are the heads of major corporations, who are highly visible to the business community at large. Employees of General Electric, wherever they work, know that the company president is Jack Welch, although to the general public, Welch is largely invisible.

Also found on the national level are *extra-sectoral celebrities*, who are well known to many people outside of their primary sector. Typically, they occupy a high position in one of the highly visible sectors, particularly entertainment, sports, or politics. Even here, a distinction can be drawn between those perceived as national *stars* and national *superstars*. Jamie Lee Curtis is considered a nationally known film star, but Meryl Streep is viewed as a superstar. In the culture sector, Joyce Carol Oates is a star, while James Michener is a superstar. Jack Reichert, chairman of the board of Brunswick Corporation, is a business star, but chairman John Akers of IBM is a superstar.

The third type of national celebrities are those who take the accidental route to high visibility. Among them are people who have committed a sensational crime, participated in an unusual event, or won a major contest. For most of these accidental national celebrities, however, high visibility is short lived, and its rewards are insignificant.

International Celebrities. The leap from national to international celebrity is not easy to make. Many persons highly visible to their national market have little or no visibility abroad. Australians do not know the names of many American baseball, football, and basketball stars. Conversely, U.S. citizens do not know the names of the stars of Australian rules football, rugby, or soccer. Except for Olympic stars, most sports celebrities enjoy only national reputations.

The same cannot be said of entertainers. Major film celebrities (and, increasingly, television performers seen in foreign markets) may achieve international prominence, as the medium in which they are distributed is exported all over the world. Current political and religious leaders such as Ronald Reagan, Margaret Thatcher, and Pope John Paul II enjoy an international reputation because they head major world institutions.

VISIBILITY DURATION

The highly visible differ not only in how widely they are known but also in how long they are well known for. There are one-day celebrities, one-week celebrities, one-year celebrities, one-generation celebrities, and finally permanent legends.

One-Day Celebrities. Andy Warhol once observed that in the future, everyone will be a celebrity for fifteen minutes, an allusion to the explosion of print and broadcast media, which must incessantly fill their space and time with people stories. Reporters are always looking for interesting stories about people; to them, everyone and every story is potential grist for the news mill. It takes only a reporter to create a one-day celebrity.

The man who rescues a boy from drowning; the woman who wins the state lottery; the educator who wins the best-teacher award—all are one-day celebrities. They will get a headline in the local newspaper or sometimes in the national press. After that, their visibility submerges again; they are forgotten by the public at large. But the one-day celebrities remember. They don't easily forget that they were once the talk of the town, recognized by others. And some of their friends remember, too. But the main feature of one-day celebrity is that it is *nonstrategic:* not easily translated into material advantage or reward.

Recently, celebrity media have been shifting to interviewing and featuring a higher proportion of unknowns in all sectors, rather than just well-known celebrities. As audiences develop an insatiable appetite for new faces, they become more interested in seeing "ordinary" people who have accomplished or been involved in something unusual. This fits Andy Warhol's speculation that more people will have a chance to be instant celebrities in the coming years.

Why are there one-day celebrities? The main reason is that certain stories have to be continuously played out to the public, for a wide variety of purposes. The media select people daily to fill these roles. But for the person featured—the brave fireman, the innovative doctor—the story is over in one day; there is no profit advantage to anyone—either the medium or an institution—in sustaining the celebrity beyond one day.

One-Week Celebrities. Some people are thrust into the public spotlight for more than one day, especially if they are part of an unfolding drama that the public desires to see resolved. The woman who is on trial for murdering her lover; the man who received the first artificial heart; the politician who is steeped in scandal—the public wants a daily report on the progress of the trial, recovery, or investigation. Eventually a resolution is reached. The public is satisfied. And the one-week celebrities go back, if they can, to their ordinary lives.

The actual length of the "one-week story" depends on several factors. The media will draw it out if it "sells." If it is a favorable story involving an important institution, it may last longer, as the institution drives the story forward for its own commercial purposes. Essentially, the story will be played out for as long as it is in the driver's self-interest to do so.

One-Year Celebrities. Each year, some people stand out as the celebrities of the year, managing to evoke extremely high levels of media attention or public interest. They make the cover of *Time*'s "Person of the Year" issue or the issue of *People* magazine entitled "Twenty-five Most Interesting People of the Year" or the few chosen for the major Nobel Prizes that year. Clearly, 1927 was Charles Lindbergh's year, as 1984 was Michael Jackson's. In the political world, George McGovern had his year, as did Bella Abzug. In the literary world, Mary McCarthy had her year, and so did John Irving. One-year celebrities usually retain their visibility for more than one year—but in one of those years, they achieve a peak of public recognition that will probably not be repeated.

Major time landmarks—month, year, decade—are important in the minds of audiences, just as is the desire to know who is on top. This supplies the media and institutions with the incentive to promote certain celebrities as the month's, year's, or decade's most prominent. That's why the drivers use a variety of selection criteria: those who made it big quickly; those who took decades to make it but finally are recognized; those who head a sector that was just discovered; and those who had a special event occur in a long career.

One-Generation Celebrities. A small elite enjoys visibility for a whole generation. They are the generation's heroes, movers, shakers, idols, icons. Clara Bow, Huey Long, Buddy Holly, Brigitte Bardot, Jim Brown, Peter Max, the Reverend Ike—they define their eras. During their eras, their future status as permanent celebrities may be widely assumed. But predicting who will gain a lock on the memory channel is not easy. History provides a perfect case: that of Antonio Salieri, the villain of the movie *Amadeus*, one of the most popular music composers of his day and age. A contemporary of Mozart's, Salieri had hoped that he, and not Mozart, would live in people's memories. But he was mistaken. Hardly anyone in subsequent generations heard of him or of his music, a circumstance predicted by Salieri who, upon learning of Mozart's death, said, "It is indeed a pity to lose so great a genius, but his death is a good thing for us. If he had lived longer not a soul would have given us a bit of bread for our compositions."[3] Salieri, indeed, was a one-generation celebrity.

Sometimes, the images of generational celebrities are kept alive by institutions. J. C. Penney, the founder and namesake of one of the world's largest department store chains, died many years ago. This is a fact. But his company, by continuing to use his name, promoting his principles in its advertising, and constantly chronicling his humble origins and his founding of the first Penney's store in the West, continues to fuse Penney's image with the modern chain's.

Moreover, a one-generation celebrity can extend his or her earning power through skillful promotion. Though he hasn't danced for years, Fred Astaire has capitalized on his generational celebrity by making cameo film appearances, giving infrequent media interviews, and gracefully serving as the honoree at retrospective functions. Norman Mailer is still a generational hero, even though his most significant writing was done years ago. Often the heroes of one generation try to stretch into the next by changing their style and content, not always with success. Bob Dylan, a generational hero of the 1960s, has often changed his song style and message. In fact, some of his transformations, such as to gospel singer, actually cost him his share of the music market. More recently, Dylan made a major strategic move, linking himself with the more contemporary music celebrity Tom Petty and generating intense fan attraction. Nevertheless, Dylan has yet to fully regain his former market share. Similarly, Jane Fonda has changed with the times and gathered momentum—leading protests against the Vietnam War, appearing on the half-time show for the Superbowl, and becoming an icon for women in the 1980s. Little Richard's appearance in the 1986 film *Down and Out in Beverly Hills* didn't mean that he had leaped to permanent-legend status but rather that he was able to take advantage of the cyclical revival of one-generation celebrities.

Legends. Legends remain famous beyond their time; indeed, their visibility lasts for all time. But even the process through which legends are created is changing. In the past, many popes, kings, presidents, and generals came and went; only a few achieved immortality. These were people whose ideas or deeds shaped history, who inspired awe among the "mere mortals." They seemed to be gods or at least demi-gods, the best of mankind. Their visibility has been built upon fictions that cannot be separated from fact; nor does it matter. George Washington probably did not chop down a cherry tree and confess his complicity to his father; but whether it happened or not is irrelevant. We have a need to venerate certain people, turning them into legends, even myths.

But today, as heroism gives way to celebrity, celebrities will begin to enter the memory channel as legends as much as a result of their marketing savvy as their achievements. The Beatles, who were certainly highly talented, will undoubtedly become legends as much for the success of their brilliant image-building tactics as for their music.

How Long Will Bill Cosby Last?

If anyone seems headed for legend status, it's comedian Bill Cosby. From almost any perspective, he appears to be on a steady climb to a memory lock on legend status. He has the top-rated TV show, is ranked by advertisers as the most likeable and sincere personality, and is in such demand that he can fulfill only a small portion of the invitations he receives. For all of this output he is paid $10 million a year and is idealized as a role model for parents of all backgrounds. He is entrusted with the image campaigns of a major Wall Street brokerage firm and of a dominant food conglomerate. He is a comedian who is not only popular but who represents an entire set of values: integrity, commitment, and intelligence. Yet the history of the entertainment sector has been so novelty based and short lived that to become legends, aspirants need very particular outputs that can perform very specialized functions: films that have been knighted by critics as classics; incidents that have been mythified in the public's consciousness; linkages with other legends. But what does Cosby have that can perform these functions? Films such as *Mother, Jugs and Speed*? Comedy routines about Noah? Record albums such as "At Last Bill Cosby Really Sings"? Even his current hit TV show can scarcely be repeated in even two years without seeming dated. Clearly, Bill Cosby will need additional memory-building strategies if he wishes to be remembered forever. At any time, the most visible seem as if they will last forever, and yet few among them ever do. Cosby, without better management of his image outputs, is sure to fade.

Visibility Life Cycles

A celebrity's position on the visibility pyramid and length of stay there are not fixed. How does a celebrity's well-knownness change over time? Let's consider a hypothetical case. Table 3 shows the path of an aspirant's well-knownness over his or her life span. We see that this person achieved a low, though not negligible, level of visibility by the age of twenty; by age forty, the person's visibility had risen to a high level; it remained there until age sixty; and thereafter he was increasingly forgotten. This is the *standard life cycle pattern*, with its four stages of emergence, growth, maturity, and decline.

Table 3. The Standard Celebrity Life Cycle Pattern.

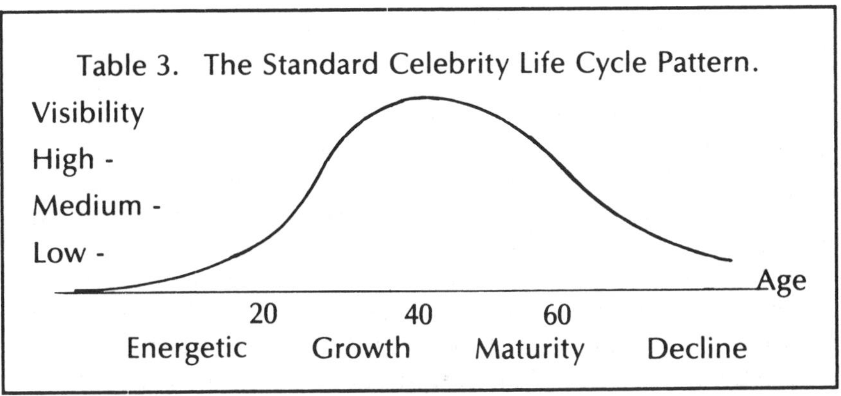

OTHER LIFE CYCLE PATTERNS

Many other celebrity career patterns exist. The most frequent patterns are shown in Figure 10. The *steady-rise-to-the-top pattern* (Figure 10A) characterizes many of the leaders of the major sectors. Cary Grant, Willie Mays, and advertising executive David Ogilvy exemplify this pattern of attaining increasing visibility during their professional careers and never fully disappearing from the public's eye.

In the *overnight pattern* (Figure 10B) someone acquires instant high visibility because of a major deed or event. Paul Revere, Sir Edmund Hillary, Neil Armstrong, and Corazon Aquino all moved from relative obscurity to sudden positions of lasting fame because of deeds that captured the imagination of the world. Jacqueline Bouvier and Lady Diana Spencer achieved overnight and lasting fame through their marriages to highly visible men.

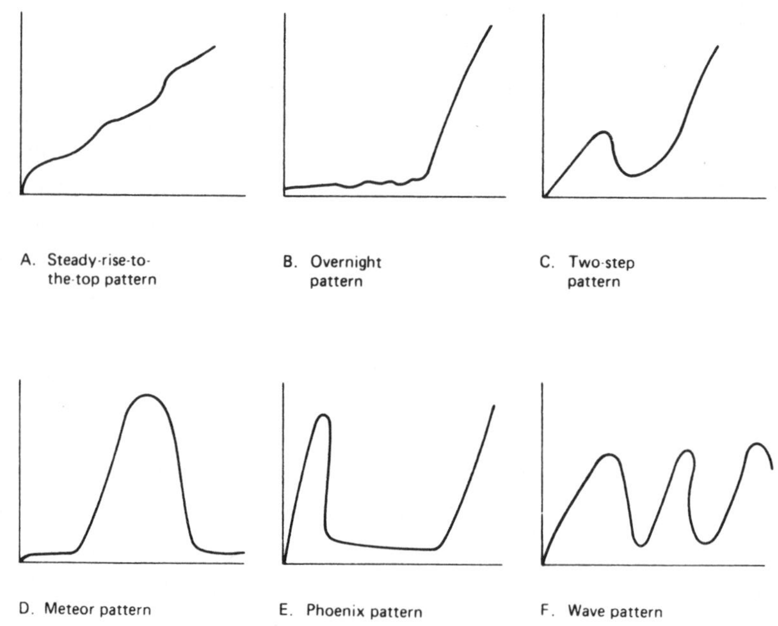

Figure 10: Other Celebrity Life Cycle Patterns.

In the *two-step pattern* (Figure 10C), an aspirant achieves a modest reputation, remains at that level for a long time, then breaks into a high level of visibility. Willie Nelson enjoyed a modest reputation for years as a country-and-western singer. A singer-songwriter who had been a regional celebrity for years, he was positioned to move quickly up the visibility pyramid when this kind of music became extremely popular. Robert Dole, long visible as a senator and briefly very visible as Gerald Ford's 1976 running mate, achieved more lasting high visibility with his tenure as Senate Majority Leader.

In the *meteor pattern* (Figure 10D), someone gains fame very suddenly and loses it just as quickly. Rita Jenrette, who rose very suddenly as a result of being married to an Abscam-related congressman, had her image forced throughout the media, writing a book, appearing in *Playboy,* making a media tour. But as soon as the story began to fade, so did she.

Figure 10E represents the *phoenix pattern,* wherein the person achieves fame, sinks into relative obscurity, then has his or her image re-marketed. Tina Turner, highly visible in the rock music sector in the 1960s and early 1970s, virtually disappeared, then reemerged in a new and improved form on the rock music scene in the 1980s with hit records and movie roles.

Finally, Figure 10F represents the *wave pattern,* wherein the person rises, falls, rises, falls, and possibly rises and falls again in public visibility. This patterns is common among political celebrities who rise with one administration, fall, then rise with another. David Stockman rose and fell a number of times while with a single administration; then shifted sectors into writing and business and attempted to rise again. Chinese leader Deng Xiao Ping, Bert Lance, and George Wallace have all ridden the wave pattern.

In a society divided into many classes, specialized occupations, and diverse interests, it is hardly surprising that our analysis of celebrity focuses on the different visibility sectors, for each has its own rules and conventions that must be factored into any aspirant's marketing strategy. The entertainer is free to endorse popcorn, appear on "Entertainment Tonight," and drive a Lamborghini Countach. In contrast, the scientist will be hard pressed to justify any of these activities and will probably want to continue publishing in the traditional journals to maintain sector credibility. As society's values and interests change, so do the sectors with the most celebrity-making potential. Finally, the management of celebrity careers is directly related to celebrity life cycles. One-week celebrities need to be carefully managed to break out of their status as mere media curiosities and the celebrity of the year needs to worry about overexposure and lack of long-term visibility.

All of these factors should be weighed in the celebrity marketing plan, but above all else, aspirants must realize whom their marketing is ultimately directed toward: an audience. Potential celebrities need clients to seek them out, people to watch them, consumers to buy their products, and fans to talk about them. The next chapter places the audience into the marketing equation.

CHAPTER SIX

The Consumers: Audiences

Aldo Gucci, patriarch of the Gucci fashion empire, strolls into his Palm Beach store, inspecting it, in the words of the manager, "as if it were the first time he ever saw it."[1] The patrons, despite their best efforts, lose their reserve and gawk as they would at a pop star or senator. But who is Aldo Gucci?

Gucci is the son of Guccio Gucci and the founder of Gucci Limited, which started out as a four-employee saddle factory. Today, he is an international symbol. The Gucci empire consists of many different audiences, all of which Gucci must address. There are Gucci's customers, his worldwide staff, his business partners, his family. Given the nature of his business, there is the critical audience of the world community of image opinion leaders: the fashion writers, designers, socialites, and entertainment stars. For Aldo Gucci, all these audiences must be satisfied.

When Gucci was indicted for tax evasion, his carefully cultivated image came under attack. Though no longer the chain's operating manager, to the Gucci audiences, Aldo still symbolized the company's elite status as retailer of expensive leather goods. His jail sentence, and his family feuds, will force Gucci to address the threat of a changed relationship with his audience, and act strategically to minimize the damage to his enterprise.

No industry can exist without customers. In modern-day manufacturing and marketing, finding the customers and matching them to the right products has become an all-consuming passion.

It is a passion so complete that many products are now fine-tuned to the most subtle variations in customer needs, desires, and expectations.

The results can be impressive, as the discovery and segmentation of markets assumes a sophistication that is mathematically precise. Ask General Motors for a comparison of buyers for a Pontiac Firebird and a Buick Park Avenue, and a mountain of data emerges to distinguish the two buyer groups on the basis of attitudes, lifestyles, and buying approaches—with estimates that project the numbers and needs of automobile buyers ten years into the future. Ask the Red Cross how Americans feel about making charitable contributions and they produce a Harris poll on age groups, income levels, and the status of competing charities. Ask American Broadcasting Company how many people tune in to the first fifteen minutes of one of its programs and accurate, comprehensive information spews forth. But ask the data collectors if veteran singer Eddie Fisher can re-ignite his career, whether current pop star Michael Jackson can widen and deepen his market and not burn out, or why George Burns made a spectacular comeback in his eighties, and the computer screens go blank. "Consumers are too fickle," say the analysts. "They change their motivations all the time. There are too many variables. You just can't predict which celebrity they'll buy."

Often, the so-called experts' discussions on audience perceptions and attachments degenerate into esoteric discourses on magic, charisma, presence, or luck. To most commentators, the reasons why Shaun Cassidy rose as the prince of pre-teens, why Oprah Winfrey ignites TV viewers, or why Pat Robertson has the highest profile in religious celebritydom are unknowable and mysterious.

But to use efficiently the marketing process, the aspirant cannot afford to be distracted by these myths. To effect the transformation that will bring the aspirant and the market together, the aspirant must fully understand the market. To do so, aspirants must answer the following questions: Who are the consumers—the audience members—that make up my market? What kinds of people are they? What do they want—and get—from celebrities?

The relationship between celebrities and audiences has always been controversial. The cliche that "only the public can make a star" expresses the popular myth that audiences capriciously decide whom to elevate to high visibility. It's indisputable that audience tastes *do* change, something we notice when some celebrities are unceremoniously abandoned and others launched without warning or apparent cause. But the relationship between the celebrity and the fan is far more understandable and predictable than common wisdom claims. To best predict fans' attractions, celebrity-makers must understand the different levels of interest and intimacy that audiences bring to their relationship with celebrities.

The Audience Intensity Ladder

Ultimately, a celebrity's marketing costs must be recouped, whether by encouraging audience members to purchase records, attend sermons, or buy tickets to games. That's why the celebrity's ability to move audiences from low levels of interest to more intense levels of interest is so important to the marketing plan's success. The Audience Intensity Ladder (see Figure 11) places audience members on a scale according to the strength of their involvement with celebrities to show how different types of audiences can be best used by the celebrity industry.

Even the few people on the extreme ends of the scale—people who have no interest in celebrities at all, and fanatics obsessed with celebrities—are of potential use to celebrities. Still, celebrity-marketers are far more concerned with those whose interest in celebrities lies between the extremes. Just as celebrities occupy a status pyramid based on higher and higher visibility, so can audience members be placed on a ladder of increasing interest in, involvement with, and dependency upon celebrities.

"INVISIBLE" CONSUMERS

Everyone has an Uncle Fred or Cousin Jane who not only disdains the latest pop stars but who seems to live behind a celebrity-proof shield. A mention of Barbra Streisand or Paul Shaffer invites only blank stares, indifference, or hostility. Fred and Jane symbolize the least-useful audience on the ladder: invisible consumers, who supposedly despise media manipulation, dislike identifying with personalities, or lack the capacity to idolize. Whereas they likely did have heroes during childhood

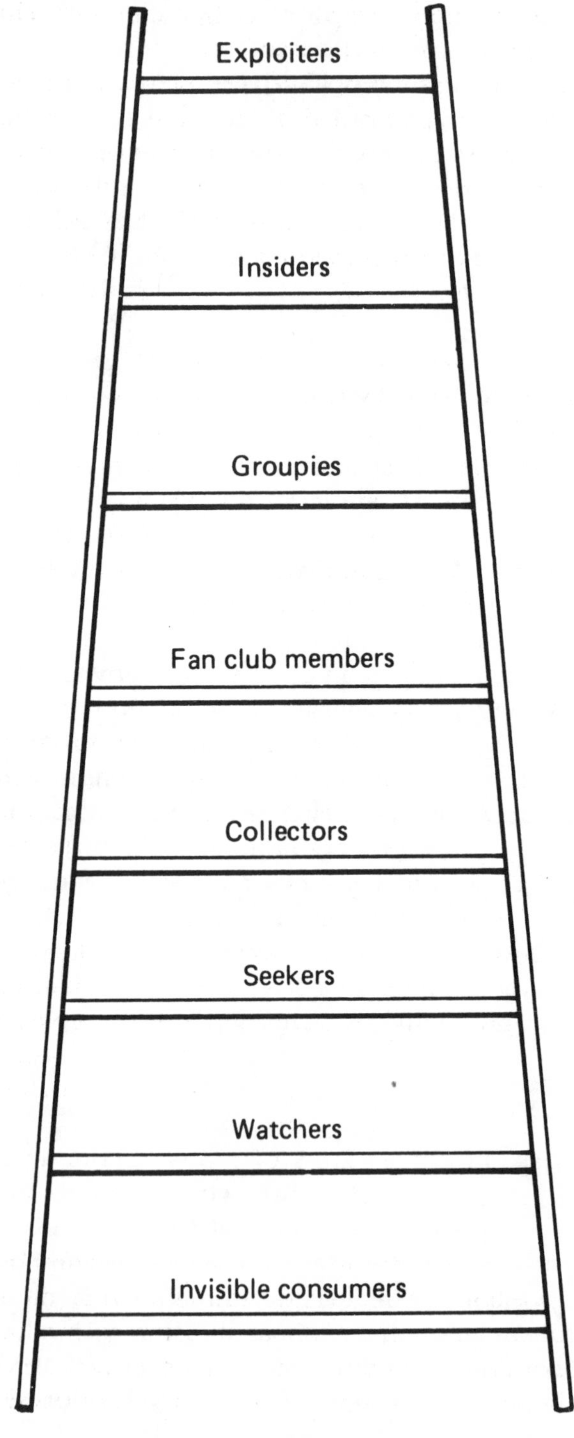

Figure 11: Audience Intensity Ladder.

and adolescence, they "grew out of it," seemingly slamming the door on celebrity worship forever.

But invisible consumers are not *non*consumers. In reality, the celebrity interests of invisible consumers are just so far out of the mainstream as to *appear* invisible. The housewife who worships the host of a PBS gardening or cooking show, the engineer who collects electronic music and would give his micrometer to talk to RCA's leading sound technician, the fisherman who yearns to meet the world-champion flycaster: All *are* celebrity-consumers.

Other consumers hidden from celebrity-marketers are those who worship celebrities in unusual ways or places. These people may not go to the movies, but they're first in line at the women's club luncheon honoring a pioneer traffic-flow designer. They dislike entertainers, yet they seek out locally celebrated ministers. They *appear* celebrity-less, but they are really just invisible because of their sectors' obscurity. The person who is truly devoid of all interest in all celebrities is rare indeed.

WATCHERS

Many people will consume celebrities if the price charged and commitment required are low. These are *watchers,* who tune in to see the president speak, who read *People,* or who go to an occasional blockbuster film or play. Their celebrity-consuming behavior is *passive*. They are observers, not aggressive celebrity-seekers.

With the increase in such celebrity-based programming as "Wide World of Sports," "Wall Street Week," and "Prairie Home Companion," the ranks of the watcher class have swelled. Watchers, already predisposed toward celebrity worship, can be seen by the marketer as prime targets, ready to be maneuvered into becoming *active* celebrity-consumers.

SEEKERS

Watchers who feel a stronger attraction to celebrities may move from casual/accidental celebrity-viewing toward more intentional contact. They begin to seek out celebrity performances. They eagerly attend their favorite singer's concerts, their favorite politician's speeches, their favorite artist's gallery openings. When it's not possible to experience the celebrity's performance "live," they settle for the next best thing: the singer's albums, the politician's book, the artist's poster reproduction. Of course, not all such purchases are made by celebrity seekers; many Boston Pops records are bought just for the music, not in conscious homage to conductor John Williams. Yet the celebrity appeal of such performers is the main reason why many *do* buy the records, especially when they choose the Pops over a different orchestra performing the same piece. Going to the auto show may or may not be a decision to see a particular celebrity; the cars alone may attract viewers. Others go to see drag racer Don Garlits or Indianapolis 500 winner Danny Sullivan.

Seekers spend money on celebrities. This earns them the undivided attention of the celebrity industry, whose tracking methods, based on sales, make seekers the first group to gain the undivided attention of the industry. But it's a fair exchange. In return for their higher expenditures, seekers receive rewards, whether it is enjoyment of the sacrifices that their worship entails, enhanced self-images, or improved fantasy lives. Seekers drive to concerts in rainy weather, wait in long lines for playoff tickets, and wolf down hurried dinners in exchange for closer seats at the Marketer of the Year dinner. Each act demonstrates commitment to the celebrity, earning the seeker a psychological return on his or her investment.

COLLECTORS

The class of audience members known as *collectors* not only attends events but also consumes physical reminders of the celebrity and event. The souvenirs and memorabilia they treasure includes everything from Grateful Dead scarfs, to Eddie Murphy's Mumford High T-shirt (from *Beverly Hills Cop*), to the autographed program from a business lecture by CBS's Ray Brady.

Manufacturers of celebrity merchandise give collectors ample opportunities to express their dedication. Collectors can obtain merchandise at events, through mail order, or via high-tech delivery systems.

A CALL FROM THE KING

Elvis Presley is dead, but the opportunities for collectors remain alive. They receive unsolicited phone calls from a computer that relentlessly dials all working numbers in areas of the country where country-and-western music is popular. When the potential collector picks up the phone, what he or she hears is an operator, saying, "I have an important telecomputer call from J. D. Sumner." When the consumer agrees to listen, a deep voice intones, "Hello, I'm J. D. Sumner, Elvis Presley's bass singer and closest friend for over twenty-five years, going back long before 'Heartbreak Hotel.' " The voice pointedly asks the consumer, "I understand that you're one of Elvis's real fans. Is that right?" So smoothly do the computers conduct the conversation that many people don't even realize they are talking to a machine. "There is something that Elvis, I know, would want you to have. The one thing besides being able to hear Elvis sing that his fans cherish most is an Elvis scarf." Avid collectors, flattered by the contact with celebrities and impressed with the seance-like quality of the call, agree to buy. "Elvis," intones the talking disk drive as music eerily swells, "wants you to have this scarf. *He* would have wanted it this way."

Why do collectors collect? On one level the motivation is fairly straightforward: to express appreciation for the experience, to preserve it, by giving it a physical manifestation that keeps the experience tangible and fresh. Although some collectors are less fans than investors, buying out of an expectation that an item will multiply in value, most collectors would never dream of parting with their prizes. They gain great enjoyment by communicating with others who feel the same way. The attendance and enthusiasm at collector "swap meets" are evidence of the strength of this attraction. Ultimately, collectors achieve a sense of physical closeness to the celebrity that seekers do not experience—and offer the marketer a chance to multiply the celebrity's earnings.

FAN CLUB MEMBERS

One step up the ladder, fan club members are distinguished by their need for *interaction*—to receive communication from the celebrity, *and* to send it back. Not satisfied with anonymously watching the concert, attending the race, or buying the T-shirt, fan club members want their idols to recognize them *as fans*. Seeking reinforcement and comfort in the company of those who feel as intensely as they do, fans at this level band together to form clubs. For the considerable time and energy they invest, the "return"—a note from their idol, preferred seats at concerts, or a brief backstage meeting—is more than a fair exchange.

According to Blanche Trinajstick, editor of *The Fan Club Directory*, the fan club class is exploding, with "millions of members" in more than 1,200 active clubs.[2] The clubs cover a vast range of sectors, including soap opera stars, musicians, actors, dead stars, race car drivers, and many others.

In an attempt to understand why this class is so huge and what draws people into it, ten fan club presidents were interviewed.[3] It was discovered that club members tend to belong to more than one club, although they limit themselves to clubs of similar type; one fan specializing in popular singers like Diana Ross and Patti LaBelle, another belonging to clubs dedicated solely to dead celebrities such as James Dean and Sal Mineo.

Fan clubs serve their members and their stars in different, but intertwined, ways. That's because almost any club activity that benefits the star psychologically rewards audience members as well. Even though most of them never get to meet their idols, fan club members serve their own and their celebrities' interests by buying the best tickets to concerts, calling in record requests to radio stations, and traveling great distances for conventions or conferences. At the same time, their activities generate media attention that heightens the celebrity's visibility to fans on a lower rung of the intensity ladder, helping to convert them to more intense status.

Fan clubs serve an important social function for their members, too. Attending luncheons and meetings to discuss their celebrity, members are able to form social relationships that are eased along by the common interests that all members share. A few celebrities have managed to use this wellspring of adoration quite skillfully by actively associating with club members. But the majority of celebrities only occasionally communicate with their clubs, and then mostly with the club presidents.

> ### "SAVE THE LAST WALTZ FOR ME"
>
> Fan club favorite Englebert Humperdinck has made an institution out of his relationship with his fan clubs. While on tour, Humperdinck attends special luncheons at which members of the local Humperdinck chapter pay for the privilege of having lunch with their idol. With each member receiving a red rose, they wait. Finally, Humperdinck sweeps into the room to the sound of his trademark song. Even though he treats his fans with a certain aloof disdain, his loyal corps swoons in his presence. Humperdinck tells of his future plans, confides in the loneliness of the road, and makes personal asides to the more visible hard-working fans gathered around him. They, in turn, pore over every phrase, ever nuance, renourished in their loyalty, even more fiercely dedicated to the selling and consumption of Englebert Humperdinck.

Conventional wisdom holds that fan club members suffer from erotomania—an obsessive need to love someone.[4] This notion supports the popular vision of wild-eyed fans storming the celebrity's car or mobbing the hotel in a frenzy of love and lust—scenes that actually occur less frequently than the celebrity press would have us believe. Our interviews suggest that fan club members are not often fanatics. Rather, we find that as the appeal of celebrities supersedes the traditional unifiers of church, school, or professional society as a provider of common ground, fan clubs serve as catalysts to provide group associations and friendships.

Not all fan clubs are warm, spontaneous movements born out of fans' love. Moving to higher degrees of sophistication, the celebrity industry has begun to synthesize the development of celebrity-audience interaction. Recognizing the potential in exploiting these groups, celebrity-marketers are usurping fan prerogative by starting "corporate" fan clubs of their own. Lionel Richie's fan club is run by his wife Brenda, with the sale of Richie merchandise handled under subcontract by a marketing house that specializes in organizing, sustaining, and exploiting fan clubs. The rock group Journey orchestrates a fan club that offers its members not just the usual T-shirts and membership cards, but also engraved sunglasses, concert ticket privileges, and "the very latest information on developments in the Personal Lives of Steve, Neal, Jonathan, Ross, and Steve."[5] It is an example of the celebrity industry's tactic of building structures that *appear* to be genuine and audience driven, but are actually marketing driven.

Take the case of Terri Flasch, who founded a Jimmy Connors fan club at the age of thirteen. Flasch not only worshipped Connors but also managed to capitalize on her personal commitment to him. Seeking experience to put on her résumé, and sensing a genuine business opportunity, she continued to serve as president of the club after her teen years' exuberance had subsided. Through careful management, she eventually built the club into an organization with 4,600 members from twenty-four different countries. Initially ignored by the celebrity's own management, the club grew so large—and potentially profitable—that Connors' brother John attempted to wrest control of it away from Flasch. In the tradition of celebrity-related litigation, she first heard about the overthrow while reading *World Tennis*. Flasch, reluctant to give up what she had so painstakingly built, took the matter to court, convinced that Connors was the one man in the world who didn't deserve a fan club. The point is that fan clubs can be a tremendous asset for enhancing celebrity, as long as they retain their genuine grass-roots flavor.

GROUPIES

Near the top rung of the audience intensity ladder are those who move from communicating with the celebrity through fan clubs to communicating directly—and, they hope, intimately. Popularly known as groupies (in the words of the immortal Cynthia Plastercaster, "a person who regularly chases groups"), these audience members may even cross the barrier that separates celebrities from audiences and achieve visibility in their own right.[6] Mostly, though, groupies seek to achieve the ultimate form of identification, to penetrate their idols' security shield and see the world from the celebrity's perspective. Desperately pursuing intimacy, groupies sleep with celebrities, offer them drugs, or hound and harass them until admitted—however briefly—into their inner circles. (Ms. Plastercaster, a celebrity in her own right, achieved *her* visibility by casting the genitals of popular male entertainers in a mixture of plaster and alginate.)

The groupies' compulsion to be close to the celebrity is observed in all sectors of American life. When teenage actor John Cusack became celebritized for his role in the film *The Sure Thing*, groupies camping out on his front lawn forced him to leave his home. When race-car champion Rick Mears shows up for a race his ubiquitous contingent of racing-circuit groupies is there to cluster, curry favor, and implore. The list of groupie targets is endless. Chief surgeons, astronauts, professors, business executives—all have the potential to attract devoted followers who crave intimacy and celebrity-by-association.

INSIDERS

Insiders are just that: audience members who move inside celebrities' inner circles, playing significant roles in their lives, or occupying legitimate, authorized positions in their support systems or entourages. Although some insiders are culled from the ranks of groupies, most insiders are those who, in the performance of ordinary functions in the celebrity's life, have become fans. In the process, they show such a compelling combination of loyalty and attachment that they earn special insider status. This list includes barbers, hairdressers, clothiers, and landlords, as well as brothers, sisters, agents, and business managers. In return for their dedication and service, insiders often receive privileged information that boosts their egos and self-esteem or gives them a degree of power. The barber who knows that the religious celebrity is thinking of running for office . . . the first cousin of Kenny Rogers' manager who learns in advance that the concert replacement for Dolly Parton is Dotty West and the Oak Ridge Boys . . . the politician's communication consultant who becomes the first to know the senator is switching positions on arms control . . . in a society obsessed with the belief that knowledge is power, such disclosures can make for a substantial return on the insider's investment of time, dedication, and service.

One special type of insider who associates with a wide range of celebrities is the *celebrity connector*. By virtue of their social status, connectors know everyone who the celebrity is likely to want to meet, and can arrange within the high-visibility network to broker favors and arrange introductions. Connectors include everyone from the owner of the hottest Manhattan disco, to the trusted bartender at the exclusive resort, to the wealthiest socialite philanthropist in the state capital. The tasks of landing a celebrity for a charity, providing discreet lodgings during Derby Week, or finding a private school for a celebrity's child often fall to the connector. The rewards are the same for the connector as for the Beverly Hills dentist who charges celebrities double for bonding their teeth: Discretion and personal service is rewarded by ego-boosting contact and, often, opportunities for profit. By orchestrating relationships between celebrities, insiders can, like groupies, attain celebrity status of their own. In return for their persistence, dedication, and sacrifice, they reach a level of celebrity involvement that those lower on the intensity ladder may only dream about.

EXPLOITERS

The watcher sees the celebrity's movie; the seeker buys his album; the fan club member writes him letters; the groupie trails his band across the country; the insider takes his telephone messages; the connector throws parties in his honor. Each successive rung of the intensity ladder is marked by increasingly strong—and intimate—fan-celebrity involvement. The final class of audience member, the *exploiter*, has the most intense relationship of all. Unfortunately, it is *so* intense that the relationship can become negative, threatening, or even fatal.

There are many different subclasses of exploiter. The first consists of the *obsessed*: fans who are guilty of such indiscretions as disrupting a celebrity's dinner, endlessly calling a private residence, gate-crashing a party, or incessantly hounding for autographs. Most of the obsessed remain invisible; some pyramid their obsession into their own peculiar form of celebrity. Morgana, the "Kissing Bandit," has gained high visibility merely by rushing onto playing fields across the country to embrace sports figures.

Far more dangerous to the celebrity is the second type of exploiter, the *muckraker*. Unlike the obsessed fan, the attitude of the muckraker toward the celebrity is calculated and professional. These are the journalists and others who make their livelihood by exploiting the visible. So pervasive is celebrity in today's society that muckrakers are thriving in all sectors:

- A. J. Weberman, stealing and analyzing garbage from Bob Dylan's home, allegedly for the purpose of "compiling a concordance of every word from every song Dylan has written "[7]
- Albert Goldman, sensationalizing the life of Elvis Presley
- "Paparazzi" photographer Ron Galella, ordered to keep a minimum twenty-five-foot distance away from Jackie Kennedy Onassis after repeatedly harassing and taking thousands of photographs of her [8]
- Bob Woodward, building his reputation on unraveling the lives of Richard Nixon and John Belushi
- Kenneth Anger, author of *Hollywood Babylon* and *Babylon Revisited*, capitalizing on the worst examples of entertainers' behavior

The muckraker has evolved a *modus operandi*: looking for inconsistent or excessive celebrity behavior, and exposing the manipulative strategies employed by celebrities and their handlers.

Muckrakers are at worst career-threatening. But other exploiters, psychologically disturbed, become extremely dangerous. These are the *destroyers*. Some are content merely to send the celebrity worshipful letters, threatening suicide if not responded to. Some stalk the celebrity, professing undying love and commitment, or file highly publicized paternity lawsuits. Others actually adopt the celebrity's appearance and mannerisms, going so far as impersonation or passing bad checks in the celebrity's name. The destroyer often blurs all the lines between private delusion and public reality. According to Dr. Lawrence Z. Freedman, a researcher of aberrant personalities, "Killing is a peculiarly and intensely intimate act."[9] These final exploiters are people so possessed by the celebrity that they attempt the ultimate act of consumption: murder. It was the obsession to achieve intimacy with actress Jodie Foster that fueled John Hinckley Jr.'s attempt to kill President Reagan; Mark David Chapman's compulsion to become John Lennon was held to be his motive to murder. In fact, Chapman's identification with Lennon was so complete that he taped Lennon's name over his own on his employee ID badge, adopted Lennon's handwriting, married an older Japanese woman, and was totally immersed in the persona of his idol.[10]

Although aiding fans who have deteriorated into destroyers can involve complex psychiatric treatment, the origins of the phenomenon are relatively easy to understand. In a celebrity-intense culture like ours, the ultimate selling strategy is to foster audience identification. Product-marketers understand the process well: Measure consumers' self-images, demographics, and psychological needs, then provide them with products that embody characteristics which match and meet them.

Honing their power to produce celebrities with whom audiences strongly identify, celebrity-marketers are beginning to use sophisticated communication systems to duplicate the product marketing process, monitoring audience feedback to produce ever more seductive, compelling messages. Unfortunately, having led the audience toward strong identification, celebrity-manufacturers and -marketers can lose control of the process. The passion that inflames fans is not like the passion we have for our Norelco razors or Amana freezers. Marketing and advertising can impart to a freezer the qualities of reliability, compassion, and likeability. But it's not the same as inspiring fans to immerse themselves in the "charisma" of rock singer Bono Vox or evangelist Billy James Hargis, or passionately to despise talk-show celebrity Alan Berg or Martin Luther King Jr. There is a multidimensionality to a person that a freezer cannot have. Audience members can project anything onto the celebrity that people project onto one another, which is how the identification process gets taken to dangerous extremes. That the celebrity-audience relationship sometimes ends in the ultimate identification of the murderer with the victim should come as no surprise.

Up The Ladder

Fans at different levels of the intensity ladder receive different types of rewards. They also receive far different treatment by the industry. Seekers are generally the first class that the industry even recognizes, because their purchases of tickets and records are measurable. To date, the industry has largely failed to cultivate invisible consumers and watchers into active seekers—to get the buyers out of their armchairs and into the stores. It has also lagged in developing profit-earning worship opportunities for higher-intensity fans. But this is changing:

- In the religious sector, evangelists are becoming adept at moving passive viewers up the ladder. An offer of a free pamphlet, accepted by a viewer, leads to a request for a one-dollar donation, which leads to a personalized direct-mail appeal, which leads ultimately to total involvement by the viewer in the evangelist and his cause.
- In the entertainment sector, radio stations now routinely maneuver audience members up the ladder. Stations in large markets, seeking new revenue sources, begin to feature the music of an unknown group and support it with glowing reviews and incessant patter by disc jockeys. Then, a "budget show" is announced, where the group appears at a prestige venue for a fraction of the normal ticket price. The whole idea is to move passive listeners into the physical presence of the aspirant and rely on the galvanizing live experience to move the audience members from watchers to seekers and beyond.
- In the sports sector, teams create venues such as spring-training "fantasy" camps, which allow baseball fans of the collector and fan club classes to actually train with their sports celebrities. The Chicago White Sox have even combined the fantasy camp with investment seminars. A fan can now play baseball with pitcher Billy Pierce, trade small talk with outfielder Minnie Minoso, and write it all off as a deductible business expense.

These developments hint at a new era in audience-building, making the accurate, sensitive measurement of audience involvement ever more necessary to the aspirant or celebrity-marketer seeking the competitive advantage.

Measuring Celebrity Power

Aspirants and celebrity-marketers have available five traditional methods to measure their drawing power with audiences. Importantly, all describe outcomes—or, at most, suggest benefits. They fundamentally fail to explain popularity-level differences. Most of the standard measuring tools are based on some form of mathematical computation—capable of measuring, incapable of revealing root causes.

The most basic indicator is *paid attendance*: box-office receipts, numbers of concert tickets sold, attendance at political fundraisers, or contributions to celebrity-fronted charities. The marketer adds up the box-office receipts, factors in how much was spent on promotion and advertising, considers the drawing power of the venue (Broadway versus a loft stage), and comes up with a rough concept of a celebrity's power to draw audiences. To rank one celebrity's drawing power relative to others, it's best to have all conditions fixed—same venue, season, promotion—such as in the Brookfield Zoo charity benefit in Chicago in July, 1984. The booking agency, Paramount, hired three acts—Donny and Marie Osmond, Johnny Cash and Larry Gatlin, and the Beach Boys.[11] In the same 12,000-seat house, the Osmonds drew 3,000, Cash and Gatlin drew 10,000, and the Beach Boys sold out. The attendance figures gave a good read on the local audience's preferences. Yet the reasons for the audience's purchase decision—and what it implies about celebrity preference in general—remained unclear. These same celebrities, under different circumstances, in different venues or locations, might draw far larger or smaller audiences.

Suppose, for example, that Johnny Cash's manager wants to measure the intensity of Cash's appeal to his audience, to help discover what can be done to improve it. For Cash's manager, discovering a formula to maintain a large, loyal audience would be invaluable. Even a formula to deliver a small but prestigious and influential audience would be an advantage. But such formulas are not revealed by the pure numbers. Popularity measures such as box-office receipts also tell nothing about the best use to which a celebrity may be put: as an endorser of sportswear, political causes, or vacation cruises. Clearly, better measures than raw attendance size are required if celebrity-marketing strategies are to be improved.

One step in the right direction is the rating scale called the *Q–Factor*. Developed for the entertainment sector, the Q–Factor purports to measure how much a celebrity is liked or disliked by the public, and how familiar the public is with the celebrity—critical information for advertisers and producers trying to hire the most effective celebrities to endorse their products, star in films, or host TV shows. Under the Q Rating System, a celebrity is graded by the public on a scale of six indicators.[12]

UNDER YOUR OPINION WRITE:
IF THE PERFORMER IS:

1 one of your favorites
2 very good
3 good
4 fair
5 poor
N someone you have never seen or heard

The Method: The questionnaire shown [above] depicts the rating scale for a sample of personalities. This scale yields two important dimensions: FAMILIARITY and APPEAL.

Each year, over 1,000 personalities are evaluated by a national sample of individuals aged six years of age and older. In its 20th year, Performer Q categorizes personalities into seventeen groups: comedians, sports announcers, fashion designers, etc.

The entire syndicated report on over 1,000 personalities costs under $10,000. Data on one personality can be purchased for $900.[13]

The Q rating is intended to give celebrity users information to help make intelligent choices. The most extreme case would be choosing between an Alan Alda, with one of the highest Q ratings, and a Howard Cosell, who is at the bottom of the scale. Both have high familiarity ratings: They are well known to the public. Alda is well liked, Cosell is not. But when selecting celebrities as endorsers or as stars of entertainment vehicles, these two measurements are of limited use. The advertiser, political committee, charity, or other celebrity-user must know what *kind* of impression the celebrity makes on audiences. The Q–factor sheds some light on this. But familiarity and likeability are only a small part of what makes up the celebrity's all-important image. The Q–factor is of little help to the celebrity-user wondering if the celebrity's image—the way he or she strikes an audience—will make the endorsement or film more or less effective. Fitness celebrity Richard Simmons may have only limited general familiarity and likeability, but such an image may be very effective in a Citibank commercial featuring his mother. Sylvester Stallone may have high familiarity and likeability ratings, but be hardly suitable as a spokesman for BMW or Save the Whales.

The third traditional tool used to measure popularity is *polling research* that attempts to detail audience perceptions about celebrities and their characteristics. Athletes, entertainers, comedians, singers, cooking experts, emcees, astronauts, journalists, politicians, corporate executives—all are potential subjects for public-opinion polling. With elaborate pre-testing and post-testing designs, independent research firms scan public attitudes about particular celebrities' believability, compatibility with causes or products, overall communication skills, and potential to change public attitudes.[14] Poll results are potentially vital, as buyers of celebrity talent can steer away from athletes who are held in low esteem, actors with little credibility, charity spokesmen without perceived warmth, or corporate executives thought to lack leadership qualities.

But the findings from polling, while sophisticated, are still limited. They cannot explain the successful endorsement touch of gap-toothed model Lauren Hutton, the popularity of off-beat comedian Albert Brooks, or the long-lived usefulness of unflashy chicken champion Frank Perdue. Polling and other measures might help make the decision between Barry Manilow and Rick Springfield as possible leads for a feature film but tell nothing about why either attracted the following necessary to become celebrities in the first place. Even such popular entertainment-sector polls as Audience Studies Incorporated's (ASI) only measure a celebrity's audience pull in a specific role; they do nothing to predict the vehicle or role in which a celebrity would be most successful.

The fourth standard indicator consists of the rating services, primarily Nielsen and Arbitron, that measure the number of TVs or radios tuned to a particular media broadcast. If the numbers show that "Wall Street Week" dramatically outdrew "Strictly Business," a possible explanation is that Louis Rukeyser is a bigger celebrity than Jack Cafferty. But such an assumption is just a leap in logic. What about such crucial elements as the shows' formats, types of guests, press reviews, network or independent distribution, or preceding "lead in" shows—none of which are measured by rating services?

The fifth indicator consists of the vast accumulation of

subjective, incidental measures that together form a sort of folklore of celebrity popularity measurement. These include:

- size and number of fan clubs
- letters to the celebrity in a week
- convention keynote speaking invitations
- posters sold
- mentions at West Los Angeles cocktail parties
- degree to which dress and mannerisms are imitated
- membership in All Time, All Star, Hall of Fame groupings
- mentions in gossip columns—*People, USA Today, Tiger Beat*—as well as in the professional press (*Fortune, Venture, AMA Journal*)

Indicators as indirect as baseball-card exchange ratios tell much about fans' celebrity interests. In 1984 it took nine baseball cards of Minnesota Twin Ken Hrbek to obtain one card of Chicago Cub pitcher Rick Sutcliffe—bad news for Hrbek, and a caution to anyone negotiating with him for endorsement services. The celebrity industry monitors such informal signs as carefully as it can. The Topps Company, manufacturer of baseball cards, surveys and ranks the popularity of players. The rise of New York Met Dwight Gooden, for example, is evidenced by the $50 value already placed on his first-year card. But card value itself doesn't tell us why Sutcliffe out-traded Hrbek so dramatically. We can guess that Sutcliffe's pitching record in a division championship year, and his dramatic, tall, red-bearded appearance, combined with the mix of a perennial underdog team, coverage by superstation WGN, and the long suffering of Cub fans, all conspired to elevate Sutcliffe's visibility. But neither the exchange ratio nor the conventional measures proves this. It's the kind of conjecture that cannot be quantified.

Discovering who is celebrated and why can involve studying something as informal as restaurant walls. In a widely practiced tradition, the walls of The Palm restaurants are covered with celebrities' faces. But The Palm's walls are especially interesting, proving how deeply celebrity has invaded all sectors. Building on a staple of sports and entertainment figures, the roster features highly visible lawyers, publishers, businessmen, clerics, editors—even fashion designers and aerobics instructors—a recognition by the restaurant's management that these images have the power to attract a clientele.[15]

All of the above indicators help the celebrity industry understand and predict celebrities' appeal to audiences. Yet there are major problems in drawing from numbers alone any conclusions about *why* celebrities catch on. Traditional ways of measuring audiences can determine their level of interest in existing celebrities, *not* the underlying motivations that predispose fans toward celebrities in the first place.

The Great Dinner Party

A different way to gain insight into audience preferences and motivations is to reproduce the fan-worship response. In the Great Dinner Party survey, interviewees would be given the following instructions: "You have been invited to three dinner parties, all scheduled for the same night. You can attend only one. Of the hosts listed below, chose the one whose party you would attend, and the reason for your decision:

1. Whitney Houston: popular entertainer
2. Ronald Reagan: president of the United States
3. Jonas Salk: prominent physician and creator of the polio vaccine."

Although limiting their choices to these three, the survey might reveal the motivations behind the respondents' choices. Some possible answers:

1. A desire to visit the most prestigious institution: select Reagan.
2. A desire to see the hottest media figure: select Houston.
3. A desire to learn from or pay homage to: select Salk.

In an actual test of the scenario, respondents were asked to name the celebrities they would most like to have dinner with, and why.[16] The answers revealed a wide range of motivations:

- curiosity ("DeLorean sounds really interesting")
- desire to debate ("I'd like to argue with Reagan")
- raising self-esteem by being in their presence ("What could be higher than to be in the Pope's company?")

- thirst for knowledge ("There are a lot of things I'd like to ask Freud")
- romance ("I don't care if Richard Gere is famous; he's still the man of my dreams")
- have an elegant experience ("The queen would throw a marvelous dinner")
- desire to prove you can hold your own with the experts ("I'd love to talk baseball with Reggie Jackson")

The dinner party scenario was designed to reveal the mechanisms that attract us to celebrities. On the most fundamental level, the scenario proves that such mechanisms are knowable. Why is this so important? Because once the reasons why fans are attracted to celebrities are known, the range of strategies open to the celebrity-marketer becomes wider, and the optimum strategy, clearer.

A Celebrity's Diagnosis

Another source of insight into audience preferences are celebrities themselves. A common belief is that celebrities are unable to analyze their audiences. It's true that when asked about it, they often describe the relationship in romantic, vague ways: "I have a love affair with my fans" or "I just feed off their energy." In keeping with the specialization of the industry, many celebrities *are* leaving the audience analysis to their agents, managers, and producers. But not always. One celebrity, popular singer Bobby Vinton, was especially adept at analyzing his audiences' attraction to him. When asked why people come to hear him sing, Vinton immediately broke his audience down into three major categories.[17]

The first audience, according to Vinton, grew up with his music in his Top 40 radio days a quarter-century ago, people who were in their impressionable teens when he recorded such hits as "Roses Are Red" and "Melody of Love." These fans, now in their forties, have a special sensitivity to songs and entertainers who evoke memories that are frozen in time. To these fans, Vinton is *still* Top 40. To them, today's rock music may not even exist.

The second group analyzed by Vinton are people of Polish origin who identify with his ethnic background. (Vinton solidified his trademark as the "Polish Prince" when he appeared in 1975 with Chicago's Mayor Richard Daley at a large ethnic rally where he was informally crowned.) Although the ethnically conscious audience was far larger earlier in the century, in local markets ethnic emcees, singers, politicians, and businesspeople still flourish. In Vinton's marketing mix, these fans still play a major role.

Vinton's third audience encounters him in his current incarnation as a Las Vegas attraction. Along with such Las Vegas perennials as Wayne Newton, Sammy Davis, Jr., and Dean Martin—celebrities who also once appealed to a younger audience—Vinton is considered a hot Vegas act. But the Vegas audience's attraction to Vinton, although initially nostalgic, quickly translates into admiration for his and other performers' modern, fast-paced, spectacular shows.

Both dinner party–type fan interviews and insider analysis such as Vinton's make clear that, contrary to industry folklore, the causes of a particular celebrity's appeal to audiences *can* be uncovered. But such information, in order to be of real use to celebrity-marketers, still needs to be more detailed, more textured. One way to get at the more subtle factors that drive audience attraction is to look not at the characteristics of single individuals but those of whole segments of society; to analyze audiences using the same type of information that manufacturers use to identify and categorize target markets: demographics and psychographics.

Audiences, Demographics, and Psychographics

Demographic and psychographic analysis, already being put to limited use by the entertainment, political, and electronic-ministry sectors, is a potentially powerful tool for all celebrity-marketers. Demographics is used to divide the public into measurable categories—sex, age, region, institutional identification, political affiliation. Psychographics, a newer tool, divides the population into categories according to attitude, values, and lifestyle—"achievers," "need-driven," "societally conscious," "followers," and other more subjective categories. Both demographic and psychographic categorization have been used to try to measure and describe political candidates' appeal or to identify likely contributors to religious causes. But the potential of such analysis has only just begun to be tapped. Even the mere breaking down of an audience into its demographic and psychographic components can help celebrity-manufacturers identify existing audiences or discover possible new ones.

SEX AND THE AUDIENCE

A look at a major demographic category—gender—leads to some interesting observations about psychographics and celebrities. Fan club expert Trinajstick reported that 80 percent of fan club presidents that she surveyed were female, and that a large share of fan club membership was female as well.[18] This fact suggests some interesting questions for celebrity-manufacturers. Why do men find fan clubs unattractive? Why is their celebrity-worship behavior less demonstrative? One possibility is that mainstream celebrity-manufacturing is so biased toward fostering female fan bonding that it excludes men.

Seeking an insight into this issue, focus-group interviews were conducted to flesh out the psychographic differences between male and female attitudes toward celebrities.[19] Females, asked to describe the characteristics that drew them to their favorite celebrities, highlighted looks and popularity. Males, however, emphasized celebrities' possession of money, respect, charisma, and masculinity. A follow-up survey based on the focus-group data revealed that none of the men selected a female celebrity as one of their top three favorites, while in contrast, 59 percent of the females polled selected a male.

Such a survey is of course preliminary. But any way such findings are viewed, it's clear that males and females bond to celebrities in different ways. It's also clear that there is tremendous potential in raising men's celebrity involvement to the same level as women's. What is also indisputable is that demographic and psychographic data can provide celebrity-manufacturers with fundamental manufacturing and marketing information. How can record companies most efficiently determine—and target—the audience for a new all-black, all-female rock band? How can corporations, seeking the most value from a CEO, select a person with the right characteristics to appeal to audiences within the business sector? Conducting demographic and psychographic research before the dollars are spent can preserve shareholder confidence or save millions in ill-conceived promotions.

AGE AND THE AUDIENCE

Another useful demographic category is age. An obvious fact is that many celebrity fans are young. The young girl who idolizes a young male entertainer is by now a cultural fixture. To young girls, celebrity worship is part of the solution to the problem of growing up. As the objects of a fantasy relationship, the celebrities whom young girls dote on fulfill a real need, enabling them to say, "This is my special person." Importantly, young fans feel this way not only as a reflex ("My parents can't stand them; therefore I like them"), but because celebrities such as Ralph Macchio, Corey Haim, Rob Lowe, and Aidan Quinn are the right match for young females: slightly older, more experienced, physically attractive, and nonthreatening because of their inaccessibility. Because of the teen female market's high per-capita spending on celebrity-linked records, movies, clothes, and other products, this market is one of the few that the celebrity industry uses demographic analysis to track. So lucrative is this market, and so short-lived the period that any one group of girls is in it, that the celebrity industry has learned to manufacture young male sex symbols on demand.

TUNE UP

The creation of the Puerto Rican musical group Menudo is the ultimate extension in meeting the teenage female market's needs. The group is composed of thirteen- to fifteen-year-old boys who are automatically retired when they reach their sixteenth birthdays. As interchangeable as spark plugs, the members sing, live, and exist wholly for their teenage girl audience, a market that responded to them with near-hysterical behavior. The basic elements of the Menudo marketing mix—superficial wholesomeness, tight clothes, and syrupy formula love songs—are engineered and orchestrated with precision. Members who are rotated out of the group are quickly forgotten. "Menudo was originally a lovely concept," said Dr. Neftail Sallaberry, the father of two former group members. "But it's become a monster, a marketing thing with a life of its own."[20]

Not only young girls bond to celebrities; young boys express attraction to them, too. They buy Los Angeles Dodgers' jackets and Greg LeMond cycling shorts, call sports talk shows, and attempt to throw footballs with the same spin as John Elway or to serve like Boris Becker. Tracking this group's tastes is important to celebrity-industry subdivisions from television to fashion.

A good example of exploiting the young male demographic group is the marketing of Air Jordan, basketball star Michael Jordan's personally endorsed shoe—a celebrity endorsement campaign considered responsible for the financial rescue of Nike Shoes. Until recently, sports footwear was routinely endorsed by celebrity athletes, but rarely dramatically and emotionally portrayed. The Air Jordan changed this process, an excellent example of analyzing market needs, then imbuing a product with qualities that meet them. The Jordan campaign features the basketball star leaping and bounding to spectacular dunk shots, then defiantly and confidently facing the camera. He is heroic, embodying his young fans' fantasies. It is personality-based advertising superseding mere product-based advertising. And it was spectacularly effective.

PSYCHOGRAPHIC SHIFT: THE AGING FAN

In American society, age plays a large role in how we perceive our peers. As a person matures, we expect his or her choices in celebrities to mature, too. The forty-year-old who still worships Fabian and the sixty-five-year-old who finds punk rock originator Iggy Pop irresistible are disparaged as cases of arrested development and stunted emotional growth. For most of us, aging gracefully in terms of celebrity admiration means shifting from entertainment and sports celebrities to those in the religious, academic, business, fashion, and other more "serious" sectors. Even within sectors there is aging-related shifting: from rock music to adult contemporary, or from Ronald McDonald to T. Boone Pickens.

Several other changes in celebrity involvement are expected of the aging fan:

1. The move to a new set of celebrities more closely reflecting "mature" interests and values.

2. A lessening of the intensity of attraction to celebrities, and the abatement of the worship process: less willingness to jump on stages, listen to 475 playings of the same song, or dye one's hair in emulation of idols.
3. Greater longevity in fan loyalty, and less fickleness in tastes.
4. The onset of nostalgic feelings toward the earlier celebrities one grew up with.
5. Far less vulnerability to manipulation. The strategies of the celebrity makers that are so effective on young fans—staging events, designing images, floating phony stories—are expected to be far less successful on older fans.

Most adults realize that society expects them to alter their behavior this way. But that doesn't mean that they always do. Because of the celebrity industry's power to expose people to such pervasive, persuasive messages, celebrity worship among maturing fans is no longer abating on schedule. Distribution-channel changes such as the move of soap operas from daytime to far more widely watched prime time, and the huge support such shows receive from the celebrity press, help extend the lifespan of celebrity involvement from youth right through middle and old age. On this issue, our entire society may well be playing an adult game of celebrity deception.

This deception was clearly evident in our focus group of women in their thirties and forties.[21] Group members spent the first half of the interview session claiming how immature and wasteful most celebrity worship was. Denouncing the power and attention accorded pop-culture idols, they preferred, they said, to admire high-culture types (authors, chefs, ballerinas). But their responses simply did not ring true. After considerable prodding, we found that the celebrities that the women *really* worshipped were not at all consistent with their ages and self-images. The second half of the focus session was spent in animated discussion about one of their admitted favorites—Tom Selleck. Eventually, the group revealed that it did a great deal of popular TV watching. Although lacking the full intensity of younger fans' willingness to bond with celebrities, the women were not nearly as blasé about celebrities as they had first claimed.

The trend *is* for older audiences to narrow and de-intensify their involvement with celebrities. But to some degree this is a false front. Many adults remain almost as intensely involved with celebrities as when they were children. Instead of papering their walls with Matthew Broderick posters, adults consume Linda Evans' "Krystle" perfume, read Joan Collins' autobiography, wear clothes from the "Dynasty" fashion line, or attend celebrity-fronted charity events. Children seem unembarrassed to worship their celebrities in groups: to attend the concert in mobs, or rush en masse to imitate the newest celebrity-spawned hairstyle. Adults, conscious of public image, prefer more discreet consumption: reading *Soap Opera Digest*, watching "Hollywood Insider," or devouring the latest bestselling exposé.

Many adults, however, *do* experience a reduction in celebrity interest. Why is this so? Perhaps it is because, when we are young, it seems as if our individual horizons are limitless. We believe that we *can* grow up to be another Sally Ride, Wayne Gretzsky, or Sherry Lansing. But as we age, and the realities of life assert themselves—as our sense of the possible narrows—such cheerful fantasies can no longer be sustained. In the end, we drop our fanciful celebrities and adopt new ones who parallel our new interests, who are more serious, more representative of mainstream adult life and values.

Demographic and psychographic analysis may be the fastest, least ambiguous route to mastering some of the basics of efficient celebrity-marketing. These measures show that there are areas of the country that are obsessed with country-and-western singers and could not care less about rock. They also show that urban college students in certain areas have little interest in country–and–western. Analyzing the preferences of different demographic and psychographic groups can make the celebrity-developer far more savvy at constructing viable celebrities and at matching them to target audiences. In the film *The Idolmaker*, Vinnie, the producer of instant singing celebrities for teenagers, expresses it perfectly. "You have the face," he says to the busboy. Understanding his audience, Vinnie knows how to pick the right venues, the right song formulas, the right image. The right face is all that his aspirant really *has* to have; the rest—voice, movement, presence—can be added on.

Demographic and psychographic consciousness has been on the rise in the entertainment sector; but it can boost the profitability of celebrity-manufacturing in the other sectors as well. Analyzing audiences can help gallery owners seeking the right types of artist to promote, government agencies auditioning for appealing spokespersons, and charities looking for a front person with the most empathy with the donors.

Forging the Audience Bond

Monday morning, 6:00 A.M., Eastern Standard Time. "Today" show hosts Bryant Gumbel and Jane Pauley are talking with their producer. What's the menu for the week? The baseball rookie dominating sports pages across the country; the author who's popped up on every talk show; the actor whose profile adorns half the covers on the magazine stand. The week to come will see the senator leading the filibuster, the seven-year-old star of the latest Spielberg blockbuster, and the doctor whose miracle diet has been banned by the government.

This is what the celebrity industry calls "hotness"—celebrities being simultaneously forced through every conceivable distribution channel at once. Drumming up tremendous interest, the hot name briefly dominates a sector, reaches huge numbers of potential fans, then often quickly fades before the onslaught of the next hot name. What are some of the strategic scenarios that generate audience appeal?

ROOM IN THE CHANNEL

Because audience interest and enthusiasm are not unlimited resources, each sector has the capacity to support only so many highly illuminated aspirants. Thus our baseball rookie of the spring season is highlighted because he fills a traditional niche in media coverage. The media don't have the logistical capacity to elevate too many hot-hitting rookies at a time. Effective celebrity-marketers understand the concept of scarcity and work hard to move *their* aspirants into the front row.

A good example of the "Room in the Channel" factor is the rush for visibility by medal winners after each heavily televised Olympics. Invariably, a few athletes become marketable, while others complain of neglect and mistreatment. Selection is dependent, of course, on the athlete's being able to marshal the right strategy mix: talent, coached charm, luck, timing, and story. But, understandably, limitations on the media's coverage capabilities and limited appetite of audiences for celebrity athletes restrict the number of aspirants who have an opportunity to capitalize on their victories.

"WHO IS MARVIN ZONIS?"

Marvin Zonis, associate professor in the Department of Behavioral Sciences at the University of Chicago, is an excellent example of room in the channel. A teacher of Middle Eastern politics, he was elevated to celebrity during the Iranian hostage crisis. ABC-TV's "Nightline" (then called "America Held Hostage") needed an expert to talk to about the crisis. The Chicago professor, one of a handful of American specialists on Iran, was based close to an ABC affiliate in Chicago. He proved to be articulate, presentable, even mildly dramatic. Night after night, Zonis analyzed the unfolding story. The fact is that without the crisis, Zonis was not necessary; with it, the media needed to find an expert that the audience could understand. Zonis filled that narrow niche, then extended his visibility by becoming the all-purpose expert on international politics for CBS's affiliate in Chicago. It was an accident that the opportunity arose in the channel. Zonis, however, was able eventually to create a permanent media position from the exposure.

"SHE TOUCHED ME"

Another factor that excites fans about celebrities is a special event or outstanding performance that draws the audience member closer to the celebrity. In some cases the situation can be accidental, as shown by this newspaper item:

> **PINCH HIT HERO**
>
> Robert Redford, who stars in the movie *The Natural,* in which he plays a baseball slugger, says Hall of Famer Ted

> Williams was his hero as a boy. In the movie, Redford says he tried to copy Williams' stance.
>
> "The first time I was in New York, it must have been about 1957, I found out the Boston Red Sox were playing the Yankees in Yankee Stadium," Redford recalled. "I went to the ballpark and got a seat in the bleachers. But Ted wasn't in the lineup. Then he came up to pinch-hit in the ninth inning. I'll be darned if he didn't hit a homer which landed right in back of me. I had some good days myself, but that had to be my biggest thrill in sports."[22]

The triggering factor that can make a celebrity especially hot for a particular fan can be hearing a song on your birthday that seems meant for you, being bumped by a television star in a hotel lobby, or eating in the same restaurant with a celebrated business leader. Even celebrities whom the fan had never before noticed can imprint themselves on the fan's consciousness with just a touch.

The strategy for the celebrity-marketer is to stage situations that will provide personal contact between celebrities and fans. Singer Englebert Humperdinck, a practitioner of this technique, communicates personal intimacy by throwing sweat-drenched handkerchiefs to his fans from the stage. Other celebrities write their fans "personal" notes with the aid of signature-copying word processors. Other attempts to foster close contact include live tours, shopping-mall appearances, and talk show chats. Talk show appearances constitute an especially subtle use of the "she touched me" strategy. The fan sees a relaxed, supposedly nonperforming celebrity. The scene is reenacted every night at 11:30. Alan King leans over to Johnny, winks, slaps his hand affectionately, grins, and mumbles a half-funny aside. It's hard not to like Alan—he's a real person. Without even being in the celebrity's presence, the fan has been touched.

"I MARRIED THE PRESIDENT'S DAUGHTER"

Celebrities can generate intense audience interest by linking themselves with a highly visible person or institution: the young lawyer representing a large company in a big case; the aspiring political consultant writing speeches for Los Angeles Mayor Tom Bradley; the sophomore halfback carrying the football for the top high school team in Texas. Being elected pope, buying a football team, or marrying the heiress to a film-company fortune are natural associations that can make one hot with audiences.

"POPPING OUT"

Jerry Reinsdorf, chairman of the Balcor American Express real estate company, was wealthy, powerful, a mover and shaker, but at a low level of visibility. Then he bought baseball's Chicago White Sox and, later, basketball's Chicago Bulls. In short order Reinsdorf was making the gossip columns, associating with film celebrities, and being quoted as an authority on sports matters. Reinsdorf was hot. Like George Steinbrenner, a shipbuilder who bought the New York Yankees, and Jerry Buss, a doctor who bought the Los Angeles Lakers, Reinsdorf understood that linking up with a highly visible institution can inspire audience interest.

THE MEDIA AS AUDIENCE

Celebrity-marketers try to draw media interest because the media and its enormous audiences need celebrities to humanize and symbolize complex issues and stories. During the 1970s, local taxpayer revolts were breaking out all over the country. Needing an instantly recognizable symbol of the revolt to interest readers and viewers, the media chose to highlight controversial curmudgeon Howard Jarvis, leader of California's Proposition 13 movement. The elderly Jarvis was extensively covered, becoming the media's all-purpose expert on tax revolts.

Media coverage produced a similar result in the press conference preceding the 1986 NCAA Final Four basketball championship. Duke University's team members distinguished themselves with the media by their modest display of intelligence and wit. How did the media package the story for their audiences? That Duke's players would be the future leaders of America, including one writer's claim that one player would some day be president.

An example of how the media can singlehandedly create a hot celebrity is the flood of coverage that turned apparent drowning victim Jimmy Tontlewitz into a nationwide seven-day wonder.

Rescued with the aid of a TV news crew after almost a half hour under freezing Lake Michigan waters, the little boy became the subject of a media blitzkrieg, complete with TV station-sponsored hospital funds, coverage of his first words upon awakening, in-depth investigative reports on the marital problems of his parents, and press conferences with doctors and police. In the same year, many people were rescued from drowning, but only one achieved "hotness." Because Tontlewitz was in the competitive Chicago media market and was rescued in full view of a TV minicam, the story was exploited for its drama. What makes this kind of "hotness" particularly effective is that people not only watch what the media present to them but automatically assume that the very fact of its transmission *by* the media makes the information, person, or story important. The lesson for the celebrity-marketer is clear: It helps to sell your product first to the media.

MADE BY ACCESSORIES

Sometimes celebrities become hot because the audience becomes fascinated with their trademarks. Whether the trademark is an object or accessory, or an odd wrinkle in behavior, the strategy is to take advantage of fans' desires to identify and bond with celebrities. Some cases—Dizzy Gillespie's pretzled trumpet; Paul Volcker's cigar; Bella Abzug's hats—appear inadvertent. Others—Madonna's clothes; the Sex Pistols' safety-pin earrings; Tom Wolfe's white suits—are clearly intentional, designed to spawn a fashion rage and propel the celebrity into the audience's consciousness.

"WHAT DID YOU DO IN THE WAR, DADDY?"

Often audiences will be attracted to celebrities by the force of an event: General Douglas MacArthur, who dramatically staged his return to the Philippines; Alan McDonald, the Morton Thiokol engineer who testified in the aftermath of the space shuttle disaster; Tom Hayden in the Chicago Seven trial; Colonel Charles Beckwith during the failure of the Iran hostage rescue mission.

What all six of these strategies have in common is that they generate audience interest in celebrities. But what successful celebrity-marketing requires is raising this interest up to higher and higher levels of intensity, to achieve the optimum bond between audience and celebrity. What is the most powerful means by which to accomplish this? Through the design, manufacturing, and delivery of the story line.

A Brief Historical Interlude: An Introduction to Dramatic Reality

THE STIGMA

In 1935, Dave Garfinkle, owner of a Minneapolis barbershop called the Artistic, inadvertently became a celebrity as a witness testifying in defense of suspected bootlegger Kid Cann. Cann was accused of murdering a Minneapolis newspaper reporter who was investigating his business activities. Garfinkle and other witnesses stood up and testified to Cann's presence in the barbershop at the time of the killing—and he was acquitted.

When the newspaper story broke, Garfinkle became a classic celebrity-by-association. His barbershop was dubbed The Alibi. Coverage, complete with quotations and pictures, was intense. When the novelty of the event cooled—as happens in all events of this sort—there were repercussions that lingered.

The nickname "The Alibi" barbershop was used matter-of-factly by Garfinkle's and Cann's contemporaries. By the time of the following generation, the facts of the case had begun to blur with retelling. Garfinkle's and Cann's celebrity were now sustained not by any immediacy in the story but by its inherent drama, aided by the continuing association of the barber and his celebrated customers. Most mornings found members of the Cann family ensconced at The Alibi, getting the works—haircut, shave, manicure—whether they needed it or not. The appearance of the family members fueled the shop's celebrity status.

By the *next* generation, the participants in The Alibi story had become little more than colorful characters of a bygone age, their lifestyles and idiosyncrasies the subject of reminiscences and "remember when" speculations.

Today, Minneapolis residents rarely hear about Kid Cann or his contemporaries. Unless the subject is raised by someone old enough to remember the events that gave the barbershop its name, mention of The Alibi barbershop evokes little emotion.

Dave Garfinkle never seemed to capitalize on his celebrity. His business remained the same. Only occasionally would Garfinkle surface in the news under one of the following circumstances:

- when nostalgic "local history" retrospectives on the case would appear in the media
- when Garfinkle, having become a fight manager for a featherweight contender, was mentioned in association with a well-known sports figure
- when his death turned attention briefly back to the highlights of his life

For Dave Garfinkle, the curtain came down on his visibility after a run of some forty years. His story reads like a piece of fiction: trial, scandal, drama, association with celebrities, and local visibility. It has some of the dark drama of *The Godfather* and *Once Upon a Time in America*.

The case of The Alibi is an early demonstration of the one concept that increasingly dominates the celebrity-marketing process: that stories have power over audiences. At the same time that Garfinkle's story did have an impact on the people of Minneapolis, he was never able to translate his celebrity into earnings. Today, a story such as Garfinkle's might well earn a large advance from Random House, sell to ABC as a "Sunday Night Movie," or turn The Alibi into the first of a nationwide chain of franchised barbershops. It is this dramatizing of reality that is now so important to celebrity-marketing.

WHAT IS DRAMATIC REALITY?

If there is one thing that serves more than any other to involve audiences with celebrities, it is the storyline.[23] The conscious design, manipulation, and promotion of storylines in celebrities' lives—up to the point of creating realities more dramatic than real life—constitutes the celebrity industry's major breakthrough in the 1970s and 1980s. Not content merely to wait for real life to supply drama, celebrity marketers, realizing the power of drama to propel aspirants to high visibility, have begun to manufacture it. Dramatic Reality consists of either (a) the highlighting of the dramatic elements in celebrities' real lives, or (b) the deliberate and strategic mixing of celebrities' real lives with fictional story elements. Its purposes are fourfold:

- to stimulate the audience's imagination
- to reinforce the celebrity's credibility
- to heighten the audience's interest in the celebrity
- to create in the audience's consciousness the illusion that it has a relationship with the celebrity

The ultimate goal of Dramatic Reality is to make more commercially exploitable the audience's involvement with celebrities.

Examples of the strategic use of Dramatic Reality abound:

- *The Tom Selleck Syndrome:* the strategy of promoting a TV series star on talk shows and in other media, in order to build a portrait of the star as a "real," just-plain-folks person. The portrait begins to blur as Selleck (the real) and Selleck (the star) become interchangeable in the audience's minds.
- *The Serious Star:* the popularity of "socially conscious" entertainment vehicles—nuclear war movies and such—that purport to show reality. The strategy is to use the seriousness of the theme to cover up the fact that the celebrities involved are in fact acting. The audience is riveted by the compelling real-life ambience. The entire storyline is fictional, but its evocation of real life helps color the actors as real, substantial people. Jane Fonda's role as a crusading reporter uncovering a nuclear accident in *The China Syndrome* and Jane Alexander's appearance as the heroic mother in the nuclear war drama *Testament* enhance their credibility as actresses in other, more overtly commercial film vehicles.
- *Identity Crisis:* stars pretending to become so wrapped up in their characters that they lose their superficial acting identities and become "real." When Farrah Fawcett reemerged from relative obscurity to star in the TV drama "The Burning Bed," the media used the rhetoric of reality to foist the idea that she was merging her acting and her real life for maximum authenticity in the part. There were lengthy feature articles describing how Fawcett "got inside" her character, lived with battered women, and finally *became* the character she portrayed.

  A similar technique was used to promote Ann-Margret's performance as Blanche DuBois in 1984's TV version of *A Streetcar Named Desire*. Ann-Margret received tremendous publicity from her claim that during filming, her character, "had completely taken

> over."[24] As she reported to *Life*, "One morning I started crumbling. I had to call my doctor. 'The walls are closing in on Blanche,' I told her, 'and I'm Blanche.' " Quoting the film's director as saying, "Her emotional investment was overwhelming," *Life* went on to report that: "At no point was the line between acting and reality more difficult than when Blanche is raped.... Only the director and camera crew were present during the scene. Other staff members sat out of sight, wincing at the screams and crashes. 'It was devastating,' says Ann-Margret.... 'It was too real.' "[25] As soon as the interviews are over, and the curtains fall, Ann-Margret and Fawcett cancel the storyline and move on.

Each of these—talk shows, nuclear war films, "The Burning Bed"—are examples of how celebrity-fan attachment can be enhanced through the mixing of drama and real life. In some cases, the system blends reality and fiction *too* well. The celebrity world blurs into real life, and we try to become part of it. Many audience members forget that Tom Selleck is only an actor, and that Lee Iacocca is only a businessman. Speaking of Iacocca's tumultuous welcome by New Yorkers during the 1986 Statue of Liberty Celebration, even Cardinal John O'Connor was moved to remark on the gap between image and reality: "I just think the people see and hear what they perceive to be authenticity.... It has that fundamental appeal that nothing else has."[26] As the celebrity industry gets better and better at creating dramatic reality, the audience's ability to distinguish between image and reality is diminishing.

What sparks the rise of Dramatic Reality is celebrity-marketers' increasing skill at blurring the lines between real and scripted life. The more proficient they become—the better the methods of teaching celebrities to "act naturally," the more precise their use of demographic and psychographic analysis—the more seductive and persuasive Dramatic Reality becomes.

The underlying principle that makes Dramatic Reality so effective is described by communication philosopher Don Idhe.[27] According to Idhe, the more transparent a message-delivery system gets—the less its imperfections (telephone static, TV picture interference) interfere with its use—the less aware we are of the way that the technology alters the communication process. As the sound quality of phone calls has improved, the less we are forced to think consciously about the subtle ways that the telephone changes the way we converse. Similarly, the more sophisticated that celebrity-marketers become at creating Dramatic Reality, the less aware we are that the "reality" presented to us was not a product of nature but was invented over lunch at the Polo Lounge of the Beverly Hills Hotel.

WHAT MAKES DRAMATIC REALITY WORK?

What permits dramatic reality to function is the audiences' increasing dependence on having information transmitted in story form. As these stories become imprinted in the public's consciousness, the celebrity-marketer is almost forced to convey information about his client in the designated story formats.

Aware of the power of Dramatic Reality, the first question that the perceptive celebrity-maker asks an aspirant is: "Tell me about yourself. Any unique experiences in your past, any tragedies? Any interesting family angles? Were you tutored by any colorful characters?" Developing the aspirant's ability to manipulate audiences is largely based on discovering—or manufacturing—the storylines that best foster fan bonding and attachment.

What other methods are available to marketers to achieve Dramatic Reality, to make the visible more authentic by adding texture and making them more familiar?

The first is to *broaden sector appeal*—promoting the celebrity in so many sectors that different stories have a chance to "catch on" with different audiences. Media business celebrity Ted Turner promotes his involvement in yachting and baseball to build a multidimensional image. Having Henry Winkler star in his own series to reach the young adult audience, appear on TV as a young child's hero boosting the value of education, make summer-stock theater appearances in Shakespearean roles to reach serious adults, and co-host the Statue of Liberty Centennial to reach the entire country give Winkler wide opportunities to try out different versions of Dramatic Reality. In the religious sector, evangelist Jim Bakker's appeal is broadened by his use of a variety show format that, combined with his preaching on political, social, and moral issues, gives his audience the chance to respond to different stories.

A second strategy is to *broaden channel distribution*, to ensure that the stories reach the widest number of fans within one sector. Tom Selleck, acting on "Magnum P.I.," confessing his insecurities on a Barbara Walters special, revealing his dreams in *Time*, playing a different "type" in feature films, and being irreverent on "The David Letterman Show" reaches many different types of entertainment fans, each vulnerable to bonding with different stories. Another advantage is that delivering the celebrity's image through a wide variety of channels creates the illusion that the celebrity has a deep, multifaceted character. He becomes more knowable, likeable—and dramatically real.

Implementing this strategy may even entail inventing whole new venues for celebrity appearances ("Battle of the Network Stars"; "ABC Wide World of Sports 'Up Close and Personal' ") or having the celebrity start new, highly visible institutions (The Dave Winfield Charity Foundation; The Hugh O'Brien Youth Foundation).

A final strategy is to *bring a denser story to the public*, making sure that the PR staff continually reveals additional details about the star's life and career. The outline of the celebrity's character is filled in by discussing his fishing trips, loves lost and forgotten, meetings with the queen, and special moments with his or her children. If the story is compelling enough, it serves the vital function of "holding a place" for the celebrity in the audience's consciousness during those periods when the celebrity is temporarily out of sight.

ELEMENTS OF DRAMATIC REALITY

In the best-selling biography *Robert Schuller: The Inside Story*, the story is told of the celebrity evangelist's trip into the unknown as a newly ordained minister heading to the promised land of California[28]:

> There was snow on the ground that February day as Bob and Arvella Schuller loaded their old Chevrolet with their few meager belongings and lovingly tucked three-year-old Sheila and baby Bobby into the back seat. Their breath hung in puffs of steam as they carried their things from their little parsonage. This was it. There would be no turning back now. . . .
>
> . . . Just before their departure, a denominational representative had phoned him to say that there were simply no halls to rent for their new church.

> ... "There's bound to be some place where we can hold services for the church," Bob determined. "I know it can't be impossible." Without another word, he grabbed a white paper napkin from the table, pulled a pen from his pocket, and began to write. . . .[29]

It's a wonderful story. Is it true? It really doesn't matter. The point is that it *is* a compelling story, imbuing Schuller and his quest with high drama. The audience sees itself in Schuller's shoes—on a mission, alone, facing the unknown. There is mystery: What did Schuller write? There is suspense: Where would he find a church? It's a perfect illustration of how Dramatic Reality is one of the most potent of the celebrity-audience attachment strategies. Yet it is also one of the least well utilized and understood. Clearly, certain combinations of stories and character types have great power to draw audiences into deep involvement with celebrities. But although we know that stories have lesson-giving power, often serving as models of behavior, little analysis has been devoted to understanding what makes them work. Examining stories for their persuasive power, it is possible to break them down into their key components, to help achieve the best match between story and aspirant. Most celebrity stories contain a mixture of six major elements:

- *drama:* a beginning, middle, and end revolving around some sort of conflict
- *adversity:* a roadblock that has to be overcome
- *crisis:* sickness, drugs, divorce, an event that brings the adversity into focus
- *mentors:* trainers, advisors, parents, or agents who provide some form of guidance
- *unrelenting talent:* some skill that simply *must* be used or understood
- *a final reward or climax:* public acclamation, a tremendous audience, charity work, or even a noble death

In Schuller's case, the elements virtually leap out of the story:

The Drama: the search for a place to preach, his eventual selection of the last possibility Schuller had written on that fateful napkin—a drive-in movie theater.

The Crisis: his poverty and inexperience, the absence of parishioners ("His self-confidence was shattered, he had already spent all the money, the advertisements had run."[30])

The Adversity: the local clergy's opposition to his preaching in a drive-in ("One pastor came over eight days before the opening service and proceeded to lambaste Bob for holding services in a 'passion pit' "[31]).

The Mentors: the "heroic" support of Dr. Norman Vincent Peale ("Bob admits to grabbing onto Norman's coattails"[32]).

The Unrelenting Talent: Schuller's "booming theatrical preaching style."[33]

The Final Reward: worldwide celebrity, culminating in the construction of the Crystal Cathedral.

Interwoven, the six elements in Schuller's story form several classic themes or storylines. But they are far from the only possibilities. The storylines which use these six elements have become so stereotypical that they can be categorized.

The Twenty-Two Major Celebrity Story Lines

Listed here are twenty-two of the most popular story lines, followed by the names of some of the celebrities most closely associated with them:

1. *First of a Kind:* Geraldine Ferraro, Jackie Robinson, Sally Ride
2. *Talent Wins Out:* Enrico Caruso, Barbra Streisand, Nadja Sonnenberg
3. *Success/Adversity/Success:* Mickey Rooney, Pierre Trudeau, Judy Garland, Bob Dylan, Tina Turner, Freddie Laker, pitcher Tommy John
4. *The Fatal Flaw:* Ted Kennedy and morality; baseball player Jimmy Piersall and depression; Janis Joplin and drugs; Richard Nixon and paranoia; Vanessa Williams and indiscretion
5. *Restrained from Greatness:* Loretta Lynn, Mary Kay Ash, H. Ross Perot
6. *A Great Rivalry:* boxers Joe Louis and Max Schmeling; comedians Jack Benny and Fred Allen; artists Picasso and Braque; tennis players Bjorn Borg and John McEnroe; cyclists Greg LeMond and Bernard Hinault; surgeons Michael DeBakey and Denton Cooley
7. *Mom or Dad's Footsteps:* Julian Lennon, Hank Williams Jr., Candice Bergen, Senator Albert Gore, archeologist Richard Leakey, Martin Luther King Jr., Liza Minnelli

8. *The Big Break:* Billy Graham in Los Angeles; General George Patton in Italy; Whoopi Goldberg in *The Color Purple*
9. *The Accidental Meeting:* singer Laura Branigan and manager Sid Bernstein; actress Shirley MacLaine and director Hal Wallis; Diana Ross and the Jackson Five
10. *The Great Teacher:* Norman Vincent Peale and Robert Schuller; Roman Polanski and Nastassja Kinski; Ion Tiriac and Boris Becker; John Wooden and Denny Crum; Walter Cronkite and Dan Rather
11. *Moved by Religious Power: Chariots of Fire*'s Eric Liddell, the Osmonds, Chuck Colson, Oral Roberts
12. *The Great Sacrifice:* Sacco & Vanzetti, Jesus Christ, Vincent Van Gogh
13. *The Incredible Feat:* Peter Ueberroth masterminding the Olympics; Alan Ladd Jr. signing *Star Wars*; Phyllis Schlafly leading the successful opposition to the ERA; S. I. Hayakawa putting down the rebellion at San Francisco State, positioning himself for a run for the Senate
14. *Young Dramatic Death:* James Dean, Steve Prefontaine, Marilyn Monroe, Buddy Holly, Rudolph Valentino, Roberto Clemente, Freddie Prinze, Karen Silkwood, Jim Croce, Amelia Earhart, Medgar Evers, Baby Fae
15. *Small Person Takes Over Big Office:* Harry Truman, Pope John XXIII, Coach Jerry Faust at Notre Dame
16. *The Pure Archetype:* actor Clint Eastwood, baseball manager Earl Weaver, sex symbol Raquel Welch, designer Yves St. Laurent, Lt. Colonel Oliver North
17. *Revenge:* Lee Iacocca, Budd Schulberg, Jackie Collins, Los Angeles Laker Mitch Kupchak
18. *Need to Prove Something:* Maria Shriver, Senator Christopher Dodd, William Zeckendorf, Jr.
19. *Risks All:* Flo Ziegfeld, Sugar Ray Leonard, Ivan Boesky, Sir Edmund Hillary
20. *Pawn in a Game:* Lt. Robert Goodman shot down over Syria, Brigadier General James Dozier kidnapped by the Red Brigades and dramatically freed, Dorothy Stratten murdered by ex-lover, Eugene Hasenfus shot down over Nicaragua
21. *Outrageous Behavior:* publisher Larry Flynt, dancer Isadora Duncan, activist Abbie Hoffman, writers Oscar Wilde and Henry Miller, Benihana founder and sportsman Rocky Aoki, entertainers Liberace and David Bowie, rabbi/politician Meier Kahane, artist Christo

22. *Little Guy Makes Good:* Woody Allen, Mayor Fiorello LaGuardia, pizza king Jeno Palucci, basketball player Spud Webb, comedian Pee-Wee Herman

Clearly, when trying to match aspirants to the most useful storylines, some generalizations can be drawn:

- Certain aspirants are more fitted to play the roles necessary to bring certain kernel stories to life.
- Few celebrities use only one story; many different stories are used over time to appeal to different audiences.
- With the media transmitting more images—of clothes, faces, walks, hairstyles—marketers are able to tell and reinforce a story more effectively.
- With the decline of traditional family units and communities, we are relying more on celebrities—not grandparents and neighbors—to embody, to make real, to transmit our stories and moral tales.

The key is story control. The celebrity and his or her developers seize the initiative, selecting the story, refining it, and managing its distribution. Is the story appropriate to the sector and aspirant? Is it memorable? Can it be widely distributed? Are the channels efficiently used? Are relations with the press exploited? These are the questions that the successful exploiters of stories ask. If they don't, someone else—the unfriendly media, the professional muckraker—may do it instead, with far less favorable results.

Ultimately, successful celebrity-marketing demands perceptive audience analysis. The celebrity must not only create interest among potential fans but also move them up the ladder to intense worship. For visibility seekers, this means developing the stories that will bond them to their markets. For celebrity-marketers, it means understanding which stories are the most appropriate ones for their clients to express.

Once aspirants understand their audience's perceptions and how to generate intense audience interest, the next step is to transform themselves to meet the audience's demands. The first issue to consider is the myths that obscure and mystify the transformation process.

CHAPTER SEVEN

The Myths of Transformation

At the age of twenty-one, college student Carter Christian Brydon celebrated his birthday with a party for 700 of his closest friends. Instead of the traditional dinner or night on the town, Brydon chose to make a costly investment in his future. A seeker of visibility, Brydon had been engaged for years in a process of transformation, methodically attempting to position himself for future celebrity. He had linked himself with charities and social organizations, run for campus office, mastered news media management, and improved his interpersonal skills. The party was designed to be a leap forward in the execution of his strategy. Staged in the grand ballroom of a hotel renowned for its elegance and exclusivity, the affair turned Brydon into the subject of intense local media attention. The story of his origins and accomplishments was spread throughout the community.

Inevitably, Brydon's strategy generated controversy. Letters to the university newspaper attacked his new-found prominence and the methods he had used to achieve it. But to Brydon, staging the party was a calculated risk. And it served its purpose: moving him a step closer to high visibility. Unlike many of his fellow students, Brydon understood the value of making an investment in his future. He understood visibility's benefits and realized that obtaining it involved strategies well beyond the customary résumés and job interviews of his fellow students. Brydon, in promoting himself to visibility, was taking an expensive gamble he hoped would pay off.

Carter Brydon was putting the Pygmalion Principle into action, marketing himself to make himself appealing to potential employers. The strategy paid early dividends. Within two years, Brydon had risen to the position of management assistant in Communications Services, serving as spokesperson for Commonwealth Edison, one of the largest utilities in the country. In doing so, Brydon not only demonstrated the value of self-promotion but exposed the fallacy of many myths about achieving success. Instead of relying only on conventional methods (mailing résumés, networking), Brydon used visibility as his tool. His tactics illustrate a crucial shift, for although highly visible people have been used to sell soap and cigarettes for more than fifty years, only recently have they begun to transform, market, distribute, and promote *themselves*, taking charge of decisions about their own visibility, viewing themselves in the detached way previously reserved for decisions about products.

Persons as Products

It was advertising expert Rosser Reeves who was among the first to confront the idea of marketing people as products. In 1952, he applied his expertise at selling Anacin to the selling of presidential candidate Dwight Eisenhower to the American public. Reeves used clever jingles, contrived man-on-the-street interviews, and repetitious slogans to package the unflashy general. Reeves' self-admitted strategy was quite basic: Survey the public to discover its needs and desires, then deliver commercials that showed Eisenhower clearly voicing the public's concerns. These early commercials, featuring a chant of "I like Ike," seem primitive by today's standards. But they broke new ground in treating people as products.

In the past, the person-based advertising that *had* been done was usually centered on promoting entertainment figures. It wasn't until Reeves' advertising campaign for Eisenhower that Madison Avenue began to adapt product advertising methods to nonentertainers. It was one thing to promote a movie with a photograph of actress Lana Turner in a revealing sweater; it was quite another to sell business leaders, presidents, sports heroes, and preachers with the same strategies. Reeves' actions stimulated the debate about treating the highly visible as products and manipulating audiences into believing in such products' authenticity. Today, with the entire celebrity industry now based on the manufacturing and marketing model, aspirants have come to be viewed as raw material, to be transformed into products that satisfy audience expectations. As a result, the industry is accused of disguising aspirants' low intelligence, lack of moral character, or absence of good will, choosing instead to highlight whatever characteristics the product must appear to possess to appeal to audiences. This criticism has dogged the industry's own image. It has also created some reluctance on the part of aspirants in the more recently celebritized sectors—business, law, religion—to undergo the process of transformation: the changing of an aspirant's identity to meet market and sector expectations.

The problem goes beyond aspirants' misgivings about the techniques of the transformers. Despite all the progress the celebrity industry has made, audiences still feel that there is something unethical about turning a politician or a preacher into a product. For the most part, the public is uncertain about how to judge leaders of the nonentertainment sectors. Is it on the basis of credibility, intelligence, sincerity, leadership ability—or image? The idea of designing the ideal aspirant on a drawing board, finding a malleable candidate, then transforming him or her into the blueprint through speech lessons, media hot boxes, image design, structured press conferences, or plastic surgery implies fakery and illusion. For a business leader to appear more competent than he or she really is, for a politician to appear more wise, a preacher more humane, a doctor more experienced, constitutes a real threat to the traditional trust between leaders and their audiences.

Another problem with treating people as products rests with the products themselves. No matter how much the celebrity industry may wish to change it, aspirants have feelings; they are human, and are therefore fallible. No matter how successfully they are transformed, few, if any, will perform with the machine-like consistency of a Toyota Celica. CEOs will be caught in drug scandals, junior partners will speak out of turn, debating candidates will lose concentration and commit gaffes, fast-track surgeons will lose patients, or pop singers will decide on impulse to change managers. Given this human factor, it's not surprising that celebrity-manufacturers go to great lengths to display their products in controlled situations, to prevent the audience from viewing any aspect of the person/product that is unappealing or inconsistent with the image plan.

This need to control celebrities' images has spawned such specialized channels as the tightly scripted talk show and the carefully orchestrated press conference, and it has brought public relations principles to bear on the problem of orchestrating person/product exposure. Though aspirants may never perform with perfect consistency, PR works tirelessly to shield the public from finding this out. But this is just one part of the industry's effort to gain complete control of the celebrity-manufacturing process.

The application of traditional product-manufacturing expertise to the production of celebrities is revolutionizing the celebrity industry. This change is being made possible by the celebrity industry's assumption that the characteristics and elements that make an object into a promotable product can be found in, or added onto, aspirants as well. At Kellogg, the researchers, marketing personnel, and product managers conduct exhaustive tests into an existing or proposed snack's inherent characteristics and appeal—a testing program that leads to the efficient design of successful products. Of course, if celebrity-makers could design and manufacture people in exactly the same way that Kellogg designs and manufactures Pop-Tarts, there would be no need for the celebrity industry to recruit aspirants at all. But because aspirants are just beginning to be built to specification, the industry still must rely on its ability to find people with the right inherent, minimal characteristics required for the transformation process to work.

Finding these minimally qualified aspirants and selecting the most promising ones to transform are among the least scientific processes the celebrity industry still relies on. Clouding and confusing this process are seven long-lived myths: the myths of right attitude, pure motivations, natural ability, necessary talent, inborn charisma, good timing, and the lucky break. Before aspirants begin transforming themselves to achieve high visibility, they need to separate the facts of transformation from the myths.

MYTH ONE: THE RIGHT ATTITUDE

Celebrity-marketers always look for clues to an aspirant's potential to be manufactured and marketed as a celebrity. One of the first questions asked is: Does the aspirant have the right attitude? Is he cooperative? Is she driven enough? Will he be willing to make the sacrifices? Will she stay with the program? These attitudes are thought to be inherent in the development of the aspirant's personality.

Closer to the truth, however, is that attitude is a shapeable, strategic element—one that aspirants must carefully understand. The attitudes that aspirants need to display actually depend heavily on their sectors and are closely related to market analysis. The successful aspirant is not always the most driven or obsessed but must be the most strategic—the person who can analyze which attitude is required and produce it on demand.

In most sectors, the people who search for the raw material of unknown aspirants speak with a sort of folk wisdom about attitude. In their conception, the term *attitude* means, "Do you want celebrity badly enough to endure the rigors of learning, practice, long hours, and the tempestuous behavior swings of your coaches, mentors, and support staff?" But this view is too narrow. Although aspirants do require commitment, they must also display attitudes that are seen by the sector's power structure as compatible with audience expectations—as well as nonthreatening to the sector decision-makers' own agendas.

An excellent example of how attitude management can aid the quest for visibility was observed by one of the authors during auditions for the 1984 made-for-TV film, "Reaching for the Stars." The concept of the film was to select four or five women from a pool of aspiring singers and dancers and subject them to an extensive remanufacturing phase involving training, coaching, and polishing. At the end of the process, they would be sent out on the road as a touring rock group. The producers suspected that the trials and tribulations of the group, "Girls Rock Club," would make a fascinating documentary-style film. Originally, 1,800 women auditioned. Each received a grade from a panel composed of the producer, staff, and casting director. It was at the cut-down to the final twenty-four candidates that attitude surfaced as a key factor. For the screening panel, having eliminated those candidates who lacked the minimum ability or appearance standards, the issue of attitude now became paramount: "Will she fit in?" "Will she interact well?" "How will she act on the road?" During these crucial final evaluations of cast members, one of the producers of "Reaching for the Stars" singled out a singer because of an attitude flaw. An agent who was attending the auditions had circulated party invitations without permission. The producer, seeing this as a suspicious come-on to the auditioners, confiscated the invitations. One aspirant claimed she had never received one (in actuality, she had). This behavior alone helped disqualify her. It was not that her sector qualifications (looks, voice, type) were inappropriate or thought to be too limited. But when making their final judgments, the panel members emphasized three factors—desire, the ability to fit in, and character. Perceived as having an uncooperative attitude, she didn't make the group.

In answering the panel's questions, the aspirants all attempted to display a mature attitude, downplaying the intensity of their desire for stardom. Many, seeing through the interviewers' loaded questions—"Did you ever see such a nice group of girls?" or "Didn't you think there was a supportive atmosphere during the auditions?"—spoke of the beauty of cooperation and the "good feeling" among their fellow auditioners. One aspirant who eventually won a position in the Girls Rock Club actually said that experiencing the warmth and camaraderie among the aspirants was more important than being selected. It was preposterous! But the evaluation panel, looking to humanize the businesslike auditioning process, liked it. Throughout, the aspirants tailored their responses to generate positive feedback from the panel and were careful to position themselves as earnest but not tedious, responsible but not obsessed, old-fashioned in virtue but not unwilling to be flexible.

The aspirants also expressed their attitudes to the panel through the care and design of their appearance. Most of the candidates dressed strategically, sometimes dramatically, for their interviews. One aspirant who admired Diana Ross's professionalism and self-confidence dressed like Ross and had Ross-like sweptback hair. Another, an Ann-Margret lookalike, evoked that famous actress's red-haired, cheerleader sexuality.

The aspirant who fails to address attitude as a strategic management issue is operating at a handicap. In all sectors, there are attitude rules and expectations that are often silent but potent. The aspirant who doesn't analyze the expectations of the sector evaluators—professionalism, consistency, compliance, adaptability—is conceding a major advantage to more marketing-oriented competitors. In the final analysis, aspirants need to shape their attitude strategy as they shape the other more obvious elements of the visibility plan.

OBSESSION

How badly do you want visibility? One aspirant seeking country-and-western singing fame planted herself at a heavily traveled intersection in Nashville and sang. As motorists whizzed by, there she was, dressed in an ingenue's gingham dress, performing an animated dance and belting out her songs to the traffic. The reaction of Nashville's professional music community was, to say the least, hostile and unsympathetic. Though she displayed in her street performance and on-camera comments an intense, unrelenting desire to be a star, she was rebuffed at every turn. Under the prevailing myths about attitude, the singer's raw desire would eventually result in success. But she had, in reality, failed to understand her sector's rules and conventions, neglected to develop the necessary interpersonal skills, and ignored the subtleties of audience analysis. In so doing, she had effectively sabotaged her quest for celebrity. For this aspirant, the intense desire for visibility wasn't enough.[1]

MYTH TWO: THE SEARCH FOR EXCELLENCE

It has become a cliché of popular self-help literature that the search for excellence is all-consuming and sufficient for becoming a leader in a sector. The misconception is that aspirants achieve high visibility just as a by-product of their efforts to be "the best they can be" at a particular activity. More realistically, however, aspirants are usually driven to become celebrities by somewhat more complex motives.

Human Motivators. One major influence on an aspirant's motivations are parents, coaches, and close friends. Most parents do not start out with the attitude "You know, I could make a fortune with my six-year-old!" But the rewards of visibility can corrupt parents' attitudes toward celebrity, causing them strongly to drive their children to achieve it. The little girl showing up with her mother to audition for the community production of *Annie* illustrates the problem. Though the child actually does the singing, it is the mother who inspires, begs, or orders her to do it, and who arranges for the voice and dance classes, braces, summer at Interlachen music camp, scheduling, starched dress, coiffured hairstyle, and cute bow at the waist. And the girl's mother is not much different from the local baseball coach who decides that the tall, left-handed, fifteen-year-old pitcher has "what it takes" to make it to the major leagues. It is the coach who supplies the motivation: getting the pitcher out of bed early, putting him on a diet, driving 150 miles round trip to small towns to play games, sending videotapes to scouts—maybe even adopting the player. It is the mother and the coach who cajole the little girl and the baseball player into desiring visibility. So strong is this impulse to enjoy celebrity vicariously that many aspirants seem little more than stand-ins for their coaches, mentors, or parents. Whether young aspirants can take this artificial motivation and replace it with a genuine motivation of their own may well determine whether they can withstand the pressures of transformation.

Situational Influences. Other factors that shape an aspirant's motivations are situational. Where aspirants are born, what schools they attend, and what media or local events they are exposed to all influence the strength and nature of their motivations. The Harvard University atmosphere, by deifying alumni success and mythifying Harvard's principal role in the universe, encourages its students to seek visibility. Large cities, as major media markets, are likely to motivate aspirants in entertainment, sports, and broadcasting. Aspirants who live in specialty celebrity centers such as Nashville (country-and-western music), Aspen (skiing), and others are exposed to specialized motivations as well. Others are influenced by regional strengths. For example, not many areas of the country have velodromes for bicycle racing; those that do produce almost all of the country's cycling celebrities. It's the equivalent of the retailing expression "unseen is unsold"—if you are not in contact with a sector and its activities, the right latent motivation may never be triggered.

Media Influences. Also affecting aspirants' motivations is the power of television and films to magnify perceptions of opportunity. The compressed dramatic nature of media makes certain sectors seem romantically attractive. One of the authors, invited to help evaluate actors who were auditioning for the role of host of a lip-sync contest TV show, "Puttin' on the Hits," was struck by the large percentage of aspirants who had given up promising careers in other parts of the country to gravitate to the TV center of Los Angeles. Interestingly, many of the aspirants claimed to have been motivated not by their parents or high school drama coach but by TV celebrity Dick Clark. For years, they had absorbed images of Clark: interviewing singers, telling jokes, making warm asides. They wanted desperately to be like him. "I've always watched Dick," said one aspirant, who proceeded to drop his voice, twinkle his eyes, and convincingly imitate his idol.

The powerful role that media play in motivating aspirants seeps into our unconscious through such programs as "Lifestyles of the Rich and Famous," celebrity golf tournaments, capsule celebrity interviews, and the endless media portrayals of celebrities showing opulent offices, palatial residences, and pampered lives. The parade of celebrity models—arms merchant Adnan Khashoggi entering his corporate jet, evangelist Billy Graham flying to Moscow, actor Michael Landon strolling the Malibu beach—magnified by the media, whets aspirants' appetites in all sectors.

The Main Motivator: Money. In the folklore of celebrity, many aspirants are thought to be entirely motivated by the love of the activity that, only incidentally, brings them visibility. This is undoubtedly true of many young aspirants. Benjamin Bloom writes that children, introduced by their parents to various visibility sectors (music, art, dance) at first find the pursuit of success to be challenging and fun.[2] Even many older aspirants in politics, religion, sports, and other sectors continue to be primarily motivated by the joy of accomplishment—not by the other rewards it brings. But most aspirants find that their motivations, initially pure, do change. This conversion from achievement for achievement's sake to the pursuit of visibility for reward's sake is the natural result of the commercialization of the celebrity industry. It is, after all, a business, revolving around the profit motive. So attractive are the rewards to successful aspirants that it is difficult for them, no matter how pure their love of their work, to resist losing their original motivations and adopting more commercial ones.

The difference in monetary rewards between different sectors is actually determining the activities that young people choose to pursue, as well as hardening their attitudes toward the importance of success. Money is forcing aspirants to abandon competitive roller skating for ice skating, speedskating for cycling, or bluegrass singing for rock and roll. There are still purists who select a field out of genuine, unshakable love for it; who are content to stay in the background, singing folk music in small clubs; or laboring anonymously in business as a top systems analyst. But such altruists are seemingly fewer and farther between.

As high visibility itself becomes a more important profit producer for industry, law, and other professions, the pressure to achieve celebrity status as a route to reward, and not personal satisfaction, increases. So widespread is the emphasis on celebrity generation that a whole new class of folk heroes is being created. As Lester B. Korn, chairman of Korn/Ferry International, executive recruiters, has said, "I expect to see the day when, just as most Americans can name ten or fifteen major entertainers and ten or fifteen major athletes, they can name an equal number of corporate executives."[3] The reason is illustrated by business celebrity Rocky Aoki, founder of the Benihana restaurant chain, who uses his own celebrity to promote his line of Oriental frozen foods. Traveling throughout the world, Aoki receives celebrity media coverage for his daring stunts and quotable quips. Messages on boxes of his frozen dinner entrees recount his career of daring sports and adventure exploits, enabling buyers to fantasize while they eat. His name, coupled with his feats, gives his Roast Pork Lo Mein its identity and memorability in the minds of the consumer and encourages others in the professions to duplicate his success.

Another sector in which motivation has been strongly altered by money is the art sector, which was long known for limiting the number of highly visible artists, elevating painters and sculptors to celebrity status only after their deaths. But today, newly minted art aspirants with scarcely a dry canvas are being hailed as virtual name brands. Far before artists' deaths, promoters and gallery owners are using visibility-building techniques to market their wares. Artist Julian Schnabel was promoted by his gallery owner, Mary Boone, who used a number of traditional marketing techniques. According to *Newsweek*, these included:

> . . . mounting shows at which most of the paintings were sold before the opening and were then exhibited to the public with the name of the purchaser proudly posted alongside. She [Boone] spread the word about the scarcity of Schnabel's art in *People*, *Life*, *Esquire*, and other popular magazines.[4]

The result was an increase in the prices paid for Schnabel's work from $3,000 to more than $60,000 per canvas. In the closely related world of design, Ralph Lauren's high visibility to consumers of all types is the key ingredient in producing sales of more than $450 million for manufacturers of clothes, shoes, furnishings, and cosmetics that bear his imprint.[5] With such high potential rewards, artists are more pressured than ever to let commercial considerations, not aesthetics, guide what they produce.

Even in such formerly celebrityless sectors as academics, aspirants are motivated to achieve visibility to enhance the image of their home institutions. In the case of Stanford and other highly visible universities, academic superstars have been strategically used to increase a school's prestige. This strategy involves finding name-brand professors who will attract other professors and students, and stimulate alumni gift-giving. In addition, institutions are urging their name-brand professors to cooperate with public relations, write for popular journals, and appear on television and radio talk shows. The pressure is subtle but unmistakable: If young professors want to succeed in the new academic world, they need to offer their institutions opportunities to promote them.

An example of how universities use celebrity scientists is the University of Minnesota's treatment of its Nobel Prize winner Norman Borlaug. A major story in its alumni newsletter praised Borlaug's remarkable history of discovery. Many of the kernel stories listed in Chapter 6 were skillfully interwoven: #3 (success/adversity/success), #5 (restrained from greatness), #8 (the big break), #12 (the great sacrifice), and #13 (the incredible feat). The glow of Borlaug's visibility is used to cast the university as the mentor of a pioneer humanitarian:

> Since the late '50s Borlaug has received a stream of honors from the University of Minnesota, where he earned a bache-

> lor's degree in forestry and master's and Ph.D. degrees in plant pathology. . . . [Recently, Borlaug] spent a week on campus, breaking away from speaking engagements in New York and Arizona, then jetting back to Minnesota. The University prevailed on him to deliver two public lectures and filled his days nonstop with meetings that continued well into the evenings. He spent two hours one afternoon in an interview for this article.[6]

The University of Minnesota, in the same issue, points out to its alumni that eleven other Nobel Prize winners, including Saul Bellow, Arthur Compton, John Bardeen, and George Stigler, had touched down at some point on university soil.

The motivation for celebrity operates at differing levels of intensity. In the most extreme cases, someone will commit a crime (John Hinckley, Jr.), cheat (marathoner Rosie Ruiz), or lie (*Washington Post* writer Janet Cooke) to become visible. In her "Reaching for the Stars" audition, one aspirant revealed that she so starved herself while pregnant that the day she gave birth she looked show-business fit. She explained that her career aspirations gave her so little time for mothering that she had immediately turned her baby over to her mother. For many of us, such desperation for high visibility might be unthinkable. But what *is* thinkable is that strong forces are at work reshaping, refocusing, and ultimately repositioning aspirants' motivations for embarking on the quest for celebrity. As celebrity sectors become more diverse, and money and opportunity continue to dominate activity within them, aspirants in *all* sectors are coming to be motivated more by money than any other single force.

MYTH THREE: THE NATURAL

In the sectors chapter, we discussed the minimum physical and mental characteristics required for aspirants to compete in the celebrity industry. *In the age of the Pygmalion Principle, it is the ability to develop, polish, and selectively emphasize these characteristics that causes aspirants to be perceived as talented.* Aspirants must possess the minimum abilities; beyond that, other factors become more important. That is why, in evaluating their potential for celebrity, aspirants must consider their sector's minimum ability threshold. In some sectors, the level of minimum abilities required to compete is relatively low—for example, in rock music or abstract painting. In other sectors, such as opera or surgery, the threshold is so high that aspirants who can't reach it should try another sector entirely. Aspirants need to measure these non-improvable characteristics: A baseball player should have good hand-eye coordination; a business leader a reasonable facility for math; a fashion model, height. It would be madness for a person lacking quick-twitch muscle fiber to seek visibility in track and field through sprinting. The aspiring actress without some ability to role play comes up short of the minimum-ability threshold. All aspirants need to consider carefully whether their natural or trainable abilities surpass the threshold minimums; and if so, whether they have the resources to achieve transformation.

Visibility-seekers have, of course, been taking informal inventory of their characteristics for years. But with the growth of the celebrity industry, the inventory process has become far more sophisticated. Interviewers no longer grill business aspirants primarily on their college grades but increasingly on their ability to project an appropriate and seamless public image. Medical tests are now routinely conducted on potential track-and-field aspirants to determine if they have the basic heart-pumping capacity to withstand training and competition. Training camps that act as discoverers and developers of potential sports celebrities dot America. Music, dance, and computer camps are supplanting the old YMCA summer camps. These camps filter and winnow out the aspirants with good tone and pitch, flexibility and balance, logic and analytical skill. Their goal is to identify those who meet or surpass the minimum-ability threshold, to justify the investment now required to compete. The tap dance teacher used to say, "The kid's got ability, Mr. Scott. Why don't you send her to La Flair Dance Academy?" Today, the modern dance instructor suggests, "A couple of years in New York, Mr. Scott, then I think Europe."

In the high-money sports sectors, specialized training camps have become even more crucial to obtaining scholarships than playing in the regular high school season. In basketball, screening camps invite outstanding high school prospects to duel against one another. Not only do college scouts attend the games, but there are rating services that rank top prospects on the basis of performance, with players moving up and down the rating scales like the Dow Jones Industrial Average. So intense is the competition among colleges to sign top players that the opportunity for a school to land a "sleeper"—an unknown but highly skilled high school player—has virtually disappeared.

The theme that underlies many of these developments is *discovery*. Discovering aspirants who already exceed the minimum mental and physical requirements for their sectors gives a celebrity-maker the advantage over the competition. Law firms recruit those who've made law review; in politics, local parties look for candidates who've demonstrated leadership in other fields. In TV news, stations review tapes of anchors from small markets. It is refining these natural minimum abilities into polished skills that earns aspirants the status of celebrity.

MYTH FOUR: ALL YOU NEED IS TALENT

It is remarkable how many aspirants believe that merely by possessing the right attitude, motivation, and basic abilities they can begin climbing the visibility pyramid. But these three elements will barely gain one entry to most sectors. To effect the transformation required to achieve high visibility, an aspirant needs *talent*.

Talent is one of the most misunderstood factors in the celebrity-manufacturing equation. Almost universally, it is believed that talent is God-given—bestowed at birth, fixed, unimprovable. For all who aspire to high visibility, no other myth is more pervasive. The fact is that talent is *not* usually fixed but is instead the product of such controllable forces as role modeling, expectation management, mentoring, timing, luck-seeking, strategic positioning, and geography. Although still largely viewed as a divine gift, talent *can* be dramatically improved.

WHAT IS TALENT?

The lights dim at the Howard Johnson's Motor Lodge in Portage, Indiana. Mary Sue walks on stage with self-assurance. She is leggy, svelte, beautifully coiffured and gowned. She begins with Cole Porter, moves to a little Jerome Kern, and concludes with contemporary Manilow and Bacharach. The crowd in the room loves her. She has a strong, throaty voice evocative of Whitney Houston's, and theatrical moves reminiscent of Dionne Warwick's.

But Mary Sue is just a lounge singer in a local market. Does she have the talent to be a major pop music celebrity?

On any given night, there are a thousand Mary Sues singing in bars and supper clubs from Portland, Maine, to Seattle, Washington—many with pleasant voices and pleasant, sometimes striking, physical presences. But only a few will make it to the peak of the pop music sector. Is it a question of God-given talent—or of attitude and strategy?

Consider the celebrity fate of two talented singers. The first, Sam Harris, was mass marketed by "Star Search," the national talent search TV program, and used this vehicle to build a lucrative career in the pop music sector.[7] The other, Vicki McClure, seemed to peak with her very first national TV appearance: the opening ceremonies of the 1984 Los Angeles Olympics. Both of these singers have at least the minimum skills that, when properly developed, make for sector talent: the abilities to hold a note, sing on key, project, and enunciate. Clearly, both had access to widely seen venues. Harris used "Star Search" as a vehicle to become a recording and performing star, as his energetic renditions of ballads such as "God Bless the Child" and "Over the Rainbow" became national hits. McClure, after singing "Reach Out and Touch Somebody's Hand" to the largest TV audience ever assembled for an entertainer, ended up back at her old job bagging groceries at a Hughes supermarket in Canoga Park, California—occasionally reprising her feat at such events as a memorial service for Dave Zinkoff, the Philadelphia '76rs public address announcer—and singing in a trio in small Los Angeles clubs. Harris converted visibility into commercial reward; McClure has so far failed to—not because of differences in talent, but in strategy and attitude. It is a matter of choices.

Harris, recognizing the need to break out of nine-day wonderhood, struck quickly, capitalizing on his initial publicity by diversifying into recording and live performances. McClure, in contrast, remains comparatively invisible. What McClure might have done more effectively is to consider the possible choices: how to distribute herself through available channels, how to appeal to fans, which story to use, which archetype to embody, which audiences to target, whether to put out a record or assemble a small-scale tour. McClure clearly could have profited from a comprehensive marketing plan and product development strategy if she so desired. But her fundamental attitude toward high visibility ruled these out. Refusing to adopt a marketing orientation, or even consider the possibility of stretching her current image, McClure observed of image-makers and promoters, "They're interested in what sells, in the offbeat, in gimmickry, so maybe [they] don't think there's a market for me." McClure went on to explain, "I know people are crying out to hear what I have to say . . ."[8] But, according to McClure, the market glorifies undesirable, bad elements. Whether McClure is correct about the market eventually discovering her, or is simply a wishful thinker, she is at minimum taking the slowest possible road to high visibility. Like McClure, many people are slow to recognize that marketing savvy and image stretchability are components of an aspirant's talent quota. But with celebrity marketing becoming ever more sophisticated, the components of sector talent are expanding all the time.

What Constitutes Talent in a Sector? What talent is varies not only from sector to sector, but also within sectors. Within the religious sector, "talent" includes the ability to master one of the popular archetypes (fire-and-brimstone preacher, wise old rabbi, serious-but-humane minister), to maintain a weighty tone in conversation, to analytically explore a Biblical text, and to write appropriate remarks for funerals, confirmations, and weddings. In the higher reaches of television preaching, additional talents are required: advanced public-speaking and theatrical skills and an ability to communicate parasocially through the media. Parasocial communication skills are particularly important for an aspirant because, by effectively mimicking the characteristics of face-to-face communication in a media setting, an aspirant can inspire a media audience to feel a strong personal bond. *Given that an aspirant has the threshold abilities appropriate to a sector, aspirants can achieve "talent" by mastering learnable skills that can be taught by advisors, coaches, and teachers and perfected through practice.*

What talents does a minister really need in order to appeal to a suburban congregation? Not merely a spiritual soul and empathy with parishioners. Today, a minister needs to communicate effectively during sermons, weddings, and funerals—and during business lunches, media appearances, and charity fundraisers, too. An understandably agitated minister once sought help with this talent area. He had recently moved from a small Oregon church to a prestigious Midwestern one. In his large new quarters he found he could hardly be heard and that his throat was aching with the strain. His voice, which had filled the room in the cozy Western facility, now sounded like a weak sparrow's chirping. The solution to his talent deficiency? A series of consultations with a speech therapist on how to breathe properly and change the method of articulating certain key sounds. He remanufactured his voice to meet the new talent specifications. This is a small but telling example of how the process of transformation is diffusing throughout the culture. Not many years ago, the minister would not even have considered seeking help, let alone been able to find it and successfully execute a transformation. The ability to sound authoritative on the six o'clock news, to impress business associates with practiced eye contact, to parry hostile questions from the press—these have become standard talent-enhancement practices in all sectors of public life.

What is mystically thought of as pure talent is often nothing more than the upper range of basic skills. The real determinant of a surgeon's success is how effectively and successfully he operates. An intelligence level that can acquire and retain medical knowledge, good hand-eye coordination, and an organizational skill in the operating room constitute the minimum threshold abilities that all surgeons require. But the extra dimension that propels some surgeons to high visibility is easily identified: the ability to inspire confidence—an eminently teachable talent. A note-taking patient, Mary Gohlke, observed that celebrity heart surgeon Michael DeBakey "couldn't have been nicer." His waiting room, she observed, "was packed with all kinds of sick people, some on rolling beds barely able to move. But I looked around and realized that everybody was clutching the same book, Dr. DeBakey's biography."[9] Are DeBakey's "natural endowments" as a surgeon so many orders of magnitude greater than those of other qualified surgeons? More likely, his special premium is earned in part through his attention to communicating with the public through the media, and intelligently managing his image. DeBakey has appeared on the cover of *Time*, been photographed by celebrity photographer Yousef Karsh, lobbied visibly for medical issues on Capitol Hill, and has performed operations in most countries of the world.

A TALENTED PATIENT

How do you measure the talent of Mary Gohlke? She attained visibility on the strength of her "first into the channel" status as the first heart/double lung transplant patient of another celebrity surgeon, Dr. Bruce Reitz of Stanford University, and lived long enough to tell about it. Gohlke was truly an accidental celebrity, making the leap into full public consciousness by co-writing a book entitled *I'll Take Tomorrow* that detailed her ordeal. Obviously, Gohlke had the courage and determination to undertake the operation. Moreover, she had the observational skills to tell her story to a professional writer. But are these necessarily talents? For the most part she was a celebrity because of modern medicine's technical skill to transplant organs, and because she was the first to have a particular operation. Her talent lay in pursuing a visibility-generating vehicle: authorship of a book.

It's clear that even with religious, medical, and accidental celebrities, the importance of so-called pure talent becomes quickly overshadowed by skills that can be learned, mastered, or purchased.

In another important way, talent is more influenced by a sector's professional members and audiences than it is bestowed by God. Critics, producers, venue managers, and judges, as well as fans, peers, and admirers, all help set the criteria for talent. And they may not all agree. People are always arguing about who has the better operatic voice—Beverly Sills or Marilyn Horne, Luciano Pavarotti or Placido Domingo. True, an opera celebrity is evaluated by a set of criteria unique to that form of music. But the voice and its pitch, timbre, and clarity are assessed along very specific guidelines. Other factors such as interpretation, projection, and ability to embody the role convincingly are held against well-known, long-held standards. Yet even here the judges may not all agree.

In other sectors, the standards may be even more ambiguous. An example is performance art, a relatively new art form that consists of mixed media and live enactments using such contributing art forms as dance, painting, theater, video, music, sculpture, and mime. The audience for performance art *seeks out* inconsistency, unpredictability, and novelty. That is because these are fundamental characteristics of performance art: a wide variety of styles, subject matter, and means of presentation. It is a sector that has an extremely complex hierarchy of participants, evaluators, and professional critics. Different "schools" exist—the German, the Visual, the Technological—and vie with one another for audience support. But as diverse and complex as this emerging sector is, its talent requirements *can* be identified, and aspirants *can* be transformed in order to embody them.

To demonstrate that the skills necessary to succeed in a sector are not necessarily God-given but can be isolated, assimilated, and perfected, two college students launched a sudden career in performance art.[10] Ultimately, their self-marketing project revealed a great deal about the interrelationship between sector talent and audience expectations.

Jason Sikes and Jeff Cory, with no experience in art presentations, managed in one short month to begin careers in, and reach the local summit of, the performance art sector. Their visibility vehicle was a performance piece called *The J. Alan Throbbing Zero Hour*, which featured throwing paint at three large canvases covered with pop-culture artifacts, accompanied by multiple video screens, slides, home movies, flashing lights, and an ear-splitting live rock band. What made their success so remarkable was that not only did Sikes and Cory have no experience in the art sector, they also had no training in art, either. But so accurately did they analyze the talent requirements expected by the performance art sector's decision-makers, filters, and audiences, and so successfully did they transform themselves to mimic these talents, that their act was accepted for presentation in the N.A.M.E. Gallery, the most prestigious performance art venue in Chicago. It was even televised by cable TV, underwritten by business sponsors, and covered by radio station WXRT, the *Chicago Tribune*, the *Chicago Sun-Times*, and the *Reader*.

Sikes' and Cory's transformation, based on their analysis of the performance art sector's talent and behavior criteria, included the following key features:

1. A physical look based on iconoclasm and avant-garde clashing of clothing styles.

2. An artistic concept—in their case, the "generative chaos of a multi-media throbbing explosion."
3. Audacity—the willingness to take great risks with little fear for the consequences.

Sikes and Cory struck such positive chords in the audience that the sponsoring gallery even asked them to return. This development led to the art community's acceptance of Sikes and Cory as legitimate artists, which led to other invitations to reproduce their *Zero Hour*.

One key to Sikes' and Cory's success was that they understood the need to affect different transformations in order to appeal to different audiences. To convince the N.A.M.E. Gallery that they were legitimate performance artists, they studied the code words, signs, and symbols of the sector: being avant-garde, spontaneous, brooding, moody, intense, with a seeming disregard for commercial success. They then incorporated these signs and moods into their presentations of self.

But in order to succeed, Sikes and Cory needed the support of another driver—financial backers and patrons. Rather than tap the resources of already overtaxed art patrons, they decided to seek funding from the local business community. Understanding the expectations of this audience, they dressed conservatively, acted eager and deferential, and emphasized their enterprising, entrepreneurial spirit in trying to get their project off the ground—all attributes they never revealed to the N.A.M.E. Gallery. The final product they delivered—their performance—presented to the sector the cues that the sector's audience valued: contrasting visual images, clashing sounds, and unstructured audience participation. Sikes and Cory's program for celebrity confronts the fundamental issue of not only transformation, but also of how standards of performance vary from sector to sector and are controlled by many different groups.

Talent Gatekeepers. Sometimes, the mass paying audience has little, if anything, to do with determining what constitutes talent in a sector. In these cases, it is the sector's professional members—its producers, agents, managers, venue operators, and others—who decide what talent is. What do general audience members know about judging physicists, architects, or fighter pilots? Not much. Consider gymnasts. The public may have a basic eye for their performances, but it is the sector's managers and organizers who, for their own purposes, develop the talent criteria. The ten-point perfect score rests in the judges' perception of talent and quality execution—not upon what the audience considers talent to be.

Often the talent criteria set by the sector's gatekeepers are more stringent than the standards set by its paying audiences. This can create some unusual problems for aspirants, who first must tailor their transformation to appeal to the sector's professional gatekeepers, then modify themselves in order to appeal to the mass audience. In the business sector, aspirants may rise to leadership by developing the talents considered important by their bosses. Once installed there, however, their audiences change dramatically. Shareholders, government regulators, and reporters often have different ideas from those of business executives of what makes for a talented CEO. A musician who makes a hit record in an isolated recording studio, trying again and again to get the song right, may be immediately faced with the need to perform live in front of a live audience of thousands or a TV audience of millions.

It's clear that aspirants have to analyze the talent criteria held by their different audiences. But ability and talent are not the only criteria upon which sector gatekeepers judge aspirants. Ability and talent are critical in that, without them, an aspirant cannot compete. But baseline abilities, and the flexibility to develop them into talent, will not drive an aspirant to the top of the pyramid. Many aspirants possess the minimum baseline skills. Thus, in the quest for celebrity, similarly talented aspirants need to distinguish themselves from their competition. How do they do it? With something even more malleable and teachable than talent: charisma.

MYTH FIVE: BORN WITH CHARISMA

In our culture, charisma is thought to be just as critical a prerequisite for high visibility as talent—just as fixed at birth, just as unimprovable. This Greek term, which stems from early Christianity, meant, literally, "gift of Grace." In the modern era, social scientist Max Weber redefined the term as having more than a religious connotation. In Weber's view, charisma came from a person's office or status, as well as "from the capacity of a particular person to arouse and maintain belief in himself or herself as the source of legitimacy."[11] Though this statement referred to what he termed "charismatic authority," it slowly began to refer to leadership in general and eventually was adopted as a term common to all celebrity sectors. Charisma began to imply a mysterious appeal. Even inanimate objects could have it; a car, if popular, had charisma. Soon, the term was being used to describe popular things and people anywhere.

It is now common to find salesmen, PTA chairpersons, doctors, or hot-dog-stand owners being referred to as "charismatic." In this use, the term usually refers to personality—a "certain something" that sets some people apart. In this most popular use, the term encompasses such ambiguous terms as "style," "charm," "looks," and, finally, the undefinable "presence." Like the Supreme Court justice who said that he could not define obscenity, but "I know it when I see it," many who evaluate and select aspirants claim that, while they can't define charisma, *they* know it when *they* see it. This view, which pervades the entire celebrity industry, is typified by the following expert advice from a popular magazine's article on how to become more popular:

> Charismatic people come on stage or into a room and you can't take your eyes off them. . . . Anyone can improve his presence with a little concentration. Vibrancy, enthusiasm, and animation all create presence. Cultivate these qualities. The pelvis is a source of energy and drive—a personal nuclear power plant available to feed vitality to the rest of you. By connecting your upper and lower body into one line, you release a force that will enhance your charisma.[12]

This self-help mysticism did not appear in a gossip newspaper or occult pamphlet, but in *Success* magazine, targeted to a wide audience of businesspeople. In the entertainment sector, charisma is just as undefined. Speaking of charisma and casting, the president of a Hollywood studio told us:

> It's just a feeling. When you look and hear somebody and it feels right, you should generally go with it. We may read fifty actors for a part. When it's really right, everybody in the room looks at each other and knows it's right. It just works. I don't know why. . . .

In interviews with casting directors, charisma always surfaces as crucial—the most powerful element in the mix of factors that make for a successful pursuit of visibility.[13] Casting director Dick Kordos claims that it determines whether an actor will be cast, and that he knows when it's there. To hear casting directors tell it, something in the aspirant's manner transmits a sense of the unusual or the exciting.

Even in fields where sophisticated selection criteria would be expected to be used, charisma is defined just as ambiguously. Political leaders often use the term to describe a candidate who they think has extraordinary potential. Many political types applauded the abundance of charisma in Ronald Reagan and bemoaned the absence of it in Walter Mondale. Reagan was "three-dimensional," "touching," and had a "commanding presence." Mondale, on the other hand, looked "flat," lacked "punch," and failed to appear "presidential."

In all sectors, aspirants are lamented for their lack of charisma or lauded for possessing it. Seldom, however, do talent evaluators recognize where charisma actual originates: *from within their own expectations*.

The Roots of Charisma: the Audience. Charisma, like talent, is thought by many to be a primal force radiated by aspirants. But the fact is that without audiences to define and perceive it, there would be no such phenomenon as charisma. *What makes for charisma is the discovery by audiences of favored or intriguing traits and behaviors in aspirants who already possess the talent minimums.* As part of our cultural heritage, we are taught to gravitate toward people in whom we perceive such qualities as competence, ability, assertiveness, friendliness, intelligence, and empathy. We are also subject to captivation by negative qualities, such as arrogance, rudeness, and disdain for authority. Both positive and negative qualities, projected by aspirants either singly or in combination, are often enough to cloak the aspirant in charisma.

Of course, unless aspirants possess their sector's threshold minimum abilities and can hone them into sector talent, the issue of charisma is moot. The businessperson must be able to coordinate subordinates' activities; the basketball player to make the layup; the politician to remember his lines; the surgeon ably to wield a scalpel. But given these minimums, there are several types of charisma that the aspirant can learn.

One way aspirants can project charisma is to learn the subtleties of sector behavior. For lawyer F. Lee Bailey, it's cracking a microphone cord like a whip to punctuate dramatic points in his defense of the Boston Strangler. For quarterback Jim McMahon, it's appearing out of control before the Superbowl, then transforming into a cool leader the moment he steps on the field. For actor John Malkovich, in "Places in the Heart," it's adding to his character's impact by stripping away the standard gestures of a blind man. (Playing the blind man, said Malkovich, was "... really one of the easiest things I've ever done. One of my eyes floats a bit so I just let it go. A lot of actors playing a blind person go to the Lighthouse for the Blind to do research, which I did for only one day."[14])

Even in so sacrosanct a sector as piano virtuosity, the tiniest details of behavior can pay off in enhanced charisma. As ICM president Lee Lamont recalls of celebrated client pianist Emanuel Ax, audiences were put off by the pianist's manner of walking on stage. "He looked like a cute teddy bear," said Lamont. "But when he sat down to play, you were drawn to listen to him. So part of my job was to say, 'Perhaps there's a better way of walking on and off.' "[15]

An even more intense charisma comes from the aspirant's ability to master a sector's behavior and personality expectations—and go beyond them, to develop a trademark twist or spin. By distinguishing the aspirant from competitors, trademarks can increase an aspirant's charisma with audiences. These personal touches can be as innocuous as an unusual story line, a quirky, interesting speaking style, or a characteristic walk. Tennis player Bjorn Borg's unflappable calm, actress Bernadette Peters' merger of sensuality and humor in her songs; celebrity businessman T. Boone Pickens' ability to define his takeover battles in cowboy and western metaphors—all are small gestures that have paid large charisma dividends on little investment.

Learning Charisma. Given that aspirants possess the minimum ability requirements and can develop these abilities into sector talent, charisma can be approached as a set of behaviors to learn and master. Celebrity-marketers now know so much about audience expectations that, given a sound marketing plan and a flexible aspirant, charisma can be programmed. Where do these audience expectations about charisma come from? From parents, myths, literature, religion, high school—everywhere. The result is that we all carry notions about what the charismatic person will sound, look, and act like. And these notions give the celebrity industry its blueprints for the design of charismatic personalities.

Fifteen years ago, a candidate for state representative sought professional help for his image. The candidate had noticed that successful candidates had the ability to enter a room and magically "light it up." Could he develop charisma in order to impress the electorate?

The candidate was turned down. At the time, "teaching" charisma was thought to be improbable. Today, we know better. In retrospect, had the candidate taken the time to analyze his charismatic peers, he would have realized that nothing mystical was actually going on. In our new age of transformation, the creation of charisma can even be broken down into steps.

First, the charisma-seeker must be evaluated. How well does he or she display the behaviors and personality traits that constitute charisma in the political sector? A professional would observe a videotaped simulation of the politician entering a room of voters, and study him or her for strengths and weaknesses. How well does he or she project the images appropriate to success in the political sector? The performance might be rated and studied through focus groups or reenactments before a variety of voters. The videotape simulation might demonstrate that the candidate enters a room without a purposeful stride or fails to make eye contact for an appropriate period of time with each guest. Further study might reveal that the aspirant does not project his or her voice with the requisite authority, or lacks the assertiveness deemed appropriate for elected officials. The candidate's ability to remember names—a hallmark of perceived charisma in politics—would be tested and improved. A session would be devoted to dress, grooming, and movement. When the testing and evaluation phase was completed, and the training, coaching, and behavior modification concluded, our candidate would be able to light up the Carlsbad Caverns—or, at the minimum, qualify for the run-off.

Charisma Engineering. A whole subdivision of the celebrity industry is devoted to helping aspirants develop charisma.[16]

These organizations range from such companies as ProServ, Inc., and the aptly labeled Charismedia, to speech specialists like Dorothy Sarnoff, to wardrobe consultants, public relations counselors, and image specialists. In the business and political sectors, employing these organizations to engineer charisma is rapidly becoming as common as taking tennis or golf lessons. But even these firms, while capable of instilling the behaviors that make for a charismatic appeal, often fail to understand what makes the appeal operate. Central to any charisma-engineering effort must be an understanding of the basic charisma-enhancing techniques:

- The ability accurately to analyze audiences, to uncover their expectations, biases, and desires.
- Familiarity with identification-building strategies: revealing to audiences some key factor about oneself, making eye contact, using people's names, addressing audience values, smoothly blending in accounts of dramatic reality and kernel stories and appealing to audiences' feelings.

Given that the aspirant has analyzed his or her audience and mastered these techniques, the next step is to apply the strategic choices. Recently the president of a small public relations firm sought assistance. Her complaint: that her voice was too low and didn't command respect in meetings. Her model for charisma was a rival who was a high-profile, dramatically dressed public relations company president. Subsequent probing revealed her real concern: that she lacked charisma. Analysis revealed that charisma in the PR sector consisted of several knowable behaviors—the ability to project authority, appear witty and analytical, select stylish clothes, and seem highly interested in client problems.

A twelve-week program was developed to intensify charisma for this aspirant. It began with an intensive scrutinizing of all of her public appearances: meetings, lunches, speeches, employee one-on-ones. On the basis of these observations, the aspirant was advised not only how to speak effectively but also to alter her signs: change her hairstyle, drive a more appropriate car, and refine her mannerisms. The components of charisma were further implanted with lessons on communicating in small groups and making effective presentations. Further enhancing her charisma were such strategic choices as selecting a high-profile charity to ally herself with, networking herself onto the board of the local museum, and serving as panelist for area PR industry conventions.

For this aspirant, charisma was shown to be no mysterious force but rather the distillation of the classic behaviors and images associated with success in her sector. However, once she was transformed, the aspirant's task was not over. Sectors continuously evolve, changing their success criteria, and these changes need to be closely monitored. When necessary, aspirants must make modifications in behavior, story, and signs. In the case of the public relations aspirant, she continues to receive professional image counseling, checking her speaking style, dress, story use, and other transformation cues. Enhancing charisma is not a one-time prescription but a long-term process.

Radical Redesign. Though our PR firm president was significantly transformed in order to achieve her goal, generating charisma can involve far more extreme measures. When automaker John Z. DeLorean first reached a mass audience, he was hard to believe. The General Motors executive had that long, lean, gray-haired look reminiscent of Cary Grant. If the J. Walter Thompson agency were casting for a macho car man, it could not have come up with a better type. This type, however, was refined in the gym and brought to a high gloss in the operating room. DeLorean, as a young candidate for business celebrity, concluded that he looked wrong for the role he wished to play. He knew that the business sector had specific ideas about what a charismatic leader looks like. So DeLorean began a transformation, reengineering himself to generate charisma: hiring a plastic surgeon to install chin implants and square his jaw, and using the latest in hair technology to "correct" his widow's peak. He lost weight and shaved his legs for what he considered the correct look. The new DeLorean, like his new model car, had all the latest features. Now in the comeback phase in the aftermath of his drug trial, DeLorean needs to effect a whole new transformation. Unfortunately for him, the first sector he chose to shift into—evangelism—was hardly appropriate to his desired image as a high-tech sports car producer.

So much can now be learned about a sector's expectations, and so much done to transform aspirants to meet those expectations, that little stands in the way of creating charismatic personalities. New methods and technologies can change faces, pummel bodies into sensual perfection, or make one appear thoughtful, sensitive, and intelligent.

Still, the aspirant needs more than a bag of voice and surgical tricks. Just as important is a broad plan to guide the charisma-seeking effort. Following are the four basics strategies.

Strategy One: The Impressive Stranger. Visibility-seekers are, by definition, not well known. While the audiences they encounter might be vaguely familiar with them ("He's a Wharton man," "I heard she trained with Uta Hagen"), their appeal to audiences has usually not been boosted by "pre-selling." Their reputations do not precede them. It is this invisibility that allows for the first type of manufactured charisma. The executive promoted to headquarters from the field, the divinity school graduate, and the TV anchor recruited from St. Cloud, Minnesota, usually find audience expectations to be quite low. Merely by meeting their sector's behavior and personality standards, unknowns can project charisma. Of course, this works only for as long as the aspirant continues to operate at low visibility. Once they begin rising in visibility, charisma-seekers have to shift to one of the following charisma-generating strategies.

Strategy Two: Charisma Pre-sold. So widely distributed are images and information that many audience members "know" aspirants by reputation before they ever meet them. Such preconceptions strongly influence perceptions of charisma. An extraordinarily wealthy corporate takeover specialist, having reached the summit of the financial sector, developed a desire to achieve visibility in the national political and social policy sector. His staff members, who considered him to be shy and withdrawn, were greatly surprised when the wizard's first public speech received an overwhelming response from an audience of financial analysts. The audience members not only responded enthusiastically to the speech, but they also excitedly raced to the platform to touch him and receive a personal word. *The key was pre-selling.* The audience had been so indoctrinated as to the financier's genius at staging corporate raids that they had granted him charisma before even laying eyes on him. His every utterance took on cosmic significance as he worked methodically through a speech that would have put an uninformed audience to sleep. Yet to an audience pre-sold on the wizard's reputation as a legendary money-maker, his charisma was electrifying. But who were the audience members? Mostly they were young Wall Street corporate analysts who saw in the low-key, whispered delivery a commanding style, who perceived in the restrained figure on the podium a towering presence. The wizard didn't need excellent eye contact, varying vocal inflection, or a square jaw. His charisma flowed from his audience's knowledge that he had exceeded the success criteria of his sector as almost no one else ever had.

It is not only a *person's* reputation that can greatly influence an audience. The reputation of the office, group, institution, venue, or distribution channel can deeply alter the way audience members process the impressions they receive. That is why we respond differently to an IBM salesman than to a salesman from an unknown computer company. Aspirants can always destroy this foundation of granted good will through poor performance, and they sometimes do. But with the worldwide ability of the media to deliver images, pre-selling the aspirant to audiences becomes a crucial tool for visibility-generators.

Strategy Three: Charisma Through Audience Mastery. Another form of charisma is that acquired by understanding the conventions of a sector's communicator/audience relationship. In all performance venues, audiences have become trained to expect certain strategies and tactics. Clinton Sanders points out that folk singers acquire a "charisma of performance" when they project to the audience, "both verbally and through facial expression, as being seriously concerned with emotional and technical artistry."[17] He specifically cites the ability of the performer to define the situation by explaining the music's history, amplifying various songs' backgrounds, and then explaining whatever is unusual about the piece.

This example of how folk singers project charisma can be broadly applied. The success of a political rally is often determined by the speaker's ability to use a particular cadence, discover and amplify the right themes, cite particular names and institutions, and use gestures and facial expressions that fit the crowd's expectations. What creates charisma for executives giving media interviews? First, they show mastery of the details of the issue under discussion and communicate a sense of easy familiarity with it. Smoothly, they define and redirect the issue firmly toward their own agenda. To accomplish this they establish strong interpersonal rapport with interviewers, appearing neither condescending nor cowed. They use the interviewer's first name, repeat questions thoughtfully, and risk using humor. The goal of these strategies is to break through the confines of the one-on-one situation and deliver a message directly to the viewing audience. When used together, the techniques give business-people, or any aspirants, mastery over their audiences.

That charisma can be engineered by helping aspirants meet audience expectations is demonstrated by the experience of an aspiring rock singer who was mired at the level of local celebrity. The aspirant was able to ignite intense fan attraction, but unable to parlay it into national stature. A powerful singer backed by a quality band—all of the requisite elements for national celebrity seemed to be in place. Why didn't he have a major recording contract? Why wasn't he on MTV? Where was the *Rolling Stone* article and "Entertainment Tonight" coverage?

Analysis revealed that his major weakness was a tendency to withdraw, shutting down communication with the audience while on stage and failing to project a coherent image in media interviews. In comparing the aspirant's characteristics with the sector's expectations, it was apparent that what the singer really needed in terms of product development was to demonstrate more presence by mastering the conventions of this sector. This meant achieving a distinctive physical image, aggressively talking to the band and interacting with the audience during performances, and adopting such sector conventions as spectacular lighting and special-effects technology. In addressing his problem with media interviews, it was apparent that he spent most of his time answering "yes" or "no" to questions that could have been used to build a compelling story and to communicate that the singer was the right type. The strategy decided upon was not to fabricate a new story but to build up his real one: his colorful origins, his struggle to form the band, his unusual musical experiences. The aspirant had a number of experiences that lent themselves to modification into Dramatic Reality. He had left home at an early age, played in rough, tough bars in the South, and had numerous interesting associations and encounters with well-known celebrities. By rehearsing his stage and media styles and practicing his story-telling, the singer began to develop the hallmarks of rock charisma. By mastering the conventions of his sector, he began for the first time to radiate character, seem alive, and have depth.

Strategy Four: Charisma through Counterprogramming. Should the first three strategies fail to generate perceptions of charisma in audiences, aspirants have a high-risk alternative: *intentionally failing to meet audience expectations*. In this strategy, the aspirant deliberately constructs a character type calculated to surprise, provoke, even shock the audience.

In the political sector, audiences have been conditioned to expect politicians who are smooth, slick, and polished, who speak in vague generalities, never take risks, and restrain the authentic emotional content of their speeches. But consider New York Governor Mario Cuomo's keynote speech at the 1984 Democratic National Convention. Speaking with pride of his ethnic origins, Cuomo saluted labor, spoke compassionately about welfare recipients, and with unashamed emotional exuberance talked of his family and his deepest personal feelings. The result was startling. The audience, so accustomed to homogenous, bland speeches, was struck by Cuomo's frank and direct counterposition. Using counterprogramming, Cuomo overnight became a leading candidate for the 1988 Democratic nomination for president.

In business, the use of counterprogramming can quickly thrust a person and his or her company to high visibility. Victor Kiam, chairman and owner of Remington Products Incorporated, habitually turns business sector conventions inside out. Kiam, taking over Remington at a time of intense foreign competition, made hard work and personal marketing the centerpiece of his efforts to revive the company. "I can't work and also be a social gadfly and charming to my wife," said Kiam.[18] Defying modern business's marketing consciousness, within weeks of taking over, Kiam had fired most of Remington's marketing experts. Kiam didn't even go along with the idea of consensus management, claiming it would lead to mediocrity. The most controversial feature of Kiam's management was his decision to make himself the be-all and end-all of Remington's advertising campaign. Most CEOs still do not pitch their own products on TV; when they do, they assume a very professional, almost detached image. But Kiam appeals to audiences by trumpeting his personal involvement with the company as loudly as a late-night car-lot commercial. As Joseph Poindexter wrote, "Kiam's recitation of how he bought the company because he liked the product plays on everyone's fantasy of gratifying a whim with a grand gesture."[19]

Kiam continues to develop charisma by reversing sector expectations. Not content with mere paid advertising appearances, he has diversified into publishing, writing a biography that he promotes heavily with his own funds and even pitching a line of Remington leisure clothes. The result of this intensive image campaign was Kiam's leveraging of his visibility into a worth of perhaps $100 million.

Public relations executive David Finn cites a case which can explain why the counterprogramming style works so well in business:

> One company chief executive I have known for some time is a good example of a businessman who is not afraid to be himself even when it gets him into trouble.... His competition consists of companies much larger than his, but because of his natural showmanship he more than holds his own in the marketplace.
>
> His dramatic bent and expensive tastes are sometimes accompanied by a short temper and disdain for critics, creating difficulties with governmental legislators who follow his industry and with reporters who cover stories about his activities. His advisers try to steer him away from controversial statements, and although he tries to listen to their counsel, he feels that if he can't be himself he might as well give up his job.
>
> Because he is always so candid about how he feels, and because he always insists on the best no matter what he does, he has built up a tremendous loyalty among employees and the people with whom he does business. He has given a decisive and dynamic character to his company. It is not colorless and impersonal. Its leadership is not seen as remote and institutionalized.[20]

Finn is addressing the value of unusual, distinct behavior in business. But the same principle can apply to all sectors of life.

For charisma to be manufactured in the new celebrity industry, it must be audience-based. This is not to say that aspirants do not embody it; they do. But we now know that figures "light up rooms" not by glowing with a primal force inherited at birth but by understanding and transforming themselves to meet audience expectations. If the charismatic figure is skilled at anything, it is in the art of communicating the right behaviors, signs, and mannerisms to audiences.

MYTH SIX: GOOD TIMING

"The reason she made it and I didn't," lamented the unsuccessful aspirant, "was her timing was right." Like talent, timing is a pseudo-mysterious force. Like charisma, it disguises more than it reveals, because what good timing really consists of is being alert to opportunities and being ready to act.

Examples of timing and aspirant development abound. In politics, Jimmy Carter arrived on the scene just as society was reexamining its values in the aftermath of Watergate. Ronald Reagan and Margaret Thatcher both benefited from poor economic conditions. Radio host Bruce Williams joined NBC's nationwide Talk-net network with a finance and money advice show just as business began to explode as an object of national fascination.

Often, celebrities who appear to have gained high visibility in mysterious ways had merely made intelligent choices about timing. Consider William F. Buckley:

> At age eighteen I was an officer in the infantry, so I had sort of formal authority over a fair number of people. And then when I was a sophomore at Yale they had a shortage of Spanish teachers. So, since Spanish is my first language, I was appointed to the faculty. So at age 21 I was a member of the faculty at Yale. That year I was elected chairman of the Yale Daily Review, which in those days was a preeminent extracurricular activity at Yale. That sort of catapulted me into the public view. [Since] my position was pretty conservative, I was all the more noticeable. And then I wrote my book the year I graduated. As I think back on my own life, there was never a point where I really *became* a celebrity, having been that almost from the age of eighteen in whatever circles I moved.[21]

At several key junctures in Buckley's early career, he executed well-timed decisions that from an outside view appear as mere happenstance.

The fate of an aspirant often depends on how the timing issue is viewed. Comedian Richard Kind finds himself sought after by television, theater, and film but has to be careful which vehicle he elects to use to seek higher visibility. Currently a star performer in Chicago's prestigious Second City theater—producer of such celebrities as Elaine May, John Belushi, Ed Asner, and Bill Murray—Kind has watched others leave Second City and plummet to obscurity. It is a terrible dilemma. Does he stay and maintain his visibility but risk running out of his promising upward momentum? Or does he leave to seek national visibility and risk becoming the victim of a poor role or vehicle choice?

Clearly, for Kind as well as for aspirants in all sectors, timing is intimately bound up with risk. Virtually any move that Kind can make involves risk, and the success of any move depends on how well timed it is. Kind has to ask himself the following questions:

1. Where does he want to be on the risk/innovation curve? Does he go for a great leap in visibility, risking much, if not all, of his current stature? Or does he spend more time at Second City—risking a decline, in the market's view, of his value as a potential celebrity? Does he pioneer the opening wedge of a new trend, such as a new kind of comedy TV show or a particularly daring film role? Or does he want to ride a proven wave to a secure, but lower, level of reward?
2. When will the window of opportunity open for his particular strength, which is improvisational comedy? Can he develop new strengths if needed?
3. Will the vehicle he selects close off access to other vehicles? Could television stardom eliminate any chance for film roles? What if the vehicle he selects fails? Can the vehicle increase Kind's visibility in other sectors?

Such timing-related risks can be daunting. An aspirant may act to move up too quickly, with necessary skills still undeveloped and valuable associations not yet made. Similarly, failing to act may strand the aspirant in a worn-out vehicle or cause audiences to perceive him or her as a has-been. In the early '80s, "Saturday Night Live" viewers were confronted with a brand-new cast of young comedians. Performers like Brad Hall and Gary Kroeger, who had been performing at their storefront theater for twenty people the week before, were now performing for millions. It was on the job that they improved their craft, gaining experience, and producing better and better television performances. Unfortunately, they might have made the jump too soon, possessing too little experience at the time they moved to national TV. They were, in fact, eventually released from the show. Should they have taken the "Saturday Night Live" jobs when they did? Would they have been better off staying in a small market, improving their product, gaining more experience before making their move? Then again, what risks were involved in passing up such an offer? These are the types of timing questions that should influence all decision-making.

MYTH SEVEN: THE LUCKY BREAK

For most aspirants, a persistent misconception is that luck is mysterious, fixed, and impervious to influence. Many nonvisibles blame bad luck for their misfortune and credit the success of the highly visible to "just being in the right place at the right time."

The "lucky break" has always been a fixture of celebrity lore, the force credited when the aspirant is the beneficiary of a fortunate accident involving no strategy whatsoever. It might be walking down the street and bumping into a movie producer, pitching a one-hitter while a major league scout happens to be in the stands, or writing your doctoral dissertation on Grenada six months before the United States' invasion.

But a claim of luck is also used to mask strategies that successful professionals would rather not discuss. Speaking about British industrialist Sir James Goldsmith, a source quoted by *Fortune* said, "Jimmy is in the grand tradition of gamblers who will bet whether someone coming through the door will wear red or black." A less romanticized view was expressed by Ambroise Roux, former chairman of France's Compagnie Generale d'Electricite, who credited Goldsmith's success to "prodigious intellect and intuition."[22] The image of gambler may be more strategic than the image of financial analyst, but not as accurate.

Another popular use of luck is as a way to allude to the corruption and unfairness of many of the celebrity industry's actions. In these uses, crediting luck serves the purpose of preventing people from probing into what you really did. Using the term allows friendships and professional associations to be maintained and keeps those who have been wronged from crying foul. But what is the real nature of luck?

Manufacturing Luck. What luck really is, is positioning. So-called luck can often be manufactured by doing little more than intentionally placing yourself wherever it is most likely for luck to occur.

Garry Marshall, producer of the TV series "Happy Days" and "Laverne & Shirley" and director of the films *The Flamingo Kid* and *Nothing in Common*, tells the story about how he cast the blonde female lead in *The Flamingo Kid*.[23] After an extensive search for the right athletic girl to play opposite Matt Dillon, Marshall attended the Carl Reiner Celebrity Tennis tournament, a tournament in which the Dick Van Patten family participated. The Van Pattens are a show business family with a reputation for good tennis-playing sons with beautiful acquaintances. One of the Van Patten sons' girlfriends, Janet Jones, caught Marshall's attention. Marshall recalled that as he approached the court, Jones's back was toward him. "I turned to my wife," said Marshall, "and said, 'If that girl turns around and has a face to match that body, she's it.'" Jones was cast in the film and went on to appear in the film *A Chorus Line* and play the lead in *American Anthem*.

Telling this story to a class full of college acting students, Marshall clearly upset his audience. Though Jones had done some modeling and had been a regular on "Dance Fever," her acting experience was minimal. Where was the traditional accompanying story of sacrifice, years of waitressing and auditioning, dues-paying in regional theater, and harrowing experiences in New York? How, the students wondered, could someone get so lucky while they were studying, sacrificing, preparing for their sector in the traditional manner? The fact is that Janet Jones had positioned herself strategically. She was living in the right town to be discovered and associating with people who were likely to be known by sector decision-makers and appraisers. Marshall was only half-joking when he said that he used a celebrity tennis tournament as a casting call. He also kept a special casting eye on the Van Patten sons, because he knew they dated beautiful, wholesome-looking, athletic women (Jimmy dated Farrah Fawcett, Vincent dated Kelly Lange, and Nels, Janet Jones). There are many beautiful blondes in America, but not many who can stage themselves in the Van Patten family troupe.

The fact is that luck is usually preceded by positioning, often something as simple as finding the right locale. A woman aspiring to visibility in business, analyzing the relative opportunities in different specialties, would be better off entering finance or publishing than the petroleum industry or the coal business. It isn't much harder to get into summer stock in the Berkshires than in Minnesota, but it's far more likely that Broadway talent appraisers will see you in the Berkshires. As an artist, you will get much luckier if you hang around Chicago's Superior Street than if you work the suburban malls or rural art fairs. Selecting the right schools, mentors, friends, and entry-level jobs are also part of the positioning that precedes luck. "Do I work for CBS for free as a summer intern or on a construction job for $380 a week?" "Do I go to Washington as an aide for a congressman at considerable inconvenience or do I stay home and work at my mother's friend's travel agency?" "Can I endure the ranting, raving, and competition of a high-powered tennis camp or do I go hiking in the Grand Tetons?" These are the dilemmas that are often posed when position is necessary to produce luck.

Making strategic decisions about positioning can often produce tremendous "luck." Unknown college dropout Lili Fini decided that Los Angeles was a lucky platform. As *People* magazine tells the story:

> Lili got an administrative position at the Carnation Company and began dropping in at pricey [Los Angeles restaurant] Ma Maison with her friend. "We thought of it as our local diner," she says. The move paid off. Pierre Groleau, one of Ma Maison's owners, noticed Lili right away. . . . Groleau decided to set up a blind date between Lili and [movie studio head] Dick Zanuck, his recently divorced friend and weekly tennis partner."[24]

The two were later married. Not long after, Lili found a movie script she liked, co-produced the film with her husband, and had the big hit *Cocoon* to her credit.

Luck and Dramatic Reality. Often, the place where luck plays the biggest role is in how aspirants handle discussing it. After all, the luck dimension is a key element in all celebrities' stories. In looking at some random stories, it's clear that luck should be handled with the objective of making aspirants look as if they had not planned, used strategy, or manipulated reality. Using luck in this manner produces such traditional celebrity story lines as:

- "Good thing I went into podiatry just before this running thing started."
- "Of course I married Sandra for love; her modeling career had nothing to do with my magazine job."
- "They needed an expert on booster rockets, and I was the only man in town."

Beneath the claim of serendipity there is usually a story of clear purposefulness. The singer Sam Harris, supposedly so lucky as to have been scouted in Santa Monica and allowed to audition for "Star Search," actually was an ambitious performer who staged an elaborate production as a student at UCLA and was considered a likely winner by "Star Search"s' producers. Celebrity editor Michael Korda of Simon & Schuster wasn't merely lucky; he was the beneficiary of a company strategy that encourages the promotion of highly visible editors.

Of course, the predominance of positioning-oriented luck doesn't preclude the possibility of genuine, plain dumb luck. It *does* suggest that the term often serves as a mask for some of the more puzzling machinations of the celebrity industry. When a comedy aspirant showed up at the "Reaching for the Stars" auditions two hours late, talking at a pell-mell pace and breaking every convention of audition practice and demeanor, it wasn't just dumb luck. The producer had a slot for a fast-talking, neurotic type, and her audition performance beautifully matched the role that was being cast. She got the part.

"I'm Joel Hyatt"

It's not hard to imagine what happens when Joel Hyatt of Hyatt Legal Services enters a room. Most people, despite their resolution to be reserved, stare or gape. They watch his every movement—judging, evaluating, wondering, "How did he become so famous?" Why Hyatt, indeed. Why not other lawyers who had won a number of sensational trials and significant decisions?

The truth is that Joel Hyatt understands the fundamentals of visibility and transformation. He was able to leapfrog over his competition by associating his name with low-cost legal services. His firm, through TV advertising, has become the largest law firm in the country, with 20,000 new cases per month. He placed his name on the venture because he realized that brand visibility demands the credibility of his face. In his commercials, he moves around the law-office set clad in a conservative business suit and looking very comfortable. He speaks reassuringly and decisively. He looks directly into the camera, calm and professional, reassuring us that Hyatt will do your legal work fairly and with integrity.

Hyatt wasn't born with these qualities; his talents were improved through practice, and his charisma was at least partly a creation of marketing. Hyatt perceptively analyzed his market and positioned himself accordingly. And like all successful aspirants, he worked on his relationship with his audiences. In short, Hyatt went beyond the myths of celebrity to understand the type of transformations he would have to make to obtain it. The next chapter goes beyond these myths and common wisdoms of celebrity to describe the four-step process of transformation.

CHAPTER EIGHT

The Techniques of Transformation

It might have struck some people as odd when the once sweet and demure pop singer Olivia Newton-John became the young, vibrant seductress in her hit single "(Let's Get) Physical." The old Olivia, prim and proper, with clear blue eyes, milky skin, and blonde hair, gave way to a new image: smoldering seductress of the '80s. The old Olivia had been photographed smiling sweetly and holding kittens; the new model wore tight pants and was photographed on a red satin sheet surrounded by flames.[1] The old Newton-John had also clearly peaked and begun to decline as an entertainment sector leader. She needed a change of image to regain her high visibility.

The transformation of Newton-John was not some mysterious force propelled by luck or fluke. It was the state of the art in the techniques of the Pygmalion Principle. The fitness craze of the '80s had created an opportunity for a performer to symbolize the energy and pace of a new social trend. So Newton-John was transformed to meet the *market fulfillment* strategy devised by her producer. Not unlike the development of Federal Express or large-breasted turkeys, Newton-John was changed and fitted to a newly developing market.

In the process of transformation, she used a number of techniques becoming quite common in celebrity-seeking. Newton-John not only changed her clothes and appearance but altered her behavior as well. Her Dramatic Reality story line was enhanced by her marriage to a muscular actor ten years her junior and by her pronouncements to the press that she and her husband were acting like kids again. An entertainer refitting herself to a new set of marketing expectations is hardly news. What *is* news is the thoroughness and efficiency of the changes and the spread of the transformation style to other sectors of life.

The idea of transformation is not a new one. We all realize that people undergo changes in age, occupation, geographic location, and lifestyle. What is different about transformations undertaken in pursuit of high visibility is that they involve audience- and market-centered concerns that revolve around public image. The image of a celebrity needs to be acceptable to a target audience. Unfortunately, many well-known people have characteristics that, if exposed in their unrefined state, would damage their relationships with their audiences—or prevent one from ever developing. One problem is that the process of eliminating unwanted traits calls attention to the fact that they existed in the first place. It has become conventional wisdom among image-planners and their clients that the disclosure that a change process is underway compromises an aspirant's image, a problem particularly acute in such sectors as politics and business, where getting transformation help is often considered a sign of falseness and a lack of authenticity. As a consequence, the transformation and image-building processes are rarely seen in full light by the audience.

Interviews with hundreds of aspirants and celebrities confirmed a broad tendency to deny the existence of the transformation process. William Simon, former secretary of the Treasury and among the most visible leaders of the conservative movement, said it clearly:

> I have never been interested in merchandising myself or perpetuating a public image. Indeed, it is always difficult to ascertain just what your image is and it is almost impossible to improve or diminish how people view you other than through direct personal contact. I simply work hard and try to be successful at what I do—whether it's as a businessman, a banker, an author, philanthropist or father and husband. I'm not attracted to the kind of society that competes for positions in 'Suzy's Column' and I'm not out to prove anything. In the end, it only matters to me that those whose

> friendship and partnership I value in life think well of me—and benefit somehow from our association.[2]

Senator Bill Bradley of New Jersey also denigrated the celebrity-manufacturing process:

> I don't worry about my image. . . . I have no strategist to work on my image. My role is to work for the country. I'm involved in the missing children campaign, these [things] all say who I am. . . .[3]

Even someone as intimately involved in the creation and distribution of celebrity images as Steve Rubell, former owner of Studio 54 and now owner of Morgans Hotel and consultant to the Palladium nightclub, said of his own public image:

> I have a public relations firm for each project, but no one for me personally. I just think you have to be sort of real. . . .[4]

Finally, Geraldine Ferraro, the first vice presidential candidate to sell soda pop, is alleged to be unsullied by her move to high visibility in commercial advertising. Her aide and fundraiser, Addie Guttag, maintained that, "[Ferraro] hasn't been changed. She is herself."

All of these interviewees downplayed any work done on their image, claiming that they were basically "naturals." Naturals, not unlike Robert Redford's home-run-hitting movie character, supposedly need no embellishment to succeed in their celebrity sector. Celebrities desire to be seen as naturals even in fields that emphasize transformation. Female impersonator Chili Pepper, in as transformation-intense a sector as there could be, claims that, "There has never been a transformation for me. I've always looked the same and done the same things."[5]

There is little question, however, that transformation processes are being undertaken by aspirants and celebrity-developers. In most cases, however, the process is based on myths, is haphazard, or lacks clear leadership. We advocate instead a process that adapts concepts from marketing and communication and uses long-term development strategies.

The Four Phases of Transformation

A development plan to transform people into celebrities requires *concept generation*, *concept testing*, *concept refinement*, and *concept realization*. Though the results of the Pygmalion Principle are often perceived of as overnight, sudden, dramatic success, the opposite is in fact true. In most cases, successful transformations take place over a period of time, preceded by planning, patience, and persistence.

CONCEPT GENERATION

In each celebrity sector, certain roles are played. For example, in the entertainment sectors, there are singers, dancers, comedians, and other roles. For most people attempting to transform themselves into celebrities, the choice of role is limited—because it has already been made. The surgeon is not going to change roles and become a politician simply because a market opportunity presents itself. By the same token, the surgeon *does* have the option of becoming a different *type* of surgeon. He or she may change types into a sports medicine specialist, a pediatric specialist, or an expert on a very specialized, risky procedure. The surgeon may even write a book on malpractice or become a media expert for a television network. All these different types are options.

The same principle applies to all sectors. Those who play the role of singer include different types of singer: wholesome folk singers, defiant political singers, sensuous torch singers. But even within a certain type of singer—for example, sexually oriented torch singers—different individuals will tailor themselves to project a distinct identity or character. Tina Turner and Sheena Easton both play the role of singer. But Tina Turner's character as a sexy singer is different from Sheena Easton's: Turner elicits the image of a woman of vast experience and deep sexual strength; Easton projects herself as the young sex kitten and ingenue. Both singers solved their concept problem differently. But each composed an arrangement of role, type, and character that distinguished her marketing position.

In the concept-generation stage, aspirants and their transformation teams (managers, agents, friends, spouses) must brainstorm to generate different possible concepts. *The idea is to select or invent a unique, or at least distinct, combination of factors that will distinguish one aspirant from the rest.* In pursuing high visibility, an aspirant needs to find a concept that will appeal to the intended target audience.

Of course, aspirants in a particular role, say politician, may not accept the need to alter type and character. He or she might say, "I don't need a new concept. I am what I am, and that's what I will be to the audience." An example would be an ideological politician who does not hide or sugarcoat ideas but presents them to all who will listen. This is the mark of a leader rather than a marketer, although he or she may lead very few. Such a politician searches for his or her natural market, rather than adjusting his or her ideas to appeal to various voter groups. The politician is interested in pure selling, not marketing.

Most aspirants, on the other hand, would accept the need for some adjustment or transformation: "I am capable of being and feeling many different ways, and I will choose the type and character that will lead to the most success." This attitude, which Erich Fromm has labeled the "marketing orientation," has predominated among aspirants in the older celebrity sectors for years and is gaining ground in the professions, arts, religion, and others. Politicians have always adjusted their ideas and personalities to please the voter group they are addressing at the time; aspiring actors have tended to cast themselves in the mold of some currently hot star. Today, religious aspirants are latching on to the issue most likely to propel them to high visibility, just as aspiring artists are altering their styles to capitalize on fashion and design trends.

An example of the new marketing consciousness in the religious sector is the decision of Reverend Cecil Todd, founder and president of the World-wide Revival Fires Ministries, to recognize the potential in marrying religious beliefs and political conservatism on television. In 1965, Todd convinced a Kansas television station to feature him in a show that eventually reached forty-seven states. Todd, in recalling his opportunity, said:

> Oral Roberts and Rex Humbard were the only two on television and neither one of them were touching these things [political issues]. I think Jerry Falwell was on in the Lynchburg area, but nothing of a national voice.[6]

Todd, seeing the opportunity to become a sector leader, was willing to adapt himself and his ideas to the media. Even more telling of Todd's market orientation was his decision to move his television production operations to California. Todd, originally from a small town in southeastern Oklahoma, knew he needed to take advantage of California's expertise and access to celebrities.

Marketing-oriented aspirants like Todd have the desire, and often the flexibility, to shape their characteristics to the marketplace. It is a process well illustrated by actors, who provide the best evidence of the adaptability and stretchability of one's personality. They can play many roles and perform as different types of people. Most actors, of course, can be "recognized" from one performance to another. But great actors such as Robert DeNiro, John Malkovich, and Geraldine Page are highly moldable, demonstrating a wide range of character plasticity. It's often hard to recognize them from one film or play to the next. And this ability to alter type and character isn't limited to the entertainment sector.

WILL THE REAL DR. BERGER PLEASE STAND UP?

Who is Dr. Stuart Berger? To his patients, he is a life saver who has mastered techniques no one else understands. Some of his peers are not so sure. ("He did not take a single course in nutrition and he did no research on the psychology of dieting," said Dr. Fred Stare, former nutrition department chairman of the Harvard School of Public Health. "I am greatly offended that he is using the good name of Harvard as part of his sales pitch."[7]) To the public, he's a great "Today" show guest. To the publishing world, he's the best-selling author of *Dr. Berger's Immune Power Diet*. Clearly, Dr. Berger is flexible enough to move smoothly between different types within his primary role as a doctor. It is an ability that even less highly visible physicians need, to express different types of behavior depending on their audiences: patients, peers, and public.

At fourteen, said Berger's mother, speaking of her son's flexibility, "[He had] the potential to be an actor."[8]

The literature of social psychology confirms the wide range of types that all people play in their daily lives. A man may be very upbeat and friendly at work, and a tyrant at home. A woman may be one person to her superior, another to her associates, a different person to her subordinates, another to her friends, another to her husband, and still another to her children. In most cases, we make our personality adjustments almost unconsciously as we seek to behave in the ways most appropriate to the variety of situations we face.

In establishing that people can play different roles and types, we are not arguing that every aspirant can play *any role or type.* Illiterate, inarticulate twenty-year-olds would find it hard to pass themselves off as doctors, lawyers, or executives. The starting point in concept generation is the *person,* with his or her particular looks, intelligence, moods, talents, and personality. The degree to which the aspirant can learn to stretch these characteristics limits the potential roles and types that he or she can play. Some characteristics, being fixed (height, race), are given; but many others may now be modified or completely changed. Some people accept the changes so thoroughly that they overidentify their real selves with their created characters—losing their identities in the process.

"I'M CLAYTON RANGER"

Clayton Moore, the original Lone Ranger, completely immersed himself in the character he created in order to flesh out the role of the Lone Ranger. When the corporation that later purchased rights to the Lone Ranger character tried to ban him from portraying the cowboy hero, he sued and won. Moore argued persuasively that he could no longer separate himself from his role. Now, long after his primary career has ended, Moore still remains the Ranger, making personal appearances, visiting trade shows, and patrolling the lonesome trail. Recently, a car accident victim was startled to find himself being rescued by the masked man, who had just happened upon the accident while traveling in full costume. The startled motorist found himself an accidental national celebrity, as he glowingly reported the providential encounter with the Lone Ranger. Hi-yo Silver!

The celebrity-maker's task in the concept-generation stage is to help the aspirant to go through three steps: *defining the target market, selecting the appropriate type to play,* and *fully developing the character*.

Target Market. Aspirants cannot transform themselves until they decide on the target market in which they covet success. As discussed in the Sectors and Audiences chapters, each target market has different characteristics and requirements. The three areas that need to be examined by aspirants and their supporters are audience size, marketing requirements, and available resources.

1. *Audience Size*. All sectors are not created equal; some are better candidates than others for supporting visibility-seekers, and for rewarding them. Consider a young female singer who could perform for either jazz or Christian music audiences. Currently, she would have a better chance of achieving high visibility in Christian music. Although jazz has a loyal audience, it is not nearly as large as the potential audience for gospel music. In fact, contemporary Christian music, as performed by such artists as Amy Grant, Steve Taylor, Andre Crouch, and Sandi Patti, is already outselling many of pop music's bestselling genres.[9] In 1984, contemporary Christian artists sold 20 million albums of their blend of rock and gospel music.[10] Assuming that she has the stretch potential, an aspirant who desires visibility is far better off selecting Christian music fans as her target market than accommodating the expectations of the smaller jazz target market.

   Consider the same issue in the sports sector. A capable athlete has a far better chance of achieving national renown in such audience-intense areas as football, basketball, gymnastics, or tennis than in minor sports such as rugby, crew, or the biathlon. Though interest varies from country to country, it is only the sports with money potential that can create a Martina Navratilova, who earns millions and is comprehensively covered by the media. Contrast Navratilova's success with that of equally skilled athlete Nancy Lieberman, a women's basketball star who is denied access to the highest-paying venue in her sport, the NBA. Navratilova could easily have excelled at basketball—or at track, soccer, or rowing. By choosing tennis, she entered a sector of intense audience interest. *To achieve the greatest rewards, aspirants must enter sectors with the most intense audience interest.*

2. *Marketing Requirements*. There may be tremendous interest in a sector—Christian music, porn films, pop psychology, economic forecasting—but special features in each that make the marketing of a celebrity particularly difficult or easy. A sector, for example, may be very attractive but may already be oversaturated with competitors. When singer Hattie Titus tried to break into high visibility through the Motown factory, she encountered only frustration:

> I was a member of a singing group in Detroit called the Bluebirds. We were signed up on a smaller recording label called D-town. . . . Among the singers in Detroit a rumor had started about Berry Gordy and his need for new talent. He threw a big party at a lavish place in which anybody who was anyone showed up. I was introduced to Berry and then he turned around and announced he had a new singer. Everyone (including me) thought he was speaking of me. But he wasn't, and that blew my little acquaintance with Motown.[11]

Though Titus was talented and had stage presence, her type was already filled by a young singer named Diana Ross. If Titus wished to break into fame with the help of Gordy's organization, she faced an insurmountable obstacle. She needed to change her type, move to a new geographic location, or find a subsector of popular music where there was less intense competition.

A similar problem exists in the business sector, where different constraints operate. The fact is that most positions in the corporate world do not lend themselves to high visibility. As a manager of Union Carbide, frustrated at his inability to become noticed, lamented, "120,000 people can't be Warren Anderson [Carbide's CEO]." The majority of people in the corporate world who desire visibility will probably have to get it through the leadership of local charities, managing the church baseball team, serving on the park board, or heading up the local United Way drive. While serving to build the image of the company, such personal publicity seeking also translates into higher visibility for the aspirant within the company. *Business Week* refers to this as the "visibility quotient." As Andrew Sherwood, a corporate recruiter, said of an IBM manager, "He claimed that his image at the company was so improved that he recouped his expenses several times over."[12]

For most people, the best opportunities for visibility in the business world are not in the boardrooms of *Fortune* 500 firms but in the far more numerous car dealerships, real estate firms, fashion boutiques, or insurance companies. The Ford dealer and real estate developer can define their own relationships with the media—and finance it for relatively low cost.

3. *Resource Availability.* When considering a range of possible concepts, the aspirant has to take into account the availability of funds and sufficient expertise. In certain sectors, these resources can be inexpensive and home grown, as in the case of the rock music sector celebrities REM. When first starting the process of generating concepts, REM, by operating from a small base like Athens, Georgia, did not have to endure the great costs associated with launching in a major market such as Los Angeles.

THE SINGING FORD MAN

It's 1:00 in the morning on late-night TV. Humphrey Bogart has the Falcon almost within his grasp. The screen goes blank, and up pops . . . Harry Schmerler, the Singing Ford Man! Sitting behind his desk in his cluttered car lot office, Schmerler, the dealership's amiable owner, breaks out with a verse of "Danny Boy." By the time the viewer begins to get annoyed, Schmerler, cheerfully acknowledging his lack of vocal talent, launches into a pitch for the qualities of his dealership. These commercials, shot in large numbers and responsible for making Schmerler a local household name, each cost Schmerler less than the parts for a tune-up.

Selecting the Type. The second step in the concept generation process is to *define the social type that the aspirant should present to the target audience*. In his book *Heroes, Villains, and Fools*, Orrin E. Klapp defines hundreds of types of people found not only in American society, but almost universally.[13] Klapp classifies them into three major categories: heroes (winners, independent spirits, charmers), villains (rebels, rogues, sneaks), and fools (incompetents, boasters, weaklings). From this repertoire of social types, as well as some subtly shaded subtypes, the visibility-seeker should choose the one that he or she can effectively project to the target audience.

Consider an attractive young woman who has chosen the role of actress and who has the intelligence and range of talent to play either a "seductress" or "ingenue" type. Her visibility advisor thinks that she has greater potential as the former rather than the latter. "Seductress" and "ingenue" are social types; in fact, according to Jung, they are *archetypes*—a collective representation of a type of being that lies in the unconscious of all people. Everyone, in relating to relatives, friends, and strangers, forms ideas in the unconscious of certain types of beings, such as "earth mothers," "wise old men," "witches," and others. These archetypes remain in our unconscious, occasionally becoming crystallized through chance meetings with people who match these idealized characteristics. Often audiences, seeking to "type" or peg an aspirant, project an archetype onto the living person, whether these persons are consciously living out the archetype or not.

The "love goddess" archetype is exemplified in myth by Aphrodite, and by such subtypes as nymph, beautiful witch, harlot, siren, and vamp. One of the most perfect personifications of this archetype in recent times was Marilyn Monroe, who consciously adapted her appearance and behavior to bring the archetype to life. As Penny Stallings documents, "At the insistence of her mentor, super-agent Johnny Hyde, Monroe had her jaw remodeled and the tip of her nose bobbed at the age of 23. Love hadn't blinded Hyde to the fact that Monroe would have to improve on nature a bit before she would be ready for stardom."[14] According to Edward Whitmont, "her identity with the archetype, and its consequent compulsiveness, made her the companion of many male figures, to the exasperation of her various husbands."[15] Eventually, the archetype's compulsive power took almost full possession of Marilyn Monroe as a person.

A new aspiring actress knows that she cannot become an exact replica of Marilyn Monroe; she is not interested in being a throwback—that is, trying to evoke the exact image power of a previously successful star or icon. Most aspirants intuitively realize that subtle distinctions are necessary. Both Jayne Mansfield and Mamie Van Doren consciously typed themselves after Marilyn Monroe and yet were not confused with her, representing alternative personifications of the love goddess. It is interesting to look at how the archetype of love goddess has evolved in the '80s. With raised consciousness and the new equality, today's love goddesses embody far more toughness. Kathleen Turner and Kim Basinger are also "love goddess" types. But although the look is similar, the attitude has changed. No longer the "dumb blonde," today's love goddesses are complex, aware, and demanding—characteristics not valued in Monroe's era.

The aspirant's need to adopt a type, or live out an archetype, is found in many sectors of society. Consider the politician who is challenging an incumbent. The challenger can adopt one of several archetypes: the "white knight," "underdog," "dark horse," "thinking man," "angry man," "idealist," or "statesman." The challenger will need to think through which type has the greatest vote potential and whether he or she has the stretch and adaptability to reach it.

Consider how differently this problem of typecasting was handled by two politicians, Senators Bill Bradley and John Glenn, who had strong images from their pre-political lives.[16] After Bradley was elected to the Senate, he faced the problem of countering the negative impact of his star-athlete past. His solution was to decline to discuss that past and to work hard to prove himself a loyal, hardworking member of the Democratic team. His strategy was to specialize in narrow, technical issues, where he could exhibit his expertise and enhance his reputation as being substantive. It must be noted that Bradley would probably not have been elected to the Senate without his sports background, and that his sports celebrity opened many doors for him as a Senate newcomer. However, in establishing a type, he purposely emphasized *scholar* and not *athlete*. In contrast, Senator John Glenn of Ohio failed to reposition his typing as astronaut hero. When running for president in 1983 and 1984, he clearly was counting on a film about the early astronauts, *The Right Stuff*, to launch his candidacy. "They're waiting for that movie," said a Mondale strategist with disgust of the nascent John Glenn presidential campaign. "They're hoping that it will sell John Glenn to this country like *E.T.*"[17] But the film did little for Glenn's flagging presidential aspirations, demonstrating that the typecasting problem needs to be carefully thought through.

Sometimes an aspirant is too successful in choosing a type. After all, the need may arise to completely shed the type. But type erasure is not that easy. Many aspirants become "stuck" in their initially adopted type. They suffer from overtyping and rarely succeed in escaping. Yankee owner George Steinbrenner, real estate magnate Donald Trump, and former United Nations ambassador Jeane Kirkpatrick cannot shed their typecasting as tough guys; Sean Connery has a hard time escaping his James

Bond typing. On the other hand, aspirants who avoid type choice suffer from undertyping; by failing to select a clearly recognizable type, they reduce their chances for immediate identification. The lesson is that aspirants have to carefully sail between the Scylla of overtyping and the Charybdis of undertyping.

Developing the Character. After choosing the specific type to play, such as the "tough guy" type of businessperson or the "girl next door" type of singer, the third step in concept generation calls for filling out the type with a rounded, believable character. "Tough guy" is only an abstraction; it must be fleshed out, made whole, and given texture. That different characters might exemplify tough guys is clear; there are striking differences between film tough guys Humphrey Bogart and Clint Eastwood, between business tough guys Sam Walton, chairman of Walmart, and Harold Geneen, former chairman of ITT. Richard Dyer, in his book *Stars*, listed nine qualities that can contribute to creating an effective and believable character[18]:

1. *Particularity.* The person should have characteristics that are distinct.
2. *Interest.* The person's concrete traits should command interest.
3. *Autonomy.* The person should not be perfectly predictable; he or she should create "the illusion of life in front of us."
4. *Roundness.* The person should not be one-dimensional but have many traits, not all of them apparent at first.
5. *Development.* The person should reveal change or new aspects over time.
6. *Interiority.* Characters should communicate their thoughts or attitudes not only through their words but also through their actions; observers should be able to discern these attitudes without the characters' explaining them directly.
7. *Motivation.* The person's behavior should be motivated, rather than appear random or habitual.
8. *Discrete identity.* The person should be seen in part as playing a role and also be seen as having a self apart from the role.
9. *Consistency.* The person carries an overall consistency in spite of multiple traits and development over time.

An excellent example of developing character in a celebrity is Miss Piggy, the inanimate creation of author Frank Oz and puppeteer Jim Henson.[19] Miss Piggy's typing is well set; clearly, she is a heroine who gets what she wants through competitive, sometimes unorthodox, strategies. Miss Piggy, labeled by her own creators as "a femme fatale gowned in satin and blessed with a pulverizing left hook," fits Klapp's "love queen" type.[20] It is not incidental to her typing strategy that Miss Piggy is a popular pin-up who is seen in all manners of porcine pin-up poses.

More important, the character of Miss Piggy demonstrates that different traits are important in communicating character. Although she is a complete fabrication, Miss Piggy has most of the characteristics and reactions of a person: Unlike many puppets, Miss Piggy is a multidimensional pig. Besides her girth she has many of the traits that define *roundness*. Although Miss Piggy finds herself drawn to the security of family life with "Kermie," her beloved frog, she also likes the glamour and fame of her position. In her personal life, she struggles with all the insecurities and self-doubts that mark most of our lives.

Miss Piggy also demonstrates *autonomy* through her notorious unpredictability. Like many humans, she displays a wide range of reactions to situations. *People* magazine observed of Miss Piggy:

> One instant [she is] playing the Arrogant Superstar snarling at her beefy litter bearers as she finishes her big Cleopatra scene: "Awright, meat! Let's move it!" The next she is Daddy's little darling, giggling and cooing: "I'll only be an eeeeentsy-teensy minute! Kissy, Kissy!" Then without warning she drops a karate chop on a luckless reporter who has enquired about her weight problem.[21]

In the area of *character development*, Miss Piggy continues to grow and change. She was, after all, the first pig to move into a writing career. Finding a need to grow beyond her television and film career, Miss Piggy moved into diet and exercise guides. It would not be unexpected to see Miss Piggy, finding celebrity a chore, move to Switzerland or take up with an European count.

Clearly, concept generation involves choosing a specific type within the given role, and then making the type distinct and memorable by creating a unique character. That even an inanimate object like Miss Piggy can be so convincing demonstrates how complete the development process can be and how important each step is.

CONCEPT REGENERATION

The concept generation stage can begin at any time in a person's career. It can be a pure start with few preconceptions. Or the process can be used to remake a person after their original concept has worn out.

To help understand how concept generation might operate, consider the possibilities which face dancer Juliet Prowse. Prowse had enjoyed a long, lucrative career as a Las Vegas headline showdancer. A native of South Africa, the long-legged, red-haired dancer had an elaborate performance aided by her support staff of personal manager Mark Murdoh, choreographers, and musicians. But the career of Prowse was endangered when her physical aging began to affect her ability to perform the high kicks of her trade. What new concepts could be generated to help Prowse remain highly visible?

There are many. Prowse still enjoys high name recognition and can be counted on to draw attention across the country. A first regeneration choice might be a relaunching as a Broadway musical performer who sings and acts—and dances very little. The opportunities for marketing Prowse as this type are excellent because of the similarities between the audiences in her new theater venue and her old Vegas one, and her experience in London theater of the same type. A second choice might be to move Prowse into the soap opera sector following the typing strategies used by other aging performers. Prowse might even be repositioned as a cable TV talk show hostess, a commercial spokesperson, or the inspiration for a chain of dance studios for students of ballet. As for anyone in any sector, if Prowse decides to pursue any of these possibilities, each choice will have to be weighed in terms of the degree of transformation required, and the expense necessary, to make her concept operable.

Just as athletes must generate new concepts as their abilities decline, so does the need for concept regeneration arise when a person has been overtyped. Jamie Farr, a journeyman and unemployed actor who had been writing game shows, had spent many years in training for fame when he was cast as Corporal Maxwell Klinger in the hit TV series "M*A*S*H."[22] His eleven-year stint as the idiosyncratic soldier brought great success, yet it left him overtyped. Farr's problem was to generate a new concept to overcome "Klinger's" seemingly indelible imprint on the audience's conception of Farr. The goal was not impossible: Sally Field landed after her stint in "The Flying Nun" and played Norma Rae, while Ronald Reagan, who played a multitude of lightweight types, evolved to become General Electric's spokesman on entrepreneurship and, eventually, President of the United States.

How might Farr actively change his type, should he decide to do so? First, he would have to consult with the various contributors to the concept design process, including agents, PR people, mentors, venue managers, and others. They might agree that Farr should be evaluated in a number of different roles, some not in acting. Does he have political potential? Can he start a business around his name? What types of game shows might be interested? Can he launch a career as a professional speaker? All these concepts need to be winnowed to the final few that can be tested.

Just as is concept generation, concept *re*generation is an essential part of the pursuit of high visibility. The people involved need to be open-minded, not limited by preconceptions or conventional thinking. Can religious leader Pat Robertson reposition himself after his shift to politics? Can a Los Angeles businessperson be launched with the same concept of public-service-minded New York business leader Felix Rohatyn? Having absorbed John Cougar Mellencamp, can the pop music sector absorb yet another Bruce Springsteen imitator? The way to answer all these speculations is through *concept testing*.

CONCEPT TESTING

Once the aspirant has selected the most promising concepts, the next step is to test them for feasibility: Can the aspirant convincingly play the role and type? Will the result attract a sufficiently large-size audience? Some concepts are not easily testable because the stakes are too high. When Lee Iacocca was hired by Chrysler after being fired from Ford, there was little foreshadowing of his potential to become a business icon. In its dark days of threatened bankruptcy, Chrysler's ad agency gambled that Iacocca's feisty, straightforward style, aided by his visibility, could sell cars. This was hardly a low-risk trial. Iacocca was chairman of the board, and his ad pitch was the only thing standing between solvency and Chrysler's joining Packard and Studebaker as famous extinct car names.

The risks and costs involved in testing a concept are, for most of us, considerably lower. In most sectors of public life, there are inexpensive, low-risk venues in which to test if your concept is workable and attractive to audiences. If Juliet Prowse wants to find out if she is Broadway star material, she can go to Houston or Mobile and test her new concept in a road show. In fact, her personal manager might not inform the media of her appearances in these trial venues so that Prowse could try out her new role in relative safety and seclusion.

The number and range of trial venues is vast. A trial venue can be as simple as football giant William "Refrigerator" Perry appearing on local radio and television shows to test his media personality before appearing on the David Letterman and Johnny Carson shows. In actuality, Perry, approaching the peak of his popularity, appeared at a tiny barbecue establishment, Hecky's Bar-B-Q. in Evanston, Illinois, so that his planners could gauge public reaction to Perry's concept. The experiment yielded encouraging results. Said Hecky, "I got a million dollars' worth of advertisement for $300"[23] (the contractual fee for which the forward-looking Hecky had signed the Fridge before he achieved visibility). Evidence of a successful test, twenty-five-hundred people showed up at the corner rib shack to see the Fridge.

Ideally, rising celebrities should test their concepts at higher and higher levels of exposure. Many politicians, trying some new ideas or even a new image, first appear in small, non-media covered rallies to test for a reaction. An excellent example of effective testing is celebrity hair stylist and beauty consultant Vincent Roppatte, who not only styles the Miss America pageant but also serves Jamie Lee Curtis, Phyllis George Brown, Liza Minnelli, and Kathleen Turner. Roppatte began testing his concepts in high school, finishing 1,000 hours of hairdressing experience before graduating. He tested his concept again at seventeen years of age by entering the World International Hairdressing Competition and winning.[24] At the contest, he met celebrity hair stylist Enrico Caruso. While serving as style director for Caruso, for Bergdorf Goodman, and finally at Salon Vincent's, he tested a still more sophisticated concept—a total beauty program accenting skin care as well as hairstyle. He wrote a book, *The Looks Men*

Love, which featured a typing system that would make Klapp proud, breaking down his clients into eight different types—from sensual woman to girl next door. The key is that only after testing his program on thousands of women did Roppatte write a book and market his concept nationally. The rigor with which he refined his concept is now apparent in his reward: frequent talk show appearances and introductions as the "world's most famous hair stylist." It is a long way from New Jersey. As Roppatte says, "I was seventeen, and me being . . . not too tall, I looked like two. It made things quite a problem . . . because I didn't look quite authoritative and they wondered just how much experience I had."[25] Roppatte just wasn't ready for national exposure during the early stages of his career. It was only through continuous concept testing that he developed his techniques to the point where he was ready to go public.

There are other ways to test a concept. One highly useful technique is to test the concept with *focus groups:* groups of people who are invited to discuss in detail a product, person, place, organization, or idea. Usually six to ten people meet for a few hours in a comfortable setting and are paid a small fee for their time. The invitees are often selected to match the characteristics of a celebrity's target market, be it a demographic or lifestyle group, or some mix. The discussion is led by a moderator and is audio- or videotaped for later analysis by skilled interpreters. In the political and entertainment sectors, focus groups are commonly used to generate feedback on a concept. In most cases, the focus group is used to react to specific proposed products and images. Depending upon focus-group reactions, a concept can either be refined or discarded. Aspirants who can afford focus group testing will find the groups to be a valuable resource.

There are other testing procedures for different components of the concept. An aspirant can test a new look by appearing at basketball games or charity affairs. A party attended by opinion leaders can be the site of a test for a particular look. Some planners will look for such events to use as a test situation. New concepts can also be tested on family members and friends.

TEST FLIGHT OF THE PHOENIX, PART I

Pia Zadora was in trouble. Despite massive investment by her husband, Meshulam Riklis, Zadora, a petite blond with a baby-doll's face, had found her film and popular music careers savaged by the critics. After appearing in the critically reviled *Butterfly* and *Lonely Lady*, Zadora had a career decision to make. Looking back on her concept options, Zadora said, "I could have done a whole other row of sleazy movies that everybody called me for after *Butterfly* and *Lonely Lady*. But I said no. . . . I could have become the Marilyn Chambers of the R-rated movies, or done TV. I've been offered a lot of TV offers: soap operas, 'Dynasty,' and all that stuff. But it's nothing I would really want to do."[26] Given her sector goals, she generated a brand-new concept: to reappear as a traditional songstress, using Barbra Streisand as her concept model. To try to avoid the failures of her past concepts, Zadora and her advisors decided to approach the new concept strategically.

A new album of old standards recorded by Zadora and the London Philharmonic Orchestra, "Pia and Phil," provided the material that Zadora would test. But *where* to test? Rather than open the show, titled "Standards of Excellence," in New York or Los Angeles, or even in downtown Chicago, Zadora did her experimenting in the Chicago suburb of Oak Brook, Illinois. The scene at the Sunday-afternoon matinee was a prime demonstration of the testing mode: a handful of people sitting inside the commodious Drury Lane Theater, virtually outnumbered by the forty-piece orchestra arrayed across the stage. Zadora, striding on stage to faint applause, went through her act as if playing to a packed house of loyal fans. In her dressing room later, Zadora described the choice of Drury Lane as a "test site" in which to work out the kinks in her act while incurring the lowest possible costs. And kinks there were. As critic Patricia Smith wrote, "Pia should travel no farther than her shower with these intricate song stylings. . . . The well trained (and obviously well paid) orchestra did a great job making her sound like Streisand. If you closed your eyes, that is. And your ears."[27]

Responded Pia, "These reviews weren't reviews, they were personal attacks. . . . Sure I'm not Barbra Streisand. She's different. I'm different. I'm just starting, and it's scary, but I'm doing it." Saying the critics loved to "rain on her parade," Zadora spoke of her successes in Europe, and of her conviction that with additional testing and fine tuning, her new concept would succeed.

Concept testing can defy the logic of publicity and media exposure. Under normal circumstances, aspirants seek the greatest reach possible. In testing, however, the aspirant desires a small, controlled exposure. Media vehicles such as *Rolling Stone* magazine might be *too* highly visible to serve as a test-marketing device for an experimental concept; if *any* medium is used for testing, it should be a local medium, with the lower circulation and entry cost that can help aspirants test a new image, story, or concept without serious consequences if the concept is rejected.

Many successful celebrities have resorted to test situations as they evolved. Garrison Keillor, who for most people suddenly emerged as a modern-day Will Rogers on his radio program "Prairie Home Companion," began testing his concept in Collegeville, Minnesota, on a local radio show. Moreover, Keillor was writing his homespun pieces in *The New Yorker* years before he broke through as a nationwide phenomenon and bestselling author. He was testing. And, as we will soon see, he was transforming.

CONCEPT REFINEMENT

Once aspirants have found and tested an effective concept, they need to refine it carefully. In many cases this process is conducted by coaches, trainers, and consultants who are retained for specific tasks. The retinue of advisors may include media consultant Jack Hilton, who says, "I can make virtually anyone more acceptable and more palatable on television"[28] or, someone like Nadine Bowers, who, while serving as fashion advisor for Miss Illinois, selected the right clothing and appearance for the candidate.

The necessary advice, for a price, is available for aspirants in most sectors. There are people who can teach you to walk, talk, sit, argue, cross-examine, reflect, preach, paint, or drive race cars. The strategy is to coordinate these coaching skills to produce a cohesive product. To help ensure that the aspirant's concept is refined as thoroughly as possible, seven areas must be addressed:

- Signs and symbols
- Name
- Appearance (face and hair, stature, clothing)
- Voice (tone, accent, diction)
- Movement (gesture, walk)
- Behavior
- Material

We will examine each in turn.

SIGNS AND SYMBOLS

According to Erving Goffman, people "infuse [their] activity with signs which dramatically highlight and portray confirmatory facts that might otherwise remain unapparent or obscure."[29] They enact behaviors designed to signify something and to produce desired responses in others. This is the first way that an aspirant communicates his or her type and character: through signs and symbols.

Consider someone who wants to project the image of "tough guy." No matter what the sector, the aspirant must choose signs that communicate this type and that identify the aspirant as having a distinct character. The signs include clothing, gestures, facial expressions, walk, and many others. In Western culture, a black leather jacket, a sneer or growl, a swaggering walk conveys the tough guy. Oakland Raiders owner Al Davis acts and dresses like a tough guy to reinforce his personal, and his team's, image. Colonel Harlan Sanders's old-fashioned clothing symbolized quality and attention to value. Symbols are particularly useful for organizations that wish to make specific impressions on their audiences. Purdue University's marching band, the largest in the country, features the Golden Girl, the lead twirler whose image includes a gold-sequined outfit, white boots, and, most prominently, long, blond hair. These symbols add up to a complete impression. According to Bill Moffett, director of bands, the Golden Girl represents "...what Purdue stands for, and young girls and Americana everywhere."[30]

By choosing the appropriate signs, aspirants convey their types to the audience. Some signs by themselves, however, may be ambiguous. A black leather jacket may evoke an image of a tough guy, but it can also conjure up an outdoorsman or a person who appreciates fine goods. A fist can signify an act of defiance or challenge; it could also signify a person in pain. Symbols may have a number of possible meanings, and that is part of their richness.

The aspirant, however, should try to avoid clichés (overused, stereotyped symbols that lack freshness and bore audiences). For the tough guy, too much scowling, swaggering, or threatening may interfere with projecting a believable character. Actress Susan Hayward, in the early stages of her career, relied on exaggerated sultriness and overdone gestures in an attempt to satisfy her conception of audience expectations. But it was not until she abandoned such behavior for a more natural style that she achieved greater fan loyalty, attracted more media coverage, and ultimately won an Academy Award.

Name. One's name is a particular sign, one that can convey a great deal about the name's owner. For this reason, many aspirants change their birth names in pursuit of high visibility. In the entertainment sector, name changing is an established tradition; in other sectors, such as business and politics, name changing may produce more costs than benefits. In 1984, candidate Gary Hart suffered adverse publicity when it was revealed that he had changed his name from Hartpence to Hart—a clue, according to some commentators, that Hart wasn't "authentic" enough to be president. In business, name changing is even less tolerated, unless it is minor: substituting the friendly Bobby for Robert, or using formal initials instead of full names. In sectors where name changing is more acceptable, aspirants should choose names that are congruent with their characters. Certain names would be clear liabilities for a planned character. A male actor whose first name is Fran might not even be considered to play a tough guy. An actress whose name is Zelda Dinkelheimer might have credibility problems trying to project the archetype of love goddess. If an actor's name were John Smith or an actress' Jane Adams, these names would not necessarily impede success in playing these types. The drawback is that neutral names neither reinforce aspirants' types nor create distinctiveness.

A name change can have a dramatic effect on the audience's perception of an aspirant. Early in his career, Keillor "changed his name from Gary to Garrison to create a pseudonym worthy of [*The New Yorker*'s] august pages."[31] The name Garrison carries with it impressions of a bygone era. The name suggests that Keillor was part of the bucolic countryside where his quaint tales are based. In reality, Keillor grew up in the Minneapolis suburb of Anoka, where parents would be hard-pressed to get away with calling their son Garrison. Keillor is a performer who has adeptly refined his concept, transforming himself into what America always needed—another Will Rogers.

Name changing is a very common step for aspirants in the entertainment world. Natalie Wood was born Natasha Gurdin, a name that would have served her well had she aspired to be a writer, but would have been a hindrance in her pursuit of film sector visibility. Following are the original and new names of well-known entertainers. How many of us would know these celebrities if we saw only their birth names at the left?

• Allen Konigsberg	Woody Allen
• Charles Buchinsky	Charles Bronson
• Bette Joan Perske	Lauren Bacall
• Issur Danielovitch Demsky	Kirk Douglas
• Joseph Levitch	Jerry Lewis
• Mladen Sekulovich	Karl Malden
• Benjamin Kubelsky	Jack Benny
• Catherine Dorleac	Catherine Deneuve
• Melvin Kaminsky	Mel Brooks
• Elliot Gouldstein	Elliott Gould
• Bernard Schwartz	Tony Curtis
• William Henry Pratt	Boris Karloff
• Maria Calogeropoulos	Maria Callas
• Henry John Deutschendorf, Jr.	John Denver
• Truman Streckfus Persons	Truman Capote
• David Green	David Ben-Gurion
• Josif V. Dzhugashvili	Joseph Stalin
• Robert Zimmerman	Bob Dylan
• Maria Rosario Pilar Martinez Melina Baeza	Charo

• Arnold Dorsey	Engelbert Humperdinck
• Leslie Hornby	Twiggy
• Yitzroch Loiza Grossberg	Larry Rivers
• John Paul "Jack" Rosenberg	Werner Erhard
• Roy Halston Frowick	Halston
• Demetrios George Synodinos	Jimmy the Greek
• Henri Donat Mathieu	Yves St. Laurent

Some of these aspirants changed their names to conceal their ethnic origins, others to shorten their names. Interestingly, aspirants within certain sectors have begun to change their American names into foreign names to gain character and credibility. They perceive that an ethnic name carries more weight in their sector, and this is the very reason why British ballerina Lillian Marks changed her name to Alicia Markova. Young American violinists could go further if they changed their names to Russian or Eastern European names such as Horowitz, Perlman, and Oistrakh. One of the authors met an art appraiser who went by the invented name of Sigmund Rothschild, a name that suggests a European of great taste and wealth.

The aspirant whose name is a liability needs to generate a list of new names, just as a company does when it needs a name for a new brand of soap or ice cream. Thus an American ice cream company chooses "Haagen-Dazs" to suggest northern European origins for its ice cream, even though the words are meaningless in any language.

Once names are generated, they have to be evaluated according to certain criteria:

- *Memorability*: Names that are easy to remember and pronounce are preferred. Generally, shorter names are easier to remember. Names that call up pictures, such as Evel Knievel or Slim Pickens, are also easier to remember.
- *Suitability*: Names that reinforce the aspirant's chosen character are preferred. Some people are fortunate to be born with names which project their later images: Oscar Renta reverted to his family name "de la" to sound like a designer; John Kenneth Galbraith was born with an academic sounding name. Many others need to change complete names to achieve suitability, as in the case of Marion Morrison's changing his name to John Wayne. Such name changes help to round out the desired image.

- *Distinctiveness*: Actors John Hurt and William Hurt can easily be confused. There are more than a dozen Johnsons in the National Basketball League, but only one Spud Webb.

An example of a name change that was memorable, suitable, and distinctive is that of the former Steveland Morris Hardaway, a young blind musician who auditioned for Berry Gordy, was signed to a contract, and was given a new name on the spot—Stevie Wonder.[32]

Ideally, one or a few names will pass these tests. If not, the original name may have to stand. Currently, more aspirants with ethnic names are keeping them: Daniel J. Travanti, Rosanna Arquette, and Harvey Fierstein, among others. In sports, players often stick with their names but acquire or create nicknames that give them memorability: Babe always meant Babe Ruth; Chrissy, Chris Evert; Charlie Hustle, Pete Rose; and Dr. K, Dwight Gooden. Aspirants have to decide whether their names are signs that support or subtract from their intended characters; if the latter, changing the name might be warranted.

Appearance. Many of the cues to character are visual, including impressions that come from an aspirant's face, hairstyle, stature, and clothing.

Certain types require certain faces to play them. A woman wanting to be cast as a seductress should probably have a beautiful face, clear skin, straight teeth, and fine features. On the other hand, a tough-guy type enjoys a broad range of faces: They can be weathered as Chuck Norris's, baby-faced as Tony Perkins', handsome as Sylvester Stallone's. In politics, business, or religion, the appearance latitude is even greater. For the first fifteen years of his career, evangelical celebrity Josh McDowell spoke mostly to students.[33] But as he was forced to adapt to an older audience, he altered his facial appearance and clothing to project a more businesslike image.

Aspirants may attempt to enhance the impact of their appearance through such extreme techniques as plastic surgery. Sometimes, the surgery is narrowly targeted, as when Mariel Hemingway had surgery to increase her breast size for her role in Bob Fosse's *Star 80*. More often, aspirants attempt to bring their features into line with classically accepted notions of beauty or good looks.

Many of the techniques that can change appearance come from the old Hollywood factory system, whose fashion designers, makeup artists, and body rejuvenators were the best at their trade. Their laundry list of innovations, according to Penny Stallings, included "lip gloss, false fingernails, hair sprays, setting lotions, toupées, body makeup, many hair dyes and lighteners, hair weaving, cold cream, skin freshener, and false eyelashes, not to mention various kinds of prostheses for augmenting body parts."[34] It was in Hollywood that it became common to fix noses, straighten teeth, eliminate body hair—to generally create "perfect" people.

Today, appearance modification is common in many non-entertainment sectors. The refinement of a football player often includes the use of appearance transformation. William "Refrigerator" Perry had a gap-toothed look that damaged his potential as an endorser. He needed the gap look for identity and comic effect; yet for long-term career goals he needed a mainstream, mature look. The answer was a removable tooth.

As for an aspirant's stature, not much can be done. A person's body type, whether ectomorph, mesomorph, or endomorph, is pretty much given. Dudley Moore, Michael J. Fox, and Linda Hunt, aside from elevator shoes, are going to remain quite short, which, because of their intelligent positioning, has worked to their advantage. Other performers with unalterable physical characteristics require adroit camera work to disguise their problems.

Even with advances in surgery, an aspirant's body type is relatively fixed. But there are many opportunities to transmit messages about character through adroit clothing choice. Color, style, fabric, texture, and other elements can all be manipulated to create distinct "looks."

DRESSING FOR EXCESS, PART I

Artist Robert Fischer looks the part. Cloaked in a tentlike bag of burlap, his head covered in a Che Guevara–style beret, Fischer enters a room jangling from dozens of necklaces and chains hung with odd objects, looking for all the world like the dictator of some imaginary Third World country. His clothing projects the character of a man outside not only mainstream society, but even outside the art world. His unique appearance has helped him position himself as a guru of art in the urban environment, allowing him to reinforce and give depth to his credibility in his primary sector. Fischer's clothes become more than just a sign, but an active prospecting tool for new work, as his appearance communicates his confidence, playfulness, subversiveness, and willingness to take chances.

Politicians usually wear business suits—unless they are trying to project the image of a different type of politician. When Jimmy Carter wore blue jeans, it suggested his Southern informality and peanut farmer origins and helped distinguish him from his competition. The point is that each role and type has a cultural dress code. Depending on whether they are seeking to meet audience expectations or strategically break them, aspirants need to obey or ignore these codes accordingly. For example, clothing can be used to alter impressions of size. What can a short political candidate do to appear authoritative? James G. Gray, Jr., an image and wardrobe consultant who runs a Washington, D.C., firm, Image Impact, says, "The small person needs to appear more authoritarian to maximize status and minimize lack of height. They also need to create a presence. I always suggest high authority, dark clothing—a pinstripe suit, a white, button-down shirt—because contrast is very important for a small person. It adds dimension and depth."[35]

At the same time, the politician must show some flexibility within the cultural code, depending on the event. Attending a large fund-raising Texas barbecue in a pinstripe suit would probably draw negative comments. Candidates, as well as all aspirants, generally try to wear the clothing appropriate to the setting.

Although adjusting one's clothing to different settings is called for, dress consistency is just as important. The political candidate who wears a regular tie one day and a bow tie the next will send inconsistent signals; these, when magnified by the media, can dilute image impact.

Ideally, when clothes are used well to define character, they become an extension of the aspirant's personality. In their best possible use, they become trademarks: Franklin Delano Roosevelt's cigarette holder, Dan Rather's sweater, T. Boone Pickens' cowboy boots, Senator Paul Simon's bow tie, Cyndi Lauper's orange hair and jangling jewelry, and Red Auerbach's cigar.

Voice. "You see this creature with her kerbstone English, the English that will keep 'er in the gutter to the end of her days," says Henry Higgins. "Well, sir, in three months I could pass that girl off as a duchess at an ambassador's garden party."[36]

The aspirant's voice—its tone, accent, and diction—is another important conveyor of character. It can also be a liability. We mentioned earlier that John Gilbert, the great lover in silent films, lost his career when his voice on his first "talkie" sounded thin and whiny, not deep and masculine. A frequent criticism of Walter Mondale was that he spoke in a monotone, a charge so widely echoed that many politicians are questioning their own vocal impact. Fortunately, training can alter voices within limits.

Accent is also important. To be candidates for national anchor positions, TV newscasters must shed their Southern drawls or Boston accents; the Midwest accent is the broadcaster's norm. Foreign accents can be a liability in some careers, while in others, they can be an asset. Henry Kissinger sounds more profound and worldly because of his German accent. The same words uttered in unaccented, American English would not make as deep an impression.

Another dimension of voice is diction, the ability to speak the language correctly, clearly, and effectively. We saw how Eliza Doolittle was doomed to be a flower girl all her life if stuck with her Cockney dialect. Diction is still perceived as an indicator of one's class origins and, thus, character. Mayor Richard J. Daley of Chicago, with his "dems" and "deys," clearly was a favorite of the Chicago working class but could not run for president without a more refined style. Many aspirants of lower-class origin consciously learn middle-class language as they rise in visibility. Conversely, middle-class actors who want to play "street" characters need lessons in language downgrading. With the increasing importance of media to celebrity-manufacturing in all sectors, a premium is placed on language skills, and voice trainers have emerged as a sub-industry.

I CAN'T HEAR YOU

Business magazines are strong advocates of voice enhancement, advising people to go to acting teachers and coaches, to stand on their heads and chant, to invest heavily in voice improvement. The reason is that as we move in our society from content and substance toward image and style, people are taking voice as an indicator that the person has all the necessary *real* characteristics for success. Resolution, conviction, and moral character are all thought to be revealed in the voice. How far has this gone? One of our researchers was interviewing a leading CEO, a man well known for such old-style qualities as intelligence, leadership ability, and evaluation skills. Despite it all, the CEO turned to our interviewer and pronounced, "I'd never hire you! You have a weak voice."

End of interview.

Movement. What is the relationship between movement and character? In most sectors of visibility, movement has three general dimensions. First, there is usually a premium placed on naturalness, on movements which show that aspirants are at home in their sectors. Secondly, movements need to communicate a sense that aspirants are in control over whatever situation is at hand. Thirdly, movements are used to create a personal style.

In the business sector, one enters an office and immediately begins to collect impressions from people's nonverbal cues: How comfortable does he seem in his environment? Does she have a brisk walk that suggests youthfulness and determination? Or is it a slow, shuffling style, communicating that she is unhappy in her job? An example of how all three dimensions work together in a different sector is TV celebrity Bryant Gumbel. As host of the "Today" show, Gumbel must appear relaxed and aware, but he achieves this impression only through skillful handling of movement. His easy swiveling between interviewees, his inconspicuous style of looking at his lists of questions, his natural way of hunching forward on the couch to probe an interviewee more deeply—all add up to impressions of credibility.

In the sports sector, consider how movements vary among major basketball coaches. They can be fuming like Bobby Knight of Indiana, laid back like Dean Smith of North Carolina, or theatrical and dramatic like Jerry Tarkanian of the University of Nevada–Las Vegas. Yet in spite of these movement differences, all three coaches express an alertness, an awareness of contact, orchestrating the relationship among the court, the bench, and the officials. They point, they rally the crowd, they kneel with their players, and, in packed stadiums, they manage to close off distractions and discuss strategy. All three coaches, while using very distinct broad styles, have all mastered the key movement requirements of their sectors.

Behavior. That one's behavior communicates one's character was well expressed by the great acting coach Konstantin Stanislavski. As explained by Sonia Moore, Stanislavski believed that:

> It is important for an actor to see the character he builds in terms of actions. In two and a half hours on the stage, an actor must project 'the life of a human spirit'; during every moment, therefore, he must use actions which will express that life. [In the Stanislavski System], if an action helps to express the character, it is artistically right; if it does not, it is wrong. An action cannot be accidental or superfluous. The choice of actions must be guided by the main idea of the play and of the role.[37]

In achieving their transformations, aspirants should try to convincingly portray their characters not just on stage, but in all facets of life. Still, the acting principle applies: Certain behaviors are culturally consistent with certain characters, others not. Queen Elizabeth is not going to curse, gorge herself, or dance in discos. It is appropriate for her to act with dignity, coolness, even aloofness. Yet this would be counterproductive behavior for other highly visible people. When Adlai E. Stevenson III was running for U.S. Senator in Illinois, the political strategists counseled him to be less aloof. They felt that he couldn't draw votes and excite the precinct captains unless he started showing up at local ward meetings, picnics, and fish frys, where he could seem more like a people's candidate. His behavior did not contribute to the goal he wanted to reach.

HAIL TO THE CHIEF

Behavior can severely affect the public's attitudes toward celebrities. There are, after all, behaviors that accent and support an image, and those that can destroy it. Ronald Reagan, in his first presidential debate with Walter Mondale, seemed confused. He frequently lost his place, spoke haltingly, and ended his presentation with a strange, rambling, unfinished tale of a drive down California's coast.

Before the candidates had walked off stage, questions were being urgently raised. Was a single public debate too much for the seventy-three-year-old president to handle? Could the public put its trust in someone who might be approaching senility?

To counter the impact of this negative voter perception, Reagan's strategists immediately put a plan into action. The strategy was to dramatize Reagan's physical energy, communicating a sense that he was mentally energetic as well. The result was Ronald Reagan in perpetual motion: springing from helicopters, striding at full speed, dashing pell-mell from one appearance to the next. Purposeful, dynamic, assertive, aware—all these qualities were transmitted by simple behavior. He quickly recovered his old ratings in the polls.

The definition of culturally acceptable behavior changes over time. In business, the range of acceptable behaviors has widened considerably. More organizations are adopting the independent behavior of entrepreneurism. Even office romance is increasing, as more companies tacitly approve of such behavior. In politics, divorce among leaders is now routinely accepted by voters. Even film stars find more liberal public sentiment toward their behavior. When Elizabeth Taylor drew Eddie Fisher away from Debbie Reynolds and broke up their marriage, her popularity fell. Ingrid Bergman's career plummeted when she abandoned her husband and child to live with Roberto Rossellini. Today, the public's attitude toward these affairs of the heart is totally different. Actors and actresses not only live together out of wedlock but some are proud to have their babies born this way: Farrah Fawcett had Ryan O'Neal's baby and preferred to live with O'Neal rather than marry him. Still, there are limits to public acceptability, and failure to heed cultural taboos can be disastrous for the aspirant. When Vanessa Williams was exposed as a former nude model, she not only lost her crown as Miss America but was barred from many venues in her sector, entertainment.

A highly visible person can use a change in behavior to reshape an entire institution. During the early 1980s, many consumers saw Ford Motor Company's cars as frumpy, staid, and not in tune with the marketplace. The new chairman of the board, Donald Petersen, decided to change Ford's image and ordered the design and manufacture of futuristic-looking, European-handling cars. He also signaled to automobile journalists and writers his company's new image by personally attending Bob Bondurant's race driving school. The new Ford president learned the fine art of heel and toe shifting and cornering at high speed. The automobile industry took his unusual behavior as clear evidence that Ford was serious. He was refining his concept and also affecting the image of his institution.

Painter Ed Paschke modified his behavior in order to project a certain character.[38] Early in his art career, Paschke realized that his introverted personality was impeding the promotion of his art. To improve his success in selling paintings to galleries, Paschke took to going out on the street with a tape recorder and conducting newspaper-style interviews with strangers. By doing so, he was able to improve a critical area of his behavior—his interpersonal communication and presentation of self—and more clearly express the artist's character. He is now one of America's most celebrated contemporary painters.

Material. "Material" is the content that the performer brings to the public. A preacher needs attention-getting material for his sermons. He needs to incorporate controversial interpretations, inspiring stories, community concerns, or political issues to help refine his image with his congregation. Actors and actresses must also choose their material carefully. If an actor plays comedy roles early in his career, this material may get in his way later when he wants to switch to playing drama. Politicians must also develop their material carefully. Their messages—speeches, press conferences, statements, and advertisements—must carry the content and tone that will win the most votes.

The refinement of Miss Piggy exemplifies the importance of material. Her performance material—songs, scenes, books, interviews—allows her to exhibit a number of human feelings. In addition, Miss Piggy's communication settings feature her relationships with people and not just puppets. Her writers and string pullers have an excellent sense of audience perception of real feelings.

Paschke, too, conveys his character through his adroit choice of material. According to Paschke, "Everyone likes a sick artist."[39] So, at one point in his career he specialized in grotesque paintings of burlesque performers, lady wrestlers, and a range of deformed adults. He followed this series of paintings with a fairly sudden move into painting nothing but shoes for two years. The shoes were featured as suffering from many of the ailments of contemporary man—acne, varicose veins, even flashy tattoos. Paschke's material was essential to projecting a certain character: the somewhat unpredictable artist at the cutting edge—a character that is extremely effective with audiences in the art sector.

TV evangelist Reverend Cecil Todd's use of material is a textbook case of helping refine character.[40] In his press releases, books, and statements, Todd emphasizes his humble origins, his close companionship with his "lovely wife, Linda," and his upstanding lifestyle. These are, of course, the kinds of pronouncements that are required material for most preachers; but Todd's material is considerably better than most. Early in his career, to build his reputation as a crusader, he excoriated sinners with special verve, going so far as to write sermons with titles like "Four People in Town That I Would Like to See Go to Hell." It is hard to imagine better hellfire-and-brimstone material than that.

Todd has always produced interesting, character-reinforcing material. "I was the first person to put Reagan on national television in a Christian setting. . . . I put him on two hundred stations prime time in 1973 and then I came back and did another interview with Reagan when he was running for president."[41] In his fight to restore prayers in the schools, Todd not only wrote speeches arguing for the change, but submitted one million petition signatures to President Reagan, which was the largest number of petitions ever brought to the White House on any issue. Todd even used atheist Madalyn Murray O'Hair's son Bill, who disagreed with his mother, to give testimony. Following in his father's innovative footsteps, Todd's son Tim learned to throw his voice, and now preaches with the help of his puppet, Friend Freddy.

Auditing the Transformation. Aspirants need to undertake considerable work to develop and refine a fully believable character. They must understand the role, choose the most fitting type of person to project, and distinguish themselves from competitors by developing a convincing character through the choice of signs, name, appearance, voice, movement, behavior, and material.

But this process never ends. Aspirants and celebrities must periodically reassess their public images to see whether the image they are trying to transmit and the one the audience receives are the same. When the public image departs too much from the intended one, work must be undertaken to repair or revise it. Image-makers must help aspirants both monitor their images and improve them.

TEST FLIGHT OF THE PHOENIX, PART II: THE PHOENIX FLIES

Pia Zadora's test site performances in the Chicago suburbs revealed a number of serious problems. Her performance was marked by amplification levels that were ear-splittingly loud, awkward moments between songs where the audience was left baffled by jarring transitions, stage movements that at times seemed pointless or misdirected, and exaggerated gestures that seemed to parody other singers rather than be part of Zadora's authentic character. The cumulative effect was that Zadora had failed to refine an image that had been so painstakingly launched.

The act needed to be brought back into the shop. Zadora needed confidence-building reinforcement, as her new image was about to be delivered to major venues. After seeing her performance, we were skeptical.

Imagine our bafflement when the critical reviews from Zadora's New York and Los Angeles openings were spectacular. According to esteemed *Los Angeles Times* critic Leonard Feather, the concert was "a musically impeccable evening. . . . She has it all: the range, expert intonation, a sensitive feeling for the lyrics and dynamic variety."[42] Music critic Peter Bloch called Zadora "this year's most pleasant musical surprise." In New York, she sold out

Carnegie Hall. Soon, there was Pia on "Good Morning America," receiving the congratulations of an obviously impressed and somewhat taken aback David Hartman. What had changed?

Because the original concept had been well thought out, it was in the refinement that the mileage was gained. Zadora had the minimum abilities and the proper concept. With her manager, Tino Barzie, Zadora fine-tuned her concept by addressing several of the seven categories of image. Adjustments were made in the amplification of her voice; more realistic stage patter was built in; she was made more conscious of the expansiveness of her gestures; she moved less self-consciously. She may not have been the new Barbra Streisand, as Feather suggested, but she was no longer a lonely lady.

CONCEPT REALIZATION

The question of how extensively and permanently the aspirant is transformed is central to the pursuit of high visibility. The drafting of the blueprint—selecting the right signs, name, appearance, behavior, and other factors—is only part of the creation of the celebrity. To complete their quests for high visibility, aspirants have to realize (make real) the transformation within themselves in order to bring the blueprint to life. Critically, the completeness with which one believes in one's own transformation helps determine how credible the transformed self is with audiences. But first, the most appropriate transformation method must be chosen. There are four primary methods by which aspirants can be helped to realize their transformation.

Behavior Modification. The most common means aspirants use to achieve transformation is behavior modification: the skilled use of rewards and reinforcements to effect changes in behavior. One reason it is so popular is that it is a process with which we all have experience. And it can lead, efficiently, to skills improvement. Trainers instruct aspirants to conduct meetings with authority, sing in a certain manner, walk with long strides, use certain debate tactics, greet patients a particular way. When they perform the "right" way, they are rewarded with smiles, applause, a hundred different ways of encouragement. When they don't carry off the requisite behavior in the right way, there is silence, criticism, or even rebuke. Gradually the aspirant modifies his or her behavior, adopting the characteristics of the role and type desired.

Unfortunately, even when behavior modification is successful, some aspirants do not feel comfortable with the new self: The transformation has not been made "real." Perhaps the changes made are superficial, or the transformer is unskilled or lacks commitment to the process. Aspirants may be *told* that they are transformed but sense a discrepancy between their new selves and the never truly abandoned old selves. When this happens, a deeper transformation technique might be tried.

Role Modeling. Some of the problems of behavior modification are addressed by the second method of transformation. In role modeling, the aspirant is presented with one or more persons to emulate. This can be done in two ways. The role model may work directly with the aspirant as a mentor (coach, teacher, advisor) whose talents and behaviors the aspirant is taught to mirror. According to Mark Morrison, "a mentor relationship involves someone of talent and ability who is attracted to and nurtures someone of talent and ability, and it is reciprocal."[43] The second way consists of aspirants' studying the film clips, recordings, speeches, or writings of established celebrities and modeling themselves after those celebrities.

Direct mentoring is typically more costly and more effective. The mentor can show a great deal of patience, add encouragement, and set the pace for change. As Morrison quotes personal manager Monique James, discussing actress Sharon Gless:

> "Nothing fit," said James. "Her voice, her walk, the way words came out of her mouth." The starmaker [James] used her influence to help get Gless TV guest-starring roles, then took her to watch dailies, helped her refine her talent, and groomed her for larger TV roles.[44]

With James present and involved in every stage of the transformation, the changes made in Gless could be accomplished methodically. They could also be designed with the best interests of the aspirant in mind. Ideally, the aspirant will find a mentor who will place the aspirant's interests above the mentor's. "Mentors are people who are willing to give away a lot of what they know in a noncompetitive way," says psychologist Marilyn Ruman.[45] In such cases, the result may be a more carefully conducted transformation—not the rush to market that may characterize transformations supervised by those with a financial stake in the aspirants' success.

The second type of role model transformation is accomplished when role models mentor aspirants through the media, with the role model never even knowing of the relationship. Singer Elvis Presley arrived at Sun Records in Memphis with a style honed through years of listening to country-and-blues radio programs. He was self-taught and already knew many of the conventions of his sector. While hardly the transformation method of choice, electronic role modeling is often the only method available.

HOW TO SUCCEED IN BUSINESS . . .

Tickets to the LaSalle Street Management Theater are expensive. For $45, audience members get no elaborate sets, costumes, special effects, or show tunes. What they do get is a new form of role modeling transformation for business aspirants. Karolus Smedja, a training consultant, produces thirty-minute plays that display typical corporate situations, featuring power plays, victimization, and miscommunication. The audience members, sent by their sponsoring employers, are then led through a discussion analyzing the actions of the professional role models on stage. Smedja is taking mentoring one step further, institutionalizing the role-modeling experience. He also demonstrates that business and theater are very much alike, and that aspirants who wish to become corporate leaders need to learn acting and stagecraft. No longer relying on the person-to-person mentoring found in companies, Smedja is a subcontractor who delivers quality-controlled mentoring for a price.

One danger of mentored transformations is that they often lead to an excess of imitation. Such was the case with tennis celebrity Andrea Jaeger, who was mentored by her ex-boxer father. Jaeger, noted as a combative and explosive tennis player, was both highly criticized and admired for her tactics. Jaeger's style may well be explained by the mentoring and role-modeling process her father conducted, an influence Jaeger acknowledges with her comment that, "My dad and I are so much alike, it's a joke. We're both hot-tempered and we're both stubborn."[46]

Situational Transformation. Situational transformation involves placing aspirants in new situations to help develop their new images. For example, instead of the aspiring comic undergoing behavior modification or role modeling, he or she goes right onstage and performs. The idea is to make the environment as realistic as possible.

Although reminiscent of the "sink or swim" method of swimming instruction, there are a number of situations in celebrity-marketing when the best strategy is to totally immerse the aspirant in highly visible environments. Comedy clubs all across the country provide the opportunity for insurance agents, nurses, or policemen to get up on stage in a starkly realistic setting. The clubs provide the audiences and the setting, allowing the aspirants to test under fire whether they can sink or swim. In the business sector, the same principle applies. The young commodities broker is told to appear on cable TV and pitch the firm's services, or the product manager is thrust into the spotlight during a liability crisis or product recall. These aspirants instantly need to analyze their markets, prepare their material, and deliver it. In such cases, the pragmatic need for rapid adaptation to high visibility can be a powerful transformer.

Acting-based Transformation. In behavior modification, the aspirant is encouraged to develop behaviors through a rewards and punishments system. In role modeling, the aspirant emulates a mentor. In situational transformation, the aspirant is placed in an environment that forces the aspirant to experience, absorb, and reproduce the appropriate behavior. All these methods attempt to inculcate certain behaviors and values into students. Acting-based transformation differs from these methods in that the agency of change is primarily within the aspirant, with the transformer attempting to draw *out* of the student the maximum flexibility and adaptability to change. The coach or transformer has a blueprint type in mind; but it is the aspirants who place themselves in the frame of mind in which transformation can most effectively be achieved.

In acting-based transformations, the goal is to encourage the aspirant to achieve a state of mind where the person's own style—composed of actions that are automatic, "second nature"—can be viewed objectively, isolated, and at least partially set aside. Then, the mentor and the aspirant cooperatively select the actions that will most convincingly project the new character. As Stanislavski believed, "The choice of actions, then, is the foundation on which character is built. . . . The value of an action lies in the inner content that it expresses."[47] The operating principle of acting-based transformation is that the aspirant, once acquainted with the broad outlines of the new character to be expressed, can most convincingly bring the design to life by being involved in the transformation process as an equal. Of course, the transformation needs to be closely monitored by the mentor or coach.

The success of the numerous actor-training techniques that use it proves that acting-based transformation works. "The actor is himself a human being," said Lee Strasberg, the famous acting coach, "and can create out of himself. The actor is the only art material capable of being both the material and the reality so that you almost cannot tell the two things apart."[48]

When the acting coach tells the student, "I want you to express the feeling of walking on the beach," the student has no clear model of how to react. But by freeing themselves from inhibitions, by visualizing how the beach *feels*, aspirants begin to see this larger action as being composed of a great number of discrete, individual actions. It is through this process—of focusing the aspirant's attention on the minor, even insignificant actions through which a particular concept should be brought to life—that acting-type transformation operates.

The problem with acting-based transformation is that in the selection of the actions that express the new character, the aspirant may take on only the surface characteristics of the new self. Unfortunately, creating a new self for a transitory role in the theater is not the same as truly expressing the full range of characteristics of the new self in real life. A theater director might cast for an actor to play Lee Iacocca, find someone with the necessary physical resemblance, clothe him in the right suits, teach him the right walk, even bring out in him Iacocca's trademark behaviors. Acting-based exercises can make all this possible.

But what they cannot do is make him *believe that he is* Lee Iacocca. That distinction—between *expressing* the new self and believing that one *is* the new self—is critical. Aspirants who use acting-style transformation must be monitored for proof that their transformations are deep and complete.

Adjusting to Transformation

An incontrovertible fact of transformation is that the trip through change is often accompanied by self-doubt and the need for great adjustments. The aspirant has to come to grips with a wide variety of change issues. Why did I transform? Who am I now? How do I relate to people in my new status? Will I be able to handle fame?

The central idea that connects these questions is, How do I live with the illusions I have helped create, the illusions that I now live out in my life? One field that has great experience with handling this issue is clinical psychology, which for years has assisted people to adjust mentally to their environments and their self-concepts. The idea of wealthy or famous persons' constantly running to psychiatrists, gurus, astrologers, and mystics is a cliché, but it has a root in truth. These people are trying to explain, anchor, or deal with transformations that may have come gradually or suddenly—and live comfortably with them. Apart from its undeserved negative stigma, psychological counseling may be a valuable additional tool to help aspirants adjust to their transformed selves.

Also to help aspirants to deal with the wrenching changes of transformation, an entire sub-industry of celebrity support systems has evolved. Its purpose is to provide an atmosphere that enables aspirants to immerse themselves totally in their new public personalities without the distractions and annoyances of ordinary life. The celebrity hotel suites, private planes, exclusive spas, and custom-designed trips help effect, preserve, and deepen the immersion into a new identity.

WOE IN LAKE WOEBEGON

Consider Garrison Keillor, the man who invented an idyllic Minnesota community where modest, self-effacing characters live out wholesome lives completely separated from the modern world. Keillor, in weaving his stories, had become to his audience almost a twentieth-century bard. To listeners gathered around their radios on Saturday night, Keillor seemed that rare person whose authenticity was impervious to change. He was the natural.

Imagine the surprise of Keillor's fans when they became aware that Keillor had been transformed—but not into what they had thought.

"I was shocked to learn the salary of Keillor," said Edward L. Henry, a longtime supporter of Minnesota Public Radio. "That kind of money to people in Lake Woebegon is a salary that can't be imagined. [Keillor's] own personal life doesn't reflect the values of Lake Woebegon. He's on his second wife and abandoned one other gal. He was in a position to be a role model. But with details of his personal life now so public, I don't know. . . ."[49]

What Keillor did not take into account is that learning to project the new self through change of name, appearance, behavior, and material is only part of projecting a new image to audiences. Only by internalizing the transformation—convincing oneself that one *is* the new self, as well as orchestrating all the elements of the new self with consistency—can one guarantee that public image and private behavior will match.

The Three Degrees of Transformation

The degree to which one can be transformed depends on the aspirant's stretch potential and drive, the resources available to assist in the transformation, and the sector's requirements for success. Let's consider how three major levels of transformation—minimal, moderate, and extensive—work.

MINIMAL TRANSFORMATION

Johnnie Whitaker achieved national visibility as Jody on the television series "Family Affair."[50] The young boy fit the role so well that he had no need to transform himself to achieve high visibility. He was discovered at the age of three while singing in a children's church choir:

> ...Anyway, what happened was this little girl got the chicken pox, and so the only other person who knew anything about this was myself. ...Well, as I remember, I got the first verse fine but when the second verse came I stuttered and stammered and started making up my own words...but I just kept on singing like there was nothing wrong.... So later on, a lady in the congregation whose son had done one or two commercials came up to my mother and said "You've got a talented young boy there.... Why don't we see if we can send him to an agent and get a job."

Whitaker then began his career under the management of Mary Grady, a well-known children's agent. After doing several commercials, he matched the "breakdown services" description—a published casting list advertising for types—for a minor role in the film *The Russians Are Coming, the Russians Are Coming.* The formation of a strong on-the-set friendship with fellow actor Brian Keith, who was cast as Bill Davis in "Family Affair," led to Keith recommending Whitaker for the part of Jody. Whitaker, who attributes 80 percent of his getting the part to his friendship with Keith, said, "...if I didn't have any talent and good looks, they wouldn't have decided to cast me."

For six television seasons, Whitaker played the part of the wholesome Jody, entertaining millions of viewers. But his career, which included four Disney films and the promotion of a Jody line of clothes, ended in the mid–1970s when he essentially grew up. During this period he always remained little Johnnie Whitaker. He projected the proper cues for the role: innocence, cuteness, precociousness. Of course, as Whitaker admits, a certain amount of transforming was inevitable, since, unlike most kids, he "got to meet presidents, kings, and important people that everybody dreams of meeting."[51]

The transformation problem for Whitaker can aptly be expressed in his attitude toward his fans. "In a sense," he argues, "our fans regard us much as they did the dolls and clothes made in our likenesses." The problem is that dolls never grow up—but Johnnie Whitaker did. He became a teenager who could never return to the child star's appearance or behavior. Although Whitaker was changed as a person by his high visibility, the changes were reactive, not strategic. In the beginning, he was the natural, who fit his role perfectly because he *was* the part. But as he matured, and his child-role fans lost interest, Whitaker needed to generate a new concept and undertake the transformation required to bring the concept to realization.

Throughout his period of early success, Whitaker failed to prepare to make the shift from child star to adult star. Had Whitaker wanted to reposition himself for a new market, deeper transformation steps would have been called for. He might have branched into another sector of entertainment, such as music or TV hosting. The accompanying sector changes would have required an investment in concept generation, testing, and refinement.

MODERATE TRANSFORMATION

An example of moderate transformation is that of Christie Hefner, president of Playboy Enterprises. Hefner, of course, benefited from the Hefner name. But just as important to her business success was the transformation she undertook during the seven years it took her to rise from trainee to president. The process included what her associates called "the most sophisticated on-the-job training of anybody we know."[52] Says Hefner directly, "I think on the basis of education and learning, I've been profoundly transformed."[53]

The transformation of Christie Hefner included such obvious strategies as changing her name from her mother's (Gunn) to the family name of Hefner. More profoundly, she altered her appearance, behavior, skills, and other indicators of character through role modeling and behavior modification. Says Hefner, "I think it really was as simple as doing, then watching, the effect of what I did. [I'd] give an interview and watch the tape and think, 'That didn't seem to come across the way I wanted it to. Why didn't it?' "[54] This meant watching tapes of her press interviews for style and appearance, and then discussing her "performance" with advisors. The fact is that Hefner is aware of her transformation and can speak eloquently about it. But by far the most important fact is that, confronted with the need to make a significant transformation, she managed to retain control over the process. The concept behind Hefner's transformation was well thought out, appropriate to the business sector in general and the Playboy situation in particular, where the need for competent management was matched by the importance of maintaining the Hefner mystique. *Playboy*'s theme had, for years, been that of the innovator. But the company's fiscal condition had deteriorated severely in the 1970s. Its management needed a new concept to restore investor confidence and public interest. The concept of a female taking over *Playboy*—and the daughter of the founder, at that—was excellent strategy. But to make it work, the only candidate for the job had to be transformed. A moderate transformation, allowing for the credible projection of the new self to the audience, was the appropriate strategy. Today, the technological change of videocassette competition and damage to *Playboy*'s magazine distribution at the hands of the New Right continue to create new challenges for the transformation of *Playboy*, its management, and its image.

EXTENSIVE TRANSFORMATION

It was the night of the premiere of *Won Ton Ton: The Dog That Saved Hollywood*—the typical Hollywood-style event. There were two stars to the show. One was the wonder dog, who arrived in a limousine and pranced down a red carpet to the acclaim of the crowds. The second star, though not an actor, was better known than the stars of the film. He was Allan Carr, impresario and producer of *Grease*, one of the top box-office successes of all time. Carr alighted from his limo looking the quintessence of the modern Hollywood mogul: beautifully tailored European-cut suit; perfectly coiffured, blond, tinted curls; and the familiar healthy tan.

This was not, however, the original Allan Carr, who described himself as an overweight, unliked high school kid from the North Shore of Chicago. But it was only to be expected that Carr would one day be so successfully transformed, as his career in its early stages was to revolve around transforming others, such as client Ann-Margret.

Carr, who said, "If life isn't an illusion, it's nothing," is a prime example of extensive transformation.[55] He used most of the transformation strategies explained in this chapter to create an image that is well known and celebrated.

Having selected the film division of the entertainment sector as his market, Carr needed to develop a workable concept. His first step was to select a role—that of producer—and a traditional type: mogul. "I'm a throwback to the great old Hollywood producers," said Carr. "My movies are Allan Carr productions. I take responsibility for the details—clothes, hair, makeup, location; the look and feel of the film are mine."[56] His next move was to achieve a distinctive character within the type, amplifying the mogul's core characteristics of flamboyance and excessiveness. "Readers of the scandal press know all about my evenings," says Carr. "Champion partygiver, social gadfly *par excellence.* I have become known as the Bianca Jagger of producers."[57]

Having once generated the concept and tested it in early work as an agent, Carr refined his concept, working out important details. Having changed his name from Solomon at an earlier date, he also gave particular attention to his appearance. Since his physical appearance was preventing him from breaking into important social circles, he radically altered his shape by such extreme measures as having an intestinal bypass operation and wiring his mouth shut. He employed hair stylist Vidal Sassoon and changed his simple hairstyle into his trademark perm. Seeking to maximize image impact, at the time Carr developed a look and style that not only enhanced his flamboyant mogul type but that turned his appearance into a trademark. Dressing in long flowing caftans and kimonos and abandoning conventional clothes, draped in miles of junk jewelry in a style he coined "glitterfunk," Carr was so successful that when the media referred to "Hollywood moguls," they automatically turned to Carr.

Behaviorally, Carr reinforced his concept with lavish parties, boorishness, and spending what seemed to the public to be outrageous sums to promote his films. He further reinforced his mogul image by always appearing to be frantically consumed with the minutiae of his complex productions. For Carr, the mogul's task was to make reservations for ten at an expensive restaurant, change the reservations, cancel, decide to fly to Miami to see a nightclub act for a possible musical, discover on the way to the airport that the rights to a hit European novel are being auctioned in Amsterdam the very next day, and change travel plans to Sabena.

Allan Carr obviously had some advantages when it came to planning and executing his own transformation, doing for himself what he had been trained to do for his clients. Having had this experience, he was able to control and alter his transformation plans to adapt to evolutions in the environment. In the 1980s, certain elements of Carr's character fell out of fashion. Adapting to this new environment, Carr refined his concept, changing just those appearance and behavior elements that were required, while retaining the characteristics that made up his original concept: modern mogul. He abandoned his outrageous look for a more contemporary image composed of expensive suits, conservative hairstyle, and a less abrasive public manner. By executing this series of transformations so successfully, Carr demonstrated that although extensive transformation is the most risky of the different levels of transformation, it can generate the highest rewards.

Conclusion

For most aspirants, the choices and decisions about how deeply to transform are crucial. But although these choices may seem intimately wrapped up in the individual aspirant's unique situation, they are also intimately related to the three major marketing strategies: pure selling, product improvement, and market fulfillment. Johnnie Whitaker was primarily a case of pure selling: a minimally improved product who succeeded because his own intrinsic qualities matched the demands of the marketplace. Christie Hefner, modified and restyled into a simultaneous icon and businesswoman, was an example of product improvement. Allan Carr fits the market fulfillment model: a person radically made over to meet the expectations and needs of an audience. In each case, the transformation was successful, because the appropriate marketing process was followed out in detail.

The techniques of transformation are evident, however, in all sectors and levels of our culture. At the twenty-five-year Midwestern class reunion of one of the authors, the star surprise was the appearance of an attractive alumna who now lives in California. As a high school student, she had been shy, withdrawn, and certainly not memorable. In fact, she described herself as "somebody who really didn't know who she was." In her modern reincarnation, she dressed in California contemporary, tanned, trim, with radiant, highlighted hair. Quite casually, she talked about having left her Orthodox Jewish home shortly after high school and discovering herself in New York City and later in California. So dramatic a change was her new self from her old self that her high school classmates were confused and taken aback. That June evening, the results of her personal transformation overwhelmed her classmates.

The transformation of the Californian didn't occur overnight, and it was not specifically arranged to surprise her former acquaintances. She had been evolving for a long time, something that we all do to some degree. The fact is that we are all capable of transformation. "What do I want to be now?" used to be a question only for entertainers and the very rich. If they faced great difficulties adjusting to changed identities and transformed lives, it seemed divine justice, a fair cost to pay in return for their inordinate wealth and fame. But high visibility is now available to more of us than ever before. How we build our visibility in the channels of distribution, convey our images through the media, and sustain our visibility over time are the subjects of the final chapters of this book.

CHAPTER NINE

Delivery Systems

Suppose Congressman Jack Kemp wanted to take inventory of all the ways his image reached the public. They would include:

1. press conferences
2. meetings with interest groups
3. campaign speeches
4. media interviews
5. appearances at parades, ball games, and other public events
6. paid commercial advertising
7. PR-placed stories in the media
8. endorsements from other public figures
9. association with institutions
10. appearances at private functions (wakes, weddings, bar mitzvahs, teas)
11. radio call-in shows
12. book-length autobiography
13. participation in public debate forums
14. buttons, posters, and bumper stickers
15. random in-person impressions made by just walking around

These images of Kemp reach different audiences through a multiplicity of *distribution channels*. In traditional marketing, a distribution channel is thought of as any specific way in which a product or service can be delivered to a market. But the concept is just as valid when applied to the ways in which images of celebrities are delivered to audiences.

As our list shows, celebrities face a variety of choices when managing the delivery of their images to audiences. The first thing to note is that celebrities' images are distributed in four major forms: formal performances, managed impressions, mentions, and products (see Figure 12).

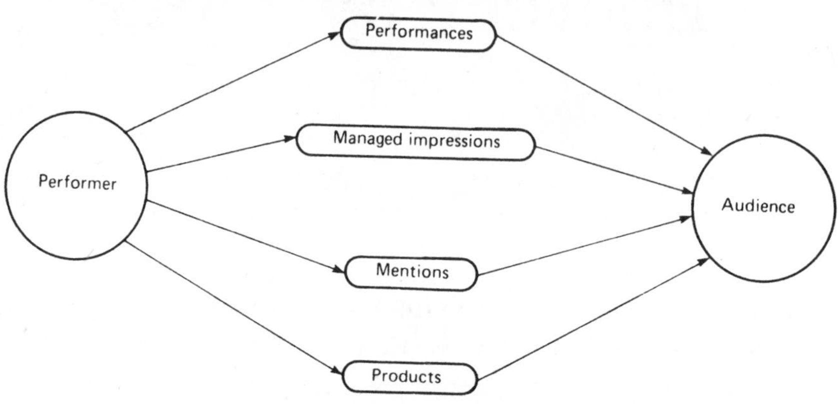

Figure 12: Performer Output

Formal performances consist of planned presentations made by celebrities to their audiences, ranging from the televised testimony of the political lobbyist, to the live concert by Waylon Jennings, to the lawyer's summation in a well-publicized trial. Formal performances include *face-to-face performances* (those presented before a live audience) and *transmitted performances* (those viewed over another medium, such as watched on television or read about in magazines).

Managed impressions are the informal images that celebrities transmit to audiences through such channels as talk shows, press interviews, appearances at charitable and other events, and in public places, advertisements, planted news stories, and photographs. The purpose of managed impressions is to maintain or attain a certain level of public awareness, create or maintain a certain image, or raise the celebrity's "price." Managed impressions are the celebrity's "sell" efforts that take place before, during, and after formal performances. The celebrity pushes informal, or free, impressions onto the audience in order to stimulate their demand for formal, or *paid*, performances. Local radio station disc jockeys who emcee the veterans' parade are transmitting informal impressions to raise their own visibility with potential listeners. The result is greater popularity for their formal performances—their radio shows—with the payoff of a larger audience and, consequently, higher ratings. *Informal impressions are not necessarily unrehearsed or relaxed ones but rather those that stimulate demand for the formal performance.*

Another type of image distributed by celebrities consists of *mentions,* impressions of celebrities that are transmitted by reporters, gossip columnists, and feature writers. Some mentions are unarranged and authentic. Many, however, are planted by the celebrity's staff in order to *appear* spontaneous.

The last kind of image consists of *products*—physical objects carrying the image of the celebrity (photos, dolls, cartoon strips) or mentioning the celebrity (buttons, bumper stickers, brand names).

These performances, impressions, mentions, and products can be delivered by different distribution channels. Amy Grant can deliver a performance in a concert hall, in an outdoor arena, over television, or on a recording. Jack Kemp can deliver a speech at a political rally, in a television studio, on a street corner, or in a neighborhood banquet hall. Managed impressions and mentions can be carried to the public through every available communication channel.

As for celebrity products, they reach the public through conventional distribution channels. Consider The Who's Pete Townshend, who abandoned the standard record distribution system in favor of distributing a full-length album, "White City," on videotape. The publisher produced tens of thousands of copies of the video, stocked them, then shipped them (via rail, truck, or air) to recording wholesalers in different cities, who stocked them and then shipped them to retailers, who stocked them and then sold them to customers. The retailers included record stores, department stores, mass merchandisers, catalogue houses, and other distribution channels.

Channel Control

Aspirants have different degrees of control over their images and the channels through which they are distributed. Aspirants generally have more control over face-to-face performances than their performances transmitted over electronic channels. The reason is that with transmitted images, someone else filters and manages the image mixture. Directors and camera crews decide on the camera angles, sound effects, and what to include and edit out—decisions that deeply influence the impressions received by audiences. By the same token, these processes *can* give aspirants better control over their packaged performances than their live ones, because of the improvements editing offers.

Channels must ultimately produce an encounter with an audience. The places where these encounters occur—churches, stadiums, conference rooms, courtrooms—are called *venues*.

Channel Choice

How does a visibility-seeker use channels? Consider two aspirants, one a young minister, the other a high school football coach. What elements do they need to consider when developing an image-delivery strategy?

In beginning a career quest for high visibility, most aspirants start with a small menu of choices. For a young minister just leaving divinity school, the channel choices include:

1. church in a small town
2. smaller church in a big city
3. public service work
4. teaching position

For the football coach, there are similar choices:

1. start as assistant or head coach in high school
2. start as assistant in college or professional ball
3. work at specialty training summer camps

Once aspirants have chosen their initial distribution channels and located available venues, they are faced with another set of options: how to communicate their images effectively to audiences. Without images to carry, channels themselves are of little use.

The minister preaches sermons and develops an interpersonal style with parishioners, all part of refining his image with his audience. He also has mass-audience possibilities: through publications, church assemblies, articles in national journals, work in civic organizations, and charity leadership. These are his channels of appearance, his ways to reach his markets and make impressions. If well designed, these impressions move him into play with wider audiences. If very well designed, the impressions he makes will distinguish him from his competitors. He will come to the attention of more powerful "casting directors": church boards and bureaucracies, and the media.

The football coach also needs to formulate a channel mix strategy. The factor dominating his image is probably his win-loss record. But the coach can go further in creating an identity that will enhance his ability to deliver his image to potential audiences. He might develop a specialty as a quarterback coach, create the image of an innovator by developing a trademark defense, or establish a reputation as a provocative lecturer at football clinics. Or he may avail himself to the media as a translator of inside terms, or as a warm, personable interviewee.

Like the minister, the coach must select the right channels to deliver his image to his different audiences. He may be forced to develop messages specially tailored for head coaches, alumni, media, community supporters, or business contacts. Each message requires a different channel, and each channel may require its own type of message.

Sequencing Through Channels

Most aspirants begin in the most accessible channel available in their sector. The aspiring politician runs for vice president of the fraternal lodge; the lawyer obtains the chair of a bar subcommittee; the dancer gains a position with the local dance troupe. It is often here that aspirants meet their severest test. Many learn at this stage that they don't desire high visibility as intensely as they had thought. The new comedian gets laughed off the stage; the new singer cannot stop the audience from chatting. The aspirant isn't asked back for a second night; the contract is not renewed. Rejected, some aspirants try to generate a new concept or undergo advanced transformation. Many more give up, quit the race, and accept a future of invisibility. Some hang on for several years in beginner performance channels, having exhausted either their flexibility, their transformation resources, or both.

The optimum strategy is to upgrade the channels while refining and polishing one's concept. For most aspirants, it is very difficult to skip the interim low-visibility channels. It is improbable that a beginning football coach could immediately become a color commentator on network college football broadcasts, or that the young minister will quickly lead the Congress in prayer. By timing their channel moves to match their transformation rate, aspirants can smoothly sequence through more powerful channels, moving up to those that offer more status, prominence, larger audiences, and higher earnings.

Even aspirants who are successfully transformed require a sound channel-use strategy to succeed in their quests. Before considering channel strategy in detail, however, the aspirant needs to understand how distribution channels evolve and change, and how one differs from another.

Channel Innovation and Change

The channels available to distribute celebrity images change all the time, with new channels emerging as old ones vanish.

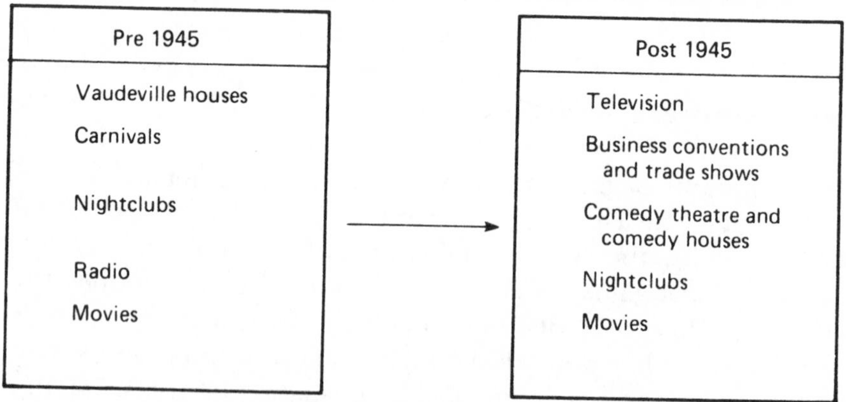

Figure 13: Comedian Performance Channels

Consider the changing distribution channels for comedians over the years (see Figure 13). Prior to 1945, professional comedians could perform in vaudeville houses, carnivals, nightclubs, movies, and radio shows. After 1945, vaudeville and carnivals disappeared at the same time that television was emerging as an important channel. Comedians such as Milton Berle, Red Skelton, and Ed Wynn made their mark in this medium. Business conventions and trade shows grew rapidly as showcases, as comedians provided businessmen with a few evening laughs between the seriousness of the meetings. In the 1960s, improvisational comedy theaters spread, based on the successful model of Chicago's Compass Players and Second City. In the late 1970s, comedy nightclubs decentralized across the country, with many new comedians performing in the hope of becoming the next David Brenner or Joan Rivers.

Some celebrity sectors have experienced a steady decline in available channels. For example, the channels for poets have shriveled up over the years. Poets used to publish their poems in dozens of major magazines; today, the few magazines that still publish poetry, such as *The New Yorker* and *Atlantic,* hardly allow it space. Poetry channels have been replaced by high-tech entertainment, particularly by the growth of twentieth-century poetry: pop music.

At the other extreme, some celebrity sectors undergo an explosion of interest, often because of major media events. Business news, for example, received only moderate amounts of media coverage until the economic slumps of the 1970s, when massive unemployment led to a greater interest among readers in economic and business news. Newspapers—the traditional channel for distributing images of business celebrities—experienced stiff competition from specialty television shows that had grown out of the development of cable TV. The result was the emergence of numerous new channels to convey images of business celebrities. One of these new channels was the business magazine. The venues that made up this channel—the specific magazines, such as *Money, Venture, INC.,* and *Success*—multiplied quickly, catering to the growing public demand for information on business celebrities and business affairs.

Three major factors contribute to the rise and fall of different distribution channels. The first is when *new technologies* create new performance channels. Television has become the most important new channel available to performers of all types—businesspeople, entertainers, politicians, athletes, even the clergy. The availability of video cameras and videocassette recorders (VCRs) made possible a new channel for viewing performances in the home. The development of special-effects lighting equipment made possible the emergence of discotheques, which provided a new channel outlet for amateur and professional dancers.

The second factor is *economic*, in that some distribution channels become too expensive for their patrons' pocketbooks. Many premiere nightclubs—such as the Copacabana and the Stork Club of New York—folded because of their high costs and declining audiences. These clubs showcased high-priced entertainers whose high cost had to be passed on to customers. When television came along, audiences found it cheaper to watch favorite performers in their living rooms than paying to see them in nightclubs.

A third factor is *changing audience tastes*. In the 1940s and 1950s, jazz clubs thrived across the country. In the 1960s, casual cafés flourished, featuring folk singers such as Woody Guthrie, Phil Ochs, and Joan Baez. In the late 1960s and early 1970s, rock enlarged its audience as people flocked to outdoor rock concerts, including the famous Woodstock Festival. In the 1980s, country-and-western music began to penetrate northern, urban markets, and country-music bars arose in great numbers.

These factors—changing technology, economics, and audience tastes—explain the emergence of new distribution channels. Both entrepreneurs and established institutions discover changing audience needs or new technologies and decide to pioneer a new channel. Their motive may be "art for art's sake" or profit; whichever, they become the agents of change.

PAINTING FOR SUCCESS, PART II

Historically, art has been distributed in very traditional manners. Only a few channels existed, and breaking in to them involved selling to intermediaries, whether galleries or museums—and then only after long apprenticeship. In the past two decades, some broadening of channels has occurred, with artists trying to deliver product directly to audiences through street fairs, open studios, and artists' colonies. But no one understands the possibilities of art channel innovation better than urban artist Robert Fischer, cited earlier for his creativity in clothing strategies. Fischer discusses his delivery strategies with the scientific detachment of a marketing executive for Procter & Gamble.

Fischer was adept at applying the counterprogramming strategy, and his first major marketing ploy was activated before he had even learned to paint well. Telephoning local society leaders, Fischer would say that he had painted their portrait and ask if they wanted to view it. If they agreed, Fischer would quickly produce the work. In the event that the subject actually liked the work, Fischer had a sale. When, as was often the case, they *didn't* like it, Fischer would ask them at least to sign the work, enhancing the value of the paintings when Fischer later offered them to other collectors. Fischer further diversified his distribution, ultimately becoming the highly visible entertainment director of a major Chicago nightclub. Fischer was even commissioned to produce the art centerpiece for the new Chicago Mercantile Exchange, which, when unveiled at a lavish party, so offended the conservative brokers that the work was instantly condemned. Fischer, undeterred, rolled up the huge canvas on the spot and calmly walked off: another controversial episode to enhance Fischer's story.

CHANNEL ATTRIBUTES

Aspirants need to understand the special characteristics of each channel, concentrating on those that best suit their abilities and can best advance their quests. To select the best channels, they need to consider the following questions:

- How much visibility do they now have?
- How much risk are they willing to assume in pursuing higher visibility?
- How high up the visibility pyramid do they eventually want to go?
- What is their time frame for reaching each successive level of visibility?
- How much will channel access and use cost?

An aspiring singer might find nightclubs to be a near-perfect distribution channel. With their small audiences, nightclubs afford singers the opportunity to experiment without risking broadcast of a costly poor performance to an audience of thousands or millions. Given a small catalogue of material, the singer can function well in a format that requires a set of music of perhaps forty-five minutes' length. The informality of nightclubs also gives aspirants the chance to polish conversation skills, as well as maintain control of the tone and content of the subject matter. Because the nightclub act is repeated nightly, aspirants can quickly perfect their act and gain confidence in the medium.

Consider, alternatively, the higher-risk talk show distribution channel. On the Johnny Carson show, a singer will receive about seven minutes of exposure, three in singing, and four in chatting with Carson. Because the singer will likely sing only one song, she cannot present a full picture of her singing capabilities. She must choose the song carefully, because it may be her only break. She must choose her wardrobe thoughtfully, because it communicates her type and character. Unable to set the agenda for the conversation, she must be skilled at smoothly integrating the material she needs to present into the flow of conversation. If she has failed to choose material well, she may fail to meet audience expectations. If she does well, she might gain access to other mass-market channels that can simultaneously distribute her image to mass audiences.

Politicians also assess the attributes of different performance channels. They much prefer giving a controllable *speech* to holding a *live press conference*. In a live press conference, they may be thrown a question that is unanticipated or embarrassing. Richard Nixon, in his successful bid for a second presidential term, sought an interview format that would have the appearance of spontaneity but be fairly well controlled; the solution was called the "Hillsboro format," a custom-designed distribution channel where Nixon appeared before a panel of citizens who asked fairly safe questions.

One of the most bizarre examples of controlling media for the purpose of impression-making occurred in France when an eighty-year-old politician, an honored member of the French Resistance, ran for political office. Because he was almost senile, he avoided all contacts with the press. Speeches were ruled out, as were public appearances. Instead, his sponsors put out press releases quoting his words and showing a picture of him taken some twenty years earlier. They were essentially marketing his reconstructed image, one that varied greatly from his real self. The campaign was purely one of managed impressions. Needless to say, he won the election.

Aspirants have to decide whether a particular channel will advance their interests or compromise them. Many well-known actors refuse to appear in television commercials because they feel that it will downgrade their image; they will appear to be selling their visibility instead of advancing their art. Some celebrities refuse interviews with certain magazines; Henry Kissinger will damage his credibility if he grants an interview to *Hustler*, as will underground rock celebrity Siouxsie Sioux by appearing in *Vogue* or *Seventeen*. Well-known fine artists will be unlikely to accept a commission to paint a graphic on the side of an office building. Some actors, such as Paul Newman and Robert DeNiro, assiduously avoid TV talk shows. (At the same time, Newman has used his name to brand–name a new salad dressing.)

Different distribution channels have different attributes. Figure 14 lists five attributes and illustrates where two performance channels—TV talk shows and nightclubs—stand on these attributes. Short audience exposure time, high conversational intensity, low performer control, one exposure only, and high visual impact characterize a TV talk show. A nightclub act provides the performer with maximum audience exposure, low conversational intensity, high control, repeat exposures, and visual impact. Our point is that aspirants have different skill levels with respect to these attributes and, through trial and error, match themselves to channels where they can be most effective.

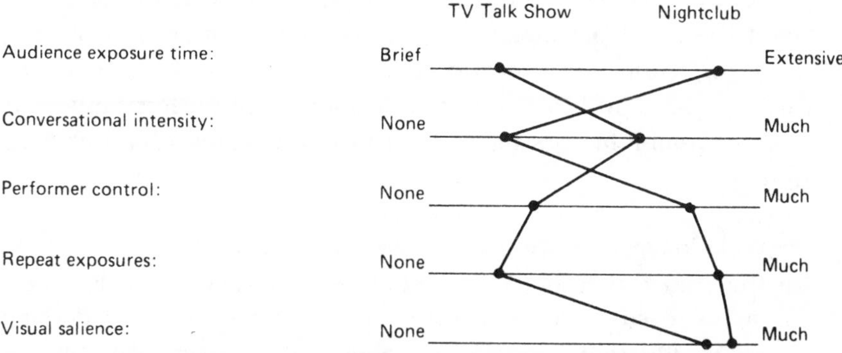

Figure 14: Comparison of Two Performance Channels

Most stockbrokers, for example, distribute their images through narrow channels that reach very small audiences—cold calling clients from lists of prospects or appearing before local investment clubs. The disadvantage of this approach is that although it emphasizes strong interpersonal contact, with feedback and immediate response, it lacks efficiency, reaching limited audiences for the resources invested. One broker who has solved this problem through channel innovation is Ira Epstein. On his TV program, "Stocks, Options, and Futures," which appears on six UHF stations and on Financial News Network, Epstein appears as the Phil Donahue of finance, fielding questions from his audience and moderating a panel of experts. What Epstein is doing with this strategy is effectively marketing his name, achieving well-knownness as a financial guru, and developing large numbers of potential clients who are identified through their requests for a free newsletter. In mimicking the traditional strategies of TV talk show programming, Epstein adapts a mass-market channel to his own purposes.

Managing the Performance Channels

Aspirants at different points in their quests for celebrity face different channel concerns. New aspirants, just starting out, are usually forced to take advantage of any channel available to them. Their opportunities are few and must be aggressively pursued. The aspiring actor will audition for new roles whenever possible. The newly ordained minister will watch for notices of churches in need of an associate minister. Established celebrities may reject all but the most prestigious channels for fear of communicating the wrong impression to audiences. Both aspirants and celebrities are seeking to build a record of successful performances.

Five major factors affect decisions regarding channel management:

- What image does the aspirant want to reinforce?
- How much time does the aspirant want to devote to performing (as opposed to concept testing, transforming, resource development, and other tasks)? How should he or she distribute this performance time over the available channels?
- In which regions and through which venues do celebrities want their images distributed?
- Does the celebrity want to distribute mostly formal performances, or does he or she want to distribute informal impressions for the purpose of building the audience?

- How many image-carrying products does the celebrity want to license?

Appropriate channels. Some aspirants find channel management easy, in that they are skilled or comfortable in only one distribution channel. Consider a president who wants to represent a company product in an advertising campaign but is overweight and physically awkward. The president may want to avoid visual channels and work primarily in recording studios making voice-overs for commercials.

At the other extreme is the multitalented celebrity such as Cher, who can give concerts, perform on Las Vegas stages, act in movies, and appear on TV talk shows. Frank Sinatra's choice of distribution channels is guided by money, favors, power, and friendships.

Performance time. Established celebrities often face an abundance of performance opportunities. Yet many want to maximize the efficiency of their public time, first to avoid overexposure and audience wear-out, and second to leave time for working on new material and conducting their lives.

Time, therefore, and not money, is often the celebrity's scarcest resource and must be guarded carefully. One ingenious solution to this problem occurred when pop artist Andy Warhol accepted multiple lecture engagements in different cities for the same evening and sent lookalikes to stand in for him. He assumed that few people knew what he really looked and sounded like and that his clones would perform as well or better—one solution to the problem of needing to be in more than one place at the same time.

Political candidates, as election time approaches, are particularly hard pressed to use their time efficiently over the wide range of audiences available to them. Major candidates use a campaign scheduler who works out the candidate's appearances each day in an effort to maximize exposure.

Regions and venues. Even after aspirants decide on the amount of time to devote to formal performances, they must decide what particular cities and venues to accept. Should pop psychologist Leo Buscaglia appear at Radio City Music Hall, or at Whittier College? In which five cities should General Motors chairman

Roger Smith debut GM's new automobiles? All of these decisions will be influenced by comparing financial offers, market size, and channel-performer fit.

Packaged products management. In the case of entertainment aspirants, many of their performances can be recorded and turned into products—records, films, audio cassettes, video cassettes, posters. Various offers also come their way for licensing their names to produce T-shirts, dolls, and other products. Finally, they might be invited to appear in commercials for replay in many locations. All this physical output must be negotiated and managed. In other sectors, packaged products may not exist, because the necessary distribution channels have not been sufficiently developed. Only recently, for example, have celebrities in the professions—lawyers, doctors, real estate developers—begun to package themselves for distribution on instructional cassettes and in self-help books.

Impression management. Besides managing their use of channels, aspirants must manage the images that they transmit over them. Some aspirants crave public attention. They will pop into highly visible restaurants, arrive in limousines at important parties and events, attend charity fundraisers, and make appearances that will keep them heavily photographed and written about. Other celebrities avoid meeting the public, preferring to wear disguises or appear in places where they will not be recognized or in places that cater to their privacy.

Without channels, it is virtually impossible to deliver celebrity images to audiences. Aspirants must understand that approaching channels sequentially and using them strategically can lead to extremely efficient and productive use of the celebrity's resources. This is because all channels are not created equal. The face-to-face small-scale "live" channels—kaffeeklatches, teas, sales meetings, public speeches, and nightclub appearances—although useful for building visibility, are not nearly as potent as the dominant channel in the celebrity-delivery system: the mass media. The mass media are the ultimate amplifier and distributor of celebrity images—the maker or breaker of most aspirants' quests.

Using the Mass Media: Breaking Out

Because the media make up the most powerful of all channels, they are crucial to winning high visibility. Other channels are capable of moving celebrity images out of the warehouse and into the marketplace, but none approaches the cost-effectiveness and audience impact of the mass media.

On any given day, the public is inundated by messages from radio, television, magazines, films, and newspapers. For most celebrities, the coverage of their activities, performances, lifestyles, and problems is routine. The celebrity might be pleased with the amount of coverage, or might even seek to dampen it, depending on the purpose it serves and the point where the celebrity is in the career cycle. In contrast, an especially hot celebrity can cycle through the media with such impact and saturation that consumers might think, for that short period, that industrialist Ross Perot, General William Westmoreland, actress Cheryl Tiegs, or astronaut Dick Truly are the only people in the world worth discussing. When Daryl Hannah appeared in the film *Splash*, she was on the cover of *Time* and *Newsweek* simultaneously. Was she really the star of the week? Of the year? Of the decade? Of the century? Or was she simply one more entertainer who met the media's needs for product? Still, for that small number of aspirants who break out into high media exposure, the opportunity may come only once. It needs careful management.

To break out means to burst into high visibility, to suddenly open up large new markets. The advantage of using media to break out into audience awareness is that they can produce a flood of opportunities. The downside is that of the aspirants who are in the warehouse, ready to ship, many are defective (incompletely transformed or tested). The danger flows from the media's tendency to amplify and highlight any aspirant's unusual features, including defects. The stakes in a media breakout are often enormous, and they must be approached just as methodically and strategically as transformation itself.

As an example, consider the meteorlike ascent of Senator Gary Hart to presidential contender in 1984. Originally, Hart was an audience-driven candidate, the choice of younger voters who resisted what they considered to be the old guard in the Democratic party. Hart's performance in the Iowa primary (he finished a distant second to Walter Mondale) suddenly turned him into a media-driven candidate as the networks and major print news sources exploited him as refreshing material to sustain public interest. They needed Gary Hart to keep alive the remaining primary races. The media built Hart into a seemingly unbeatable candidate. He fit into a traditional story slot: the vigorous, visionary, confident, and youthful candidate. With the help of the mass media, Hart broke out.

Quickly, the standard features of a media-driven breakout became apparent in the Hart story:

- That every aspect of his life would be examined and his flaws revealed.
- That he lacked the coaching and preparation to master the media barrage.
- That his support staff—writers, PR people, policy experts—were not able to provide timely information to the media and thus were not managing the media but always reacting to it.

Hart finally stumbled in Illinois as he issued contradictory statements and seemed thoroughly confused. One of his advisors described this process as Hart "going soft." But it is clear that once the media usurp the celebrity, the media themselves begin to make the decisions on how the other two drivers—audiences and institutions—will view the celebrity. In Hart's case, the media began to drive the other drivers by placing into contention such arguably goading questions as "Can Hart handle the media?" and "How old is Gary?" Media-driven celebrities run the risk of being publicly defined, psychoanalyzed, and finally drawn and quartered by media opinion-makers.

The story of another celebrity who broke out illustrates the need to manage the media and not be managed by them. Marva Collins, a westside Chicago private school principal, was praised as a superteacher on a "60 Minutes" segment and was the subject of a laudatory "Hallmark Hall of Fame" two-hour biography. Collins at this point had become a national education sector celebrity, glorified as an example of what can be done by a single dedicated person working against tremendous odds in our inner cities. Inevitably, a person so in the media spotlight could not sustain scrutiny without revealing blemishes. Accusations surfaced about her use of funds and the effectiveness of her teaching methods. Journalist Michael Miner described Collins as "perched so high and so exposed that when the complaints started coming in, the media at first didn't dare repeat a word of it—then finally reacted to bring her down. Journalism would destroy what it had created."[1] In the end, the media turned on their own media-driven celebrity, rejecting what they had once extolled.

Both Gary Hart and Marva Collins are examples of the price the media exact for driving aspirants to high visibility. The reason Hart and Collins found their journeys through the breakout phase so perilous is related to the economics of treating celebrity news. The media treat celebrities as investments that need to be nurtured, sustained, managed, and, in a final phase, sometimes discarded. As a result, media-driven breakouts generally follow a sequence. The media initially play up the reasons why the aspirant deserves attention, the aspirant's humble origins or struggle, insights on how the aspirant dresses or eats, and problems the aspirant is facing in his or her visibility sector. Many of the story lines are drawn from the 22 Major Stories discussed in the Audience chapter and are used to drive the breakout.

The more mature phases of the celebrity's breakout often devote space to the celebrity's tribulations. Stories of scandal (John Zaccaro and his trials), episodes of excess (comedian Robin Williams and drugs), or exhaustion with gossip (Priscilla Presley and salacious innuendo) satisfy the media's need to perpetuate the story. After an appropriate interlude, the celebrity may be rebuilt, using such kernel stories as a comeback from trials and tribulations (Zaccaro affirms his innocence), the rejection of excess (Williams finds fatherhood), and the achievement of stability (Presley and daughter Lisa are reconciled). The phases of the media breakout may seem to advance inexorably, and usually they do.

Sometimes aspirants are able to coordinate their agendas with the media's, appearing for a brief breakout, then disappearing from view. A celebrity who broke out very suddenly with the help of the mass media but managed to use the media to fight his battle is Richard Studer. Today, Studer's name would baffle most people, as he surfaced only briefly as an instant celebrity, then moved on to post-media obscurity. But for a short time, Studer dominated the media's treatment of a major national story.

Richard Studer is the father of a young boy who was hospitalized in Florida in 1983 needing blood transfusions. The hospital refused to allow Studer to donate his own blood directly to his son, insisting on the customary practice of drawing blood from a common blood bank. Studer vehemently protested, fearing that his son might contract AIDS from donated blood. Studer's fears were not unique, but at this point, he had little clout or following.

Studer's story was timely and controversial—two characteristics highly attractive to the media. Quickly, he moved up through channels, finally appearing on network television to discuss his ill child, often accompanied by a fundamentalist preacher. The argument, while dramatized by the father's dilemma, really turned on the issue of whether people should have the right to specify the recipients of their blood donations. The media, seeking the most dramatic story, accorded Studer the same coverage as the medical experts involved in the AIDS story. As a result, the media began to cycle the emotionally charged story of Studer and his child throughout American households.

The appearance of Studer on television forced the American Red Cross and other blood banks to defend the universal blood donation system as safe, sound, and critical to the country's welfare. These officials argued that if blood was not universally available, only the hale and hearty would receive it while the principal users, the elderly, would be deprived. Yet Studer, amplified by the media into a personal symbol, had become a crusader whose emotional arguments made a greater impact on audiences than the scientific discourse of the experts. Studer, although he did not achieve the policy change he sought, succeeded nonetheless in attaining high visibility for himself and his cause.

The Rules of Breaking Out

As our cases demonstrate, the breakout needs to be carefully managed. The basic rules:

1. Breaking out needs to have a purpose. Climbing up the side of a tall building or sending out a controversial press release can accomplish a breakout, but such sensationalism will hardly sustain a celebrity quest. Breakouts that have been thought through will be directed toward some ultimate, strategic goal: to generate an audience, sell products, or distinguish the aspirant from competitors.

2. Breakouts need to be preceded by careful preparation. The celebrity needs to have tested his or her concept, refined it, and been thoroughly coached before the media are met.
3. The celebrity needs to recognize that each phase of the breakout is part of a standard media cycle, and anticipate upcoming phases.
4. During the breakout, the celebrity needs to take the initiative in defining topics and setting the agenda. Leaving these tasks to the media will almost always lead to serious problems.

CHRONOLOGY OF A METEOR

The opportunity for a media-driven event can occur as suddenly as the case of Rosie Ruiz. The name of Rosie Ruiz is probably somewhere between ever-so-slightly familiar and tantalizingly reminiscent. That is because Rosie Ruiz faked winning the Boston Marathon.

Ruiz is an instant celebrity who broke out in the media and enjoyed a celebrity lifespan of literally nine days, from April 22 through April 30, 1980. For those nine days, Ruiz traced the arc of the celebrity-as-meteor. Covered on the front page of *The New York Times* and most other major newspapers in the country, she was the object of feature stories in countless magazines, consuming incalculable chunks of television news time. Her movement through the media constitutes a textbook case of how the media need and use celebrities.

Stage One: *The Explosion onto the Scene*

In the first stage, the anonymous aspirant explodes into the public's consciousness through a media barrage, with the coverage focusing initially on a significant accomplishment. In this case the rationale was provided by Ruiz's stunning and unexpected victory in the Women's Division of the 1980 Boston Marathon, the world's most famous race. On April 22, 1980, Ruiz commanded page one of *The New York Times* and, adding inside coverage, consumed over 25 column inches of space—more than the unquestioned winner of the Men's Division, Bill Rogers.

The coverage was thorough and intense. Expectations for Ruiz, at this point, were excellent. Unfortunately, Ruiz's breakout was doomed, because Ruiz won without running the race. Stage One was the pinnacle of Ruiz's breakout; the rest were her undoing.

Stage Two: *The Questions*

The accomplishment that forced Ruiz's name into visibility was quickly discredited. On April 23, award-winning *New York Times* columnist Neil Amdur wrote an investigatory piece whose theme was scandal. In the Ruiz case, the blanket coverage attending her victory had brought out many who doubted the authenticity of her victory. "Susan Morrow," wrote Amdur on Day Two, "a Manhattan photographer and freelance clothes designer, said yesterday that it was impossible for Miss Ruiz to have run the entire distance in the New York Marathon (the only other Marathon Miss Ruiz had completed besides Boston) last October, because she and Miss Ruiz both rode the subway together to the finish line."

Stage Three: *Protests of Innocence*

On April 24, Ruiz told a packed press conference, "I want to bring out the truth. I admit I've had medical problems. I don't mind talking about it. They are all in the past."

Ruiz acknowledged having undergone brain surgery in late 1973 for a "tangerine-sized tumor."

Saying she would not "bow down to anyone" or be victimized by rumors, Ruiz insisted again that she had run both the Boston and New York marathons from start to finish.

Stage Four: *The Testimonials*

The media quickly sought people who, though unconnected with the events that had propelled Ruiz into high visibility, could testify to her character and trustworthiness. Quoted in *The New York Times*, Maria Grovas, an aunt of Ruiz's who lives in Wayne, Nebraska, said her niece was not capable of cheating in a marathon. "But even if she told me she had not run the races," said Miss Grovas, "I would never say anything to hurt her."

Stage Five: *Get Me Legal Counsel*

On April 26, the headline in the *Times* read, "Miss Ruiz Deprived of New York Finish." Acting on the testimony of Susan Morrow and other supposed observers, the New York Marathon Committee stripped Ruiz of her status as a finisher in the New York race—thus setting the stage for an inevitable development in the lifespan of the media-driven instant celebrity:

> Efforts to reach Miss Ruiz yesterday were unsuccessful. But Susan Donegan, a friend, said Miss Ruiz "has been under friendly legal advisement."

Stage Six: *The Editorial*

On April 27, Ruiz completed a journey as indicative of celebrity as the journey from the start to the finish of the Boston Marathon: the journey from the front page to the editorial page of *The New York Times*. Using her increasingly sad case as raw material from which to fashion moralistic sentiments, the *Times* editorial, "The Scarlet 'D' " (so named after the "D" train that Ruiz had ridden to victory), commented:

> We're moved to muse on all this because of the heavy going over people are giving Miss Ruiz, the woman who did, or didn't, run the Boston Marathon. Some runners have already been spotted in Central Park wearing T-shirts that say, "We believe you, Rosie." Why not hold a special race, a "dare-a-thon," perhaps, open to anyone who has a better idea for how to finish faster, undetected. The winner might get the Abscam Trophy.

Stage Seven: *"Analysis"*

On April 28, there appeared in the *Times* a story entitled "Ruiz Case Shows Running's Growing Pains." Labeled "Sports Analysis," the article used the Ruiz case as a platform from which to make a variety of pronouncements about the "growing pains which running is staggering through." The newspaper was now grinding the Ruiz story thoroughly and resolutely through its machine.

Stage Eight: *Denouement*

On April 30, exactly nine days after her spectacular victory first placed Ruiz in the media spotlight, the final major chapter was written in her story. Having consumed untold thousands of column inches of space in the national and world press, having dominated major blocks of media air time, the Ruiz case was closed with a small note in a five-column-inch piece in the *Times,* a wire dispatch titled, "Miss Ruiz Loses Her Title."

Because she had once broken out, Ruiz remains fair game for media reprises for as long as she lives. Two years to the day after Miss Ruiz was stripped of her Boston title, *The New York Times* reported in a two-column-inch dispatch titled "Miss Ruiz Held for Larceny":

> Rosie Ruiz, who two years ago was the first woman to finish the Boston Marathon, but was disqualified a week later when it was determined that she had not run the full 26 miles, was arrested in New York on charges of larceny and forgery yesterday, a half hour before the annual race.
>
> Miss Ruiz, 26 years old, was accused of stealing more than $15,000 in cash and more than $45,000 in checks from her employer, the Stephens Real Estate Company. Conviction on each charge carries a maximum seven-year term.

Becoming Visible: Attacking the Filters

A first step in breaking out with the help of the media is learning how to get into the media's coverage patterns. The media have only so many techniques or procedures to retrieve information. They receive information from *facts, events,* from *their competition,* from *insider sources, environmental scanning of fads and cycles, experts,* and *public relations*. It is obviously in the best interests of the celebrity to understand how the media gather their information.

Aspirants have to contend with the media's tendency to turn to specific sources for their information. These sources of celebrity news—public relations, gossip columnists, promoters, agents, venue managers—understand the flow pattern for celebrity information. A story is planted at the local level and distributed up through the channels to the news wire houses to the national media. Or a story is planted at the national news level and allowed to percolate down through channels to the local media. As a celebrity rises in visibility, the normal transition is from local newspaper attention and radio talk shows to magazine articles, local TV, and, finally, national TV.

Business aspirants often try their skills at the local level before moving up to regional and national media venues. Typically, the practice for business aspirants is to rehearse and polish their concepts on nonprofit local weekend morning television interviews before moving up to higher-risk venues. In this strategy, each local performance is videotaped and then scrutinized for content and style behavior that may need to be strengthened or reworked to match audience expectations. The goal is to prepare for the media by rehearsing: learning to answer questions crisply and directly, telling the essential story, focusing on business and not on personal matters, and maintaining eye contact with the host. Many aspirants in this situation need the self-confidence-building of practice, and the improvements brought by review, to feel comfortable before a more skilled interviewer. In a sense, the local level serves as a tryout or test market for such sectors as business and religion. Aspirants, by being available to local markets, are not only practicing but are positioning themselves to be distributed by more powerful, national media.

Aspirants can also help their causes by understanding how and why the media deliver certain information about celebrities to audiences:

- The media process celebrity information on the basis of local priorities, needs, attitudes, and prejudices, and at the behest of special interest groups.
- The media have evolved a menu of story types that have proven to be reliable audience-pleasers. Aspirants who understand these story archetypes have a better chance of attracting media coverage.
- The media process information because of competitive pressure. If one venue in the media is covering a certain type of celebrity story, it is likely that other media venues will seek out a similar celebrity story to cover.

This is how media get their information. Understanding how celebrity information flows to, and through, the media is crucial.

This is more easily said than done. At the peak of breakout, chaos seems to reign. The media cover the celebrity from so many angles, in such force, that the aspirant seems overwhelmed by instant attention.

But it's at this point that the hard, crucial decisions must be made. The aspirant is suddenly faced with a tempting array of distribution channels, many of them equally powerful, and in direct competition. The aspirant finds that certain venues need to be turned down, and others pursued. During the breakout period, the aspirant feels that it will never end.

During the breakout, certain elements of the media frankly cannot be controlled. Rumors, gossip, badly edited interviews, and missed appointments are often the side products of overcommitment and a compressed time schedule. In the breakout phase, relationships can become strained, resulting in new alliances and uncertainties: The long-time manager is pushed aside; the professional coach replaces the family mentor; or the spouse finds a divorce lawyer. But many aspects of the breakout *are* controllable and manageable. That breakouts simply do not materialize out of thin air, and that they can be controlled to a great degree, will be seen as we examine the delivery of celebrities in three different sectors.

Distribution Strategy: Cases

DISTRIBUTING AN X-RATED ENTERTAINER

Earlier we discussed the X-rated entertainer Seka in terms of how effectively she transformed herself to project an image tailored to meet her audience's expectations. But Seka's quest for high visibility did not end with transformation; she also strategically managed her image's distribution through a variety of channels.

Seka's original channel was film, with her primary venues being X-rated movie houses. But with the explosion in the use of home videocassettes, she moved aggressively to capture a share of this new channel. In fact, Seka credits her success largely to channel entry timing: the decision of Caballero Control, a film company for which she had made a number of films, to release all of her titles on videocassette. Having captured a large market share, Seka retains the visibility her breakout generated by appearing at such events as the Consumer Electronics Show, the Annual Adult Film Association of America Erotica Awards, and the National Sexology Convention. Seka actively promotes her video product.

But video is just one of the channels that Seka utilizes. She also controls her own mail-order business, taking advantage of her "collector" class of fans by making available her used panties, posters, films, and Seka-endorsed novelties.

Seka especially makes use of the media-driver, frequently appearing on national media venues such as the "Today" show and "Saturday Night Live." Those media venues that do not solicit her appearances, she pursues. "I work at keeping my name in the public [eye] through PR," she says. "I think a lot of [potential media attention] is there and people sometimes don't approach it. But once my PR person approaches them, they're for it."[2] Seka estimates that 80 percent of the press she receives is generated this way.

Seka places her image before the public in a variety of other ways, too. Being associated with interests outside the X-rated sector "keeps your name and personality alive," she says. One way she accomplishes this is through charity work: "I donate money to different organizations throughout the year," says Seka. "I donate my time. I [recently] worked as a celebrity bartender for the St. Vincent DePaul's Catholic school."

The distribution of Seka is purposeful, strategic, and highly effective. It has left her competition searching for strategies to counter her lead in innovative distribution development.

DISTRIBUTING A HIGH-PROFILE PRIEST

The differences between Seka and Father Andrew Greeley are apparent.[3] But while their sectors could not be more different, their distribution strategies are strikingly similar. Both celebrities function within sectors that have their own sets of rules, conventions, and restrictions. Like Seka, Greeley specialized in countermarketing himself, pioneering the distribution of his image through channels not previously used in the religious sector. Originally an academic and theologian, Greeley diversified into broader, more profitable markets. A chronology of his activities shows how his strategy evolved.

Andrew Greeley is a Roman Catholic priest who writes popular novels that combine religious themes with enticing sexual entanglements. He is also the controversial theologian who distributes himself through the lecture and media circuit, promoting his books and ideas through such channels as "Donahue" and local newspapers. To most viewers, Greeley is a fixture of the permanent media environment. But how did he reach this position?

A look at Greeley's progress in the past thirty-five years shows a steady march through the various levels of distribution channels, culminating in a staging for breakout. In the early 1950s, Greeley was known only to friends, family, and fellow seminarians. He was just another able student, without any apparent desire for high visibility. It was in 1960 that he began to be known by what one would consider an "audience": the members of his parish and diocese, and liberal Catholics he attracted through his work with the Catholic Action Movement. This was Greeley operating in the cottage industry stage, using his connections with institutions to generate moderate visibility among a core audience.

Five years later, Greeley branched out into a new sector, academics, obtaining his doctorate in sociology from the University of Chicago, conducting original research on the Catholic school system, and distributing his findings through the media. He began to coalesce his concept—controversial priest—and to distribute his image among the national audience of non-Catholics.

By 1975, through his syndicated newspaper column, Greeley was firmly established as a media figure as well as an editorial commentator on the broader social scene. Through his continuing research, he began not just contributing to but also controlling the cottage industry of religious controversy. With his national newspaper forum, he was able to set the agenda for discussion, and lead it.

The beginning of the 1980s saw Greeley distributing himself in highly visible nonreligious channels: *Time*, *Newsweek*, and others. The force behind this new momentum was his book *The Making of the Pope*, which describes the political maneuvering which fills the papal selection process. At this point, the distribution of Greeley's image, fueled primarily by his story, achieved critical momentum as one popular media channel after another picked the story up, transporting it to wider and wider audiences. Greeley assumed the qualities of a name brand, with major media venues depending on him as a reliably controversial guest. His output of material began to overwhelm the distribution channels, with one reviewer commenting, "Every week or two, Father Andrew Greeley writes a book. Well, all right, it only *seems* like every week or two."[4] Another critic said, "Greeley is easily the most talked-about Roman Catholic priest in America, if only because he talks so much himself."[5]

At present, Greeley stands at the top of what can only be termed a one-person sector. He is a theologian-academician-pulp romance novelist—and a distribution and marketing genius. His novels are now national and international bestsellers, translated into many languages and dominating new book displays in shopping malls and airport bookstores. Even his autobiography, *Confessions of a Parish Priest,* became a best-seller, as Greeley prematurely summed up his life.

The distribution of Andrew Greeley demonstrates how channel innovation and testing are crucial to the successful launching of a celebrity. Greeley began in face-to-face venues, moved to local and regional markets, and finally refined his concept, enabling him to move his image through national and international channels.

TRANSFORMATION AND DISTRIBUTION: MARKETING A YOUNG ACTOR

To test the idea that transformations can be designed to satisfy the demands of channels, media filters, and the ultimate audience, two of the authors assisted in a project developed in a course on celebrity communication and marketing. The goal was to transform an aspirant to meet the demands of a national distribution channel, generating maximum publicity. The aspirant who volunteered to undergo this strategic transformation was Richard Radutzky, a young comic actor who, on the surface, *seemed* to get a lucky break. Although his celebrity was relatively short-lived, the transformation process he underwent typifies the principles presented in this book.

Radutzky faced the problem of most aspirants: how to obtain maximum visibility with minimal resources. While living in New York one summer, he decided to attend an open audition for the NBC network TV show "Late Night with David Letterman." Radutzky was seeking to fill the role of contestant on the show's popular "Stupid Human Tricks" segment, in which amateurs do just what the name implies: stunts and tricks. Radutzky's act was to perform pea levitation—the suspending of a pea by blowing a stream of air to propel the object into orbit. Letterman's producers selected Radutzky from among the crowd of auditioners to be a contestant and said he would be notified soon of the date of his appearance on the show.

Radutzky's overall plan was sound. He had intelligently sought out a platform that suited his talents and had offered material in line with the filter's—in this case, the producer's—expectations. Radutzky now faced an opportunity to become visible before 6 million TV viewers, an exciting prospect for any aspiring comic actor. At this stage—his selection as a contestant—many aspirants would see their work as mostly done. For Radutzky, however, selection was only the beginning. Because his deeper agenda was to make the maximum possible impact, he needed to make a strategic transformation.

The first step in Radutzky's transformation was to put together a planning team.[6] Its general charge was twofold: to test, refine, and realize Radutzky's concept (in this case, his comic performance), and to market Radutzky through all available distribution channels to augment the burst of visibility that the Letterman show itself would produce.

The next step was to analyze the show on which Radutzky would appear. For a young aspiring comic actor, there could not be a more perfectly tailored platform for visibility-seeking—the Letterman show. The demographics and psychographics of Letterman's audience virtually match the profile of Radutzky's potential fans: young, upwardly mobile, and mostly urban. Television was the right channel; Letterman's was the right program with the right audience; the issue was how to handle it.

The segment in question, "Stupid Human Tricks," presented a host of problems. The segment was designed specifically as a showcase for amateurs and not professional aspirants. Its structure makes it very difficult for performers to leave *any* image with audiences, let alone a lasting or significant one. In the space of just six or seven minutes, Letterman brings out up to four performers, generates laughs by playing off them and their absurd antics, then dismisses them. Radutzky had just seconds of air time to work with. But even seconds of national TV exposure are valuable. Clearly, gaining Radutzky maximum air time within the segment was a prime objective. Other objectives were to develop an image and material that would feature Radutzky's ability to convincingly portray a role, interact smoothly, think on his feet, display comic timing, and deliver an entertaining performance.

Although an actor with a fair amount of stage experience, Radutzky knew little about television and interviewing. He had, at the outside, two minutes to distribute his image effectively and efficiently to millions of potential fans and, even more importantly, to the talent scouts and agents who regularly monitor the Letterman show seeking new acts.

To help transform Radutzky, the development team decided to design and manufacture his image and material in as realistic a setting as possible. The team obtained a TV studio for rehearsals, and another young comic actor well known for his David Letterman impersonations was recruited. In this simulated Letterman show setting, it was possible to reconstruct the many possible ways that Radutzky's appearance could play out—and use them to plan strategy.

Before the transformation could begin, however, it was critical to take inventory of Radutzky's raw ability to handle the situation at hand. Although he was an accomplished improvisational stage actor, Radutzky's first attempts in the TV rehearsal studio, viewed in retrospect, show how dramatic his ultimate transformation would be. In his first run-throughs with the simulated Letterman (actor Richard Kaplan), Radutzky was noticeably nervous and appeared overshadowed, allowing "Letterman" to dominate the interaction. Instead of building up the drama and difficulty of his trick, he did it quickly and seemingly without effort. Moreover, his story—so crucial to making a lasting impression on potential fans—was lost in Letterman's barrage of put-downs and asides:

> *Kaplan/Letterman: "What do you do?"*
> *Radutzky: "I study acting."*
> *Kaplan/Letterman: "You hope to be on stage, on the radio?"*

> *Radutzky: "I guess this is the beginning of it."*
> *Kaplan/Letterman (sneering): "Well, many people do indeed get contracts for doing stupid human tricks . . . that's bound to happen."*

Radutzky's gambits to remain on camera longer were clumsy at first. His first was to tell the simulated Letterman, "If we have time, I don't know if we do, maybe you can give it [the trick] a try." By observing these initial run-throughs, the development team discovered that it was especially difficult for Radutzky to get across a great deal of information, evidenced by such jumbled lines as, "This is something I've learned from my family. I later developed it at school where I'm studying acting. . . . I'm going to be an actor. . . . I *am* an actor."

Having already analyzed the Letterman viewing audience, it was next necessary to analyze the primary filter. Viewing tapes of David Letterman made it clear that his humor style depended on his skill at playing off of his guests' weaknesses and lampooning them, often mercilessly. Earlier, during the inventory-taking of Radutzky's abilities, the team determined that one of Radutzky's strengths—developed in improvisational comedy—was to adopt a confrontational style. But the team concluded that such an approach, given Letterman's style, would be suicidal. Thus the decision was made to underplay Letterman, not to overpower him. Given Letterman's tendency to emphasize the amateur status of the contestants on "Stupid Human Tricks," the team decided to emphasize Radutzky's development of the trick, and not his comic acting ambitions. The strategy was to showcase Radutzky as confident and able to perform at a professional rather than an amateur level—qualities that would appeal to the talent scouts likely to be watching.

Next, the support team considered the use of signs and symbols to reinforce Radutzky's desired image. A way had to be devised to carry the pea out onto the stage. Eventually, they decided to use a plain pea can on a silver tray, suggesting put-on elegance. As far as dress, the informality of the show and the time of year dictated a gray wool sweater and dark gray pants, with Radutzky's look calculated to project the image that he was earnest, unpretentious, and ready for business.

At the end of the lengthy rehearsal sessions, the team had transformed Radutzky to satisfy Letterman's, as well as the audience's, expectations. He understood how to parry and redefine Letterman's predictable asides, how to play to the camera that was trained on him, and how to stretch out the time he was on the air. Through improvisation, various scripts were developed to allow Radutzky to involve Letterman in his act, reducing Letterman's control and superiority in the situation.

The comparison between Radutzky's initial rehearsals and his actual TV appearance show dramatically how an aspirant can be transformed. During the actual appearance, Radutzky played along with Letterman's sarcastic style with a planned answer designed specifically to appeal to Letterman's well-known attraction to "homespun" comedy.

> *Letterman: "Where did you learn to do this?"*
>
> *Radutzky: "I learned it from my Uncle Harry."*
>
> *Letterman (laughing, turning to audience): "I think it's nice how these things are passed on from family member to family member."*

Radutzky's baseline abilities were painstakingly developed to match the behaviors that pass for talent in the entertainment sector. Through analysis of audience and behavior modification he began to project an image that appealed to the market. But the transformation was only half of the experiment. The manufacturing process was a success; the next step was to determine just how widely Radutzky's image could be distributed.

The team developed a plan to take advantage of the Letterman appearance and publicize Radutzky's performance to a larger audience. The goal was to convert the two minutes of high visibility into a longer-term asset. Members of the development team were given the assignment to place Radutzky into as many media channels as possible, to attempt to generate "hotness."

Their first task was to select a story that would best appeal to the filters in the media. What were their options?

- *Story One:* Student Uses Transformation to Make an Impact on David Letterman Show.
- *Story Two:* Local Boy Does Inane but Charming Stunt on National Television.

Of the two stories, the second was clearly superior. Given the media's need to fill their standard story slots, it was far more likely that the standard "dumb stunt" story would appeal to the media's interests than would a complicated tale of transformation and image-marketing.

The assumption proved correct. When most media outlets appeared uninterested in the story, the team decided to concentrate on a single outlet, in order to take advantage of the competitive nature of media coverage. Eventually, they persuaded the features department of the *Chicago Sun-Times* that there was sufficient local interest to justify carrying the story of Radutzky's upcoming appearance on Letterman. Once the *Sun-Times* decided to run the story, the team had only to mention this fact to competitive media in order to gain remarkably widespread coverage. So efficient was the team that the day before Radutzky's actual TV appearance, the *Sun-Times* ran a large photo and story about Radutzky on page 2 of its main edition. In addition, image distribution was sharply boosted by a technological consideration: UPI distributed a story about Radutzky over its wire service, with hundreds of newspapers subscribing around the country. Through UPI, Radutzky was soon featured as a human interest story in newspapers from coast to coast.

Because of the interdependence of the channels of distribution, and because of the archetypal nature of the story, the *Sun-Times* story was rapidly picked up by major-market radio outlets. Soon, Radutzky was being interviewed live via telephone by radio stations from New Hampshire to California. The team was even able to use connections to persuade the Chicago CBS-TV affiliate, WBBM-TV, to cover Radutzky's return from New York live as he left the plane at O'Hare Airport.

With his transformation, marketing, and image-distribution process so carefully crafted, it is not surprising that Radutzky achieved excellent results. Unlike the other "Stupid Human Tricks" participants, Radutzky remained in complete control of his brief appearance. (When Letterman asked Radutzky about the notoriously poor Northwestern University football team—a question that his support team should have anticipated—Radutzky did not freeze, and instead turned to the camera and deadpanned, "We've got a pretty good team.")

So effective was the overall planning that the conclusion of the trick found Letterman doubled over in laughter. Coming to Radutzky's side, he declared, "No more calls, ladies and gentlemen—we have a winner!" And, of the hundreds of guests and contestants who appear on the show annually, Radutzky was one of the few invited back to the prestigious Letterman anniversary show.

Radutzky's self-marketing project was a success. Choosing to refine his concept through more acting training, he decided against immediately raising his visibility any higher. Had he wanted to, there were a variety of options open to him. As it was, the experiment paid handsome dividends. Radutzky acquainted himself with the transformation process and gained valuable insight into his own "stretchability" as a product.

A problem for many aspirants is stepping back and planning their path to the top of their sectors. In each of our case studies—those of Seka, Greeley, and Radutzky—the effective management of distribution channels was crucial to moving their image through to audiences. The problem for most aspirants is one of choices: "What can I do?" "When do I do it?" "And how do I do it?" The management of distribution resources is essential to gaining momentum for the celebrity's quest. But even intelligently distributed aspirants cannot sustain their distribution without support. And the most essential support for most aspirants comes from Public Relations.

CHAPTER TEN:

Public Relations: The Voice of Visibility

Business Manager, TV Production Company: "Tell me again—what is the book about?"

Author: "It's about how celebrities become visible through a large number of industry efforts."

Business Manager: "Oh, that's PR stuff. I don't know anything about that."

(Phone conversation with Aaron Spelling Productions)

If ever an industry had a public relations problem, it's PR. Integral to celebrity-marketing, the image of public relations remains caught between the high road of distributing legitimate celebrity information to the public and the low road of selecting, filtering, and manufacturing the best information possible. There is a widespread public perception that PR is the disingenuous part of the celebrity-marketing process. At Aaron Spelling Productions, according to the business manager, the job was to produce the physical product—TV shows featuring celebrities. But the razzle-dazzle hyperbole required to spark public interest in the shows was the responsibility of PR.

The role of PR is probably the least understood element in celebrity-marketing. Yet undeniably, PR's skills are essential for the celebrity image to be fleshed out—for translating the celebrity's personality into the most appealing images for the audience. With the maturing of the celebrity-marketing process, the reach of PR has steadily expanded beyond its original client list to include aspirants in all sectors:

- Dr. Daniel Silver, Los Angeles orthopedic surgeon, pays $1,500 per month to a public relations firm to publicize his practice.[1] Dr. Stuart Berger, our multi-dimensional diet doctor, pays $2,500 per month to a PR firm to guarantee his distribution over the media.[2]
- Business celebrity T. Boone Pickens, starting in 1982, paid the Hill & Knowlton PR firm $500,000 "to help shape his image as a friend of the small shareholder and a battler for investor rights."[3]
- In the CBS/William Westmoreland $120 million libel trial of 1985, both sides retained PR firms to help manage their images. Daniel Edelman, retained by CBS, said that his job was to "help present a balanced picture of the proceedings."[4]

Despite PR's obvious value, many of its users still feel guilty about retaining its services. As a result, the PR industry is constantly attempting to improve its *own* image as it produces images for its clients. This defensive posture is especially ironic, because there are logical, justifiable reasons why PR's clients seek its aid. "I've never had anyone come to me and say, 'Make me famous,' " said an executive who represents publisher Rupert Murdoch and hotel executives Harry and Leona Helmsley at the PR firm of Howard J. Rubenstein Associates. "It's more subtle than that. It's for a business purpose. Most of these people don't want [celebrity] for its own sake but for business reasons."

Public relations' dubious image is partly explained by its evolution. Historically, PR has been perceived as entertainment-dominated. Many PR practitioners were ex-newspaper writers who climbed over the fence to promote clients. News reporters have long disdained turncoats who found it expedient to sell their souls to the devil and flood their former newsrooms with promotional material. As early as 1893 a *Boston Globe* staff booklet advised that "any item is a puff which is of more interest to the firm or person mentioned than to the general public."[5] By 1908 the American Newspaper Publishers Association was already tracking the activities of the ever-growing public relations sector for its members.

It was Edward Bernays in the 1920s who began organizing and providing a body of literature for the public relations industry. Bernays, in his book *Crystallizing Public Opinion,* gave professional structure and psychological underpinnings to PR, providing a powerful counterattack to the criticism of PR as an unregulated supplier of pseudo-news.[6] Public relations textbooks over the years began to sound highly businesslike and more moralistic than organized religion. Public relations, according to textbook author Allen Center, "has evolved from outgoing information, to a two-way concept of sending messages and listening to feedback, to a concept in which character and behavior combined with two-way communications, to the present idea of character, conduct, and communications combining to adjust an organization harmoniously with all the publics on which it depends."[7]

The army of promoters, writers, press agents, consultants, and gossip-column-seeders gradually grew to view themselves as members of a profession. Still, no amount of theorizing could dramatically change the reality of stunts, fabrications, and tricks so exalted in public relations lore. The dramatic and macabre staging of Rudolph Valentino's funeral by publicist Harry C. Klemfuss and other agents is one of the classics. Every detail from fake love affairs to posed pictures of the funeral cortege fueled the mile-long crowd. And the promotions continue today. The attempts to make an American recording star of Julio Iglesias, Malcolm Forbes' never-ending efforts to become the Renaissance man, and the Harlem Globetrotters' strategic search for female team member Lynette Woodard—all are accompanied by exaggeration, hyperbole, and some distortion. Each story tends to undermine the public relations quest for image respectability.

Traditionally, the PR business has been associated with the entertainment sector, where the issues of values and ethics never seemed a central concern to anyone. After all, the effect of a dour Bette Davis suddenly becoming a sex goddess isn't of profound importance. In contrast, the spread of PR into sports, religion, science, and other sectors does raise ethical questions.

The image of today's sports figure is developed with the same professional finesse that a Bette Davis received years ago. Before television began to widely distribute such sporting events as the Masters and the NCAA Final Four, PR treatment was limited to a few professional sports and schools with intercollegiate programs. Much of the work, while occasionally brilliant, was haphazard and amateurish. Today, with the widespread availability of televised sports images, sports celebrities enter our consciousness incessantly, raising unlimited opportunities for promotion. Seeking to exploit this trend, sporting goods companies use athletes to endorse their equipment. Teams employ PR to produce the most palatable images of their players while corporations sponsor golf and tennis tournaments to humanize themselves.

Part of the support staff of emerging sports stars are their own PR specialists who will—if any good—reconstruct these celebrities into total packages congruent with their blazing fastballs or overpowering net play. This means that our pitcher may get speech lessons, media encounter training, dress-for-stardom advice, and identification with his or her very own charity. Sports celebrity-making becomes increasingly industrialized as media organizations such as Magid Associates begin to target college athletes for development as mouthpieces and public relations vehicles for their home schools.[8] The student-athlete, whom the university now sees as an important image resource, is taught how to give postgame interviews, relate to local media, appear before alumni and donors, and, above all, protect the university's image.

Today's athletes move through the media channels using many of the same promotion strategies as movie stars. When football running back Walter Payton broke the yardage record for the National Football League, his shoe sponsor publicly presented him a blue $125,000 Lamborghini sports car. National media coverage of Payton getting into his KangaRoo-sponsored car more than compensated the sponsor for its costs. See Walter break the record—see the big celebration following the event—see Walter get into his sports car at the celebration—see everyone getting free publicity.

Another athlete who underwent PR management is Bill Johnson, who was an obscure downhill skier until he won a gold medal at the 1984 Winter Olympics in Yugoslavia. As a result of that success, Johnson bought a BMW and a four-wheeler for his new house in Oregon. He traveled the country making high-fee speaking engagements and granting press interviews to promote a movie about his life. Providing news-gatherers such snippets as the possibility that actor Sean Penn would star in the film, Johnson said, "I'm earning six figures now and I'm hoping for seven by next year."[9] Johnson, promoted throughout the country on the strength of his Olympic success, used public relations strategies no different from those used to promote entertainers or products.

The PR practitioners—the chief story architects in our culture—had good raw material in Johnson. At one time Johnson spoke of himself as a "budding delinquent," having stolen a '56 Chevrolet that had a desireable 350 engine.[10] His aggressive, winning run down the slope wove many stories together: the triumph of the underdog, the hard-fought victory, the vindication of self-confidence. It was ideal material for packaging and development.

For dramatic counterpoint, consider the fate of 1932 speed skating Gold Medalist Irving Jaffee, who ended up in Depression bread lines. Where was Bernays when Jaffee needed him? In 1932, the PR industry wasn't ready to break out of its traditional concentration on business and entertainment.

Today, however, PR touches every facet of American life, *providing more than 70 percent of all information that is published as "news."* As a result, news channels have become highly dependent on PR's output. On Monday, a thirteen-year-old baking wiz—representing the flour manufacturers—makes the rounds on local radio. On Tuesday, a research scientist—funded by a chemical company—describes how a certain mosquito repellent has more resistance power than its competitors. On Wednesday, a well-known actor speaks at the local drugstore chain for Fabergé, eats at a local restaurant, attends an art opening, and makes charming, off-the-cuff remarks to senior citizens. Thursday finds the attorney general's office releasing a study on gang crackdowns. As for Friday, Saturday, and Sunday, it is the usual potpourri of football interviews, film reviews, political and social commentary—all planted and skewed by PR.

The pervasiveness of PR is a crucial aspect of how the Hollywood model invades other sectors. Entertainment-style PR is moving into formerly unadulterated sectors and using story lines, diversification, exploitation of free media, and manipulated images.

Evidence of public relations' move into nonentertainment sectors is everywhere. In the business section of *USA Today*, controversial former Bendix executive Mary Cunningham continued her invasion of every channel of American media. Having married her former boss at Bendix, Bill Agee, Cunningham had written a book that restirred the tumult. The story line this time is *prejudice against women*. Cunningham presented her views on morning shows, in magazine interviews, and in live performances. Former Olympic gymnast Cathy Rigby—now a television commentator—was chronicled in the "Lifestyle" section of the same newspaper.[11] Her saga exhausted half the available story lines: great fame, marriage, divorce, anorexia, bulimia, and now rebirth. For most of us, PR has seeped so subtly into the fabric of our lives that we scarcely realize it's there—whether it is a disc jockey at a grade-school fundraiser, a parade for disabled factory workers, or a TV weatherman speaking to golden-agers about snow predictions. Our thinking is done for us, our attitudes determined by the stories portrayed in the media.

PR has even moved boldly into creating one-week wonders and transferring them into sustained celebrity. A striking example was grade-schooler Samantha Smith, who in 1983 wrote to then Soviet President Yuri Andropov urging peace talks and who ended up visiting the Soviet Union. Smith was transformed with both Russian and American PR help into a specialty sub-industry. In the year following her visit, she began writing a book, appeared on the Johnny Carson show twice, guested on three TV specials, and appeared as a special commentator on "Good Morning America." In the days before her death in 1985, she had even begun filming a network TV series. With the help of publicity and management, Smith—unlike other one-week wonders—was positioned to profit from instant fame, a promotion so successful that she has entered the memory channel: the opening ceremonies of the Russian Goodwill Games in 1986 were dedicated to her, and the Soviet Union named an asteroid in her honor.

There are additional problems with PR's invasion of nonentertainment sectors. In entertainment, the outcome of most events can be controlled. Obviously, in many other sectors, control is a problem. This was learned the hard way by sports celebrity Carl Lewis, who, sportswriter Ron Rapoport observed, moved too quickly from the sports sector to the entertainment sector.[12] Lewis's elaborate staff had contributed greatly to the public expectation about his long-jump attempt in the 1984 Los Angeles Olympics. The public was primed to expect history to be made, with Lewis breaking Bob Beamon's longstanding record. Lewis did nothing to dampen expectations, wearing designer track outfits, living in VIP quarters, signing a contract for a book, and enjoying special interview arrangements. Lewis was now an entertainer, not unlike comedian Robin Williams, expected to deliver on demand. But an earlier event, the hammerthrow, was delayed, and Lewis's event was postponed. The temperature fell as the sun began to set. The packed coliseum crowd grew restless. Where's the record? Where's the victory parade? Endless ABC closeups of Lewis' face, not surprisingly, resembled movie shots, feeding the expectations of the home viewers. But in the cool evening, Lewis' legs began to stiffen. Having jumped far enough to assure victory, he did not make the attempt to break the record, instead withdrawing from the event as disappointed fans began to boo. The pure athlete had become the celebrated performer—but could not deliver the movie script finale. Lewis has seen the potential reward in having PR drive his image, but not the cost in overstimulating demand. As a newspaper reported under the headline "Perplexed Sprinter":

> Carl Lewis, winner of four Olympic track and field gold medals, expressed concern that his unsurpassed success in the Games has turned people against him. "It has alarmed me that many people that knew me and the type of person I was became bitter and angry with me," Lewis said. "During the Olympic Games, people were painting a picture that wasn't me. I was baffled as to why people were doing that at that time. They were creating things that weren't me. Most of them were people who had known me for years. That's what alarmed me. People had created things."[13]

What were the "created things" that Lewis complains of? Nothing but the inevitable consequences of the very forces that he—and PR—had placed in motion.

What Is PR?

PR firms see themselves as brokers that communicate information between their clients and the public. Celebrities normally hire PR firms to help control the distribution of their images to their publics. But PR's role can be much more complex. In the pursuit of transformation, PR firms might develop, control, and even implement an aspirant's entire visibility-generating strategy. In other cases, PR may only issue occasional press releases or stage press conferences when the situation demands. For the aspirant trying to understand PR's power and work out the most useful relationship with it, PR is often crucial to achieving high visibility. It also is not easy to do, given PR's tendency to mystify its working procedures and planning processes. Of course, considering the importance of keeping PR's role behind the scenes, such secrecy is justifiable. (Imagine how the public would feel if every time a piece of PR-generated "news" were broadcast, "PR" flashed on top of the screen. Or if every time a religious leader or corporation president read a speech ghostwritten by his staff, a note was added giving due credit.)

PR experts know intuitively that most people would have less respect for the industry if they were familiar with PR strategy. Occasionally, PR leaders drop their guard and publicly demonstrate their craft. One example is that of the widely respected Henry Rogers of Rogers & Cowan, who has a theory of psychorelations—"people relations elevated to the highest level." His list of ten "Rules for Success" includes Rule Number Four—"Sugar Coating the Truth."[14] This is hardly a guideline that most professions would promote.

PR also serves as the voice of celebrities, not only gaining them audience attention but also constructing their stories and defining their personalities. When actor Burt Reynolds comes to town to promote his latest film, the public sees him through the filtering eyes of public relations. What is the story line? On this trip, it's Reynolds' need to be understood, coupled with his honesty and past problems.[15]

Whether the fundamental stories are or are not true, PR *always* amplifies and distills them for public consumption. The new Reynolds' image may be accurate—it's just that the PR filter puts the most palatable spin on the story. Unfortunately, this often keeps us from fully understanding or identifying with the celebrity as a three-dimensional person. Where is Reynolds? He is somewhere amidst the itinerary, takeoff, and flight of his latest PR regeneration. To the media, he is one more quick press stop and background story. But to the public, he is unknowable, an image filtered through the mill of the publicity-generating system.

The relationship between PR and the celebrity client will always be marked by tension, because celebrities, while benefiting from the relationship, will always be uneasy with surrendering their voices to someone else. This problem becomes magnified when PR becomes so proficient at serving its clients' needs that it goes beyond image-amplifying into image redesign. "Who am I?" ought to be determined in consultation with the client, not solely by the account executive.

Why Does PR Exist?

PR exists because the media need news—news that is often free coverage for celebrities. Control of whom the news features is what the public relations business strives for.

Just as important as *who* is covered, PR exists to control *what* is covered, coordinating, refining, and delivering images of the celebrity to the free news channels. In the past, a new cherry cheesecake usually required an ad campaign to get the consumer's attention. The manufacturer had to pay for this attention. Today, however, the cake manufacturer's PR firm write a "news" story highlighting the fascinating new things to do with frozen cheesecake. The "story" is run *as news*—creating valuable free publicity for the product, supplementing current ads or freeing up advertising monies for other applications.

The same process is at work in celebrity PR. Certain sectors—notably entertainment and sports—have always enjoyed generous free coverage of their celebrities. But as more sectors become fixtures of media coverage, more opportunities develop for celebrities to exploit the coverage public relations creates. At the same time, it becomes increasingly difficult for the public to discriminate between what is PR-based coverage and what is authentic news.

Yet for PR to be effective, the news it creates must not appear artificial or self-serving. The Burt Reynolds story should not look or feel like something that was fed to a reporter but instead like something initiated and written independently. This requirement means that PR must give the story a legitimate hook that warrants news coverage. In most cases the hook relies on dramatic climaxes in the story line. For example, a baseball pitcher in the comeback script is looking back on the struggle or now has some new doubts on his trick screwball. PR copywriters spend the better part of their days trying to give their material an authentic feel. At the same time, they know full well that the celebrity may not appreciate a hook that, while successful in generating coverage, calls into question aspects of their image. There is little doubt that a story on dancer Juliet Prowse rebuilding parts of her body would get printed. There is also little doubt that the damage might outweigh the gain. How about a story on Prowse's redecorated den?

What Do PR People Do?

PR practitioners carry out a number of tasks for their celebrity clients. Each of these tasks can be seen as fundamental PR responsibilities that require special tailoring when applied to celebrity clients:

1. They stage press conferences. This involves arranging for a time and place, writing a press statement, alerting the media, and then coaching the celebrity to answer anticipated questions.
2. They prepare press kits highlighting the key ideas that the celebrity wants televised or printed, including selected quotations and suggestions on story angle.
3. They write speeches. If a celebrity has to be at an awards dinner or on a talk show, PR often writes the script. Because celebrities often do not have the time or skill to write their own material, their presentations are ghostwritten—sometimes by underpaid twenty-two-year-olds. The publicist researches the topic, probes the celebrity's knowledge, and tries to create an authentic-sounding presentation. The real problem is the tension between the publicist's material and the celebrity's own voice and tone. That's why the publicist has to be extremely careful to speak in the client's voice. Worse than an unprepared client is the client who is clearly mouthing someone else's words.
4. They plan and execute publicity tours, travel itineraries, interviews, and speeches. This function gets to the heart of PR's role in celebrity-marketing. They are the brokers of the celebrity product, offering news or persons to venues or shows that need them. PR's tour-planning role also demonstrates PR's expertise at distributing the product to the market. After all, there is serious competition to get on CNN's "Daywatch" show to talk about a new book. The aspirant pays PR to have the connections that will make it happen.

   It is often PR that provides guests for the radio and television talk shows. For many authors or on-tour celebrities, the talk show is the most efficient distribution available.

> *PR: Do you want Clint Eastwood?*
>
> *Host: Sure, but I want to talk about Eastwood* the person.
>
> *PR: No way—he'll only talk about the film.*
>
> *Host: Let's forget Clint Eastwood.*
>
> *PR: No, let's talk about it!*

5. PR tracks the movement of the client's image and gathers feedback from venues and media. One way they chart their success is by subscribing to clipping services, which scan the whole universe of newspapers and magazines and compile files containing every single mention of the celebrity's name. Ironically, it is the client who is billed for the clipping service—the very service that the PR firm uses to justify what it is charging the client. "You won't believe it," says the PR executive. "We got your story into the Hawaii newspapers!" Believe it. You paid for it.
6. They hold hands. This is a critical function, one hard to measure, but vital. One PR executive at Rogers & Cowan was described by a rival executive at another firm as a "handholder." Though the description may well have been a put-down, the ability to handhold a celebrity is not an inconsiderable asset. Celebrities often need assurances, smiles, and pseudo-intimacy. Whether actress Rosanna Arquette is lonely on tour in Nashville, or pitcher Joaquin Andujar is being hassled by his manager, the PR representative can listen and provide rationales. The disdain for handholding is due to the mundane associations with such an act. In a world where it is very hard to evaluate with any precision what you're doing from day to day, a handholder supplies an important service: confidence-building and ego maintenance.
7. They provide or arrange for skills improvement. This area could best be described as celebrity product development. It is a newly developing area for PR firms, in most cases amounting to informal counseling. Both Paul Shefrin of The Shefrin Company and Steve Lewis of Guttman and Pam, Ltd., described informal conferences with clients on how to handle a talk show host. Shefrin, upon encountering an inarticulate client, will send along film clips or seek to place the celebrity in nonconfrontative media settings. In a recent trend, PR firms have begun to stage interview simulations and provide in-depth public-speaking training, media encounter workshops, social skills development, and appearance counseling. Though some PR firms have their own experts, it is far more

common to subcontract the product development to outside consultants. Following the industrialization model, consultants now exist with specialties as narrow as the preparation of authors for media tours.

8. They manage special projects. In the quest for celebrity, large numbers of promotional materials must be developed and disseminated. A common request is for an approved biography. Frequently PR will find a writer who will grind out a custom-designed glorification of the celebrity, complete with memorable quotes. The format may be "as told to," "written with," or ghost-written, but it usually amounts to nothing but a long press release. An example of how this process can become self-serving is the best-selling book on the life of celebrity television preacher Robert Schuller. The biographers, one a member of Schuller's staff and the other a close friend, write of "staggering growth," "hauntingly beautiful strains," "birds singing," and Schuller's "brown hair moving softly in the breeze."[16] Aimed directly at the celebrity worshippers of Schuller, it too easily distorts facts and omits important information.
9. They handle interviews with the media, often interceding in one-on-one situations to act as supervisors and facilitators. This task also involves making strategic decisions on who gets the story. They make decisions based on target market, size of audience, and favors owed.
10. They act, increasingly, as the implementors of the marketing plan. In traditional product marketing, the marketing staff selects the target markets and designs strategy. PR then helps put the plan into action, writes the press releases, and arranges for talent. A recent trend, however, is for PR firms to add marketing capabilities, so that they have more influence and control over the whole marketing process. By doing so, PR is trying to move its influence closer to the decision-making point. PR firms, by adding marketing researchers, running their own focus groups, and encouraging full-service planning, are attempting to make the fundamental strategy decisions.

Why Don't Celebrities Handle Their Own PR?

The most obvious reasons why celebrities don't handle their own PR are cost-effectiveness and economies of scale. It is just not cost-effective for celebrities to do their own PR, or to train their parents to do it. Also, PR representatives are specialists at making connections. These skills are already in place, and adding one more client doesn't mean opening a new office or putting in new phones.

On a broader, more fundamental level, PR is involved with celebrities because every player in the celebrity-marketing process requires information. The media need it in order to inform and entertain readers and viewers. Venues need it to interest potential audience members in attending events. The endorsement companies need information to give the media something to say to readers and viewers other than "Kodak thinks you should buy its film." In the eyes of both the media *and* the manufacturer, it is better to promote the athletic prowess of Kodak's spokesperson Edwin Moses than the improved light sensitivity ratings of Kodak's new film.

To some critics, PR greases the skids, smooths the waters, puts out the "right" story. But for the celebrities who employ its help, PR serves as advocate—putting out the defense that, were it to come directly from the celebrity, would appear more obviously self-serving.

PR and Celebrities

The role PR plays in the celebrity industry is often that of a pure adoration machine, designing, managing, and protecting the celebrity image. Celebrities, like fresh produce, generally have a short shelf life. Skillful manipulation of the media is therefore crucial. The very reason PR exists is that there is only so much media space available, so much time to get the celebrity launched, and, unfortunately, considerable competition. From the perspective of the celebrity, the situation frequently needs a communication specialist. It may be the need to nurture the fragile career of a young actor, the difficult promotion of the concert in the park, or the preparation of an important speech by a business executive. Each of these tasks needs the image-manipulation skills of PR.

PR manipulates images partly by playing on the saleable factors of a name. It is unlikely that the chief executive's philandering, the TV producer's notorious unfairness, or the senator's temper tantrums will be voluntarily offered up by the PR staff. More often PR staffs create a blizzard of skewed information—

accentuating positives, heralding triumphs, and extolling conquests. The truth is not so much ignored as massaged.

But image-making involves more than just accentuating the positive. "When you first get started you want to get your name in the newspapers," said Steve Rubell of Morgans Hotel and The Palladium. Rubell continued:

> Public relations helps. But after that the main purpose of most PR firms, like for Robert Redford, is to keep your name out of the paper unless you have a special problem. I think PR is as much keeping your name out of the papers as getting into the papers.[17]

PR protects its clients from reports on a singer's tax problems, an actor's infidelity, or an athlete's drug habit, sometimes talking reporters out of using the items, sometimes planting corrections or denials, or counseling the celebrity on even whether to respond.

THE TRUTH STRIKES OUT

Robin Monsky handles PR for the Atlanta Braves, a pleasant job that involves providing the media with player's batting averages, pitching records, and other minutiae. But Monsky was overzealous, distributing to reporters not only the favorable statistics but also stats on "Failing to Hit in Clutch Situations" and "Pitchers' Early Innings Troubles." This dispersal of true information would strike most people as fine. After all, said Monsky, "Is it my role to provide an objective view of my team? Or is it to provide fluff?"[18]

The answer was—fluff. The team's manager, Chuck Tanner, was incensed, ordering Monsky off the field, off the bus, and off the plane. This apparent abridgement of fair play and free speech was supported enthusiastically by the club's PR and promotions director. He blithely dismissed Monsky's charge by saying, "Chuck's the captain of the ship. When you're selling something, you sell the good side."

There are other reasons for PR's importance to celebrity-marketing. We've already seen why there is more crisis in celebrities' lives. When a celebrity comes under attack because of scandal or poor performance, it is PR that is usually responsible for improving, or even salvaging, the celebrities' situation. The response might be as grand as Michael Jackson on his first Victory Tour giving gate receipts to charity to stall criticism of high ticket prices, or as mundane as arranging for the celebrity to meet with a previously shunned small-town reporter. PR is suited to putting out strategic positive information, since it has access to sources and knows how to limit damage. In this same vein, PR serves to clarify conflicting and potentially damaging stories. There are many sources developing information on celebrities. It might be a game-maker, a chewing-gum sponsor, a weekly magazine, or the barber of a close friend. Some of the information may be contradictory, wrong, or damaging. The damage-control headlines inspired by PR have included "Sonny Bono Tells His Side of the Story," "Erica Jong Fearlessly Faces Life in the '80s," "The Rebirth of King Crimson," "Eddie Murphy was a Victim in Brawl, Manager Says," and "Baron Hilton Fights for Hilton Hotels." PR usually acts as a clearinghouse and final word for clarity on the celebrity's image.

Who Does Celebrity PR?

In the informal ranking system within the celebrity industry, public relations practitioners are often rated by their clients as "A," "B," or "C" publicists. An "A" publicist represents high-priced talent such as Lionel Richie, Mobil Oil, or the Archdiocese of New York. A "B" publicist may handle successful, "almost there" clients. A "C" publicist represents newcomers or comeback candidates. Aspirants can save a lot of time by understanding where they might fit in the alphabet, given their present status in the celebrity hierarchy, their resources, and their needs.

The aspirant needs to analyze the choice of PR support with the same critical eye as decisions on sector, manager, or transformation method. Most aspirants will first approach either a solo PR practitioner or a small firm in the "C" or "B" class. In this category, the aspirant can expect personal attention, but without the research abilities and full-service facilities of the larger, higher-ranked organizations.

In contrast to small publicist operations are the large PR firms that specialize in serving an exclusive set of celebrity clients, such as Rogers & Cowan and Guttman and Pam. Far less accessible to the novice aspirant, these firms are structured much like traditional firms, with office managers, researchers, and account managers. A full-service celebrity specialty house can mount very large campaigns, exploiting established connections to obtain quality PR exposure and generally serving as the celebrity's spokesperson.

Another group of PR firms are the multi-faceted public relations firms, such as Hill and Knowlton and Burson-Marsteller, that also handle celebrities. But these PR firms represent many different levels of clients, in different sectors. Typically they have a variety of clients representing individuals in entertainment and business, as well as representing products, public-interest groups, and nonprofit institutions. An aspirant in the political, business, or academic sector often feels more comfortable with these multi-dimensional firms, possibly because they lack the show-biz profile of the celebrities-intensive organizations.

PR services are also provided within large organizations such as movie and record companies, religious organizations, and large corporations that employ celebrities. These organizations promote celebrities, not for the celebrities' exclusive benefit but for the profit-making interest of the corporation. Their promotion strategies can vary. Alberto-Culver, the personal-care products company, employed actor Billy Dee Williams to promote hair products through commercials, speeches, and personal appearances. Even firms outside the traditional consumer products sector use this strategy. Architect Helmut Jahn employs an assistant for publicity and marketing to assure that his image is promoted through PR channels as a way to keep the firm's name before potential clients.

Venues also manage their own PR, promoting celebrities for the purpose of making money for the places where they appear. It might be a nightclub, Great America theme park, the Hyatt cocktail lounge, or the Rose Bowl. Although rarely generating new PR information, such performance sites can give the celebrity's official story a boost if supplied with the appropriate PR material.

In the end, the aspirant must realize that good public relations requires cooperation and exchange of information. When novelist James Michener addresses a college audience, the local student activities board does not generate Michener material from scratch. Material may come from the in-house PR staff at the author's publishing firm or agent, or even from freelance PR professionals the author himself retains. In this sense, celebrity PR is a cooperative venture that needs careful orchestration and planning.

PR's Style

On one level—a level most of us see every day—PR is marked by a distinctive style. PR releases are characterized by writing that is flattering, anecdotal, and very selective, a style that English teachers dislike. Press releases are written to be rewritten and feature quotations that can be easily reproduced in "news" stories. The press kit from the film *Cannonball Run II* is illustrative:

> Like most young men of the period who could carry a tune, [Dean] Martin did imitations of Bing Crosby and other trend-setting radio singers and he developed a pleasant easy style of his own. By 1946, he was singing at the 500 Club in Atlantic City, New Jersey. On the same bill was Jerry Lewis, a comedian Martin had met several times in the course of their budding careers. When the club owner found himself minus an act, Dean and Jerry induced him to let them go on as a double, and the team of Martin and Lewis was born. Martin recalls, "We laid the biggest bomb in nightclub history when we first started." The following night, however, they went on and ad-libbed. The audience loved it, and them. A new chapter in show business was opened.[19]

Who is the voice of this press release? The fact is that we rarely think much about who is speaking. This voice is complimentary, easy to read, and well informed. Is the voice young? old? female? Catholic? Actually, it is none of the above. The PR style, while pleasant, has no author or accent, and very little modesty.

PR's style is typically selective in its use of facts, ignoring the negatives in sometimes confounding juxtapositions. In trying to extricate Martin from the split with his comedian partner, the release simply says, "After eight years and 16 movies together, Martin and Lewis parted company and went on to enormously successful separate careers."[20] The press release treats the parting not unlike that of two aging shoe store operators who decide peacefully to retire to Arizona. In truth, the parting of Martin and Lewis was one of the most bitter, angry breakups in the annals of entertainment. It is not hard to believe that a lot of time was devoted to that line. The line—like much of PR—is not inaccurate; it's simply not the whole truth. It is a quick, easy, and logical solution to the problem—the typical kind of solution that keeps PR's own image in difficulty.

Another of PR's stylistic devices is the use of positive action terms. In the *Cannonball Run II* press release, such terms as "a pleasant, easy style," "budding careers," "the audience loved it," "a new show business chapter," and "enormously successful" are kneaded into the prose. There is a core vocabulary of PR power words that includes "emerging," "developing," "hot," "legendary," and "multi-talented." The vocabulary becomes so much a part of our audience experience that "critical praise" seems like one word. In PR terms, "great" may only mean "workmanlike" and "earnest" may mean "forgettable."

Another stylistic device of PR is to take the basic celebrity story lines and tie them in to natural opportunities, meaning *any* media need, from seasonal to culinary. Thus we have stories about celebrity birthdays, favorite summer vacations, foods, hobbies, and charity commitments. Every year at Christmas, there are a number of stories on what the holidays mean to celebrities. "Celebrities Act Out Home-Staged Holiday."[21] "Dolly Parton Just Loves an Old-Fashioned Christmas." "Meryl Streep Likes to Do the Manhattan Thing for the Holidays." "What Is a Los Angeles Christmas Like for Kenny Rogers?"

All the above strategies, functions, and styles of PR work only in service of a larger purpose—to create, manage, and control news for an aspirant or celebrity. As a consequence, certain conventions emerge that are understood and seen only by PR. When feminist Gloria Steinem held a large, glamorous fiftieth-birthday for herself in 1984, the press coverage was massive. Most of the media seemed enraptured with the PR-generated story line: that celebrity Steinem stood for the discovery of the beautiful older woman. This "birthday story" featured Steinem in a bubble bath with a glowing gaze. The party and the observations of the media on the new, mature older woman came across as hard news. The press or media never showed the wires being pulled by PR, never hinted at the self-serving staging of the event. Nowhere does this story indicate to the reader that it is not the "hard news" that it tries to imitate. Actually, it is a series of cleverly constructed story lines with the ultimate purpose of building Steinem's image and supporting her business ventures. It is not incidental to the story that Steinem would eventually become a temporary host of the "Today Show," and be relaunched as an all-purpose media personality specializing in interviewing celebrities.

The Steinem birthday story demonstrates that almost everyone winds up cooperating with the PR machine because it is so powerful and useful. There is Steinem, the movement leader and working woman's representative, becoming a beautiful person and cavorting with other celebrities. How celebrities can be tempted by visibility's rewards can be seen in the new cooperative attitudes of former political radicals Jerry Rubin and Eldridge Cleaver. They were once the scourge of the culture—attacking and baiting, playing against middle-class sensibilities. Today, both find it far easier to cooperate, give friendly interviews, stage events, and end up on the feature page than to face the alternative of obscurity. In the 1960s and early 1970s, a viable story line was to run against the mainstream. Those who exploited this story line gained great PR coverage. But the culture—and, therefore, the most productive story lines—changes. The PR machine eases the transition, acquainting the public with the new story in the least jarring, most familiar way possible.

Selling the Story

What are PR's options in building an aspirant into a celebrity? Most of the strategies involve getting the story scripts into play. This means finding a strategy to entice the reporters to use the generated story. One seemingly simple tactic is to write the truth—that is, to find a legitimate story about the aspirant and simply report it. In the 1984 Olympics, Jeff Blatnick, a Greco-Roman wrestler, overcame cancer to win a gold medal. At the moment of victory, before millions of viewers, Blatnick leaped about the arena in a genuinely emotional expression of triumph, then broke down in tears. The story stands on its own as inspirational and interesting. It also has enough media interest to be used without distortion and requires only a minimum of PR intervention.

The second approach is to embellish a legitimate story. Here, PR highlights a factor, exaggerates a key element, or invents a motivation that didn't really exist. The evangelist from a middle-class background is portrayed as dirt poor in order to appear closer to the people. A country singer who misses her husband is said to sing her lyrics with more passion. A bright corporate president is supposedly sleeping just four hours a night, flying his own Lear jet, and longing for his spouse, all in pursuit of closing the merger. The key strategy is to highlight the little features that help audiences identify with the highly visible.

A third approach is to contrive a story, either making up one of its key elements, inventing an entirely new one, or selectively suppressing aspects of the story that do not match the strategy. The story can be as simple as denying the rocky state of the candidate's marriage during the campaign, insisting that the crusading company president has no plans to bust the union, or stating that the reason why the priest took the leave of absence was to research a new book, not recover from alcoholism. To combat rampant rumors about the state of their marriage, Buckingham Palace once presented Prince Charles and Princess Diana in a carefully staged television broadcast that displayed the royal couple as more happy and affectionate than was conceivable for *any* couple—fairytale or real.

The spread of contrivance is an international fact. In the past, when some negative event occurred in a movie star's life, the audience was shocked at the deviation from the unflawed images built up by PR. Today, PR is involved in image enhancement in so many sectors that we routinely come to believe in characters who have no flaws. When amateur runner Mary Decker fell in her much-publicized Olympic duel with South Africa's Zola Budd, it placed into perspective her entire image campaign. Decker's rise to prominence had been based partly on accenting certain positive character qualities to the exclusion of all else: the heroic Mary fighting off injury, finding love, preparing for the last mythic battle. But when she ran up on Budd's youthful ankles and fell, collapsing in wracking sobs and being carried off by her muscular fiancé, reality began to deviate from image. She looked like Elizabeth Taylor playing Cleopatra as she was ferried to the press room to reconstruct the race. At the press conference, Decker was angry, unsportsmanlike, and somewhat shrill, dropping for a brief moment her persona. Zola Budd had committed the ultimate anti-PR act—derailing the story.

A variation on contrivance is the reverse negative. PR is always looking for a hook on which to build a story, one that features a client suffering, enduring, and resurfacing healed. It's a story line so powerful with audiences that *People* magazine in its "Coping" section devotes almost weekly coverage to it. George McGovern—repudiated by the American people in the 1972 presidential election—is now at peace with himself. Former Olympic sprinter and Dallas Cowboy football star Bob Hayes, convicted of drug charges, has reached a new understanding of himself and is now fit to endorse products. Under the reverse negative, Hayes can make visibility-generating, instrumental value out of a plain negative.

Film director Francis Ford Coppola has made a career out of exploiting the reverse negative. Each of his films seems to be burdened with a powerful, behind-the-scenes tragic story that foreshadows box-office doom. Opportunistically, PR can usually generate massive amounts of coverage over the problems. Typical was Coppola's film *The Cotton Club,* whose production problems intrigued many critics, who then regaled their audiences with retelling of these tales:

- producer Robert Evans and Coppola fought like dogs
- Richard Gere left the set
- production costs were mind-boggling—$48 million
- a number of writers left the project

The film's problems became legendary as the story churned through all of the channels of media: Despite the major problems, despite haggling and warfare, art triumphs. A new story line then oscillated through the media: Coppola needs stress to produce his art.

The reverse negative operates from the cynical but plausible premise that the only bad press is no press. Though Johnny Carson excoriated Bo Derek's film *Bolero,* her interview on "The Tonight Show" only promoted box-office receipts and video rentals. The ever-buoyant Derek spoke about the problems of the film with resolution and commendable single-mindedness. The making of *Bolero,* according to Derek, consisted of a series of strange and sometimes humorous occurrences. *Bolero* was mentioned with the frequency of Tide commercials. This is the key to the reverse negative strategy: keeping the name in play. The downside risk is the danger of the media and the audience concentrating on the negative connotations—a risk that in the case of *Bolero* was well worth taking.

PR's PR

The latest celebrity promotion strategy is to write stories not about the celebrity but about the celebrity's PR. How was the publicity for Bob Geldof's "Live Aid" concert orchestrated? Who was the true brains behind the Mobil Oil anti-media campaign? Celebrities become ennobled by the amount of manipulation that their staffs achieve. The *chutzpah* of the PR aide becomes legendary.

"How can we get attention?" has always been the main agenda for PR. What hasn't been done? Can we put a new twist on an old idea? The truth is that stories and scandals are generated and then regenerated. The classical appeals—the elements of shock, suspense, sympathy—are the stock strategies of PR:

> "I've got it," cries the account executive. "Let's have a soap opera character who writes novels on the show, put her name on a real novel—her screen name, that is—and tour her in character to tout the book. If that doesn't get her attention and sell some books, let's change her name and claim she's a descendant of William Faulkner. Or, we could try to get Norman Mailer to claim that she's as talented as Erica Jong. How about renting a 747 and dropping . . ."

Building the Buzz

Whenever venue managers get together, whether they're nightclub owners, sports team managers, or executive recruiters, the subject inevitably turns to who's "hot." The discussion sounds like a combination weather report and occult religious service as magic terms pepper the conversation: "lots of steam," "generates a power," "lights up the place," "hard to describe," "high concept," "a love affair with the audience." What is usually being described is some celebrity who seems to be in high demand. Do you remember when John Travolta was every producer's dream? Or how about the flood of publicity for the Armenian place-kicker for the Miami Dolphins, Garo Yepremian? In politics, everyone said to watch Senator Ernest Hollings of South Carolina. What was a New York party without Baby Jane Holzer? Norman Vincent Peale was once a very high concept. In PR terms, when you're hot, you can sell just about anything. It is the job of PR to make celebrities hot: to get people talking, to create momentum, to build a buzz.

A buzz is really a configuration of elements that gets attention and sustains it. It generally involves a formula drawn from six key elements of PR choices:

- audience: the specific needs
- story selection: the right story
- timing: when to do it
- positioning: where to do it
- placement: what sector and venue
- staging: the exact launching vehicle

These elements are mixed to create the excitement and sense of anticipation associated with a buzz.

In most cases, a particular choice may be crucial. An example is how agent Sid Bernstein's launching of singer Laura Branigan emphasized positioning and staging. Instead of launching her in traditional venues such as nightclubs, he arranged for her to sing for small parties of entertainment-industry opinion leaders. His final staging was a very intimate recital for the president of Atlantic Records, who liked her and signed her.

PR people faced the issue of what to do with Chicago Bulls basketball star Michael Jordan. He was fortunate enough to come along in an Olympic year and possess highly marketable basketball skills—great court sense, and quick, fluid, dramatic moves. But despite all of his abilities, a marketable story was needed. In this case the story selected was that he was the new Dr. J—supertalented, good guy, citizen. Placement and staging then became crucial. Jordan made the rounds of talk shows, accepted the best products to endorse, produced high-quality commercials, and even appeared as a fashion model. The worst that could happen would be that Jordan got lost in the array of competing basketball talent, was not given playing time, or became involved in drugs or scandal—in which case, the possibility of maintaining the buzz is remote.

In some cases, marketing dominates the buzz-building process. When rock singer Bruce Springsteen first surfaced, he was marketed as the new Bob Dylan. The similarities with Dylan were extolled: They looked alike, sang alike, were real poets from the streets. When this positioning failed, PR constructed a follow-up campaign based on a newly generated concept for Springsteen: blue-collar rock singer. In this phase of Springsteen's marketing, all six buzz-building elements were used together.

- Audience: the public desire for an authentic-seeming music hero
- Story: that Springsteen, man of the streets, sang of his real life and friends from New Jersey
- Timing: his record was promoted heavily first to the trade and to the media, and only then to the general public.
- Positioning, Placement and Staging: For his new public debut, a nightclub was selected that was purposefully too small to handle the crowd, creating the impression of excitement and intense popularity

As a result of this carefully orchestrated buzz-building strategy, Springsteen simultaneously appeared on the covers of *Time* and *Newsweek*, and had a top-selling album.

Whose Voice?

Usually when celebrity-makers and aspirants congregate, the topic turns to PR. The criticism is all too familiar: PR takes too much credit, lacks content, handles too many clients, advances its own agenda, and overcharges. What's more, PR fuels its own image problems by often trying to enter a more lucrative area of the celebrity industry. Discontented with just promoting the celebrity's concept, and wanting the greater profits of ownership and control, PR often attempts to move into producing and managing talent.

For the highly visible, how to manage the relationship with PR is a critical issue. The many advantages that PR offers are balanced against the tradeoffs of loss of control, inaccuracy, and image with the audience. *PR, ultimately, by being the voice of the celebrity, defines the celebrity's relationship with the audience.* It is understandable that sometimes aspirants feel that their images have been designed by strangers. But the fact is that PR can help drive aspirants to a sector's peak and help sustain them once they are there. This critical phase of celebrity-marketing—sustaining visibility—is the subject of the next chapter.

CHAPTER ELEVEN

Sustaining Celebrity

"On with the show," Lawrence Welk earnestly implores, "and another Harry Warren song from the movie 42nd Street. *Boys, let's shuffle off to Buffalo. Ready, everybody? A-one, a-two . . ."*

The career of bandleader Lawrence Welk has spanned six decades. Starting in the small towns of North Dakota, Welk toured the plains playing the standards of the day. Moving to Chicago in the Big Band era, he was a staple of the hotel circuit. He early seized the opportunity to move into television, and his blend of old musical favorites, traditional arrangements, and musicians playing unfashionable tubas, marimbas, and accordions entertained enormous audiences over a record-breaking span of time. Even with Welk in semi-retirement, his image power remains strong. Although he is no longer seen live on television, Welk's name retains strong commercial appeal. The Welk empire now includes Lawrence Welk Village, a retirement community in Escondido, California. The 1,000-acre complex encompasses 456 mobile homes, 286 vacation villas, two golf courses, a ninety-room hotel, a restaurant, a dinner theater, a shopping village, and a gift shop where Welk fans can buy ashtrays, calendars, and appointment books with the Welk signature.[1] Although the champagne bubbles die, the beat lives on.

What Is "Sustaining" Celebrity?

Once a product's market share is established, defending it becomes the issue, and different strategies come into play. The same is true of manufacturing celebrities: The forces and strategies that create them are not the same as those that sustain them. In theory, to sustain celebrity means to stretch out one's period of high visibility, in order to prolong celebrity's rewards. Practically, however, the process is not so cut and dried. As our Lawrence Welk example illustrates, there is a wide range of possible career patterns. Some examples:

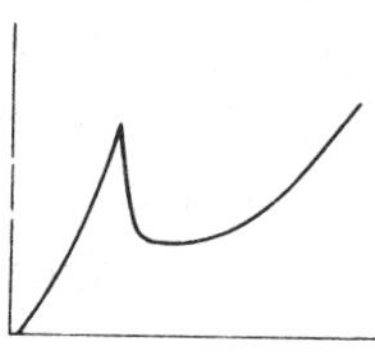

Primary Career—very short

Celebrity Durability—very high, because of youthful, dramatic, story-intense death leading to Legend Status

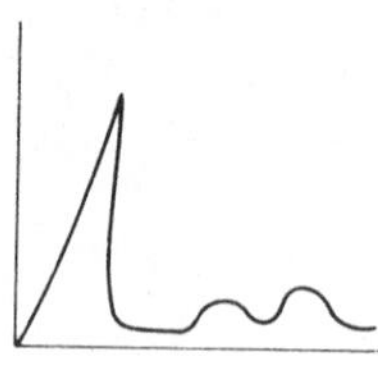

Primary Career—short, curtailed by physically outgrowing the requirements of her sector niche

Celebrity Durability—sporadic, with career re-energized by a subsequent sector-shift into politics featuring a poor choice of mentor (Richard Nixon)

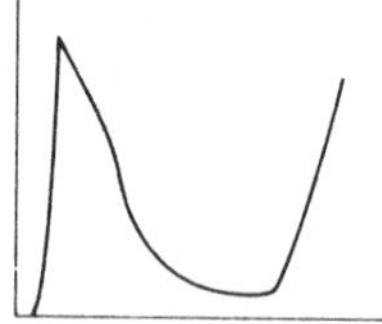

Primary Career—intense but brief; curtailed by changing styles within her original sector (fashion)

Celebrity Durability—delayed but excellent; her long period of low celebrity utility was followed by a classic shift into a related sector (theater), resulting in a secondary celebrity career with an even greater potential lifespan than the first

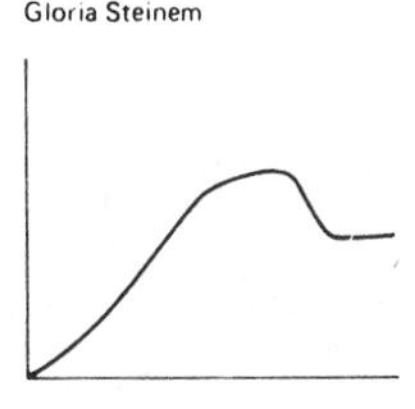

Primary Career—very long, but eventually diminished from active leadership of woman's movement

Celebrity Durability—permanent; because of successful long-term legend-building strategies, Steinem leads a life as a revered symbol of another age, lending her celebrity status to causes

Steinem's career is an example of near-perfect sustain: a steady rise; a long-lived, high-visibility plateau; followed by a lifelong, post-career coast in the limelight. But Steinem's experience is comparatively rare. There was a time when daredevil Evel Knievel seemed headed for novelty immortality; when H. L. Hunt was quoted in every business magazine; when presidential aspirant Eugene McCarthy was the number-one draw on college campuses; when parapsychologist Uri Geller was booked on every major talk show in the country; when Olympic swimming star Mark Spitz could choose from endorsement contracts offered by major advertisers. In each case, these celebrities rose to the very pinnacle of their sectors, enjoyed the rewards of high visibility, and lost them. Today, these figures exist in the twilight of celebrity afterlife, intermittently surfacing in the media, enjoying little utility from their once powerful names. *In each case, strategic errors contributed to their failure to sustain highly visible careers*.

How Sustaining Is Measured

Each celebrity sector is governed by its own unique rules, conventions, and informal understandings with its audiences. Daredevil Knievel once dramatically announced that he would pilot a death-defying rocket-powered skycycle across a gorge in the Rocky Mountains. The millions who tuned in to watch live on ABC's "Wide World of Sports" had clear expectations. After all, daredevils are supposed to hurtle fire-belching motorcycles over obstacles, plunge their shackled bodies into raging rivers, or be shot smilingly from cannons. They are supposed to succeed, or at least fail spectacularly. They are not, as Knievel did, supposed to trickle off the side of the Snake Canyon to an ignominious parachute-softened landing.

The fiasco severely affected Knievel's ability to sustain himself at the top of the daredevil sector. His decline was measurable: reduced attendance at his appearances, less television coverage, less media attention.

As the Knievel case makes clear, sustaining celebrity involves two factors: how visible a celebrity remains, and for how long his or her longevity can be extended.

Longevity can be measured simply in units of time: years in office, months on the record charts, seasons as a starter. Visibility, as we've seen, can be measured, too. Both must be maintained to stave off decline.

Causes of Decline

To avoid decline, celebrities must understand the factors that cause it. Ten of the most widespread include:

THE UNCONTROLLABLE EGO

Under the pressure of high visibility, a celebrity's self-confidence often grows into cockiness or arrogance. Partially this is due to the large entourages of obsequious support personnel that surround the celebrity. As comedian Eddie Murphy has said, "Everyone around you is telling you you're a genius. You start thinkin', 'Man, I *am* a genius. I can do anything!' "[2] Celebrity lore is replete with celebrities whose inflated egos decimated their ability to process information and make objective decisions—or listen to those who could. Legendary comedian Lou Costello became so egomaniacal that his family life suffered, his professional associations were damaged, and his career was severely affected.[3] "Miami Vice" co-star Philip Michael Thomas suffered a severe image setback after an especially egocentric interview in *People* magazine.[4] Angry letters to the editor included such comments as, "If Thomas's future goals include an Emmy, Grammy, Oscar and Tony, perhaps he had better drop his egotistical attitude and start working on his so-called talent,"[5] and "The man is a legend in his own mind."[6] One especially miffed fan wrote:

> I can appreciate a positive attitude in a person as a plus to their personality, but in Philip Michael Thomas's case it's more like megalomania. Suffice it to say that on the third day after his death, Thomas is going to be mighty surprised to realize that he hasn't risen.[7]

UNPLANNED OBSOLESCENCE

Changes outside a celebrity's control can initiate a decline. Music Television (MTV) has forced non-visually oriented rock groups out of celebrity contention. In the religious sector, local preachers have been dealt severe blows by wholesale defections to the "electronic ministry" of Jerry Falwell, Rex Humbard, and others. The advent of widespread baseball telecasts has all but destroyed the minor league baseball player's opportunity for more than local celebrity.

ADAPTATION

As sector trends evolve, so must celebrity's strategies. In the business sector, many old-style "seat of the pants, gut instinct"-type managers have been displaced by the new strategy-minded MBAs. In tennis, the traditional baseline ralliers were overshadowed by the shift to the boom-serve-and-volley game. The old-style comedian finds stand-up venues disappearing and more opportunities in comic acting.

DE-LINKINGS

Celebrities who have risen to high visibility as part of groups, or with the key help of another party, often cannot survive being abandoned. The death of Karen Carpenter . . . an aspiring boxer's rejection by celebrity manager Angelo Dundee . . . the defection of a Russian celebrity gymnast's coach to the United States: Each is a potentially career-threatening "de-linking."

THE PICTURE OF DORIAN GRAY

One legacy of the diffusion of the Hollywood model throughout all sectors is audiences' growing preoccupation with youthfulness. Highly competent business sector aspirants can age themselves right out of celebrity contention. Qualified news anchors may lose their positions to inexperienced journalism school graduates. Aspirants in the religious sector may not even have a chance at high visibility until they reach a minimum age. Child actors, rising fast on the basis of their precociousness, may find their careers terminated by age fifteen.

DECLINING ABILITY

In sectors where there are significant physical ability requirements, aging can make it impossible for the celebrity to perform up to standards or expectations—one reason why there is so much lying about age in certain sectors. Lawyers who can no longer withstand the rigors of a five-month trial ... aging sports celebrities in all areas ... Blue Angels aerobatics team fighter pilots whose reaction times slow below minimum tolerance ... rodeo stars who can no longer wrestle the steer ... dancers who lose flexibility and endurance—all are examples of declining ability.

POOR PERFORMANCE

Repeated failure to satisfy audience expectations can trigger an unstoppable decline: Sly of Sly and the Family Stone taking success for granted, giving shorter and shorter concerts, often not even showing up ... the NBA superstar with the guaranteed contract failing to maintain his level of play ... the regional sales manager whose territory falls below quota for three years in a row—these are examples of poor performance.

VENUE EROSION

The disappearance of the forums in which aspirants appear can be devastating: California self-improvement gurus find society's focus shifting to social consciousness ... sitcom actors face a network shift to action series ... business celebrities in smokestack industries see the economy changing to high tech—these are examples of venue erosion.

SELF-DESTRUCTION

Distinct from poor or uneven performances, celebrities can intentionally act against their own best interests: comedian Shelley Berman displaying his temper on national TV and rapidly declining in visibility . . . rock star Joe Cocker, at the peak of his career, suffering from alcoholism . . . evangelist Herbert W. Armstrong divorcing his wife and remarrying, despite his own church's absolute rules to the contrary.

SCANDAL

Scandal—whether true *or* false—can destroy or severely damage a celebrity career. Vanessa Redgrave's admitted sympathy for the Palestinian cause blocked her access to numerous venues, while numerous sports figures alleged but not proven to be involved with drugs may suffer, too—and damage the reputation of their sponsors in the process. Continuing revelations of impropriety in the business affairs of Bert Lance moved him out of national visibility. Even Lee Iacocca needed to move quickly to repair an image damaged by his forced removal as chairman of the Statue of Liberty centennial campaign.

These patterns and causes of decline can seriously damage or destroy a celebrity career. But the damage need not be permanent. Many celebrities, encountering decline, hit upon counterstrategies that allow them to trace career patterns as rhythmic as a sine wave. They rise steadily to prominence, encounter one or several of the factors cited above, decline to invisibility, then rise again. What are the key factors involved in sustaining celebrity?

How to Sustain: Retaining the Audience

EXPOSURE

But by far the most important factor in sustaining visibility is exposure: how often, in what ways, and in which places the aspirant's image is distributed to audiences. Because audiences' appetites for celebrities are not infinite, the key to sustaining visibility is to achieve a balance: between a level too low to produce well-knownness and one so high that it satiates audience demand, destroying fan interest. Governing all exposure strategy is the law of diminishing returns: In the early stages of attraction, fans can absorb a barrage of celebrity images and still not be satisfied. Over time, however, too much exposure becomes counterproductive. Money spent to expose the celebrity early in his or her career, while not seeming to pay immediate, adequate returns, may be money well spent building the audience base. Celebrity's marketers must understand the principle of investment spending, that more money must be spent to generate a unit of well-knownness than needs to be spent to sustain well-knownness. In other words, it is more expensive to attract audiences than to keep them. Of course, the reverse is also true: If spent too quickly, each additional dollar spent exposing the celebrity may begin to return *less* than a dollar in rewards. Farrah Fawcett, overexposed through every channel from TV to posters to magazine covers, once wore her audience out. David Mahoney, chairman of Avis, featured in a comprehensive $23 million advertising campaign, was similarly overexposed. "Mahoney gets smaller and smaller the longer you watch," said an advertising executive at the time. Eventually, he completely disappeared.[8]

Conversely, too *little* exposure forces audiences to engage in their own form of "investment spending"—pouring time and energy into a search for new celebrities. Such high-visibility candidates as professional hockey stars, lacking the exposure afforded by network television, can force potential fans to turn to other aspirants who are more widely distributed. A fan living in a region that idolizes stock car drivers may become caught up in such worship but then move to a region where the absence of racing or media coverage forces him or her to abandon these new celebrities. "Serious" stage actors, limited to small venues, may never play to enough of the public to energize mass appeal. An aspirant has to be aware of how to provide the minimal amount of exposure to satisfy, but not overwhelm, audience demand.

STOOPING TO CONQUER: COUNTERSTRATEGY

Sometimes, a decline in sector celebrity is strategically advantageous. The mobster planning to run for union leadership, seeking enhanced respectability, will gladly surrender visibility within the criminal sector in return for broader support among the larger audience of union members. Singer Linda Ronstadt traded off some of her visibility among young rock fans in return for less fanatical, but far more durable, support among a middle-aged audience. The success of her 1950s-style collaborations with bandleader Nelson Riddle bears out the wisdom of her decision.

STRATEGIC UNDEREXPOSURE

At some point, celebrities obtain the optimally sized audience for the resources they have to invest, balanced against the rewards they desire. But how can this equilibrium be maintained? One way is through strategic underexposure: deliberately maintaining a small audience because of its relatively low maintenance cost. The rock band The Grateful Dead has enjoyed extremely high fan loyalty for more than twenty years, but only by allowing its fans to feel a part of a very exclusive group. By keeping the size of their audience relatively small, by making infrequent appearances and playing many small venues, the Dead have perpetuated fan support without either letting it die out or balloon to the point where the aura of uniqueness could be destroyed.

But overexposure and underexposure are not the only dangers to long-term celebrity. Conflicting exposure and confusing exposure can be just as harmful.

CONFLICTING EXPOSURE

Trying to attract two dissimilar audiences at the same time can alienate both. Betty Ford, while First Lady, tried to appeal both to the *conservative* constituency by playing the role of loyal Republican wife, and to the *feminist* audience with her liberated, independent rhetoric. The result was a muddled public image that never achieved sharpness. Pope John Paul II has galvanized liberal Catholicism with his human, down-to-earth appeal—and simultaneously alienated it with dogmatic, traditional pronouncements and rulings aimed at the mainstream Catholic constituency.

INDECENT EXPOSURE

It is the dream of many celebrities to capture every audience member in captivity. The realities of target marketing, while clear and sensible, are never as attractive as desiring exposure to larger and larger audiences. Amy Grant, who first rose to high visibility as a Christian singer, is proof. In tailoring her message to the Christian listening market, Grant rose to the top of her sector with Bible verses sung to rock tunes. But this is where conflicting exposure began to affect her. In a move to expand her market to include secular popular music listeners, Grant downplayed the overtly religious tone of her songs and took Biblical verses out of her lyrics. In an image-altering move, she donned a leopard print jacket and assumed more pop music-style stage manners. She even gave a provocative interview on sunbathing in the nude. The results were predictable, as the pursuit of the two audiences caused a conflict. Grant was accused by her religious listeners of adopting secular ways, a charge intensified by Grant's temporary sponsorship by beer and cigarette companies. And some mainstream music listeners resisted her conflicting message as well. As a result, Grant's pastor was forced to come to her defense. In an interview in *Christianity Today*, he said, "She doesn't want to be a sex symbol, but wants sex to be seen as a good thing, a Godly thing."[9] Grant herself confronted the conflicting exposure issue directly, telling interviewers that she had thought through the problem and decided that music was a way to bridge the gap between unbelievers and the faithful. Undeterred, she continued to refine her type and rework her material to clarify her appeal to the larger secular market. While her redefinition still meets some resistance, her record sales climb, and her exposure rises.

CONFUSING EXPOSURE

Making different appeals to different audiences causes problems; making them to the *same* audience is also dangerous. Evangelist Billy Graham cultivated a loyal, conservative audience over a long period of time, then thoroughly confused it with his visits to the

Soviet Union and his claim that "religious freedom" exists there. While somewhat more tolerated in the entertainment sector, changes such as Bill Murray's, from comedian to serious actor in the film *The Razor's Edge*, sent confusing signals to his established audience.

Exposure: What, Where, How

Exposure is critical to all celebrities, but just what it is varies widely from sector to sector. In entertainment, exposure may mean promotional activities such as talk shows, interviews, and charity appearances, as well as formal performances, such as appearing in concert or in games. In sectors such as business, academia, or the professions, exposure means conference appearances, speeches, trade show visits, cocktail party attendance, or articles in journals.

Clearly, there is a quantity/quality tradeoff in managing exposure. Is it better to be seen by fewer members of the right audience or by many members of the wrong audience? A wide receiver in college may start every game and be seen by hundreds of thousands of fans, then sit out the bowl game with injuries and escape the notice of a dozen pro scouts who could control his fate. A young priest may have the smallest congregation in the county but be the youngest member of the highly visible National Council.

EXPOSURE BALANCING

For the football player, the priest, and all other aspirants, a key to sustaining celebrity status is to balance *audience-building activities* and *audience-satisfying activities*. Aspirants who fail to appreciate the differences between them do so at their peril.

Most fans meet their celebrities parasocially; not in the flesh, but as images distributed through channels. Nevertheless, the evidence is strong that fans adopt celebrities through almost the same psychological process that governs their adoption of friends and other intimates. Logically, celebrities must make themselves known to fans before they can expect audiences to hold them intensely enough to buy their records, elect them to office, or come to see them pitch or play tennis.

Exposure management means balancing the amount of energy invested in generating an audience against the reward that can be reaped from that audience. Ideally, the celebrity controls the process. More often, it seems, it is a matter of reacting to negative exposure (harsh reviews, poor performances, bad decisions) by generating positive exposure (press conferences, photo opportunities, charity appearances).

How to balance exposure depends on many factors. One, of course, is sector conventions. In the business sector, activities that build visibility overlap with performing the job. Corporate vice presidents do not take time off to campaign for the promotion to CEO, but as part of their day-to-day activities, VPs who wish to rise often stage-manage their business dealings to generate positive visibility. They make trade show and media appearances, write articles, and make sure that they are seen around town. Film actors deliver images of themselves through a strategic mix of channels in order to remain visible to their audience. Partly, this is done through intelligent venue selection (choosing good roles and projects) and producing quality performances. Unfortunately, it is impossible for actors to have good films released every three months. To remain in the public's sight, they engage in publicity-generating activities—talk show appearances, feature magazine articles, endorsements, gossip column mentions—as well as participate in new business ventures, charity work, and other activities that keep their names in play.

A second factor in balancing exposure involves physical constraints, such as stamina, family requirements, or limited funds. A celebrity has only so much energy to expend on promotional activities; spend too much and there's nothing left to sustain celebrities through their major roles, whether it is conducting a shareholder meeting, giving a sermon, or playing in the Big Game.

Another factor affecting exposure management is the fact that celebrities don't have even skill distributions: They don't do *everything* well. A politician may be wonderful at addressing small groups, yet wooden before large audiences. An artist may be dynamic among collectors at an opening, yet inarticulate in interviews. One of the celebrity industry's growth sectors involves developing strategies to cope with such inadequacies. When putting an actor with limited conversational skills on a publicity tour, public relations counsel Paul Shefrin will send a video clip from the actor's latest film so that he will not have to talk too much. The key is to balance the audience's desire to see the celebrity with the need to cover up skill deficiencies.

Another consideration involves possible conflicts. A politician may get great exposure appearing before veterans' groups yet cancel out the exposure value by offending liberal voters.

Exposure decisions are also affected by a celebrity's individual goals. One celebrity may say to his staff, "Maximize my income at all costs. Take the highest-paying venues, no matter what the majority of my fans think." The popular singer may decide to appear in South Africa for millions of dollars, irrespective of the damage done to the loyalty of her socially conscious listeners. Another celebrity may also desire maximum income yet reserve enough unpaid promotional appearances to keep the media friendly. Still another celebrity may take the long-term view, arguing that to generate strong audience loyalty, a great deal of investment spending is necessary to shore up audience support: charity work, telethon appearances, acting lessons, plastic surgery—anything that increases visibility, likability, or longevity.

Finally, in managing exposure, timing is critical. When should the promotional appearances end and the paid performances begin? In some sectors, timing has evolved into a science. Politicians follow well-tested schedules when deciding how far in advance of the election to begin campaigning. In other sectors with less-rigid schedules and less-measurable outcomes, timing is more hit or miss. Entertainers, for example, often alternate between both types of activities many times in a single day.

5 KEY RULES OF SUSTAINING

In each sector, certain events or processes invariably signal a decline in celebrity status. In politics, it's losing office. In sports, it's being benched. In entertainment, it can be scandal or low ratings that lead to cancellation of vehicle or venue. In business, it's demotion or firing.

Such outcomes are largely the result of celebrities making bad decisions or failing to adapt to changing conditions. But the exact causes of decline are rarely understood. Politicians lose office because they get fewer votes than their opponents. But why? Was it failure to scan the environment accurately to stay in touch with voter needs? Or failure to anticipate and counter their opponents' strategies? Football players may become injured because they spent the off-season selling life insurance instead of training; comedians may lose venues because they didn't prepare material appropriate to the changing socio/cultural environment; businesspeople may lose visibility because they merged when they should have divested.

There are many forks in the road to a sustained celebrity career. Each is a decision, based on rules the aspirant must clearly understand.

> *Rule One:* The more popular the sector, the more violently will a person's celebrity status fluctuate—and the sturdier the aspirant will have to be.

Insular, less-visible sectors such as accounting and architecture, without fickle public opinion to contend with, afford their celebrities far greater stability. A singer is more likely to oscillate up and down the visibility pyramid than the more stable business sector's chief executive officer; the race car champion needs more resilience in the face of adversity than the architect.

> *Rule Two:* Aspirants must understand their sectors' fundamental visibility conventions.

In the academic sector, there is an unwritten rule that the highly visible should not act flamboyantly; those who do have been unceremoniously cut off from their home universities. Artists who become too well known to the general public risk losing the support of the trend-setting art establishment that is the ultimate guarantor of their celebrity status. Entertainment celebrities may mistakenly believe that there is no such thing as too large an audience, only to find, as have Jerry Lewis and Bo Derek, that they have come to be admired by the wrong audience entirely.

> *Rule Three:* Aspirants must realize that an audience's expectations are directly linked to its perceptions about the status of the celebrity's career.

Depending on whether the celebrity is perceived of as rising, at his or her plateau, or on the decline, audiences have vastly different expectations about the quality of celebrities' performances, behavior, and lifestyles. A best-selling author who appears on Larry King's talk show confronts an audience with fixed performance expectations. Authors who stutter, freeze, ramble, or repeat themselves may permanently alienate many potential readers. Consciously striving to meet the audience's expectation level is critical to long-term visibility.

> *Rule Four:* Aspirants must understand the audience's preconceptions about celebrity behavior and age.

Through years of media exposure, venue attendance, and celebrity worship, audiences have developed a sense of how visible any celebrity should be after so many years of visibility-seeking. The public "knows" that a comedian working The Comedy Store in Los Angeles at age twenty-two is on schedule. An equally skilled comedian working the same venue at age forty-seven may run head on into fatal audience doubts: Why hasn't this aspirant made it? Is this a has-been trying for a comeback? In the same way, the music group warming up audiences for headline bands will, while still fairly new to the scene, be perceived as eager and properly positioned. But it's a status the group soon outgrows. Failing to break through to celebrity status within so many years, a group no longer fits the age stereotype. If they still seek celebrity, the group faces important strategic decisions, some involving major image changes. Or they can redefine themselves as a nostalgia band and succeed in satisfying specialized audience expectations. They can move to a part of the country where audiences' age expectations are different. Or they can reposition themselves as the purest band in their particular genre, publicly eschewing popular success and appealing to the connoisseur audience. The aspiring lawyer who fails to make partner by age thirty-five may suffer image problems throughout the law sector. And these effects may spread beyond the sector. Our culture is so conscious of prestige that the passed-over lawyer may be turned down for country club membership, school board appointment, or an officer's position with the local bar association.

> *Rule Five:* Shifting from one sector to another, in order to stretch out visibility, requires different strategies from those used in pursuing visibility in the first place.

Today, it is common for sector-leading celebrities to capitalize on their prominence by shifting into other sectors, such as politics or social causes, or to exploit their names by fronting for franchise businesses. *However, each move made in the pursuit of visibility in new sectors can initiate a decline in visibility in the primary sector.* A variation on Clausewitz's military dictum always to hold a firm base, sector shifting is fraught with hazards. Even to the public, certain sector shifts are considered dead giveaways that a celebrity's decline has begun.

In local markets, the aging athlete who advertises toupees or outsize suits might as well take out a full-page ad announcing his decline. The Hollywood leading lady who appears in a road show of *Annie Get Your Gun* in Tulsa and the novelist who accepts a teaching position at the University of Wyoming are popularly perceived as taking the face-saving route to a gentle career landing. Though any of these efforts may, given the circumstances, be strategically sound, the *appearance* of decline can trigger a chain reaction resulting in steeper decline. That's why celebrities must understand the mechanics, and politics, of shifting sectors.

Shifting Sectors

The first problem confronting the sector-shifter is that seniority in the celebrity world is not usually transferable. High-level business and political celebrities such as Alexander Haig, Drew Lewis, and others are able to shift smoothly back and forth between the peaks of both sectors. Between other sectors, however, transitions are not so easy. Celebrities shifting out of their primary sectors usually have to take a cut in visibility. The Hollywood director who has peaked in film and wishes to move to theater will probably have to start anew with less power, pay, and authority. The reasons are pragmatic: to avoid alienating the leaders and filters in the new sector, and to allow time to climb the learning curve.

Athletes often express a desire to "go out a winner." For celebrities in all sectors, it's a laudable goal—for, like a disease, a decline in visibility is best diagnosed early. Celebrities who can see warning signs of their own decline are well advised to begin their sector shift while still near the height of their commercial value. The cast of "Dynasty" didn't wait until being cancelled to start their clothing lines; they struck while their names were still marketable.

As a general rule, celebrities who see their visibility plateauing or beginning to decay ought to first consider a shift to a new role within their sector. The tradition is well established. Musicians become record producers; actors change into directors; politicians convert to lobbyists, law firm partners, or consultants. The reasons are simple: The celebrity already knows his or her new subsector, is familiar with its power structure, and is already well known to the people within it.

TV director Jerry Paris, extremely successful in the sitcom genre, suddenly found his "Happy Days" series canceled. The comedy era in television, of which he had been an architect, had enjoyed a long run but was now being replaced by action shows, soap operas in prime time, and melodramas. Paris approached his sector shift strategically, with no intention of becoming a politician or a preacher. He examined the possibilities of shifting to film, starting a small theater in Los Angeles, or taking a show on the road. When the opportunity to direct the films *Police Academy II* and *Police Academy III* arose, he accepted it, having already analyzed the relative merits of his other options.[10]

The Mechanics of Sector Shifting

In abandoning one sector for another, declining celebrities give up much of the recognition they still retain; the psychological pressures can be tremendous. That's why celebrities should divorce themselves from the past and realistically access their proposed new sector's success criteria. Do they have the necessary attributes to make it? Do any of their old skills help, or hinder? What about their support staff—is it appropriate for transfer to the new sector, or is a purge in order?

In product-marketing, these kind of judgments are made all the time. What conditions are necessary for the product to succeed? Does it have the required attributes? Can they be added on? Celebrities in decline need to make objective assessments. Whom can they really trust? Working against them is the force of inertia. Their existing support staff—agents, managers, associates—will probably lobby hard to remain in the old sector, on their own turf, where they stand to remain employed.

Celebrities who need or want to shift sectors *do* benefit from the public's perception that celebrities are more multidimensional than ordinary people. Why else are so many sports, entertainment, business, and other celebrities routinely mentioned as candidates for high positions in other sectors? Why are Charlton Heston and Lee Iacocca so often mentioned as possible senatorial or presidential candidates? Why did Clint Eastwood win a landslide victory as mayor of Carmel-by-the-Sea, and "Love Boat" actor Fred Grandy win election to Congress in Iowa? It's because in our culture, high visibility has a utility all its own. As a prerequisite for high office, one's visibility is often as important as one's qualifications.

But taking advantage of the public's acceptance of sector shifting is no guarantee that the shift will be successful. Such unsuccessful shifts as failed New York gubernatorial candidate Lewis Lehrman's from business to politics, Muhammad Ali's from boxing to fast-food franchiseship, and Joe Namath's from football to broadcasting proves that a quality performance must follow a shift.

WHAT'S IN A NAME?

One fairly low-risk strategy is to shift sectors by proxy, sending the celebrity's name into a new sector while the celebrity remains in the old one. The key is to lend one's name to an enterprise that is reasonably close in image to the image one has already developed. TV talk show host Joan Lunden's sponsorship of videotapes on raising children is a logical fit, and so is country comedian Minnie Pearl's chain of chicken restaurants. Dick Clark's line of cosmetics played on his image of eternal youthfulness and, although a failure, was an intelligent risk.

MASS MARKETING

An excellent sustaining strategy is to take a product or performance previously marketed to an exclusive audience and market it to a mass audience. Carroll Shelby, a top race car driver in the 1950s, had been forced into retirement by illness. His first sustaining strategy was to shift into race car design, a career that he became celebrated for in its own right. But the audience interested in "consuming" Shelby—race car drivers—was very small.

So Shelby executed another sustaining move, merging his European elan and romantic racing-sector aura with Ford Motor Company's American mass-production know-how to produce the Shelby Mustangs: muscle cars for the man in the street, a strategy so timeless that Chrysler was able to transfer the same elements to market Shelby Chargers in the '70s, and again in the '80s, to market a model called the GLHS Dodge Omni (literally, the "Goes Like Hell Shelby").[11] Speaking of the "halo effect" of Shelby's image, Gerald Greenwald, chairman of Chrysler Motors, said that Shelby "has helped us appeal to the driver who wants to have some fun on the road."[12] The association has maintained Shelby as a celebrity three decades after his primary career ended.

Delaying the Decline

So far, we've discussed strategies intended to sustain the celebrity at a near-peak level of visibility. But even with the best-timed moves, this isn't always possible. A number of strategies exist to stretch out a celebrity's commercial value during decline. Underlying all of these strategies is the notion that for the celebrity forced to shift sectors, the less extreme the necessary transformation, the better. It only makes sense for sector shifters to choose new sectors that make best use of the skills, stories, characteristics, and audiences that sustained them in their original sectors. Some of the most popular are discussed here.

THE BOOK

The book is one of celebrity's most enduring institutions, a channel with a long tradition of serving celebrities in all sectors. Whether it's the memoirs of a CEO, the reminiscences of a Broadway star, or the authorized biography of a president, the book serves similar purposes. It psychologically rewards fading celebrities by keeping their names in the news, extends their commercial value by generating income, and serves as a vehicle for the strategic revision of history, giving celebrities the last word, the chance to place into the memory channel the most favorable story possible, to consign themselves to immortality. It is also extremely profitable, sometimes earning celebrities more than they earned in their primary careers. Former Budget Director David Stockman was paid an advance of $2,000,000 for his memoirs, while even former House Speaker Tip O'Neill was advanced more than $1,000,000 for his book.[13]

"TO PLEDGE, CALL . . ."

Jerry Lewis, celebrity of the past, still receives treatment accorded today's star entertainers. Lewis endures because he has, more successfully than anyone, pyramided his fronting of a charity into a new career.

Charity work, implying self-sacrifice and humanitarianism, ennobles celebrities while keeping their names in the limelight. Not that their motives are insincere. But periodic television charity stints both enhance credibility and keep the celebrity before the public eye.

Celebrities' managers are capable of talking about charity work in cold terms. Speaking about the value of charity work as a visibility builder, Shelly Finkel, manager of boxer Mark Breeland, said:

> You know what I'd do with a guy like Tommy (Hit Man) Hearns? Get him one of those deals like Jerry Lewis has, a disease like MS, you know? People would see another side of Tommy and forget the "Hit Man" stuff. For all of his fame, you don't see Hearns selling sneakers on TV, do you? Roberto Duran never had much of an endorsement portfolio, did he?[14]

FOREIGN MARKETS

That wildlife naturally migrate toward available food and water has not escaped the notice of many celebrities who, in decline, move to foreign markets where the supply of authentic American culture has not yet exceeded local demand. Curiously, one of the chief exploiters of this is, once again, Jerry Lewis, whose film work attained a legitimacy in Europe that it never even approached at home. Today, in France, Lewis is hailed as a comedic genius. A trip there for him must seem like a voyage back through time.

A different version of this scenario was played out by Neil Sedaka, who, in steep decline in his native American market, was taken to England by agent Dick Fox. There, Sedaka used another strategy—linkage—and joined forces with singer Elton John. The result was a series of hit records, including the 1974 number one hit "Laughter in the Rain." For Sedaka, the move to England culminated in a renaissance in his native land.

Many American music aspirants now make the trek overseas. One highly successful group, Foreigner, launched itself on the novelty of the mixed international pedigree of its members. American groups going to Europe have an additional advantage: the promotional and story value inherent in their exotic experience when they return home. The rock group Stray Cats used this foreign flavoring strategy with enormous success.

Yet a different marketing strategy was played out by the Sir Douglas Quintet, a pop group from Texas formed during the 1960s. Finding it impossible to break out of the crowded local scene, they *faked* being from England—and rose to nine-day wonderhood on the strength of their chart-topping "She's About a Mover."

"DO YOU KNOW ME?"

Another popular sustaining strategy is to capitalize on commercial endorsements. Innumerable celebrities have extended their commercial value for decades through the timely linkage of their names with products. Actress Margaret Hamilton, who played the Wicked Witch of the West, lived comfortably for years by pitching Maxwell House coffee; aging Latin lover Ricardo Montalban kept his career energized with nightly appearances for Chrysler; Yankee Clipper Joe DiMaggio is more well known to most audiences today for his Mr. Coffee commercials than for his baseball achievements.

BIG MAN ON CAMPUS

Another strategy for reviving a deteriorating career is the academic connection. Faculties of Los Angeles–area universities are rife with "adjunct" professors of entertainment-related subjects; Washington, D.C.–area institutions feature aging politicians and lawyers. The university connection is popular because it is mutually beneficial: It cloaks the celebrity with academic respectability and spices the university's image with notables whom contributing alumni actually know. And like the best decline-management strategies, it also functions as a legitimizing process. It's a lot more dignified for aging celebrities to say they're teaching a course at USC than to admit that they're playing pinochle at a retirement village.

JUST STOPPING BY . . .

In past decades, one of the strangest celebrity afterlifes could be found in America's restaurants and casinos. Fading sports and entertainment celebrities such as boxer Joe Louis and baseball player Willie Mays were given room and board, and often a salary, just to play golf, sit around the bar, and generally rub shoulders with guests. Today, the celebrity needs to work a little harder. The new strategy is "just stopping by," as illustrated by ex-Los Angeles Rams quarterback David Humm, appearing for pay at the Monday Night Football party at Caesar's Palace. A variation on this tradition is found at shopping center openings, heavyweight fights, corporate banquets, and cruises ("just swimming by").

DOWNSIZING MARKETS

In ancient times, the man who returned to his native village from a journey to the capital was a hero. Today, local markets happily reabsorb those who've tumbled from the pyramid's peak. National news anchor Bill Kurtis, resigning from "CBS Morning News," capitalized on misfortune by returning to local TV station WBBM in Chicago, where he earns a larger salary for broadcasting to only a fraction of his former audience.

All across America, local markets employ "utility" celebrities who imbue local institutions with the flavor of their celebrated pasts: baseball players who represent banks and car dealers, former movie stars who host the local afternoon TV movie, and former radio and television celebrities who front suburban real estate housing developments.

Decline Dynamics

All of these strategies share some important characteristics. Each is based on an exchange: the celebrity accepting a variety of rewards in order to let the candle burn a little longer; the institution paying money or loaning out its prestige to the celebrity in exchange for whatever commercial value remains in the celebrity's name.

It all works because of memory filtration: human nature's propensity for recalling the positive and forgetting the negative. We remember Jim Palmer as a winning pitcher with the Baltimore Orioles, not for the long-struggling end to his baseball career. Richard Nixon's transgressions blur before a barrage of new, improved images. Helping our selective memory are institutions' memory-suppression strategies: displaying their celebrities in favorable situations, controlling events, supporting the celebrity with coaching and public relations training. And it usually succeeds. Watching their TV commercials, we think that athletes like Gale Sayers or Roger Staubach are still on top of the world. This combination of forgetfulness and image engineering has turned The Comeback into an institution.

Comebacks

Any number of events or decisions can send a career spiraling into decline. But virtually any catastrophe, properly handled, can be redefined to energize a celebrity's comeback.

Richard Pryor's domination of the comedy sector was threatened first by his heart attack, then by his admittedly drug-related self-immolation. But by highlighting both of these events in his new comedy routines, Pryor was able to milk them for their humor value, while presenting to his audience his own version of the controversial events. The publication of explicit nude photos of Miss America Vanessa Williams stimulated a flood of commercial offers that, while not the type of offers Williams might otherwise have hoped for, still rewarded her substantially.

Some of these scenarios have become virtual scripts. Watergate felon Chuck Colson features his criminal convictions as part of his comeback as an evangelical Christian. Former movie swim queen Esther Williams capitalizes on tales of how she sacrificed her career for love.

But the fact remains that in the vast majority of cases, celebrities don't manage their declines; they are managed *by* them. Sometimes the decline is slow, predictable, inexorable. Other times, it is swift, unpredictable, even ruthless.

BACKHANDED

Billie Jean King, from her first days on the tennis circuit, promoted herself as aggressive, colorful, and determined. Having dominated women's tennis in the 1960s and early '70s, she had positioned herself for a long, lucrative decline featuring endorsements, network commentator jobs, and leadership in the women's sports sector.

Then, suddenly, scandal broke: a spurned lesbian lover suing for support; omnipresent cameras; splashy tabloid headlines. King was immediately threatened with cancellation of endorsement contracts, revocation of network TV assignments, and overall audience freeze-out.

What was King's response to this assault on her celebrity? To limit the damage and regain the initiative. Going public immediately, she intelligently played a variation on her established no-nonsense image by tearfully confessing to the errors she'd made and recommitting herself to love for her husband. As *Newsweek* columnist Pete Axthelm wrote, "Billie Jean managed to turn a tawdry legal blackmail attempt by an ex-girlfriend into a personal portrait in courage."[15] She then returned to doing what she knew best—playing tennis. Soon, she had repaired her image, regained her endorsements, and repositioned herself for a sustained, profitable decline.

Whether their declines are brought about by crisis or poor management, most distressed celebrities attempt comebacks. Not all manage to return to their former level of visibility; many make it only part of the way back. Sid Caesar, vying for commerciality again after years of near-invisibility, discovered that with his old comedy venues gone, he needed to find new ones. His response was to write a book titled *Where Have I Been?*, release a fitness video, cut up 65 old episodes of "Your Show of Shows" for release to the media, and do a variety of concert, television, and film engagements. He is no longer the biggest star in television comedy, or the highest paid performer in the entertainment sector, but he has made a significant comeback.

Some celebrities engineer comebacks that propel them *past* their old visibility levels to new heights. Comedian George Burns was popular during his primary career, but he never approached the status he attained in his comeback phase. Richard Nixon told us that we weren't going to have him to kick around anymore; in the same decade, we elected him president. Singer Tina Turner, de-linked from the husband with whom she performed as a successful duo, languished in obscurity for years, then attained international celebrity on the strength of style changes and new strategic linkages.

Other celebrities achieve similar comeback success by shifting sectors entirely. Fairly well-known actor Ronald Reagan came back to become extremely well-known President Ronald Reagan. David Letterman attained local celebrity as an offbeat TV weatherman, quit, failed in his network morning talk show, and eventually came back full force as a durable leader in the comedy sector.

One of the most important considerations when mapping a comeback strategy is to assess how tangibly success is measured within a sector. Boxer Roberto Duran, reduced in promotional potential by his diarrhea-induced forfeiture of a title bout with Sugar Ray Leonard, simply had to win fights to make his comeback. Celebrity lawyers need to win cases; businesspersons, to generate profits. But in the entertainment, art, religious, and other sectors where the criteria for achieving visibility are not so clearly defined, the mix of available comeback options is far more complex.

COMEBACK STRATEGIES

Appeal to Nostalgia. In every sector, in every generation, forgotten celebrities will return to meet the public's need for living embodiments of the past. The key to success through this strategy is to do what you *did*. Chuck Berry should sing '50s songs. George McGovern should talk about peace and love. Radical attorney William Kunstler should defend social and political activists. In this way, old audiences can be retapped.

Emerge Through a New Channel. Former celebrities can come back by distributing their stories or images through new channels. G. Gordon Liddy, after a jail sentence for his participation in the Watergate scandal, became a highly paid celebrity circuit speaker (sometimes touring in tandem with '60s drug celebrity Timothy Leary). Vicki LaMotta, released from obscurity by

Cathy Moriarty's sensual portrayal of her in the film *Raging Bull*, leaped from being an ex-sports celebrity's wife to high visibility in the entertainment sector with a well-timed *Playboy* pictorial. Jerry Mathers, TV's "Beaver" Cleaver, reemerged into the limelight as a radio DJ in nostalgia-conscious California. Comedian Red Skelton drew large audiences by promoting his oil painting. Singer Rita Coolidge, de-linked from celebrity husband Kris Kristofferson, reemerged through the new high-tech distribution channel of "music television" as a host VJ on adult-oriented channel VH–1.

"New and Improved". A celebrity in decline can alter—or just pretend to alter—some key talent or characteristic. Yannick Noah, beset by physical and emotional problems, reemerged on the world tennis circuit heralding his new and improved attitude. Resigning as U.S. ambassador to the United Nations after a controversial unauthorized meeting with Palestinian diplomats, Andrew Young reemerged as a champion of concern for domestic issues and was elected mayor of Atlanta.

Ride a New Vehicle. Career setbacks or declines due to poor venue or vehicle selection may be reversed through the selection of a new vehicle. Jessica Lange, critically condemned for her performance in *King Kong* and typecast as a sex symbol by her next major film role, in *The Postman Always Rings Twice*, strategically planned a comeback. While improving her skills by taking acting lessons, she also developed her own vehicle by researching the life of Frances Farmer and then interesting producers in making a film about the controversial star. When *Frances* was ultimately produced, Lange had a compelling argument as to why she, and not a better-known actress, should play the role. With the film's success, Lange went on to greater visibility with a starring role in *Tootsie*.

Create a Controversy. Controversies are one of the most powerful ways to reawaken audience interest in a declining celebrity's career. Joan Collins has mastered this technique with the strategy of writing about the macho and sadistic men who abused her throughout her career. Billy Martin in sports, Jesse Jackson in politics, and Andy Warhol in art have consistently used controversy as a vehicle to regain visibility.

Promote Your Problems. What would morning TV be without its endless parade of fallen celebrities recounting their trials and tribulations? Of course, this technique is more popular in certain sectors than in others. Religion and business frown on it, but country music thrives on it. George Jones, Johnny Cash, and others take advantage of the "lost loves and sorrow" character of country music to promote the woe in their own lives.

Catching the Cultural Wave. Declining celebrities can re-invigorate careers by hooking up with popular trends or social movements. Senior citizen Bobby Riggs astutely exploited the new women's consciousness and created intense interest in his male/female tennis challenges—a stunt he repeated in two different decades. Colorado Governor Richard Lamm generated tremendous media coverage with his controversial positions on such trendy issues as the right to die, immigration, and the federal deficit.

Bring Back Your Old Vehicle. Many celebrities find renewal through reviving their greatest success. One version of this strategy is the farewell tour. Yul Brynner, acknowledged by the critics to be far past his prime, returned to *The King and I* for a farewell tour and set Broadway box-office records. Sometimes declining celebrities say farewell, disappear, then return to say farewell again, as the multiple swan songs of The Who, The Rolling Stones, and Frank Sinatra demonstrate.

Sudden Death. The comeback strategy of sudden death should not be considered casually. It is, however, a powerful device for reactivating faded fan attraction. The list of celebrities who have become mainstays of fan worship after their deaths is impressive: Elvis Presley, James Dean, Jim Morrison, Malcolm X, Steve Prefontaine, Sid Vicious, Jackson Pollock, Marvin Gaye, Sharon Tate, Marilyn Monroe, Sal Mineo, Jimi Hendrix, and Huey Long. Indeed, some celebrities become far more visible in death than they ever were in life. *Playboy* playmate Dorothy Stratten, moderately visible while alive, achieved high visibility after her death. Immortalized by director Peter Bogdanovich's sympathetic biography and by a major Hollywood film, Stratten accidentally became an icon for feminist groups seeking a way to personify the experience of women degraded by the *Playboy* treatment. By dying young, celebrities freeze their images for eternity, saving generations of fans from the disappointment of seeing their idols slowly fade away.

DIZZY AND DENNY

No one declined more gracefully from celebrity than baseball player Dizzy Dean. A former St. Louis Cardinals pitcher, Old Diz spent his post-pitching years spinning baseball yarns on radio and television. There was Dean, fracturing the English language, having a wonderful time. Dean's descent was exposure management at its finest: taking advantage of his storytelling talents, his audience's expectations and nostalgic longings, and his full repertoire of anecdotes, reminiscences, and wistful ramblings.

Contrast Dean's decline with that of similarly celebrated pitcher Denny McLain, the last pitcher in baseball to win thirty games in a season. At his peak, it seemed as if no force would ever dislodge McLain from honor in the memory channel. His long-term "sustainability" seemed guaranteed. But soon after leaving the majors, McLain began transforming—at high speed and in the wrong direction. His weight ballooned; he became involved with gambling and alcoholism. Eventually, he was indicted for extortion, racketeering, drug dealing and conspiracy, and was tried, convicted, and sentenced to a long jail term.

As the Dean and McLain cases illustrate, sustaining visibility can be as difficult as attaining it. Each of these celebrities was in excellent position to manage his exposure profitably over time. When a celebrity's career is over, usually there are offers to choose from. Dean used a method of distribution that took full advantage of his talent and experiences. The opportunities for McLain were just as promising: endorsements, broadcasting positions, and business associations that made use of his name. Yet in the end, one celebrity was rewarded by his visibility, while the other suffered. Ultimately, it is the appeal of rewards and danger of costs that complete the entire celebrity experience.

CHAPTER TWELVE

The Rewards and Costs of Celebrity

Leo Burnett's name is better known today than it was during his lifetime. As the founder of Leo Burnett Company Inc., he produced outstanding advertising that everyone remembers. The lonesome Marlboro cowboy, the Jolly Green Giant, and Charlie of Starkist Tuna are legendary examples of Burnett's powerful, direct campaigns.

The problem is that Leo Burnett, celebrity advertising man, finally died, taking with him an image that defined the quality and values of one of the top advertising firms in the United States. What could Burnett's company do? Burnett the man had iconic quality. His name stood for the dedicated, honest image of his company. The reward stemming from his strong image was a clearly focused, successful organization. And the potential cost? The danger of losing clients once Burnett was gone.

The solution to this dilemma was not untypical of celebrity-dependent organizations: the embalming of the image. Leo Burnett's career has been sustained long past his death by a number of strategically staged events and publications. His trademark baskets of red apples still grace reception desks in Leo Burnett offices all over the world. His birthday is celebrated every year with an elaborate party. And his quotations and advertising philosophy still infuse much of Burnett's internal and external literature.

Leo Burnett's investment in his own celebrity created a marketable icon, and like most icons, he could not be put to rest.

No one at Burnett will claim that its founder is still alive. No one is going out of his way to deny it, either.[1]

Rewards and Costs to Celebrities

For the successfully transformed, as well as for the institutions they lead and represent, high visibility is a double-edged sword. It is almost universally assumed that celebrity brings great rewards, and this is true. But only superficially understood are the unexpected costs that the highly visible often pay.

THE COST OF CELEBRITY

What sacrifices, crises, and dangers accompany celebrity?

A first problem for the celebrity is the media's need to expose every possible sordid fact of a celebrity's life, to build the media's audience. Often the media will typecast celebrities with characterizations that pervade all coverage about them: Carl Icahn and ruthlessness; Geraldine Ferraro and family crises; Johnny Cash and drugs; evangelist Richard Roberts and excessive spending.

A related problem is the overall loss of control that celebrities suffer over their own distribution *through* the media. In earlier times, celebrities could effectively separate the public life disclosed to their audiences by the press from the private life kept out of sight. The key was for celebrities to operate within certain boundaries of propriety. Were they to violate sector conventions severely, their problems became legitimate targets for coverage.

But as the celebrity machinery churned out more celebrities in all sectors, the public began to expect a steady flow of celebrity story material: news of divorces, financial catastrophes, drug addictions, drunken binges, diseases, car accidents, TV series cancellations, movie set tantrums, and other traumas. This expectation has spawned a vicious cycle: The pressure of public visibility creates private tensions for celebrities; their tensions precipitate visible crises; crises attract media coverage; coverage creates more pressures. How many times can former New Jersey Nets basketball star Micheal Ray Richardson and former Los Angeles Dodgers pitcher Steve Howe succumb to, and then triumph over, drug addiction? How many times can the media find a new angle to the quarterback-turned-broadcaster Joe Theismann/actress Cathy Lee Crosby relationship? How many failed marriages and health problems can Elizabeth Taylor endure?

Unavoidably, celebrities live in a public fishbowl. Virtually every move they make is under microscopic examination through the media's lens. The innocuous actions that invisibles get away with every day become celebrities' PR disasters. Rudeness to waiters, filing late taxes, denting a fender—each, potentially, is "news."

But the media don't just amplify incidents; they create them, too. Celebrities are more highly prone to confrontations *because* of the media. In the days before intensive celebrity media coverage, celebrities were generally known to the public through their paid performances. But not anymore. Because they are constantly revealing themselves through dramatized reality over talk shows, in magazines, and "infotainment," audiences come to know their celebrities intimately without ever having been in their presence. The result is a growing belief by fans that their celebrities are actually very approachable. An actor or politician who has discussed his favorite chili recipe on our living room televisions has lowered a barrier that might otherwise keep fans at bay. Consequently, many celebrities can no longer venture out in public.

And when they do venture out, the danger they face is not limited to mobs of "intimate acquaintances" seeking a friendly autograph or conversation. As demonstrated so graphically by Hinckley/Foster/Reagan and Chapman/Lennon, the intimacy that anonymous fans develop with celebrities through the media can have lethal consequences. Fans and fanatics can now know their celebrities, and their whereabouts, just as intimately as their own families' and neighbors'. While the strategy behind making celebrities so knowable is to raise their commercial value, it also permits the obsession-prone to dwell on celebrities, fixate on them, and sometimes even make them the center of their hallucinating world. What the celebrity industry sets in motion is sometimes impossible to control.

In reality, very few celebrities actually suffer harm at the hands of fans. Nonetheless, a cost is there for all celebrities: fear.

Frightened by perceived and actual violence, many celebrities have retreated behind the modern-day equivalent of a moat. These installations include guard dogs, security perimeters, bodyguards, bulletproof cars, evasion-maneuver-trained chauffeurs, ultra-high-security homes, and most of the other security accouterments of banana republic dictators.

Besides fearing for their physical safety, celebrities must be on constant alert against threats to the integrity of their images. Because of the media, the visual image has come totally to dominate matters of talent, ability, and substance. Gaining weight, a case of acne, an undisguised hangover—these and other travails are, in the broadcast age, dreaded like the plague.

Many celebrities are denied anything approaching a normal life. The combination of society's disregard for its public figures' privacy and the media's increasing technical ability to invade this territory leaves celebrities exposed. Apart from the impact on family harmony of crowded schedules and unusual working hours, celebrities are vulnerable to uncertainty over the very reason why their friends and family hold them in the regard they do. Is their care authentic, or cynical? Do they love him as a person, or worship him as a star? Is their motivation sincere, or exploitative? Given the rewards that await a rising celebrity's inner circle, inevitably doubt, fear, distrust, and chaos have become standard fixtures in many celebrities' private lives.

We have already discussed celebrity exploiters, those who make a living out of assaulting the celebrity's image and privacy. But there is another class of celebrity attackers, people who may be friends or acquaintances of the celebrity target. These are the insiders—spouses, maids, chauffeurs, gardeners, children, and others—who, once dismissed or grown up, may attack the celebrity's image. Joan Kennedy's secretary exposing the private life of her former employer, presidential daughter Patti Davis and her thinly veiled novel about her family, and Nora Ephron's *roman à clef Heartburn* and the subsequent film about her marriage to Watergate celebrity Carl Bernstein are examples of "kiss and tell" publishing. In the current climate, in whom can the celebrity safely confide?

These costs are factors that the media amplify and reinforce. But other costs derive from the essense of celebrity itself.

Major celebrities are plagued by alternating periods of calendar stress and abundant free time. The former occurs when the celebrity must make difficult choices among distribution opportunities. The celebrity has the same needs for rest as invisibles do.

But the celebrity's audiences—fans, charities, institutional sponsors, shareholders, parishioners, media channels, and others—do not acknowledge this reality. When visiting particular markets, a celebrity can be "on stage" nearly twenty-four hours a day. Sports celebrity Reggie Jackson, for instance, divides his limited time between the demands of his primary sector—baseball—and his obligation as fashion model, TV commentator, video recorder pitchman, and car tester for auto magazines, not to mention the appeals of autograph hounds and shutterbugs.

The opposite of calendar stress is the need to cope with free time. Between films, speeches, projects, performances, appearances, promotions, or engagements, a celebrity is often left with absolutely nothing to do—usually at just the times when the rest of the world is preoccupied with work or sleep. Where are celebrities supposed to get a good meal after the nightclub closes? What to do until the next curtain rises? Where do they work out? Taken alone, these may seem to be minor costs, especially in a society where some people cannot afford food. But when these costs repeat daily, they magnify.

Another traditional cost media intrusion provokes is performance stress. By definition, a celebrity operates in the public arena. Whether before a TV audience, a political rally, a crowded operating room, or a shareholders' meeting, a celebrity is *on stage*. In addition to its psychological costs, performance stress can lead to physical ailments and breakdowns.

Yet another cost of high visibility is the strain of coping with uncertainty and intangibility. While the celebrity-manufacturing process has begun to attain a respectable degree of sophistication, it has a long way to go before it catches up with the air freight industry or the fast food business in predictability. Today's businesspeople, with all the information management and technical forecasting skills at their command, can usually isolate which elements of their businesses are malfunctioning or failing. Within the celebrity industry, however, the state of the art is not so advanced. When is the exact moment to debut? What is the perfect costume to wear? What is the proper venue to use? What is the proper tone to take on one's first appearance on "Nightline"? Celebrity-marketers understand these issues better than ever before—better, unfortunately, than most celebrities do. As celebrities move closer to becoming pure products, they are more likely to be kept isolated from the information-gathering and -processing techniques and analytical models used by producers, headhunters, studio heads, team coaches, agents and packagers, and other industry leaders. Consequently, celebrities must cope with the pressure of deciding which move is right for *them*, and which moves are being recommended in service of the interests of others.

Finally, given all the artifice, manipulation, posturing, and positioning that the new celebrity environment requires, what about the costs to the celebrity's conscience? What happens when celebrities know, deep down, that they are just getting by on reputation, by trickery, by makeup, surgery, and mirrors? What happens when they acknowledge that they have been made by PR, refined by research, elevated to high visibility by modern image-manufacturing? How do celebrities answer their consciences? With the increasing sophistication of the industry, with its growing ability to market aspirants into high visibility, the answers are harder to come by.

THE REWARDS OF CELEBRITY

Counterbalancing the costs of high visibility are major benefits, notably profit, privileges, and power.

The reward for high visibility that attracts the greatest attention is money. Celebrities often earn exorbitant returns—salaries, fees, compensation packages, stock options—because celebrity is by its very nature exclusive. Unlike other product markets, where there is a large supply of the same or similar items, celebrities are unique. Because of the high commercial profits they can generate for others, celebrities are compensated accordingly.

Celebrities also enjoy community status. On the broad level, society looks to celebrities to display and promote role choices. One of the reasons that America is such a dynamic society is because of the high number of possible roles offered to its young citizens. Celebrities often embody and communicate these possibilities. The intense celebritization of our society maximizes the chance that each individual will encounter a role model that matches his or her potential. It is reminiscent of comedian Robert Klein's comment that the quiet kids who don't admire anybody are the ones who wind up shooting the president. Certainly, some youngsters may come to admire celebrity criminals or gangsters. But for the most part, celebrities are looked on as positive role models.

Whether it is with envy, respect, jealously, or regard, communities always pay attention to their celebrities, attention that the celebrity doctor, academic, or sports hero welcomes. While not an easily measurable factor in the rewards structure, these reactions are a continuous theme in celebrity lore. The once-poor actress who returns to her home town to enjoy the community's acclaim; the business leader who arrives in a limousine to address her high school; the lawyer who is the talk of the hotel staff because of his defense of a well-known client—these celebrities are enjoying a subtle, but important, reward.

Closely related is the respect accorded celebrities by *other* celebrities. It does not seem to matter what a particular celebrity's sector is, or even if its "essence" directly conflicts with other sectors: They seek one another's recognition.

This clustering effect also rewards celebrities by providing access to valuable information not commonly available to invisibles—a reward grounded in the tendency of invisibles to share information with celebrities in order to gain their attention or win their friendship. Such information ranges from tips on hot horses and real estate deals to whispered advice on fashion moves or negotiating strategies. Through this unlikely channel, valuable information *does* occasionally come to celebrities.

A reward similar to information access is the tradition of the free lunch. Ironically, celebrities, with greater ability to pay for goods and services than most other members of society, receive more freebies than our neediest. Here, two forces are at work. The first is the pure value of PR for the donors, who hope to receive mention of their places of business in gossip or society columns: where businessperson X lunched, where politician Y dined, where film star Z styled her hair.

The other force driving the free lunch is the familiar psychological need of fans to appease and please celebrities. Merchants derive psychological pleasure by according celebrities special favors—celebrities they may not even personally admire.

Those who pursue or achieve celebrity need to consider its personal rewards and costs. Even if they knew how much harassment, abuse, and fatigue they would encounter, celebrity sector leaders would not likely choose anonymity. "The problems of success are not hard to handle, only the problems of failure," said

Steve Rubell. "I think that people who complain about the problems of success are full of baloney. You don't have to have those problems. They choose that. I have no sympathy for the star that complains. Don't *be* a star, then. Quit! It's the man with eyes complaining the sun is too strong and the blind man next to him can't see."[2]

IMPACT: CHARGES AGAINST CELEBRITY

There is another way to evaluate the rewards and costs of celebrity: not the profits and losses that accrue to individual aspirants, but to society itself. After all, this is an industry that has many critics and few defenders. Typical of the critics is Barbara Goldsmith, who, in attacking the celebrity industry, expresses the deep misgivings of many intellectuals:

> The line between fame and notoriety has been erased. Today we are faced with a vast confusing jumble of celebrities; the talented and untalented, heroes and villains, people of all accomplishment and those who have accomplished nothing at all, the criteria for their celebrity being that their images encapsulate some form of the American Dream, that they give enough of an appearance of leadership, heroism, wealth, success, danger, glamour and excitement to feed our fantasies. We no longer demand reality, only that which is real seeming.[3]

Should we really be as concerned as Goldsmith with society's preoccupation with celebrities? Does the explosive growth of celebrity-marketing signal the decline and fall of Western civilization? Can anything positive be said in defense of celebrity-marketing? If not, can anything be done to control it? All these concerns have led Goldsmith, Daniel Boorstin, and other critics to see celebrity worship as a "cancerous growth." Their varied criticisms fall into three major charges.

The first is that *celebrities are overrewarded, overprivileged, and overempowered.* William "The Refrigerator" Perry earned millions of dollars after the overweight defensive lineman was used as a running back on the national TV venue "Monday Night Football." Once he was marketed into high visibility, businesses competed to take advantage of his promotional value. According to his agent, Jim Steiner, Perry "could generate an additional seven-figure income from endorsements, well beyond the $5,000 to $15,000 that other linemen in the NFL generally make from promotions."[4] Besides doing numerous TV commercials and endorsements, Perry was specially written into an episode of NBC's "The A-Team" to take advantage of a single free day during his busy post-Superbowl schedule. For the day of filming, Perry received $10,000. "Wheel of Fortune" hostess Vanna White earns a six-figure salary for flipping letters on the popular game show. Meanwhile, public-school teachers are fortunate to draw annual pay of $20,000 and, arguably, they work much harder. And people who have some really thoughtful things to say about public issues have to settle for nothing more than calling in on a radio talk show.

Why the grossly disproportionate sharing of the pie? In a free market, people presumably pursue the careers open to them on the basis of their educational and other qualifications. Some sectors pay more than others because of the value that people attach to these services and the relative "scarcity" of talent in these sectors. How *much* more might be paid for scarce talent? A lot—if the performer's service is valued by millions who are each willing to pay $5, $10, or $20 a year for viewing that performer. If 10 million people think that listening to a Bruce Springsteen record or concert is worth $10, then Bruce Springsteen and his sponsors are going to divide $100 million among them. And Bruce Springsteen will get the largest share. That millions of people are willing to buy Harold Robbins novels or pay to watch Wayne Gretzky swing at a puck is the real reason for the high earnings of these stars and their privileged treatment and media access.

In principle, there are only two ways in which the enhanced premiums of the high visibles could be lowered to more modest levels. One is through the free play of market forces where audiences decide to reduce their celebrity support. They attend fewer rock concerts or shift their interest to less famous and less expensive performers.

The other solution is to limit or severely tax high earnings, reducing the output of celebrities and aspirants' drives toward celebrity. But if aspirants and celebrities do what they do for enjoyment, not primarily for money, they may still work as hard.

We favor leaving the issue of high earnings to market forces. Celebrities earn what audiences are willing to pay. And most celebrities' high earnings last only briefly before they fall to normal levels. Martina Navratilova won't be winning tournaments all of her life, nor will Texas Air chairman Frank Lorenzo forever lead the airline industry. Audiences get sated fast, often switching their loyalties to the latest celebrity to dominate the distribution channels. Celebrities understand that much of their appeal is based upon novelty, part of the price to be paid for participating in person-marketing.

Another major charge is that *citizens should honor heroes, not celebrities*—that most of us generally end up worshipping the wrong people. Goldsmith and other critics acknowledge that human beings have a great need to have individuals to honor. But, they wonder, why celebrate Pia Zadora, who has spent millions to gain high visibility, instead of celebrating Peace Corps doctors who labor in the jungles of Africa or social workers trying to stop gang violence in our inner cities? There *is* something unbalanced about a society that celebrates people whose main virtue is their well-knownness rather than their merit.

This obsession with the superficial, vain, and notorious leads critics to see American society as rapidly deteriorating. The elevation of glamour, clothes, fast living, and sexual escapades to a position of honor, critics say, raises as many questions about our individual ethics as it does about society's. If these are the values that young people grow up on, they say, then it doesn't augur well for future generations.

Boorstin and others have lamented the decline of genuine heroes, people who through their words and deeds perform acts for the common good at great personal risk. Where do people who save others from drowning end up? At best, in one-day mentions in the back sections of newspapers. If we don't honor them, how will young people learn about valor, discipline, sacrifice, magnanimity, and other virtues that lift a society above the law of the jungle?

The irony is that a return to hero worship would require the same marketing tools that sustain celebrity worship. Heroes can be known only through the media. If heroic deeds were passed on only by word-of-mouth, most modern heroes would never surface to people's attention. Their surfacing actually requires the work of writers, dramatists, poets, publicists, even agents and personal managers. Chuck Yeager captured wide attention only when the film *The Right Stuff* was released. He's been a hero for more than a generation, but it took the celebrity industry to make him a household name.

Finally, the critics complain that *the celebrity industry is manipulative and devious and should be regulated*—that celebrity-makers manipulate public taste for their own financial gain. Agents, publicists, coaches, and others conspire to create synthetic personalities and illusions that pander to our basest tastes. They make the unreal real and the real unreal. They hawk make-believe worlds of "the rich and famous" and in the process distort life and minimize worthwhile values.

In this, the critics have a point. No one can deny the powerful impact of the media on our lives. Media managers have the skill to build whatever stories and quasi-realities they wish. And they build the ones that serve to advance someone's profits. Some image-makers *are* unscrupulous and unconscionable in how far they will distort reality to sell their product. At the same time, many others draw the line and act responsibly. There is no way to regulate the unscrupulous without repressing those who put their talents to more positive ends. One can only hope that the market restrains the unethical operators or that audiences will grow sophisticated enough to recognize stark manipulations and resist them.

But no matter how the critics view the negative impact of high visibility, celebrity continues to expand into all sectors of life. The reality of celebrity is contained in four judgments.

VERDICT ON CELEBRITY

Visibility Pays. Visibility clearly produces large and varied rewards for its holders. Thus Linda Evans, through starring in a popular TV show, is able to sell her image to sponsors for millions of dollars a year. She receives VIP treatment when it comes to hotel rooms, restaurant tables, theater seats, and social invitations. If she wanted to make serious pronouncements about world affairs such as hunger in Africa or nuclear proliferation, she would get instant news coverage. All said, high visibility pays off handsomely in terms of money, privilege, and power.

Visibility Isn't the Fruit of Grace But of Informed Drive. Celebrities are widely thought to have arrived at their blessed state through divine intervention, nepotism, or luck. Julio Iglesias has a "great voice," Cybill Shepherd has "outstanding beauty," Christie Hefner was "born" into a business dynasty. These explanations unfortunately ignore many men who can sing as well as Iglesias, and many women who look as beautiful as Shepherd or administrate as well as Hefner. We believe that most celebrities skillfully plotted to attain their high visibility. They went to the right schools, moved to the right cities, found the right mentors, and developed the right talent for their sector. Consciously or unconsciously, they grasped the right formula for celebrity success.

Contemporary Visibility is Manufactured and Marketed by a Sophisticated Industry that is Spreading to All Sectors of Society. Future virtuosos, whether of violin, acting, tennis, or gymnastics, must start their training as children, go to the right camps, and impress the omnipresent talent scouts who are looking for the next marketable star. Some will continue to operate in the product-improvement mode, searching for candidates with the most commitment to, resources for, and flexibility for transformation. More and more coaches and celebrity-developers will operate in the market-fulfillment mode, widely scanning for candidates with the right characteristics to fit a predetermined role. Some sectors, such as rock music, are fully industrialized, with a whole set of talent scouts, agents, personal managers, coaches, publicists, and financiers. And this corporate-type activity is occurring in other sectors such as art, politics, business, academia, and religion.

Celebrity Worship and Visibility-Seeking is in an Explosive Growth Phase. Celebrity manufacturing is exploding, thanks to the use of modern technology, particularly television and film. The public at large knows the names and faces of thousands of people whom they have never met. These high visibles are not known for heroic deeds or special merit or genius but simply for their well-knownness. As more people become aware of the high rewards going to the high visibles, more will try to achieve it. So celebrity worship stimulates visibility-seeking, which in turn stimulates celebrity worship, in an endless chain of explosive growth.

Conclusion: The Manufacturing and Marketing of Celebrities

There is naturally a heated discussion over the ethics of the Pygmalion Principle. The critics, quite rightfully, are suspicious of any process that tends to favor illusion over reality. We agree that the following would be desirable:

- That highly visible people not receive disproportionate reward and privilege in relation to their real contributions to society.
- That society should do more to nurture real talent and authentic personalities and reward *them* with higher visibility.
- That society's image-makers should restrain their distortions and manipulations of reality.

At the same time, we would prefer to rely on the good sense of audiences rather than on legislation or regulation. We must hope that the public's judgment keeps pace with the industry's growing skill in constructing illusions. We hope that this book, by making the celebrity industry's workings more visible and knowable, will contribute to greater audience sophistication. In a deep sense, the celebrity industry's critics are the public's best allies, because they continually remind us of the difference between celebrities and heroes, and that the former are no substitute for the latter. But as long as the marketplace is willing to pay enhanced premiums to celebrities, no amount of moralizing, preaching, or idol-burning will have any impact at all. Celebrities exist because we need and want them. The celebrity industry has become so huge and proficient because we buy the tickets, use the products, and pay the homage. Celebrity production will cease or moderate only when the public is satiated or turned off from the cult of celebrity. But until that day, the competitive marketplace is best served by all the participants knowing the rules.

Notes

Chapter 1

1. Richard Monturo, "The Roller Skater's Transition to Figure Skater: Risks and Rewards," unpublished research paper, *Northwestern University*, November 5, 1984. Monturo was a nationally ranked roller skater.

2. "The Rain in Spain," by Alan Jay Lerner and Frederick Loewe. Copyright © 1956 by Alan Jay Lerner and Frederick Loewe. Copyright renewed—CHAPPELL & CO., INC., owner of publication and allied rights throughout the world. International Copyright Secured. ALL RIGHTS RESERVED. Used by permission.

3. Edith Hamilton, *Mythology: Timeless Tales of Gods and Heroes* (Boston: Little, Brown and Co. Inc., 1940), p. 108.

4. Daniel Boorstin, *The Image: A Guide to Pseudo-Events* (New York: Atheneum, 1961).

5. Boorstin, p. 47.

6. Richard Schickel, *His Picture in the Papers* (New York: Charterhouse, 1973), p. 8.

7. Graphs researched and prepared by Jeffrey Colin, Northwestern University, 1983.

8. Barbara Goldsmith, "The Meaning of Celebrity," *The New York Times Magazine*, December 4, 1983, pp. 75, 76.

Chapter 2

1. *The Wedgwood Dictionary of English Etymology* (London: Tribner & Co., 1872), p. 60.
2. *The Oxford English Dictionary* (London: Ely House, 1970), p. 211.
3. Earl Blackwell and Cleveland Amory, *The Celebrity Register* (New York: Harper & Row, 1963), p. v.
4. "A Revealing Look at the Startling Sums that 57 Top Celebs Banked Last Year," *People*, March 25, 1985, pp. 92–101.
5. Marcia Froelke Coburn, "The New Darling of the Social Set," *Chicago Sun-Times*, Living section, April 29, 1984, p. 3.
6. Author interview with Chuck Binder, Benedict Canyon, California, April 5, 1984.
7. Jill Langendorff, unpublished research paper, "On Being A Local Yokel in Suburbia," Northwestern University, June 1, 1983. This study of Munster, Indiana, examined twelve residents who were characterized as local celebrities. Particularly striking was how many of the strategies of the Hollywood Model were already in place.
8. One of the authors served as communications consultant to one of the candidates in the campaign and observed close at hand Byrne's image transformation.
9. David Greising, "Two Investors Here Sue Obie, Diamond," *Chicago Sun-Times*, September 29, 1986, p. 57.
10. Author interview with Bobby Vinton, Pacific Palisades, California, April 2, 1984.
11. Shelley Berman appeared before a seminar, Evanston, Illinois, April 13, 1983.
12. Richard Schickel, *His Picture in the Papers* (New York: Charterhouse, 1973), p. 7.

Chapter 3

1. Scott Cohen, "Playboy Interview: Wayne Gretzky," *Playboy*, April 1985, p. 59.
2. Jack Falla, "The Key Man Is Sharper," *Sports Illustrated*, February 18, 1985, p. 25.
3. Aljean Harmetz, "Christmas Film Sales Set Record," *The New York Times*, January 15, 1986, p. 18.
4. Jerry Hulse, "Helping Jet-Set Celebrities Get Set on Their Jets," *Chicago Sun-Times*, February 14, 1984, p. 42.
5. Kevin Richert, "Filmmaker John Sayles: A Cottage Industry," unpublished research paper, Northwestern University, November 5, 1984, p. 1.

6. Gloria Valentine, interviewed by Michael Parker, October 28, 1985.
7. Milton Friedman, interviewed by Michael Parker, October 25, 1985.
8. Jacquie Sinclair, "Entrepreneur or Dentist?" unpublished research paper, Northwestern University, December 4, 1985.
9. Author interview with Dr. Donovan on June 10, 1986.
10. Steven Davis, *Bob Marley* (New York: Doubleday & Company, Inc., 1985), p. 70.
11. Jodie Gerson, "The Motown Formula," unpublished research paper, Northwestern University, June 8, 1983, p. 3.
12. Smokey Robinson, *VH–1 One on One* interview, broadcast August 2, 1986.
13. William Petersen, interviewed by Charles Martinez, December 6, 1985.
14. Ray Kennedy, "On His Mark and Go-Going," *Sports Illustrated,* May 12, 1975, p. 83.
15. Mark McCormack, *What They Don't Teach You At Harvard Business School* (New York: Bantam, 1984).
16. Author interview with John Wild (public relations, International Management Group), October 29, 1986.
17. McCormack, p. xiii.
18. Sarah Crichton, "The Making of Laura Branigan," *Harper's,* July 1983, p. 22.
19. Jon Pareles, "A Rock Manager's Day: Study of Life on the Run," *The New York Times,* July 14, 1986, p. 14.
20. Jack Childers appeared before a seminar, Evanston, Illinois, May 1983.
21. Vic Ziegel, "Mark Spitz: Eleven Years and Seven Gold Medals Later," *Advertising Age,* February 7, 1983, p. 32.
22. "Despite Critics and Lawsuits, HerbaLife Has Made Mark Hughes Wealthy If Not Healthy," *People,* April 29, 1985, p. 78.
23. Donovan interview.
24. Patricia Morrisroe, "Forever Young," *New York,* June 9, 1986, cover.
25. Jacqueline Thompson, *Directory of Personal Image Consultants* (Brooklyn: Editorial Services Consulting, 1984–85).
26. Valerie J. Phillips, "Image Experts Dress Clients for Success," *Chicago Tribune,* Section 8, December 29, 1985, p. 1.
27. Phillips.
28. Shirley Potter, president of Communication Advisory Services, quoted by Phillips.
29. The Consultants: U.S. Statistical Guide and Source Finder (Glenelg, North Dakota: Consultants Library, 1986), p. 41.
30. Author interview with Marvin Snyder of Dusty, Snyder, Inc., February 11, 1984.
31. Snyder.

32. Donald R. Katz, "Smart Money," *Esquire*, January 1986, p. 37.
33. Snyder.
34. John Hauser interviewed by Sue Berkey, Jeff Greenfield, Jeffrey Jacobs, and Scott Whalley, November 30, 1984.
35. Dave Anderson, "Oysters for the Fridge," *The New York Times*, January 23, 1986, p. 20.
36. "Timeout," *The New York Times*, April 4, 1986, p. 23.
37. Burton Manning, chief executive of J. Walter Thompson USA, quoted by Stratford P. Sherman in "When You Wish Upon A Star," *Fortune*, August 19, 1985, p. 68.
38. Stuart Weiss, "A Skin Cream Stock That's Working Magic," *Business Week*, January 13, 1986, p. 112.
39. "Star-Gazing and -Grazing," *The New York Times*, August 24, 1985, p. 5.
40. Joan Kron, "Is Madonna in LA? Is Sean Penn in New York?" *The Wall Street Journal*, April 8, 1986, p. 1.
41. "Maps Help Fans Swoon Near Stars' New York Homes," *Chicago Sun-Times*, August 3, 1986, p. 35.
42. David Best, "Formalizing Fame," *American Way*, June 1983, p. 175.
43. Jeff Berger and Martin Stoller, "Crowded at the Top: Celebrities and the Ambient Support System," unpublished research paper, Northwestern University, February 23, 1984.

Chapter 4

1. Garson Kanin, *Moviola* (London: Pan Books, 1980), pp. 311–32.
2. "The Wacky World of Pop Promo," *Chicago Daily News Panorama* magazine, October, 16–17, 1976, p. 4.
3. Tim Alevizos, "Seka: The Platinum Princess," unpublished research paper, Northwestern University, December 5, 1985.
4. Mary Schmich, "Seka: Star of Film Fantasies is Satisfied Staying Dressed for Success," *Chicago Tribune*, Tempo section, October 11, 1985, p. 1.
5. Kanin, p. 393.
6. Peter G. Horsfield, *Religious Television: The American Experience* (New York: Longman, 1984), p. 13.
7. Bernie Zilbergeld, "The Hugging and Unhugging of Leo," *Psychology Today*, November 1983, p. 18.
8. Helmsley Hotels ad, *Chicago Magazine*, June 1986, p. 131.
9. *Chicago Sun-Times*, August 28, 1985, p. 40.
10. Press release of the Curtain Corporation, "Christo's Valley Curtain Scheduled to Hang in June," October 12, 1972.

Chapter 5

1. Reprinted by permission of the *Harvard Business Review.* "Public Invisibility of Corporate Leaders," by David Finn (November/December, 1980, pp. 103, 109). Copyright © 1980 by the President and Fellows of Harvard College; all rights reserved.
2. James Coates, "Celebrity Sheriff Captures Few Hearts Back Home," *Chicago Tribune,* June 23, 1986, p. 1.
3. *Grove's Dictionary of Music & Musicians,* ed. Eric Bloom, Vol. V. (New York: St. Martin's Press, Macmillan & Co., Inc), 1954, p. 941.

Chapter 6

1. Felicia Rubloff, Katy Schlesinger, and Jennifer Smyth, "Gucci: The Man Behind the Label," unpublished research paper, Northwestern University, December 4, 1985.
2. Blanche Trinajstick, president, National Association of Fan Clubs, interviewed by Neil Kornfeld, Northwestern University, March 1984.
3. Interviewed were the presidents of fan clubs for Shaun Cassidy, Jimmy Connors, James Dean, Buddy Holly, Caroline Munro, Elvis Presley, Allen Tripp, Robert Redford, Johnny Mathis, and Tom Jones, Kornfeld, March 1984.
4. *The Oxford English Dictionary,* Vol. III, D–E (London: Oxford University Press, reprinted 1969), p. 274.
5. *Force Journey Newsletter,* published by Journey Force, Box 404, San Francisco, California 94101.
6. John Burks and Jerry Hopkins, *Groupies & Other Girls* (New York: Bantam, 1970), p. 105.
7. "Dylanologist," *Newsweek,* April 12, 1971, p. 123.
8. "Dossier," *Esquire,* December 1983, p. 189.
9. "Desperate to Fill an Emotional Void," *People,* April 20, 1981, p. 38.
10. "Lennon's Alter Ego," *Newsweek,* December 22, 1980, p. 35.
11. Author interview with Bryan Rusted concerning his dissertation research on Paramount's booking techniques, Northwestern University, August 1984.
12. "Syndicated Performer Q Study," copyright 1983, Marketing Evaluations, Inc.
13. Reproduced from Performer Q Rating brochure, published by Marketing Evaluations.
14. *McCollum Spielman Topline,* Vol. 2, Number 3, August 1980.
15. Jeffrey Berger, "The Celebrity System: The Image Game," unpublished research paper, Northwestern University, May 1983.

16. Some aspects of the dinner party scenario were tested by telephone by researcher Lynn Turner in Highland Park, Illinois, October 1984.
17. Vinton interview.
18. Trinajstick interview.
19. From a study using focus groups and surveys by Jane Steiner, "The Idolization of Celebrities," unpublished research paper, Northwestern University, December 1984. The groups were college students at Northwestern University. The focus groups were matched sets of 9, and the number surveyed was 122.
20. Joshua Hammer, "Say 'Cheese,' Burger," People, April 2, 1984, p. 34.
21. Celebrity Focus Group conducted by authors in Evanston, Illinois, February 15, 1984.
22. *Chicago Sun-Times,* July 14, 1984, p. 95.
23. The concept that people use stories to manage the impressions they make on others was clarified by Erving Goffman (*The Presentation of Self in Everyday Life,* London: Penguin Press, 1969). Such researchers as Dan Nimmo and James E. Combs (*Mediated Political Realities,* New York: Longman, 1983) and others have explored the idea that the media enhance and even alter stories while transmitting them to audiences.
24. Carol Wallace, "Is This Trip Necessary?" *People,* August 15, 1983, p. 99.
25. "A Fine Madness," *Life,* March 1984, p. 73.
26. Martin Gottlieb, "All Around Town, Iacocca Is the People's Choice," *The New York Times,* July 4, 1986, p. 14.
27. Don Idhe, "The Technological Embodiment of Media," in *Communication Philosophy and the Technological Age,* edited by Michael J. Hyde (University of Alabama Press, 1982), pp. 54–72.
28. Michael and Donna Nason, *Robert Schuller: The Inside Story* (Wheaton, Illinois: Tyndale House Publishers, 1981).
29. Nason, pp. 45–46.
30. Nason, p. 49.
31. Nason, p. 49.
32. Nason, p. 49.
33. Nason, p. 49.

Chapter 7

1. Documentary film *Obsession,* produced by WSMV-TV, Nashville, Tennessee, November 25, 1983.
2. Benjamin Bloom, *Developing Talent in Young People* (New York: Ballantine, 1985), p. 508.
3. Judith Dobrzynski, "Business Celebrities," *Business Week,* June 23, 1986, p. 100.
4. "Golden Paintbrushes," *Newsweek,* October 15, 1984, p. 83.

5. Marian Christy, "Lauren: Success Isn't Money, It's Loving What You Do," *Chicago Sun-Times,* November 22, 1983, p. 40.
6. "Norman Borlaug: The Peaceful Revolutionary," *Update,* University of Minnesota, February 1986, p. 1.
7. Jonathan Taylor, "Success on 'Star Search' Lands a Dream for Singer," *Chicago Tribune,* Tempo section, August 9, 1984, p. 11c.
8. Paul Dean, "Her Song Was Olympic, But Nobody's Calling," *Los Angeles Times,* Section 5, September 3, 1984, p. 1.
9. Pete Gorner, "Landmark Heart-Lung Surgery Gives Mary Gohlke a New Life," *Chicago Tribune,* Tempo section, May 17, 1985, p. 2.
10. Cory & Sikes presented their performance at the N.A.M.E. Gallery in December 1985. They received free promotion from WXRT–FM, *The Chicago Tribune, The Chicago Sun-Times, Reader,* and others.
11. Max Weber, *Economy/Society* ed. Gunther, Roth & Claus Wittlich, Vol. 1 (New York: Bedminster Press), p. 213.
12. Therese McNally, "Steal the Spotlight: Show Biz Secrets That Will Make Your Next Speech a Smash Hit," *Success,* April 1986, p. 49.
13. Class appearances by Jane Heitz, May 14, 1985, and Dick Kordos, Kordos & Charbonneau, May 16, 1985, at Northwestern University, Evanston, Illinois.
14. Jack Kroll, "A Place in the Sun," *Newsweek,* September 24, 1984, p. 86.
15. "How Stars Are Made," *Newsweek,* February 24, 1986, pp. 74–75.
16. A book that contains specific information about charisma-engineering and support organizations is *The Directory of Personal Image Consultants,* edited by Jacqueline A. Thompson (Brooklyn: Editorial Services Consulting, 1982).
17. Clinton R. Sanders, "Psyching Out the Crowd: Folk Performers and Their Audiences," *Urban Life and Culture,* Vol. 3, No. 3, October 1974, p. 268.
18. "The Chairman Never Stops Selling," *International Management,* February 1983, p. 59.
19. Joseph Poindexter, "Voices of Authority," *Psychology Today,* August 1983, p. 61.
20. Reprinted by permission of the *Harvard Business Review.* "Public Invisibility of Corporate Leaders," by David Finn (November/December, 1980, p. 107). Copyright © 1980 by the President and Fellows of Harvard College; all rights reserved.
21. William F. Buckley, interviewed by Melissa Pate and Tad Mayer, October 1985.
22. Gwen Kinkead, "Jimmy Goldsmith's U.S. Bonanza," *Fortune,* October 17, 1983, p. 142.
23. Author interview with Garry Marshall, August 29, 1986.
24. "Dick and Lili Zanuck Pledge to Mix Matrimony and Moviemaking from Here to Eternity," *People,* August 26, 1985, pp. 78, 83.

Chapter 8

1. Julie Noack, "Olivia Newton-John: Her Double Sector Crossover into Pop Music and Acting," unpublished research paper, Northwestern University, December 4, 1985.
2. William Simon, interviewed by Jane Steiner, December 1985.
3. Senator Bill Bradley, interviewed by Jane Steiner, December 1985.
4. Steve Rubell, interviewed by Jane Steiner, December 1985.
5. Benjamin Pohn, "Story of Chicago's Very Own Man-Made Woman: Chili Pepper," unpublished research paper, Northwestern University, December 6, 1985.
6. Interview for *High Visibility,* with Cecil Todd, November 27, 1984.
7. Ellen Hopkins, "Dr. Diet," *New York,* March 17, 1986, p. 46.
8. Hopkins, p. 47.
9. Timothy Blaney, "Contemporary Christian Music: In Transition," unpublished research paper, Northwestern University, December 12, 1985.
10. Kenneth L. Woodward, "The New Christian Minstrels," *Newsweek,* August 19, 1985, p. 70.
11. C. M. Titus, "Magic: The Maintenance of Motown," unpublished research paper, Northwestern University, December 12, 1985.
12. John Byrne, "How To Toot Your Own Horn," *Business Week,* November 3, 1986, p. 156.
13. Orrin E. Klapp, *Heroes, Villains, and Fools: Reflections of the American Character* (San Diego: Aegis Publishing Co., 1972).
14. Penny Stallings and Howard Mandelbaum, *Flesh and Fantasy* (New York: Bell Publishing, 1978), p. 33.
15. Edward C. Whitmont, *The Symbolic Quest* (Princeton: Princeton University Press, 1969), p. 100.
16. Jeffrey Kwatinetz and Jill Obmascik, "Bill Bradley and John Glenn: From Celebrityhood to the Senate," unpublished research paper, Northwestern University, December 9, 1985.
17. Joe Klein, "The Right Stiff," *Rolling Stone,* November 24, 1983, p. 79.
18. Richard Dyer, *Stars* (London: British Film Institute Educational Advisory Service, 1979) pp. 104–108.
19. Kerri Ginsberg, "The Study of Miss Piggy: How an Inanimate Object Can Become a Celebrity," unpublished research paper, Northwestern University, December 4, 1985.
20. Don Freeman, "Muppets on His Hands: Jim Henson," *Saturday Evening Post,* November 1979, p. 176.
21. Brad Darroch, "Screen: Miss Piggy," *People,* September 3, 1979, p. 88.
22. Cyndi Zale: "Jamie Farr's Fame: Unfortunate Fortune," unpublished research paper, Northwestern University, November 30, 1985.
23. Hecky Powell interviewed by Michael Sable, November 23, 1986.

24. Paula–Barri Whitehorn: "Vincente Roppatte: Success Hasn't Spoiled Him," unpublished research paper, Northwestern University, December 4, 1985.
25. Whitehorn.
26. Pia Zadora interviewed for *High Visibility* by the authors, and by Marilyn Hill and Christiana Tralmer, "Pia Zadora," unpublished research paper, Northwestern University, December 14, 1985. Interviews conducted Sunday, October 27, 1985.
27. Patricia Smith, "Drury Lane New Side to Pia Zadora's Non-Talent," *Chicago Sun-Times*, November 13, 1985, p. 52.
28. Martha Hawtrey: "Jack Hilton: A Study of the Packaging of Celebrities," unpublished research paper, Northwestern University, November 11, 1985.
29. Erving Goffman, *The Presentation of Self in Everyday Life* (London: Anchor Books, 1959), p. 26.
30. Clifford Terry, "The Golden Girl," *Chicago Tribune*, Tempo section, October 23, 1985, p. 3.
31. Louise Lague and Linda Witt, "Garrison Keillor Favorite Son of the Town Time Forgot," *People*, February 6, 1984, p. 44.
32. Martin Torgoff, "Stevie Wonder," *Interview*, June 1986, p. 43.
33. Martha Hawtrey, "The Transformation of a Religious Celebrity," unpublished research paper, Northwestern University, December 4, 1985.
34. Stallings and Mandelbaum, p. 38.
35. Quoted in Beryl A. Reed, "Dress Codes for Candidates: How to Look the Part," *Campaigns and Elections*, Summer, 1981, pp. 40–45.
36. George Bernard Shaw, *Pygmalion* (New York: Pocket Books, 1916), p. 11.
37. Sonia Moore, *The Stanislavski System: The Professional Training of an Actor* (New York: The Viking Press, 1974), p. 66.
38. Douglas Mazer, "The Image and Stylistic Transformation of Ed Paschke, the Painter," unpublished research paper, Northwestern University, December 1985.
39. Mazer.
40. Todd interview.
41. Todd interview.
42. Leonard Feather, quoted in an advertisement for the Pia Zadora concert at Carnegie Hall, *The New York Times*, Section 2, January 5, 1986, p. 6.
43. Mark Morrison, "Mentors," *Los Angeles*, June, 1984, p. 284.
44. Morrison, p. 237.
45. Morrison, p. 234.
46. Barry McDermott, "Oh Were It Only a Racket," *Sports Illustrated*, April 9, 1984, p. 41.

47. Moore, p. 66.
48. Toby Cole and Helen Krich Chinoy, *Actors on Acting* (New York: Crown, 1970), p. 626.
49. Richard Phillips and Peggy Rader, "Garrison Keillor: What He Did for Love," *Chicago Tribune,* Style section, February 12, 1986, p. 10.
50. David A. Harris, "Here's Johnnie and There's Johnnie: An In-Depth Study of Johnnie Whitaker," unpublished research paper, Northwestern University, November 15, 1985.
51. Harris.
52. Lally Weymouth, "The Princess of Playboy," *New York,* June 21, 1982; p. 37.
53. Nina Harlan, "If Christie Hefner Didn't Exist, the Playboy Promotional Department Would Have Invented Her," unpublished research paper, Northwestern University, November 11, 1985.
54. Harlan.
55. Richard M. Levine, "The Selling of a Used Carr," *Esquire,* November 1983, p. 189.
56. "A Day in the Life: Alan Carr," *Esquire,* January 1980, p. 86.
57. "A Day in the Life: Alan Carr," p. 87.

Chapter 9

1. Michael Miner, "The Press: Searching for Saviors," *Reader,* Section 1, February 19, 1982, p. 10.
2. Tim Alevizos, "Seka: The Platinum Princess," unpublished research paper, Northwestern University, November 15, 1985.
3. Mary K. Deeley: "Andrew Greeley as a Celebrity: A Study in Point of View," unpublished research paper, Northwestern University, October 30th, 1985.
4. "Andy's Answers," *Time,* July 10, 1978, p. 70.
5. Kenneth L. Woodward, "Trials of a Novelist Priest," *Newsweek,* August 16, 1982, p. 61.
6. The students who participated in the Radutzky team project were Audrey Shepps, Jane Steiner, Jodie Taub, Ginni Vath, and Anucha Browne.

Chapter 10

1. Jennifer Bingham Hall, "If The Doc's on TV, Maybe It's Because He Takes the PR Rx," *Wall Street Journal,* August 23, 1983, p. 1.
2. Hall.

3. Allan Dodds Frank and Lisa Gubernick, "Beyond Ballyhoo," *Forbes,* September 23, 1985, p. 136.
4. Mary Gillespie, "PR Firms Court Media in Westmoreland Case," *Chicago Sun-Times,* November 7, 1984, p. 65.
5. Silas Bent, *Ballyhoo* (New York: Horace Liveright, 1927), p. 133.
6. Edward L. Bernays, *Crystallizing Public Opinion* (New York: Boni and Liveright, 1927).
7. Allen Center, *Public Relations Practices* (Englewood Cliffs, New Jersey: Prentice-Hall, 1985), p. 2.
8. Bob Greene, "Image Makers Tackle the College Athlete," *Chicago Tribune,* Section 5, January 9, 1985, p. 1.
9. Len Ziehm, "Johnson Unspoiled by Success at Sarajevo," *Chicago Sun-Times,* August 3, 1984, p. 110.
10. Jim Jerome, "A Maverick's Moment of Glory," *People,* March 5, 1984, p. 51.
11. *USA Today,* "Lifestyle," July 30, 1984, p. 1.
12. Ron Rapoport, "The Selling of Carl Lewis," *Chicago Tribune,* August 9, 1984, p. 124.
13. Steve Nidetz, *Chicago Tribune,* Sports section, October 31, 1984, p. 2.
14. Henry Rogers, "Ten Tips to Take You to the Top," *Chicago Sun-Times,* October 21, 1984, p. 18.
15. Mary Ann Norboom, "All Reynolds Really Wants Is Respect," *Chicago Sun-Times,* August 10, 1983, p. 53.
16. Michael and Donna Nason, *Robert Schuller: The Inside Story* (Wheaton, Illinois: Tyndale House Publishers, 1981), p. 93.
17. Rubell interview.
18. "Noose Report," *The New York Times,* July 15, 1986, p. 25.
19. *Cannonball Run II,* Warner Brothers Press Packet, 1984.
20. Warner Brothers Press Packet.
21. Mark Schwed, "Celebrities Act Out Home-Staged Holiday," *Chicago Sun-Times,* December 1, 1983, p. 81.

Chapter 11

1. Jane and Michael Leahy, "The Empire That Welk and Son Built," *Los Angeles,* November 1984, p. 215.
2. Eddie Murphy, "Late Night with David Letterman," December 1984, NBC-TV.
3. Chris Costello (with Raymond Strait), *Lou's on First* (New York: St. Martin's Press), 1981.
4. Carol Wallace, "The Ego Has Landed," *People* magazine, December 9, 1985, pp. 130–131.
5. Sheena Nugent, "Letters to the Editor," *People,* January 6, 1986, p. 10.

6. Barbara Rozran, "Letters to the Editor," *People,* January 6, 1986, p. 10.
7. Linda C. Beaver, "Letters to the Editor," *People,* January 6, 1986, p. 10.
8. Joseph Poindexter, "Voices of Authority," *Psychology Today,* August 1983, p. 61.
9. Steve Rabey, "Christian Singer Appeals to Fans of Secular Pop Music," *Christianity Today,* November 8, 1985, p. 62.
10. Author interview with Jerry Paris, April 25, 1984.
11. John Holusha, "Shelby's Cars Return to Aid Chrysler's Image," *The New York Times,* June 23, 1986, p. 19.
12. Holusha, p. 20.
13. Edwin McDowell, "The Rush to Write 'Son of Iacocca,'" *The New York Times,* May 11, 1986, p. F-1.
14. John Lombardi, "The Fighter with the Glass Heart," *Esquire,* January 1986, p. 89.
15. Pete Axthelm, "The Case of Billie Jean King," *Newsweek,* May 18, 1981, p. 133.

Chapter 12

1. Mark Bloom and Jon Nemeth, "Leo Burnett: Image within Images," unpublished research paper, Northwestern University, December 14, 1985.
2. Rubell interview.
3. Barbara Goldsmith, "The Meaning of Celebrity," *The New York Times Magazine,* December 4, 1983, p. 75.
4. Thomas Moore and Michael Rogers, "The Fridge Goes to Market," *Fortune,* December 9, 1985, p. 9.

Index

I

J

K

L